THE ARCHAEOLOGY OF RITUAL

COTSEN ADVANCED SEMINARS 3

Cotsen Advanced Seminars

The published results of the Cotsen Advanced Seminars, where scholars explore cross-disciplinary themes in conferences periodically sponsored by the Cotsen Institute.

THE ARCHAEOLOGY
OF RITUAL

Edited by
EVANGELOS KYRIAKIDIS

Cotsen Institute of Archaeology
University of California, Los Angeles
2007

This book is set in Janson Text
Edited and produced by Leyba Associates, Santa Fe, New Mexico
Cover design by William Morosi
Index by Evangelos Kyriakidis

Library of Congress Cataloging-in-Publication Data
The Archaeology of ritual / edited by Evangelos Kyriakidis.
    p. cm. — (Cotsen advanced seminar series ; v. 3)
  Includes bibliographical references and index.
  ISBN 978-1-931745-47-5 (pbk. : alk. paper)
  ISBN 978-1-931745-48-2 (cloth : alk. paper)
 1. Archaeology and religion. 2. Ethnoarchaeology. 3. Ritual. 4. Rites and ceremonies. I. Kyriakidis, Evangelos. II. Title. III. Series.

BL65.A72A75 2007
203'.8—dc22

200703475

CONTENTS

ILLUSTRATIONS

CONTRIBUTORS

Catherine Bell   Santa Clara University
Religious Studies

Lars Fogelin   Albion College
Department of Anthropology and
Sociology

Christine Hastorf   University of California, Berkeley
Department of Anthropology

Caroline Humphrey   University of Cambridge
Department of Social Anthropology

Evangelos Kyriakidis   University of Kent
Classical and Archaeological Studies

James Laidlaw   University of Cambridge
Department of Social Anthropology

E. Thomas Lawson   Queen's University of Belfast
Institute of Cognition and Culture

Alessandra Lopez y Royo   Roehampton University, London
School of Arts

Joyce Marcus   University of Michigan
Department of Anthropology

Robert N. McCauley   Emory University
Department of Philosophy

Marianna Nikolaidou   University of California, Los Angeles
Cotsen Institute of Archaeology

Terence Ranger   St Antony's College, Oxford
Race Relations and African History

Colin Renfrew   University of Cambridge
McDonald Institute for Archaeological
Research

To Chip for his 50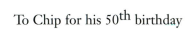th birthday

ACKNOWLEDGMENTS

This volume is the product of a collective effort of colleagues in UCLA and Cambridge, students, volunteers, and friends. The idea of a conference on the Archaeology of Ritual was originally conceived at Cambridge in 2001 in response to the need to put forward and compare ideas on the subject from a wide array of disciplines and fields within archaeology. It was realized in January 2004 at UCLA, as the third Cotsen Advanced Seminar. Thanks go to Sarah Morris and John Papadopoulos for their help and encouragement at all stages in preparing and organizing this conference.

I am most grateful to all the contributors of this volume who helped me with their patience and cooperation in bringing it to completion. My sincere thanks to the discussants of the conference who offered their views and made valuable contributions during the course of this two-day event: Mary Beard, Chuck Goodwin, Richard Lesure, Donald McCallum, Sarah Morris, and Julia L. J. Sanchez.

Special thanks go to Lloyd Cotsen for his generous endowment of the Advanced Seminar and of the Cotsen Scholars' Program, as well as to the director of the Institute, Charles Stanish, and the then assistant director, Julia L. J. Sanchez, for their assistance throughout the organization of the conference.

The organization and implementation of this event would have been almost impossible without the enthusiasm and great assistance of Ken Lapatin, the Steinmetz family, Tim Whalen, as well as Sigdem Atakuman, Sally Donohue, Leslie Ellen-Jones, Peter Evans, Helle Girey, Petya Hristova, Kathleen Louw, Mojdeh Makabi, Ben Sigman, Jill Silton, Sheryol Threewit, and Magdalena Yamamoto.

Thanks also go to Hans Barnard, Giorgio and Marilyn Buccellati, Lloyd and Margit Cotsen, Paola Demattè, Christopher B. Donnan, Richard Lesure, David Scott, Monica L. Smith, Charles Stanish, Lothar von Falkenhausen, and Willeke Wendrich for their support throughout this project.

This volume owes a lot to the expertise of the copyeditor Carol Leyba and to the sound suggestions made by the two anonymous readers; I thank them wholeheartedly. Last but certainly not least, I thank my Ph.D. supervisor Colin Renfrew for the long discussions on ritual that provided much inspiration in the organization of the conference and subsequently this volume.

E. Kyriakidis
Canterbury 2007

1.

IN SEARCH OF RITUAL

Evangelos Kyriakidis

This book is the fruit of the third Cotsen Advanced Seminar conducted at UCLA in January 2004. A wide spectrum of scholars, historians, art historians, anthropologists, students of performance and of religion, archaeologists, cognitive scientists, and linguists were all asked to think about and comment on how ritual can be traced in archaeology and also to suggest possible directions for ritual research in the discipline. The product is a fairly accurate representation of research on ritual and the archaeology of ritual: scholars from various disciplines and backgrounds putting forward sober and well-considered arguments, yet with little agreement among them. So this volume should not be seen as presenting one unified attitude toward ritual and its study in archaeology. Rather, it should be viewed as exemplifying the discourse on the archaeology of ritual today. The outcome is a collection of papers, which are individually thought provoking, often controversial, but always of extremely high quality.

It is worth stressing from the outset that the use of "ritual" in the title of this work does not imply any consensus as to what this term means. In my view, the lack of an agreed-upon definition of "ritual" has been a barrier to scholarship, as without a fixed point of reference, the exchange and cross-pollination of ideas is hindered. One of the aims of this book's concluding chapter, then, is to tentatively formulate a definition of "ritual" that begins to reconcile some of the major views on the subject.

Ritual is, by its nature, a fascinating and exciting subject. Its lure, however, can be damaging to its study in many different ways. As a category of activity, it tends to draw scholarly attention exclusively to itself and away from other related activities. Yet, when isolated from its context, ritual cannot be studied fully. As a social activity, ritual is defined by the society that practices it; as such, it should be studied in its proper social and material contexts.

1

The very appeal of ritual for both archaeologists and their audience can lead to a distorted picture of the archaeological record. That is, an archaeologist drawn to the subject may tend to interpret other "crystallized" (culturally encoded) activities such as sports and games[1]—and even perfectly mundane items or activities—as ritual.

Ritual also catches the imagination of students and incites them to reconstruct the ritual being studied even when the material at hand is insufficient for such reconstructions. The search for fame, the thirst of readers, the needs of the tourist industry, and nationalistic claims can all exacerbate this tendency. The following two excerpts exemplify the urge to reconstruct the rituals at Stonehenge:

> The faces of the celebrants would be turned in the direction of the sunset at the winter solstice. It may be supposed, then, that Stonehenge was erected after enormous labour to commemorate annually at midwinter the death of some great divinity. [Abercromby 1912:95]

> Equally, the sarsens may have been put up to be the everlasting house of such a deity whose role it was to safeguard the dead. . . . [O]ne can imagine supplicants holding axes aloft, the other hand raised with fingers outstretched, saluting the sun. [Burl 1987:214]

Such overreaching has, in turn, discouraged a great number of scholars who, by contrast, consistently avoid all reference to ritual. Thus, in archaeology, ritual activities tend to be either over-imaginatively reconstructed or avoided entirely. A "rational" approach has recently gained strength, and many of the imaginative reconstructions have been ousted from the mainstream archaeological literature.

Unfortunately, these tendencies have distracted us from what can be genuinely learned about rituals and what they can teach us about a given society when the material is dealt with soberly. For example, rituals can be seen as a mechanism for the shaping of beliefs, ideologies, and identities; or as a source of social power for those who participate in, control, or create them, thus revealing a great deal about the given society and its dynamics (Kyriakidis 2005:69–75). They can also be seen as a focal node of social networks, or as a means of illuminating the hopes and desires of a given society. There is a need for research that takes the middle line and focuses on ritual as an important and informative class of action.

The extreme approaches also have lacked a theoretical basis (Flannery 1976), whether implicit or explicit. Thus, archaeology could benefit from a greater focus on the development of theory in its study of ritual. There are a few archaeologists studying various rituals around the world whose valuable work deserves to be acknowledged (Drennan 1983: 30–32; Marcus and Flannery 1994:55–74). But being few in number and cut off from the research of current archaeological theory, their contributions cannot be compared and contrasted and their findings are not readily transferable to other areas and disciplines. With the exception of a few theorists (Bruck 1999:313–344; Renfrew 1985; Richards and Thomas 1984:189–218), most archaeologists follow an implicit theoretical approach which does not lend itself to testing and reproduction of results.

While the implicit theories share the view that ritual is a special activity, this is not sufficient for attribution because non-ritual activities can also be considered special. Often, the studies inspired by implicit theories must rely on non-archaeological evidence to make their case. Thus, Mesoamerican and South American archaeology draw on ethnohistory, the ethnographic and historical record of the Spanish colonials who recorded what they saw or were told. Greek prehistoric archaeology often makes reference to the Homeric epics or Hesiod, though these have little credibility as straightforward accounts of historic events. Classical Greek and Roman archaeology make use of historical texts to reconstruct rituals; as a consequence, the archaeological record may be slanted to comply with the historic sources. In the archaeology of the Indian subcontinent, the notion of continuity is used to such an exaggerated extent that any pattern observed in Neolithic excavation layers that has even a slight similarity to a modern ritual may be sufficient to argue for the existence of such a ritual in antiquity.

The archaeology of every region and of every period has its distinct problems, peculiarities, and needs; and each has approached ritual in a particular way and can contribute to its study in its own fashion. Archaeologists working on ritual in different parts of the world have unique experiences, and their collaboration can be very fruitful. Moreover, there is a growing number of disciplines with relevance to the study of ritual in archaeology, such as cognitive and performance studies, or paleo-ethnobotany; each comes with its own agendas and prejudices. Their incorporation into archaeological discourse not only enlivens but also enriches the discussion. And such an interdisciplinary approach is indeed one of the virtues of this volume.

This book is loosely divided into two sections. The first primarily concerns archaeological material and practice, while the second concentrates mainly on theoretical issues and could apply to other disciplines as well. The boundaries, however, are not altogether sharp, as all of the papers with primary material concerns also have significant theoretical sections. The papers in the first section are mainly reactions to the material itself, or to previous studies of it, as well as more wide-ranging critiques aimed at the study of ritual in archaeology.

The volume begins with a chapter introducing the challenges peculiar to the archaeology of ritual (chapter 2). In it, I draw attention to the similarities of individual rituals within a system, the common use of one space for the performance of multiple rituals, the disjunction between ritual practice and belief, the inseparability of the ritual and the mundane spheres, and the finding of ritual items in secondary contexts. I argue that awareness of these issues can "calibrate" the evidence and help steer research in fruitful directions.

Lars Fogelin (chapter 3) condemns the obsession with tracing the ancestry of specific gods or rituals back to the distant Indian past. He challenges the value of such an approach, which commonly takes continuity for granted and has insufficient evidence to support it. In doing so, he also casts doubt on the value of uncritical ethnography and demonstrates, with a case study on the distribution of some intriguing Buddhist cairns, how a methodical contextual approach in archaeology can enlighten our understanding of past rituals and religious landscapes.

Joyce Marcus (chapter 4) calls for a diligent, method-driven, testable study of ritual in archaeology that avoids speculation. She looks at various definitions and classifications of rituals, such as calendric versus non-calendric, and discusses their repetitive character. Marcus looks at Mesoamerican rituals and draws out their eight basic components. She opts for studying "ritual's key principles," be they at the conceptual, structural, or hierarchical level. Marcus uses Vogt's ritual replication theory (1965:342–353) and discusses these with particular reference to Aztec cosmological principles. Finally, she argues that archaeologists should look carefully for ritual regularities and patterns that will assist them in the discovery and documentation of further rituals.

Christine Hastorf (chapter 5) presents evidence for ritual in the Lake Titicaca Basin, commenting on the ways ritual has been attributed and discussed in Andean archaeology. Although she concentrates mainly on the difference between performance- and liturgy-centered rituals, which reflects different degrees of ritual establishment, she also raises many other issues, such as how ethnography and ethnohistory have been used to reconstruct ritual, how we can see the effects of ritual boundaries, and how ritual interacts with daily practice.

Colin Renfrew (chapter 6) acknowledges the existence of both religious and secular rituals, pointing out the relevance of his own previous work on religious ritual (cult) (1985, 1994:47–54) to the work of ritual in general. In so doing, he brings forth various issues related to the study of ritual: the study of the "co-evolution" of ritual and society (Flannery and Marcus 1994; Marcus and Flannery 2004; Marcus, here chapter 4) as well as the institutional role of ritual, a role that brings into being "institutional facts." Renfrew also analyzes the element of time in ritual, that is, as a repetitive as well as a time-structured activity.

Terence Ranger (chapter 7) reflects on the themes of this book and gives a lively account of the major ritual sites of the Matopos Hills and Great Zimbabwe, looking at the ways in which these sites have played both active and passive roles in the local politics, being important sites of recognition, conflict, and participation. His account is a prime example of how the roles of the historian, the archaeologist, and the anthropologist can merge.

Alessandra Lopez y Royo (chapter 8) discusses how archaeological reconstructions in India have influenced the creation of new rituals, a phenomenon that has important repercussions for our viewing of the past, as well as for the tourist industry and history itself. By looking at the ritual Odissi dance, the negotiations between its purported history and what we observe it to be, as well as the role archaeology plays in such a negotiation, Lopez y Royo reveals some of the motives and factors involved in the fabrication of a rite and its "exoticization."

Marianna Nikolaidou (chapter 9) treats technology and craft as "fields of ritually encoded action." She looks at technology as a social phenomenon that combines the social, the material, and the symbolic, as it structures the world through a nexus of links and associations. In this way, she proposes to apply the analytical tools used for ritual to the study of technology. She goes on to comment on the ritual aspects of a craftsperson's life, discussing the ritual dimension of specific materials, roles, and even the strategies of production in the technological process.

Robert McCauley and Thomas Lawson (chapter 10) offer a summary of their recent book (2002), somewhat adapted to address the purposes of archaeology and to tackle recent criticisms. McCauley and Lawson take ritual to be exclusively religious[2] and introduce several concepts relating mainly to the memorization of ritual, the use of sense arousal, and the interlinking of rituals; they also propose several avenues in which archaeology could benefit from the study of ritual.

Caroline Humphrey and James Laidlaw (chapter 11) repeat their argument that "ritual" is a quality that any action can come to have, reminding us that understanding what is distinct about ritual is separate from understanding the nature of the acts or processes that are ritualized (1994:65–67). In this article, they look at the Mongol *taxilag*, an activity that can be described by the term "sacrifice," arguing that "sacrifice and ritualization should be understood as separate processes." They make the point that although the entire sequence of a taxilag may be considered a "ritual," it does not necessarily follow that the killing of the animal is in itself a ritual, presenting relevant evidence from the Urad tradition. They describe, for example, how various Mongol rituals have been incorporated into the Buddhist tradition and how one can discern detachable or "movable ritual acts" that can be seen in various different ritual ceremonies of the same or other traditions, much like the common denominators that I present (in chapter 2).

Catherine Bell (chapter 12), on the antipode, offers her thoughts on definitions and their usefulness, particularly for the term "ritual," arguing that it is less important to define what ritual is than to delineate what ritual does. She claims that the study of ritual is in fact hampered by strict and formal rules or definitions. However, she does believe that, if anything, ritual is exclusively religious. Her views are a reminder that nothing should be taken for granted in ritual research.

In the final chapter (chapter 13), I conclude by proposing a definition for ritual activity that aims to reconcile many of the various views. I offer a discussion of and commentary on this great collection of papers and propose several topics that were touched on throughout the volume as inspirations for future research.

NOTES

1. Unpredictable outcomes are integral to sports and games; this is not the case for rituals, which are largely set; rituals should thus be considered a distinct type of "crystallized" action.

2. The conference was divided on the issue of whether there is such a thing as a secular ritual. McCauley, Lawson, and Bell argued for the existence of religious rituals only, whereas Renfrew, Humphrey, Laidlaw, and Kyriakidis maintained that secular rituals exist alongside religious rituals, examples being graduations, birthday celebrations, and inaugurations. For more on this issue, see the final chapter (chapter 13) of this volume.

REFERENCES CITED

Abercromby, Hon. John
    1912   *A Study of the Bronze Age Pottery of Great Britain and Ireland*, II.
            Clarendon Press, Oxford.
Bruck, Joanna
    1999   Ritual and rationality: Some problems of interpretation in
            European archaeology. *European Journal of Archaeology 2*
            (3):313–344.
Burl, Aubrey
    1987   *The Stonehenge People*. J.M. Dent, London.
Drennan, Robert D.
    1983   Ritual and ceremonial development at the hunter-gatherer level.
            In *The Cloud People: Divergent Evolution of the Zapotec and Mixtec
            Civilizations*, edited by Kent Flannery and Joyce Marcus, pp.
            30–32. Academic Press, New York.
Flannery, Kent V.
    1976   Contextual analysis of ritual paraphernalia from Formative
            Oaxaca. In *The Early Mesoamerican Village*, edited by Kent V.
            Flannery, pp. 333–345. Academic Press, New York.
Humphrey, Caroline, and James Laidlaw
    1994   *The Archetypal Actions of Ritual: A Theory of Ritual Illustrated by the
            Jain Rite of Worship*. Clarendon Press, Oxford.
Kyriakidis, Evangelos
    2005   *Ritual in the Aegean: The Minoan Peak Sanctuaries*. Duckworth,
            London.
Marcus, Joyce, and Kent Flannery
    1994   Ancient Zapotec ritual and religion: An application of the direct
            historical approach. In *The Ancient Mind: Elements of Cognitive
            Archaeology*, edited by Colin Renfrew and Ezra Zubrow, pp.
            56–74. New Directions in Archaeology. Cambridge University
            Press, Cambridge.
    2004   The coevolution of ritual and society: New ^{14}C dates from
            ancient Mexico. In *Proceedings of the National Academy of Sciences of
            the USA* 101 (52):18257–18261.
McCauley, Robert N., and E. Thomas Lawson
    2002   *Bringing Ritual to Mind: Psychological Foundations of Cultural Forms*.
            Cambridge University Press, Cambridge.
Renfrew, Colin
    1985   *The Archaeology of Cult*. Thames and Hudson, London.
    1994   The archaeology of religion. In *The Ancient Mind: Elements of
            Cognitive Archaeology*, edited by Colin Renfrew and Ezra Zubrow,
            pp. 47–54. New Directions in Archaeology. Cambridge
            University Press, Cambridge.

Richards, Colin, and Julian Thomas
  1984   Ritual activity and structured deposition in later Neolithic
          Wessex. In *Neolithic studies*, edited by Richard Bradley and Julie
          Gardiner, pp. 189–218. British Archaeological Reports (British
          series) 133, Oxford.
Vogt, Evon Z.
  1965   Structural and conceptual replication in Zinacantan culture.
          American Anthropologist 67 (2):342–353.

2.

FINDING RITUAL: CALIBRATING THE EVIDENCE

Evangelos Kyriakidis

This paper draws attention to the challenges archaeologists face in the study of ritual evidence. Issues include the similarity of individual rituals within a system, the common use of one space for the performance of multiple rituals, the disjunction between ritual practice and belief, the inseparability of the ritual and the mundane spheres, and the finding of ritual items in secondary contexts.

An awareness of the potential complications in the archaeological record, and of the need to calibrate the evidence, should facilitate secure attributions of ritual activity in archaeology.

Reconstructing any type of ancient practice is a challenging task for archaeology. Only a minute fraction of human actions can be represented materially. In many instances, action does not effect any perceptible change on material culture, and even when it does, the affected remains often perish long before the archaeologist has the chance to observe them. Moreover, archaeologists have only a few analytical tools to discern the actions behind a certain change in material culture, and the validity of these tools has been questioned by different factions within the discipline.

In general, archaeology attempts reconstructions on the basis of observed patterns and, as a result, traces mainly repeated activity. Ritual, like other forms of crystallized action,[1] is most often a repeated activity, the material remains of which may create patterns. In this, it has an advantage over other types of less repetitive action. Thus, in the few instances where ritual has an effect on material culture, it has a greater chance of being traced than many other activities. Without claiming that the identification of ritual in archaeology has been rigorous, this may go some way toward explaining the overwhelming presence of rituals in archaeological reconstructions. This presence may not necessarily reflect the dominant role of rituals in past societies, but rather the more physical and thus more traceable effect they had on material culture.

In the archaeology of ritual, as elsewhere, however, we should be aware of the ways in which the evidence can be misleading, so as to calibrate our data. Drawing on the author's own experience working at ritual sites, this chapter aims to facilitate secure attributions of ritual activity in archaeology, through raising awareness of frequent complications and challenges posed by the evidence.

But before we come to the issues concerning the archaeology of ritual, we should briefly address the problem of definition. The lack of an accepted definition leaves scholarly discourse without a fixed point of reference. In chapter 13, the problem and a tentative solution are discussed in greater detail. Here it will suffice to propose that "ritual" can be defined as an etic category that refers to set activities with a special (non-normal) intention-in-action, which are specific to a group of people. Until now, the main guidance for defining ritual was offered by the overlapping and graded traits proposed by Bell—that is, repetition, invariance, rule governance, formalism, and the air of tradition and symbolism (Bell 1997:138). Although Bell called these traits "non-definitive," it can be said that all of them, save symbolism, can be linked to the above definition, as they are all aspects of a "set" activity; all these traits contribute to the crystallization of activity. (For a lengthier discussion of these traits of ritual and their relation to the establishment of an activity, see Kyriakidis 2005: 32–40, 68–74.)

Beyond the inherent problems of definition—which, it is hoped, are sufficiently addressed in chapter 13—the archaeologist faces a variety of challenges in the study of ritual evidence. Issues include the similarity of individual rituals within a system, the common use of one space for the performance of multiple rituals, the disjunction between ritual practice and belief, the inseparability of the ritual and the mundane spheres, and the finding of ritual items in secondary contexts. These issues will be considered in turn.

DISTINGUISHING BETWEEN RITUALS WITHIN A SYSTEM

My main experience with ancient ritual sites has been at the Minoan peak sanctuaries. These bleak mountaintop sites are widely regarded as the most indisputable religious ritual sites in Minoan Crete (figure 2.1). The excavations there have uncovered dozens of animal and human figurines as well as drinking cups, bowls, serving jugs, and storage vessels. As a group, the material clearly points to ritual, especially compared with similar finds from non-ritual sites (for example, the figurine material is proportionally and absolutely much greater than figurine material found in settlements)

FIGURE 2.1. A Minoan peak sanctuary: (*top*) the peak sanctuary of Philioremos from the nearby Sklavokampos Minoan villa; (*bottom*) a close-up view, 2000.

(figure 2.2). One of the first challenges was to evaluate finds that might suggest ritual activity comparable with that of other sites. For instance, the evidence of ritual drinking and feasting in the peak sanctuaries (Kyriakidis

FIGURE 2.2. Human figurine fragments from the peak sanctuary of
Philioremos. (Photo by Kai Scharmer 2006)

2005) is comparable with that found at the contemporaneous Mesara tholos tombs, such as at Moni Odegetria (cf. Vasilakis 1989; Michelaki et al.
forthcoming; Vasilakis forthcoming). Animal and human figurines bearing many similarities to those found in the peak sanctuaries are also found
at ritual caves, at Piskokephalo (a rather different open-air ritual site), and
at Syme (the largest open-air ritual site in Minoan Crete). An instinctive
response is to assume that the similar material points to the same rituals
being performed in all locations. Observation of modern-day rituals,
however, tends to undermine this assumption.

There is a tendency in rituals, especially if well established, to borrow items or behaviors from one another. Moreover, rituals that belong
to the same belief or ritual system[2] (for ritual systems, see this volume,
Kyriakidis, chapter 13; Bell, chapter 12) will often employ the same paraphernalia, such as symbols or icons, songs or dances, which may identify
them as belonging to a certain ritual system and distinct from rituals of
different groups.[3] Also, through the two-way process of replication (Vogt
1965:342–353; Marcus, this volume, chapter 4), a group may copy elements of one of their rituals into another of its culturally encoded activities; and conversely, non-ritual cultural elements may be replicated into

the rituals and become ritual elements. As a result, rituals of the same system or group will most often look like one another, sharing a common denominator of elements.

For instance, the religious ritual of blessing the sea, river, or lake waters for the Christian Epiphany, which takes place across Greece on January 6, is in many ways similar to that of the Christian Church's Sunday service, not only in the material culture used, but also in its structure, chants, garments, symbolism, participants, and so on (figure 2.3). Even in less institutionalized ritual systems, there is a centripetal tendency for emulation (Barth 1987:24–37). This cross-fertilization can be a challenge to archaeology since it renders previously distinct rituals almost indistinguishable archaeologically. As far as archaeology is concerned, most material culture related to the Epiphany ritual will be virtually identical to that of the Church's Sunday service.

One other force that enhances ritual homogenization in a ritual system is what McCauley and Lawson call ritual "depth" (this volume, chapter 10). That is to say, some rituals are necessary preconditions for other, "deeper" rituals to take place. Divorce presupposes marriage. Baptism is a

FIGURE 2.3. The Epiphany ceremony in Crete.
(Copyright © *Explorecrete.com*. Reprinted with
permission, courtesy of Yiannis Samatas)

prerequisite for marriage in the Christian Church. The priest must be initiated for baptism to take place. Rituals of greater ritual "depth" (e.g., divorce) recall and refer to rituals of lesser ritual depth (e.g., initiation of a priest), as they are heavily dependent on them.

Circumcision for the Cameroon Dowayos, to offer a second example taken from Barley (1983), is a ritual of small depth, much evoked in all rituals that depend on it, which have, therefore, a greater ritual depth. Indeed, Barley reckons that most of their rituals seem to "have been 'quotes' from circumcision, reproducing exactly what happened on that occasion" (1983:171).

Thus, archaeologists may be able to distinguish between ritual and non-ritual activity (Kyriakidis 2005:28–40); but they will not be able to differentiate among specific rituals uncovered. Returning to the peak sanctuaries, although the rituals that took place there certainly seem to bear similarities to the contemporary funerary rituals at Mesara or those of Piskokephalo and Syme, in light of the above factors, there is little reason to assume that they were of the same nature. Indeed, the Mesara tholos tomb rituals were clearly funerary, whereas there is no hint of ancestor worship in the peak sanctuaries or in Piskokephalo or Syme (or indeed in other Minoan open-air sanctuaries). It is highly probable that rituals in all these sites borrowed elements from one another, being part of the same ritual system. It is always worth bearing in mind these possible other explanations in accounting for the similarity in material culture among contemporary ritual sites in the same area.

ONE PLACE, MANY RITUALS

One of the elements that may be borrowed from one ritual to another is the location of the performance itself. The more established the ritual system becomes, the more crystallized the ritual locations. This often results in the performance of multiple rituals in specific sites. And this observation challenges another early assumption made when studying the peak sanctuaries—namely, that they played host to one specific and recurring ritual.

All the features of an established ritual locale, be they man-made or natural, inevitably become associated with the rituals. Moreover, ritual paraphernalia are commonly stored there (in the case of buildings) and used in several of the respective rituals. Thus, to give an example, in a Christian church, many different rituals take place—including baptisms, marriages, funerals, communions, vespers, and confessions—which are considered different by the emic participants. However, shared elements, including the location, garments worn, paraphernalia, group of participants, and organizers, constitute a common denominator among the rituals.

A notable exception is the interfaith sanctuary in "globalized" locations, such as the Internet,[4] airports, or great natural landscapes such as the Grand Canyon. Such sanctuaries usually require little in the way of modification for ritual use, being virtually a blank space or an inspiring natural landscape in which rituals can be performed. Notwithstanding such exceptions, the majority of established ritual locations host a variety of rituals of the same system that usually have a great deal in common.

Consequently, archaeologists are often faced with identifying multiple rituals, the remains of which are mixed. In the case of the Minoan peak sanctuaries, the primarily open-air ritual sites have yielded masses of human and animal figurines, architectural models, and drinking and eating vessels found on and around flat, man-made areas. It is very possible that this material represents a number of rituals. Their common elements and location make it almost impossible to distinguish one ritual from another, as far as the material culture is concerned. Instead, the archaeological record represents a ritual pattern.

We should thus bear in mind that the evidence at an excavated ritual site will in all likelihood reflect many rather than one ritual. Archaeologists will generally have to content themselves with identifying ritual patterns of common denominators.

Occasionally, however, there are some elements that are restricted to a certain ritual, not repeated in any other. These may be rare, even unique, and sometimes immaterial (e.g., things spoken), but if traced could offer the possibility of differentiating one ritual from another. This very role of differentiation would indicate their significance from the performers' standpoint and as such places them in a central position in the ritual itself. They will thus be called *ritual cores* (Kyriakidis 2005:43). For example, the font is used only for baptisms in many Christian churches, where it is a central element. Unfortunately, at this stage of peak sanctuary research, where there is no comprehensive peak sanctuary publication, it is impossible to trace candidates for ritual cores, and therefore, at least as far as my research is concerned, these remain a theoretical concept.

CONTINUITY OF PRACTICE, CONTINUITY OF BELIEF

The peak sanctuaries were used for ritual for hundreds of years, some for almost a millennium. Initially, the constancy of the ritual deposits suggested to this author a relative constancy of ritual, which in turn suggested constancy of associated belief. Indeed, the more established the rituals of a system, the more likely they are to be attached to specific beliefs—about how the rituals are to be correctly performed, their significance, their properties, and their purpose. As mentioned earlier, ritual is a set practice, and that implies a relative constancy through time. Moreover, rituals tend to be associated with a certain tradition, thus implying a constancy across long periods of time. Although such implications have been challenged (Cannadine 1983:101–164), it is true that as crystallized action many rituals are less variable in their performance than many other types of action.

But, that is not to say that the relationship between ritual (a certain type of action) and belief is singular; the association of identical rituals with identical beliefs should not be taken for granted. The continuity of religious ritual practice may be indicative of, but does not in itself prove, the continuity of religious belief. For example, in the first centuries of the spread of Islam, the gestures and movements of prayer were (and still remain today) identical with the contemporaneous Eastern Christian way of praying (which has since altered). This may have resulted from the close historical relationship between the two religions, the fact that many of the early Muslims were previously Christians, but it may also be due to the geographical link of the two religions once Islam expanded into previously Christian-dominated areas in Egypt, Syria, and the Levant.[5] The beliefs behind these two prayers, however, were and remain, at least partly, different. Thus, in this case, ritual practice stayed the same while associated belief altered. Conversely, a change in ritual practice does not necessarily imply a change in belief. In Queen Victoria's funeral, horses accidentally bolted in the midst of the ritual; this action was then quickly incorporated into the tradition. Yet in this change of ritual, there was no significant change in the associated beliefs (Cannadine 1983:134; Ponsonby 1951:32–33, 83–94).

Thus, in the case of the peak sanctuaries and other ancient ritual sites, it cannot be assumed that the constancy of the material evidence for the ritual practices necessarily reflects a continuity of the associated beliefs. Neither is change in the ritual material culture necessarily sufficient to argue for a change in the related beliefs.

THE INSEPARABILITY OF THE RITUAL
AND MUNDANE SPHERES

Another issue to consider when identifying and interpreting ritual in archaeology is the common inseparability of ritual and the mundane. The overlap between these two activity spheres raises many questions: Is all of the material excavated in the peak sanctuaries, for example, exclusively ritual in nature? Should storage jars really be considered cult items? Are the remnants of workshop activities, such as potters' wheels, likely to be votives? Evidence found across cultures demonstrating the inseparability and overlap of the ritual and the mundane worlds argues against such assumptions.

Since there is no temporal or other limit as to what constitutes a practice or action, the term "ritual" can apply to both a "package" (a number, a group) of events and to an "element" (a single event). For instance, the classical Greek funerary festivals can be considered ritual as a package, though many of their elements may be non-ritual. For example, the Patroclus funeral (*Iliad* 23) included sport contests that Achilles organized to honor his companion. In the same way, during a Christian mass in Greece (and elsewhere), a basket is circulated in order to collect donations, a relatively unritualized event. In this volume (chapter 11), Humphrey and Laidlaw describe how the ritual ceremony of the *taxilag* sacrifice (a ritual package) has an unritualized event as its main element: the mundane slaughter of an animal. Conversely, mundane packages such as elections or university studies include a host of ritual elements, from oath taking and prayers to matriculation or degree ceremonies. This means that the two types of action, ritual and mundane, cannot usually be cleanly separated from each other, as they may form part of the same "package" or group of activities.

The same is true for institutions. Ritual institutions such as Christian churches and monasteries have a number of non-ritual rooms: offices, storerooms, activity rooms, bedrooms, even cafeterias and museums. Conversely, many civic (i.e., mundane) institutions, such as government buildings, art galleries, or port installations, also host ritual performances: inaugurations, blessings, personal prayers, and award ceremonies. Often these institutions have rooms especially reserved for rituals, such as chapels, prayer rooms, special ceremony rooms (e.g., banquet halls), or ritual assembly rooms. Thus, there are very few, if any, locations that categorically exclude either ritual or mundane activities. Location, then, does not directly dictate the type of action taking place there, though it may be indicative of that action.

In some of the peak sanctuaries, buildings were erected toward the end of the Old Palace period. These buildings bear no trace of ritual but seem to have housed storage facilities and workshop activities. Storage and workshops were in all likelihood ultimately associated with ritual practices; the buildings themselves, however, despite apparently forming part of the ritual institutions, were primarily mundane in nature

(Kyriakidis 2005:99–109). This is also very likely to have been the case in other established ritual sites.

The storage of ritual and non-ritual objects together can also contribute to the inseparability of the two spheres (figure 2.4). A great number of rituals are performed in places not exclusively used for rituals, such as the aforementioned mundane institutions or even private homes. Special items used in the performance of these rituals are often stored together with non-ritual items. An example from modern Greece illustrates this phenomenon. It is not unusual for a household to be ritually fumigated every day. This is usually carried out by the older women of the house who have a special incense burner. In the 1980s, I observed the ritual being carried out by Sophia Zographaki, an immigrant from Smyrna (today Izmir) to Athens; but variations of this practice are still taking place today in various parts of Greece. The event used to commence in a specially designated part of the house with religious icons and a candle. The practitioner would first light the candle and the incense, and then she would say (or rather mumble) prayers in each room, moving the incense burner in the air in the form of a notional cross or in a straight up-and-down movement. The incense burner was stored together with the dining plates; the incense and the candle-wicks (whether plant or artificial) together with the spices; the candle oil used was household olive oil. In other words, there was no special ritual storage space, and it would have been difficult to discern the ritual from the non-ritual objects without special, insider knowledge. In the same way, non-ritual items may be stored in primarily ritual sites such as churches. Telephones, stationery, spectacles, and other personal items belonging to the priests may be found in the sanctified areas of Christian churches, which are primarily designated (and often built) for objects used in rituals. Thus, as far as storage of ritual items is concerned, context is rarely indicative.

The storage of ritual items in mundane contexts and of mundane items in ritual ones is also evident in the study of the peak sanctuaries. As noted earlier, buildings in the peak sanctuary premises were used to store foodstuffs, tools, and possibly items for ritual use; however, few rituals, if any, occurred there. Thus, given that the ritual and the mundane spheres are often linked so closely as to be inseparable, the attribution of ritual value to an item on the basis of its context alone is difficult for archaeology.

Finds in Secondary Contexts

The excavation contexts of ritual sites can be misleading in one other way: residues from ritual performances are scarcely traceable in situ. Indeed,

FIGURE 2.4. Mundane storage at a ritual site: two storage jars from the peak sanctuary of Philioremos. The site included fragments of many such storage jars. (Photos by Kai Scharmer and Yiannis Papadakis 2006)

established ritual locales that host one or more rituals are usually cleared
before and after a ritual performance. So material residues of the ritual
activities are recycled, pushed aside, littered in wells or pits, purposefully
destroyed, or dutifully cleared away, often in a fashion not respectful to
the objects. The peak sanctuary figurines and other material were mostly
found in secondary contexts, thrown or cleared away. Many flat areas or
platforms in these sites were even constructed with fills of figurines and
broken pottery. In Aghios Georgios at Kythera, Sakellarakis found heaps
of figurines thrown off the cliff (Sakellarakis 1996:81–99), while in many
Cretan peak sanctuaries, figurines and other ritual residues were found
mainly in rock clefts and chasms. Initially, researchers surmised that the
Minoans venerated the earth and tried to push votives inside rock-clefts.
However, there is not enough evidence to support such a reconstruction,
and the fragments of figurines found rather favor the scenario that the
material was simply cleared or swept away into any space available. Rock
crevices and chasms were better protected from the rake, the broom, the
wind, and the rain and thus retained more material.

And finally, excavators studying rituals can be fooled by find context
in still another way. Consider the kind of ritual that begins in one place
and ends in another, such as a procession. In such a ritual, items originating in one place may be found in another, as residues from the ritual may
be deposited anywhere along the route. In several Minoan peak sanctuaries, for example, river or sea pebbles were found in large numbers.
Because it is obvious that the pebbles did not originate at the find spot,
we can notionally connect their place of origin and the peaks. We know
that people came from other places to visit the peak sanctuaries, and it is
possible that many of them brought along such pebbles (Kyriakidis 2005:
143–144). This connection of rivers or the sea with the peak is interesting
in many ways, but the point here is that, like the pebbles, many (if not
most) of the other items found at the peak sanctuaries may well have been
in secondary deposits. The identification of a ritual in the archaeological
record, therefore, is complicated by the fact that the items found are most
commonly not in a primary deposit.

To sum up, rituals may be easier overall to trace than many other
types of action, due to the fact that they are crystallized, often repeated,
and can form patterns in the archaeological record. Nevertheless, archaeologists should be aware of the various limitations and the challenges
posed by a ritual's material remains. Such an understanding will help "calibrate" the evidence and steer research to more fruitful directions, away
from potential dark alleys and red herrings.

NOTES

1. That is, technologically governed activity, trade, and exchange, or simply culturally encoded action; see chapters 10 and 13.

2. If "societies" can be groupings of interacting individuals of any kind, and multiple societies can exist within a population of individuals (e.g., for a population in the United States, you might have the society of U.S. citizens, the society of computer engineers, the society of academics, the society of Catholic Christians, the society of those who are of Italian decent, and so on, and one person can be a member of all of them at once), then ritual systems are groups of related rituals, and multiple ritual systems may be present within a population (e.g., British military rituals, Protestant Christian religious rituals, personal rituals, family rituals, state rituals). Often the various societies within a certain population have their own ritual system.

3. Sometimes, even rituals of different belief and ritual systems will copy and imitate each other due to a general trend of cultural assimilation or imitation. A good example is the Eastern Christian Church's wide influence on the Ottoman Islamic "institutions" in areas such as architecture and music.

4. For example, *www.paganinstitute.org*.

5. Tertullian and Origen describe kneeling and prostration for Early Christian prayer, much like in the current Islamic prayer (Burghardt 1954:226, n. 466). For more on the various positions assumed by Early Christians in prayer, see Leclercq 1913.

REFERENCES CITED

Barley, Nigel
    1983   *The Innocent Anthropologist: Notes from a Mud Hut.* British Museum Publications, London.

Barth, Fredrik
    1987   *Cosmologies in the Making.* Cambridge University Press, Cambridge.

Bell, Catherine
    1997   *Ritual: Perspectives and Dimensions.* Oxford University Press, Oxford.

Burghardt, Walter (editor)
    1954   *Origen, Prayer, Exhortation to Martyrdom.* Ancient Christian Writers 19. Paulist Press, NJ.

Cannadine, David
    1983   The context, performance and meaning of ritual: The British monarchy and the "Invention of Tradition." In *The Invention of Tradition,* edited by Eric Hobsbawn and Terence Ranger, pp. 101–164. Cambridge University Press, Cambridge.

Flannery, Kent V.
    1976   Contextual analysis of ritual paraphernalia from Formative Oaxaca. In *The Early Mesoamerican Village,* edited by Kent V. Flannery, pp. 333–345. Academic Press, New York.

Humphrey, Caroline
  1998   *Marx Went Away — But Karl Stayed Behind.* University of
           Michigan Press, Ann Arbor.
Kyriakidis, Evangelos
  2005   *Ritual in the Aegean: The Minoan Peak Sanctuaries.* Duckworth
           Publishers, London.
Leclercq, Henri
  1913   Genuflection. In *Dictionnaire d'archéologie chrétienne et de liturgie,*
           edited by Fernand M. Cabrol et al., pp. 1017–1021. Letouzey et
           Ané, Paris.
Lebessi, Angeliki, and Polymnia Muhly
  1990   Aspects of Minoan cult. Sacred enclosures: The evidence from
           the Syme Sanctuary (Crete). *Archäologischer Anzeiger,* 315–336.
Marcus, Joyce
  1989   Zapotec chiefdoms and the nature of formative religions. In
           Regional Perspectives on the Olmec, edited by Robert J. Sharer and
           David C. Grove, pp. 148–197. Cambridge University Press,
           Cambridge.
Michelaki, Flora, Keith Branigan, and Tim Campbell-Green
  Forthcoming Pottery usage in the tholos cemetery at Moni Odigitria. In
           Proceedings of the 10th Intenational Cretological Congress, edited by
           Maria Vlasaki et al. Philologikos Syllogos Chryssostomos,
           Chania.
Ponsonby, Frederick
  1951   *Recollections of Three Reigns.* Eyre and Spottiswoode, London.
Sakellarakis, Yannis
  1996   Minoan religious influence in the Aegean. *Annual of the British
           School at Athens* 91:81–99.
Vasilakis, Thomas A.
  1989   Proïstorikes theseis ste Mone Odegetria-Kalous Limenes. *Kretike
           Estia* 3:11–79.
  Forthcoming E Organose tou Chorou sto Proanaktoriko Nekrotafeio tes
           Mones Odegetrias. In *Proceedings of the 10th International
           Cretological Congress,* edited by Maria Vlasaki et al. Philologikos
           Syllogos Chryssostomos, Chania.
Vogt, Evon Z.
  1965   Structural and conceptual replication in Zinacantan culture.
           American Anthropologist 67 (2):342–353.
Xanthoudides, Stephanos
  1922   Minoikon megaron Nirou. *Archaeologike Ephemeris* (1922):2–4.

3.

HISTORY, ETHNOGRAPHY, AND ESSENTIALISM: THE ARCHAEOLOGY OF RELIGION AND RITUAL IN SOUTH ASIA

Lars Fogelin

Studies of ancient ritual in South Asia have long been dependent on historical and ethnographic sources. In most cases, archaeologists have explained past ritual by referring to particular passages in the extensive religious literature of South Asia, and/or ethnographic accounts of ritual practices in contemporary "village India." Unfortunately, many archaeologists employing historical sources have ignored that these texts were often highly scholastic products of the religious elite. As for the use of "village India" as a resource for understanding past ritual, it rests upon the fallacy of evolutionary survivals, even when phrased in the more modern anthropological language of "cultural memory."

That said, the misuses of history and ethnography are not the most serious problems underlying archaeological research on ritual in South Asia. More fundamentally, much of the research on ritual in South Asia is essentialist in orientation, using individual archaeological indicators to identify the origin of practices that resemble some element in either historical or ethnographic sources. By examining these elements in isolation, archaeological statements on past ritual become little more than factoids—decontextualized statements concerning the origin of modern religious practices.

To illustrate this point, I review the claims made concerning one common motif found on Indus Valley seals, a figure seated in a cross-legged position. Archaeologists have repeatedly identified this figure as an early representation of the god Shiva. I argue that the identification of "Proto-Shiva" has not led to any substantial increase in the understanding of Indus Valley religion, nor could it. Rather than study the origin of modern gods, archaeologists should focus on the ways that ritual articulates with other aspects of past society. This can only be accomplished by a careful contextual analysis of assemblages of material remains of past ritual practice. I illustrate this approach through studies of an Early Historic period (ca. 300 B.C.E.–300 C.E.) Buddhist mortuary landscape in Andhra Pradesh, India. Spatial investigations of mortuary features surrounding the monastery identified significant differences between Early Historic period mortuary practices, mortuary

23

practices described in early Buddhist texts, and modern Buddhist mortuary prac-
tices. Further, these differences demonstrate that an ambivalent relationship exist-
ed between Buddhist monks and local populations that directly contradicts descrip-
tions of this relationship in Buddhist religious texts. In contrast to the essentialism
that orients much of the archaeology of early ritual in South Asia, a contextual
approach allows for differences in past ritual to be explored.

Archaeology, history, and ethnography have long served to inform one
another in the study of religion in South Asia. In the nineteenth century, Buddhist textual sources guided archaeological explorations of northern India (Cunningham 1854, 1876, 1892) and of the rock-cut monasteries
of western India (Fergusson and Burgess 1880). New translations of the
Ramayana and Mahabharata led archaeologists to search out the cities and
sites that served as the backdrop to these Hindu epics, much as the *Iliad*
guided Schliemann's research at Troy (Trautmann 1997; Trautmann and
Sinopoli 2002). Throughout the twentieth century, these same historical
sources continued to inform archaeological research on the subcontinent,
to the benefit of archaeology (Fritz 1986; Fritz and Michell 1989; Marshall
1931; Thapar 2002; Wheeler 1954, 1968). However, in recent years, many
archaeologists and historians have come to view the uncritical use of historical sources as limiting the further investigation of religion and ritual in
South Asia (Chakrabarti 1997; Coningham 2001, 1998; Coningham and
Lewer 2000; Lahiri 2000; Schopen 1997; Trainor 1997; Trautmann and
Sinopoli 2002). Rather than using these textual sources, some archaeolo-
gists have advocated for a greater use of ethnographies of contemporary
South Asian villages as a source for understanding ancient India
(Coningham 2001, 1995; Lahiri 1996).

While recognizing the enormous debt modern archaeologists owe to
earlier generations, I agree that in the past archaeologists have not fully
appreciated that most texts were highly scholastic products of the religious elite and/or composed several centuries later than the archaeological material being investigated (Schopen 1997; Trainor 1997). However, I
argue that the substitution of village ethnography as a source for understanding past ritual often rests on the fallacy of evolutionary survivals,
even when phrased in the more modern anthropological language of
memory (Bloch 1977; Inden 1990; Van Dyke and Alcock 2003). That said,
the misuses of history and ethnography are not the most serious problems
underlying archaeological research on ritual in South Asia.

More fundamentally, much of the research on ritual in South Asia is
essentialist in orientation, using individual archaeological indicators to

identify the origin of practices that resemble some element in either historical or ethnographic sources. By examining these elements in isolation, archaeological interpretations of past ritual become decontextualized statements concerning the origin of modern religious practices. At best, this approach is uninformative about past ritual. At worst, these archaeological claims serve as ammunition in modern sectarian conflict (Mandal 1993; Rao 1994; Shaw 2000a). To illustrate this point, I will review the claims made concerning one common motif found on Indus Valley seals that archaeologists have repeatedly identified as an early representation of the Hindu god Shiva. I argue that the identification of Proto-Shiva has not led to any significant increase in the understanding of Indus Valley religion, nor could it.

In response to the essentialism of existing archaeological research, I argue for a contextual approach to the study of past ritual in South Asia, using historical and ethnographic sources to inform, rather than replace, rigorous archaeological investigations. Rather than study the origin of modern religions, archaeologists should focus on the ways that ritual articulates with other aspects of past society. This can only be accomplished by carefully analyzing assemblages of material remains of past ritual practice and delineating the differences among historic, ethnographic, and archaeological materials.

From the outset, I should state that I do not see my proposals as representing a new approach to the archaeology of religion and ritual. Rather, I argue that the study of religion and ritual should follow the same general methods as any other archaeological research. To be successful, the focus of research must remain on identifying material traces of religious practice rather than attempting to leap directly to more esoteric questions of symbolic meaning. I will illustrate this approach through a small example from my own research on an Early Historic period (ca. 300 B.C.E. to 300 C.E.) Buddhist mortuary landscape in Andhra Pradesh, India.

PROTO-SHIVA

In 1924, John Marshall posted a picture of an Indus Valley seal in the *Illustrated London News* (figure 3.1), asking if anyone had seen a similar seal elsewhere in the world. Within a week another reader responded, stating that similar seals had been found in Mesopotamia, in contexts dating to the third millennium B.C. With that, the antiquity of South Asian civilization was pushed back almost three millennia. It also established seals as one of the primary foci of Indus Valley investigations. Within a few years,

FIGURE 3.1. A Proto-Shiva seal. (After Marshall 1931: Plate XII)

Marshall and others had examined many seals and identified one common character that they felt had particular importance (Marshall 1931:52–56). While there is some variation in the motif, this character generally consisted of a man wearing a horned headdress, sitting on stool with his feet together, often with an erect phallus. Almost immediately, these early researchers recognized a striking similarity between this figure and depictions of the Hindu god Shiva. As stated by Marshall,

> We have, then, on this seal a god whose distinguishing attributes proclaim him the prototype, in his most essential aspects, of the historic Shiva. Of the name of this pre-Aryan god we are in ignorance. [Marshall 1931:52]

Marshall backed up this claim by listing numerous characteristics in common between depictions of Shiva and elements found on the seal. I have little to quarrel with in Marshall's analysis. The figure in the seals does strongly resemble representations of Shiva. I also appreciate the hesitations that Marshall adds in his footnotes, recognizing that there were also profound differences in the depictions of Shiva and Proto-Shiva. Thus, I agree that this figure may be, as Marshall states, an early form of a god that, over the years, was transformed into Shiva. The identification of Proto-Shiva provides a tantalizing possibility for the antiquity of modern

Hinduism. However, a quick review of modern discussions of Proto-Shiva suggests that little progress has been made toward understanding the ancient significance of this figure for the people of the Indus Valley.

> Whereas many later Hindu deities may have had their roots in earlier beliefs of the Indus Valley . . . we cannot confirm specific connections between the horned figure on the Indus seals and later Hindu deities. There are similarities in iconography, but the meaning relayed may have been significantly different. [Kenoyer 1998:113]

> There is considerable merit in the contemporary critiques of Marshall's hypothesis on the Proto-Shiva seal. He seems to have taken his thought on the significance of this figure one or two steps too far. . . . But there is something significant about this seal . . . and it would be wrong to abandon the idea that in the Proto-Shiva seal we have insight into the Harappan system of belief, [and] even later Indian tradition. [Possehl 2002:143]

> Alternative interpretations have been suggested. . . . [H]owever, it is only Marshall's explanation [of the Proto-Shiva seal] which makes sense in the light of Hinduism. [Chakrabarti 2001b:42]

These quotes demonstrate that, at best, no more is known about Proto-Shiva than what Marshall stated seventy years ago. The question I have is why. Why have archaeologists made so little progress in understanding how Proto-Shiva fits within the larger context of Indus Valley religion, from what seemed so promising a start? This is not to say that no progress has been made concerning Indus Valley religion; other avenues have been profitably explored (Kenoyer 1998; Parpola 1994; Possehl 2002). As I see it, the lack of progress on the social significance of Proto-Shiva is due to the failure to examine the differences between the figure on the seal and later representations of Shiva. Recognition of these differences is the first, though admittedly insufficient, step toward investigating the differences in the meaning and social context of Proto-Shiva to the ancient people of the Indus Valley. By focusing on similarities, we can only make questionable statements about the origin of modern Shiva.

The lack of progress in understanding Proto-Shiva is emblematic of a lack of progress in the archaeological study of religion in South Asia generally. What then, should archaeologists be doing differently? The orientation of archaeological inquiry into South Asian religions seems focused on dating the antiquity of modern religious practices rather than on the role of religious beliefs in past societies. It is not that archaeologists do not see that differences existed; rather, they often do not seem to be interested in them.

HISTORY

In recent years, several archaeologists and historians studying religion in South Asia have identified an over-reliance on historical sources as a major factor limiting archaeological inquiry (Chakrabarti 1997; Coningham 2001; Schopen 1997; Trainor 1997; Trautmann and Sinopoli 2002). For example, Robin Coningham (2001:63) argues that many misinterpretations of Early Buddhism were "created by the extreme focus on textual readings, that is the sayings of the Buddha or those of his followers, to the detriment of archaeology." In those cases where archaeological evidence directly contradicts texts, Coningham argues, archaeology is rejected out of hand. More problematic, in Coningham's view, is the way that over-reliance on historical sources leads to research methods that eliminate the possibility of recognizing differences in the first place. For example, Buddhist religious sources declaring all monks were to be vegetarians have led archaeologists to forgo collecting faunal samples in all but a few Buddhist monasteries (Coningham 2001:88). My one criticism of Coningham's argument is that at times he seems to set archaeology in opposition to history, knocking down historical claims through reference to archaeological evidence. I favor a more balanced approach, best illustrated in a recent article by Thomas Trautmann and Carla Sinopoli (2002). That said, I agree with his critique of the archaeological use of historical sources, and my own critique of the use of ethnographic sources follows in much the same manner.

Dilip Chakrabarti presents a differing view on the relationship between archaeological and historical sources. In a study of the archaeology of Hinduism, Chakrabarti states:

> The textual roots of Hindu religious tradition go back to the four
> Vedas . . . which are conventionally dated to between 1500 and
> 1000 BCE. More reflective of reality is the belief that these are
> composite texts containing diverse traditions of diverse periods
> and cannot represent any specific period in the Indian historic
> sequence. What is clear . . . is that the first textual phase of Indian
> philosophical and religious tradition has to remain undated and
> that archaeology has to be kept out of it. In such a situation

archaeology can do only one thing: try to trace different ritual behaviors which Hindus traditionally associate with Hinduism. It is not a question of beginning with a checklist of rituals and looking for their archaeological manifestations. Rather, it is a question of looking at the early archaeological record as a whole and pointing out the categories of evidence which make sense from the point of view of later, well-documented Hinduism. [Chakrabarti 2001b:35]

In my view, this approach has the same failings as those I discussed for hypotheses concerning Proto-Shiva. Even if present and past people followed the same ritual practice, this does not demonstrate that the meaning of that practice was in any way similar, or even that there are necessarily ancestral ties between the earlier practice and later ones. This method only serves to identify those elements of modern Hinduism that appear potentially to have some antiquity. It does not explore how those elements were understood at the time in which they existed. Contrary to Chakrabarti's dismissal of making a "checklist of rituals," only a checklist would reveal the differences between past and present religious practices. Chakrabarti's approach, therefore, fails to study ancient ritual, while providing only questionable antecedents for modern Hindu practice. Just as in the case of Proto-Shiva, the essentialist nature of the evidence can only be used to support or counter modern religious arguments based on dubious claims of antiquity.

VILLAGE INDIA

In response to the perceived difficulties of using historical sources, some archaeologists have turned to modern religious practice in South Asia to assist in their investigations (see Coningham 2001, 1995; Lahiri 1996; Shaw 2000a, 2000b). The reasons for this are twofold. First, many archaeologists and historians recognize that South Asian historical sources were the product of a small, literate minority (Schopen 1997; Trautmann and Sinopoli 2002). It is unlikely that they provide an accurate portrayal of the typical religious practices of the majority. Following from the recent emphasis on popular Hinduism and religious practice in South Asian ethnography (Fuller 1992; Ortner 1989), archaeologists and historians have begun to focus much of their attention on more quotidian aspects of religion and ritual (Coningham 2001; Schopen 1997; Trainor 1997). My own research is informed by the very same concerns, and I have found it to be a fruitful approach (Fogelin 2006, 2005, 2004). I would argue, however, that there is a second, more problematic reason behind archaeologists' embrace of village ethnography. Relying upon the writings of an earlier generation of ethnographers, archaeologists have unwittingly come to accept village India as a survival of the India of antiquity. As with the studies of Proto-Shiva, modern similarities from ethnography are compared with archaeological data, providing questionable antecedents for modern religious practices. That these practices are of a more quotidian nature does nothing to improve their veracity.

Studies of village India had their peak from the 1950s to the 1970s in the work of Srinivas (1989, 1976, 1966), Marriott (1955), and others (Mayer 1960; Wiser and Wiser 1969). Underlying these studies was the conviction that, unlike the metropolitan centers in South Asia, villages were distinct microcosms, retaining their earlier lifeways and connections with the distant, precolonial past. By the 1980s, this position was heavily criticized, principally on the grounds that the imprint of colonialism was far more extensive than those who studied village India had accepted (Inden 1990; Ludden 1985). Further, rapid population increases and the adoption of new technologies had resulted in profound changes in the size and locations of settlements both before and after colonialism (Morrison 1994; Talbot 2001:77–79).

From an archaeological perspective, the critique of village ethnography does appear overdone. In case after case, the antiquity of some villages, and some religious sites, has been clearly demonstrated (see Chakrabarti 2001a; Coningham 1995; Shaw 2000b, 2000a; Lahiri 2000). However, it is also clear that many other sites have been forgotten over the years, their location and significance having faded from memory by modern times. Even in those situations where specific ritual locations have persisted for several millennia, it is often the case that the meaning, if not their religious affiliation, has profoundly changed. As with most things, some aspects of village India have remained the same, while others have not. There is value in the archaeological use of village ethnography and studies of popular religion, but archaeologists cannot assume that continuity always exists between the past and present, or that similarities always show historical ties between ancient and modern inhabitants of a region.

Recently, memory has become a focus of archaeological research, emphasizing the dynamic and creative use of memory—that people choose to remember, forget, or modify elements of the past depending on their own present concerns (Sinopoli 2003; Van Dyke and Alcock 2003). Thus, the orientation of these studies is how earlier iconographic motifs or material patterns are appropriated or reimagined in later contexts.

These later appropriations of material symbols may, or may not, have relevance to understanding the meaning of those material elements in their original context. Given the fluidity of memory, it should not serve as a basis for assumptions about the past.

An example of this problem can be found in Julia Shaw's (2000b; Shaw and Sutcliffe 2001) archaeological survey near the Buddhist site of Sanchi in central India. Her survey method was centered on villages, surveying the neighboring hills and using local informants to direct her to nearby sites. The benefits of this strategy, she argued, were that it helped her to more efficiently find archaeological remains while allowing settlement continuities to inform landscape interpretations:

> The area was surveyed on a village-to-village basis, whereby modern settlements . . . formed the foci for following up local leads and carrying out systematic exploration in the surrounding fields and hills. This method is popular in India because of a tendency toward settlement continuity, and the practice of reinstalling archaeological material as objects of worship within the village itself. [Shaw 2000b:776]

Shaw's research questions required the survey of a large area with limited time and money. In this regard, I understand her desire to use a more efficient method of survey. However, my concern is that Shaw does not accomodate the modern biases built into her survey methodology. By centering her survey around villages and using local leads to identify sites, to a large extent her survey methodology removes the potential for identifying differences between the past and present. It remains unclear if the long-term continuities she identifies in the region are genuine or are the product of her survey strategy. As Shaw suggests, archaeological survey can benefit from the information provided by local informants, but attention still must be paid to exploring those areas where no such continuity is suggested. Again, as with interpretations of the Proto-Shiva seal and the uncritical use of historical sources, assumptions of continuity serve only to address questions of the origin of modern religious practices rather than explore the broader context of past ritual.

A CONTEXTUAL APPROACH TO THE ARCHAEOLOGY OF RELIGION AND RITUAL

Ancient religion and ritual can be best investigated archaeologically if we abandon approaches that emphasize comparisons with modern religious doctrines, origin myths, and practices. It is important to note that I am not suggesting that these aspects of religion are uninteresting or unimportant. Where sources concerning them are available—in texts and oral traditions, for example—they provide critical insights into the broader social world in which a particular religious tradition existed. However, we must examine ancient religions within their own context, not simply as precursors to modern religions. This approach will still allow for similarities and continuities to be identified, but will also permit the differences to emerge.

Given the material focus of archaeology, it is difficult to recover origin myths or the specific meaning of religious iconography. Archaeologists will never figure out the true name of Proto-Shiva. Rather, archaeology can look at the effects of religion on the social life of the people who were involved with it (a similar argument can be found in Hays 1993). How does religion serve to strengthen or weaken ties between social groups? In what ways did religion serve to legitimize or contest positions of authority? It is not necessary to know the specific name and origin of a statue of a god to realize that its placement next to a throne served to associate a ruler with the divine. The approach I advocate here relies heavily on the spatial relationships and layout of religious structures and sacred landscapes. It is not the individual elements, but the patterns of association among the elements that provide meaning and allow my investigations to proceed. Of particular importance to this process is the recognition that religious ritual is particularly amenable to this form of archaeological study.

In my research, the key element of ritual is its regularized, or habitualized, performance (Bell 1997:150–152). As with any regularized human action, rituals are likely to leave patterned material traces of their practice. It is these patterns of material traces that allow me, as an archaeologist, to reconstruct and investigate past ritual. Once the relationships among ritual elements are identified, archaeologists can employ a wide variety of anthropological approaches to study their social role and examine their broader social implications. Importantly, this can be done without precise knowledge of the ritual meaning or content of the rituals performed.

MORTUARY RITUAL AT THOTLAKONDA MONASTERY

Between November 2000 and March 2002, I led a team that conducted six months of archaeological survey in the area surrounding Thotlakonda (figure 3.2), an Early Historic period (ca. 300 B.C.E. to 300 C.E.) Buddhist monastery in north coastal Andhra Pradesh, India (Fogelin

2006, 2005, 2004). During this time, we intensively surveyed 7.3 km^2 and identified 328 archaeological features. In the process, we directly investigated the broader social context in which Thotlakonda was situated. The fieldwork culminated in a map of the social landscape of Thotlakonda, containing walls, paths, reservoirs, a *stupa* (a Buddhist reliquary mound), and one Early Historic period village. The most common features recorded during survey were small, mortuary cairns constructed of unmodified cobbles. In total, 231 cairns were found across the top of Thotlakonda Hill, two adjacent hills, and in the floodplain below Thotlakonda in areas peripheral to the Early Historic period village.

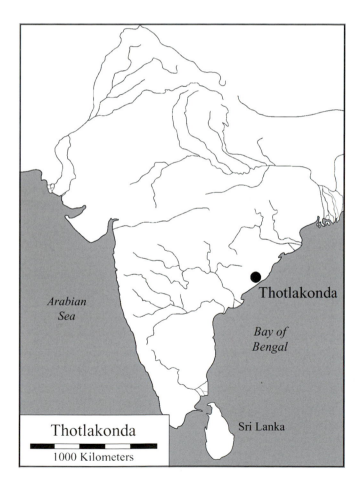

FIGURE 3.2. The location of Thotlakonda monastery in South Asia.

Here I discuss one small question in regard to these cairns: who was memorialized within them? There are three possibilities. First, the cairns may memorialize monks from Thotlakonda who were not important enough to warrant larger memorials within the monastery. A second possibility is that the cairns memorialized the local, non-monastic dead. Finally, it is also possible that the mortuary landscape blended monastic and non-monastic memorials (figure 3.3).

Following the tradition of relying on historical sources, it would seem likely that the cairns memorialized monks. Within the *Mulasarvastivada-vinaya* (Schopen 1995a, 1995b), a fifth-century C.E. Buddhist text from China, there is a description of the funeral of an ordinary monk. In this account, monks who were not important enough to warrant burial within the monastery were cremated and memorialized outside of it. This account provides rich documentation of the process of removing the body from the monastery, cleaning and preparing the body for cremation, the prayers said over the deceased, and the ritual baths mourners went through before re-entering the monastery. The critical elements of the passage in terms of understanding the cairns at Thotlakonda are (1) we should expect memorials for ordinary monks to be located outside the

FIGURE 3.3. A well-preserved cairn near Thotlakonda monastery.

monastery walls, and (2) these memorials should be far simpler than those found within the monastery. The cairns on the hills surrounding the Thotlakonda fit both of these elements. Thus, it is possible that later Buddhist mortuary practice, as described in the *Mulasarvastivada-vinaya*, may have greater antiquity, appearing four centuries earlier in South India. At least this would be the conclusion if one were to follow the strategy employed in the examination of Proto-Shiva. A closer examination of the spatial distribution of the cairns provides, I think, a more compelling understanding of this mortuary landscape, one that emphasizes its position vis-à-vis the monks and laity who created and used it.

Buddhist monastic texts do not mention funeral procedures for the Buddhist laity beyond the occasional statement that monks were to perform funeral rites for the laity even when this required the monks to leave the rainy season retreat (Schopen 1995b:105–106). What is known of these rituals is derived almost exclusively from inscriptional and archaeological sources. Hundreds of small, haphazardly placed, votive stupas are found surrounding the primary stupas at several Early Historic period pilgrimage sites (Schopen 1997:118–120). Inscriptions on some of these votive stupas document that they contained the remains of Buddhist monks, while others name members of the Buddhist laity. Thus, the mortuary population at Buddhist pilgrimage centers comprised both monastic and lay memorials. In terms of understanding the cairns at Thotlakonda, the implication of the pilgrimage sites is that not all of the cairns necessarily memorialize monks. Some, or all, may be for the laity.

This interpretation is supported by the spatial distribution of the cairns recorded during survey (figure 3.4). If the cairns were intended to memorialize monks, it seems likely they would be found on the same hill as the monastery. This is not the case. Numerous cairns were found on the hills next to Thotlakonda, and several others were located in the floodplain below Thotlakonda Hill, adjacent to an Early Historic period, non-monastic settlement. It seems unlikely that those monks who lived in relative seclusion within the monastery would be interred next to a local village or on hills distant from the monastery. These more distant cairns are more likely to be the memorials for the local Buddhist laity. This is not to say that Thotlakonda is not important in their placement.

Seventy-five percent of the cairns identified during survey were located in positions with a clear view of the monastery. Interestingly, this percentage is higher on neighboring hills than it is on Thotlakonda Hill itself. This pattern is most clearly demonstrated on a hill west of Thotlakonda and directly above the non-monastic settlement. During

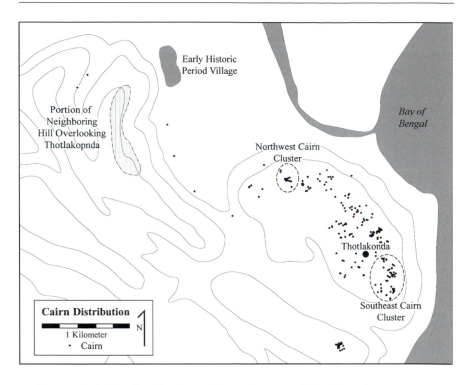

FIGURE 3.4. The distribution of the cairns near Thotlakonda monastery.

exploration of the side of the hill facing Thotlakonda, we found roughly fifty cairns. On the opposite side, where Thotlakonda monastery is not visible, not a single cairn was found. Based on this, it appears that the monastery was the center point of large mortuary landscape and that the local laity placed a value in erecting their memorials with a view of it. The distribution of the cairns suggests that local laity recognized, to some degree, monastic authority over mortuary ritual. In this context, textual accounts stating that monks should perform funeral rites for the laity begin to assume a more concrete form. Still, the question remains: what is the significance of the remaining 25 percent of the cairns that were placed out of sight of the monastery? Whose remains are buried here?

Of the cairns concealed from view of the monastery, almost all are located in two clusters on Thotlakonda Hill, one in the northwest and one in the southeast. In both cases, the significance of these cairns is best understood in terms of the other archaeological features associated with them—that is to say, by their context. The southeastern cairn cluster is centered around a reservoir. In addition to the cairns, there are four, poorly made structures as well as several areas of smoothed stone and mortars used for washing clothes and grinding seeds, respectively. Based on these material remains, as well as analyses of the ceramics collected at this site, I have previously argued that this area was used by laborers who worked at the monastery (Fogelin 2006). I have also suggested that its placement out of sight of the monastery was not accidental. The monks at Thotlakonda, desiring isolation, distanced themselves from the non-monastic people who worked for them. Given the proximity of the cairns to the reservoir and structures, and their similar concealment from the monastery, it is likely they memorialize lay Buddhists, perhaps those who worked at the monastery. Their position suggests that in death, as in life, their interaction with the monastery was kept to a minimum. This pattern is further demonstrated in the northwestern cairn cluster.

Within the northwestern cairn cluster was a quarry and an unfinished column, similar to columns found within Thotlakonda. From this evidence it appears that the area was used by the people who quarried and carved the columns used in the construction of the monastery. Like the southeastern cairn cluster, this portion of the hill is not visible to Thotlakonda. Thus, it seems that the laborers who quarried stone for the monastery were kept out of sight of the monks, just as those who worked around the southeastern reservoir were.

There is one other important archaeological feature present within this cairn cluster: the only stupa found outside of a monastery in the entire survey area. More importantly, the layout of this stupa follows a pattern that I have previously identified as serving lay, rather than monastic, ritual interests (Fogelin 2003). As with the rest of the archaeological remains within this area, it is concealed from direct view of the monastery. In contrast, it is prominently visible to the Early Historic period village in the floodplain below. The form, placement, and association with the quarries suggest that this stupa and cairn cluster created a distinct ritual space created by and for those laity who worked for the monks. Unlike the cairns on neighboring hills, these cairns were hidden from the monastery. Overall, it appears that the local laity had an ambivalent relationship with the monks at Thotlakonda: they worked for the monastery, they placed their dead in memorials on neighboring hills overlooking the monastery, but they were kept at a distance from the monastery. This distance extended even to the creation of separate ritual spaces.

But what of the cairns close to the monastery? Here my interpretation is left in the same state as our understanding of Proto-Shiva. The cairns may memorialize monks, as suggested by the *Mulasarvastivada-vinaya*. Or, they could be memorials for the local laity, perhaps those who gave larger donations to the monks. Without further information, it is not possible to decide between the two possibilities. However, based on the contextual evidence of the cairns, there is no reason to assume any continuity between the mortuary rituals of Thotlakonda and those described in the *Mulasarvastivada-vinaya*.

CONCLUSION

This example is only one small part of a larger study of the material remains at Thotlakonda which includes examinations of monastic architecture, ceramics, and the spatial distribution of other archaeological features. With this additional contextual information, I was able to investigate the ritual ties between the monks and laity with greater detail (see Fogelin 2006, 2005, 2004). I concluded that while there were strong ritual and economic ties between the monks at Thotlakonda and the local populations who lived near it, for the most part these social relationships were highly ambivalent. These conclusions address one of the ongoing problems in the textual study of Early Buddhism (Schopen 1997). Where some passages in Buddhist religious texts suggest monks should isolate themselves from local communities, others imply greater monastic interaction. My research, then, has implications for understanding these conflicting textual readings, demonstrating that contradictions in the texts reflect real tensions in the broader social role of Buddhist monasteries during the Early Historic period. This illustrates my final concern about using textual and ethnographic sources to interpret past ritual. These sources are often more ambiguous and conflicting than archaeologists have recognized (Trautmann and Sinopoli 2002). We have failed to realize that our investigations of the material world can inform historical and ethnographic debates just as much as these sources can assist in formulating archaeological interpretations of past societies.

As stated earlier, I do not see this paper as developing a new approach to the archaeology of religion. Attention to material context and difference is bread-and-butter archaeology. Archaeologists in South Asia have long been seduced by the richness of historical and ethnographic sources. I am not proposing that these sources be entirely ignored, only that archaeologists should be wary of projecting modern religious practices or motifs into past contexts. Rather, archaeological research on ancient religions should focus on material remains and the ways that religion and ritual articulate with other aspects of past societies. It is not necessary to know the precise symbolic meaning of a ritual, or the precise manner in which it was performed, to infer some of its social significance. In all of my research on the cairns at Thotlakonda, I have never learned what specific rituals were performed for the dead. Despite this, I feel that I have come to learn how these mortuary rituals served to promote and retard social ties between the monks at Thotlakonda and the local populations who lived below it.

ACKNOWLEDGMENTS

I thank the Andhra Pradesh Department of Archaeology and Museums and the Archaeological Survey of India for their assistance with the research on which this paper is based. Funding for this project was provided by the Wenner-Gren Foundation for Anthropological Research (Gr. 6597) and the University of Michigan Rackham School of Graduate Studies. Additional logistical support was provided by the American Institute of Indian Studies. The assistance of Praveena Kumar, Smita Sahay, Chhaya Bhardwaj, Hemanth Kadambi, Garima Misra, Abhishek Singh, Dilip Sebak, N. Sivakumar, and R. Chumbeno Ngullie made the fieldwork in Visakhapatnam possible. I also thank Carla Sinopoli for her suggestions on this paper. Finally, I thank Evangelos Kyriakidis and all the participants in the conference for the lively debate on issues regarding the archaeology of religion and ritual generally, and issues addressed in this work specifically.

REFERENCES CITED

Bell, Catherine
    1997   *Ritual: Perspectives and Dimensions*. Oxford University Press, Oxford.
Bloch, Maurice
    1977   The past in the present. *Man* 12:278–292.
Chakrabarti, Dilip K.
    1997   *Colonial Indology: Sociopolitics of the Ancient Indian Past*. Munshiram Manoharlal, Delhi.
    2001a   *Archaeological Geography of the Ganga Plain: The Lower and the Middle Ganga*. Permanent Black, Delhi.
    2001b   The archaeology of Hinduism. In *Archaeology and World Religion*, edited by Timothy Insoll, pp. 33–60. Routledge, New York.
Coningham, Robin
    1995   Monks, caves, and kings: A reassessment of the nature of early Buddhism in Sri Lanka. *World Archaeology* 27:266–281.
    1998   Buddhism "rematerialized" and the archaeology of Gautama Buddha. *Cambridge Archaeological Journal* 8:121–126.
    2001   The archaeology of Buddhism. In *Archaeology and World Religion*, edited by T. Insoll, pp. 61–95. Routledge, London.

Coningham, Robin, and Nick Lewer
  2000   Archaeology and identity—Interpretations and consequences.
          Antiquity 74:664–667.
Cunningham, Alexander
  1854 [1997] *The Bhilsa Topes or Buddhist Monuments of Central India.*
               Munshiram Manoharlal, New Delhi.
  1876 [1962] *The Stupa of Bharhut: A Buddhist Monument Ornamented with
               Numerous Sculptures.* Indological Book House, Varanasi.
  1892 [1998] *Mahabodhi or the Great Buddhist Temple under the Bodhi Tree at
               Buddha-Gaya.* Munshiram Manoharlal, New Delhi.
Fergusson, James, and Burgess, James
  1880 [1988] *The Cave Temples of India.* Munshiram Manoharlal Publishers
               Pvt. Ltd., New Delhi.
Fogelin, Lars
  2006   *Archaeology of Early Buddhism.* Altamira Press, Walnut Creek, CA.
  2005   Recent Research at the Buddhist Monastery of Thotlakonda. In
          South Asian Archaeology, 2001, edited by C. Jarrige and V. Lefevre,
          pp. 483-490. Editions Recherche sur les Civilisations-ADPF,
          Paris.
  2004   Sacred architecture, sacred landscape: Early Buddhism in North
          Coastal Andhra Pradesh. In *Archaeology as History: South Asia*,
          edited by H. P. Ray and C. M. Sinopoli, pp. 376–391. ICHR,
          New Delhi
  2003   Ritual and presentation in Early Buddhist religious architecture.
          Asian Perspectives 42 (1):129-154.
Fritz, John M.
  1986   Vijayanagara: Authority and meaning of a South Indian imperial
          capital. *American Anthropologist* 88:44–55.
Fritz, John M., and George Michell
  1989   Interpreting the plan of a medieval Hindu capital: Vijayanagara.
          World Archaeology 19:105–129.
Fuller, Christopher J.
  1992   *The Camphor Flame: Popular Hinduism and Society in India.*
          Princeton University Press, Princeton, NJ.
Hayes, Kelley A.
  1993   When is a symbol archaeologically meaningful? Meaning, func-
          tion, and prehistoric visual arts. In *Archaeological Theory: Who Sets
          the Agenda*, edited by Norman Yoffee and Andrew Sherratt, pp.
          81–92. Cambridge University Press, Cambridge.
Inden, Ronald B.
  1990   *Imagining India.* Basil Blackwell, Cambridge, MA.
Kenoyer, Jonathan Mark
  1998   *Ancient Cities of the Indus Valley Civilization.* Oxford University
          Press, Islamabad.

Lahiri, Nayanjot
   1996   Archaeological landscapes and textual images: A study of the
           sacred geography of Late Medieval Ballabgarh. *World Archaeology*
           28 (2):244–264.
   2000   Archaeology and identity in colonial India. *Antiquity* 74:687–692.
Ludden, David
   1985   *Peasant History in South India*. Princeton University Press, Princeton.
Mandal, Dhaneshwar
   1993   *Ayodhya: Archaeology after Demolition*. Tracts for our Times. Orient
           Longman, Hyderabad, India.
Marriott, McKim (editor)
   1969 [1955] *Village India: Studies in the Little Community*. University of
           Chicago Press, Chicago.
Marshall, John
   1931   *Mohenjo-Daro and the Indus Civilization*. Arthur Probsthain, London.
Mayer, Adrian C.
   1960   *Caste and Kinship in Central India*. University of California Press,
           Berkeley.
Morrison, Kathleen D.
   1994   States of theory and states of Asia: Regional perspectives on
           states in Asia. *Asian Perspectives* 33 (2):183–196.
Ortner, Sherry B.
   1989   *High Religion: A Cultural and Political History of Sherpa Buddhism*.
           Princeton University Press, Princeton, NJ.
Parpola, Asko
   1994   *Deciphering the Indus Script*. Cambridge University Press,
           Cambridge.
Possehl, Gregory L.
   2002   *The Indus Civilization*. Altamira Press, Walnut Creek, CA.
Rao, Nandini
   1994   Interpreting silences: Symbol and history in the case of Ram
           Janmabhoomi/Babri Masjid. In *Social Construction of the Past:
           Representation as Power*, edited by George Bond and Angela
           Gilliam, pp. 154–164. Routledge, London.
Schopen, Gregory
   1995a   Deaths, funerals, and the division of property in a monastic code.
           In *Buddhism in Practice*, edited by J. Donald S. Lopez, pp.
           473–487. Princeton University Press, Princeton, NJ.
   1995b   Monastic law meets the real world: A monk's continuing right to
           inherit family property in classical India. *History of Religions* 35
           (2):101–123.
   1997   *Bones, Stones, and Buddhist Monks: Collected Papers on the Archaeology,
           Epigraphy, and Texts of Monastic Buddhism in India*. Studies in the
           Buddhist Traditions. University of Hawaii Press, Honolulu.

Shaw, Julia
  2000a   Ayodha's sacred landscape: Ritual memory, politics and archaeo-
          logical "fact." *Antiquity* 74:693–700.
  2000b   Sanchi and its archaeological landscape: Buddhist monasteries,
          settlements and irrigation works in Central India. *Antiquity*
          74:775–776.
Shaw, Julia, and Sutcliffe, John V.
  2001   Ancient irrigation works in the Sanchi area: An archaeological
          and hydrological investigation. *South Asian Studies* 17:55–75.
Sinopoli, Carla M.
  2003   Echoes of empire: Vijayanagara and historical memory,
          Vijayanagara as historical memory. In *Archaeologies of Memory*,
          edited by Ruth M. Van Dyke and Susan E. Alcock, pp. 17–33.
          Blackwell, Malden.
Srinivas, Maisur Narasimhachar
  1966   *Social Change in Modern India*. University of California Press,
          Berkeley.
  1976   *The Remembered Village*. Oxford University Press, Delhi.
  1989   The cohesive role of Sanskritization. In *The Cohesive Role of
          Sanskritization*, edited by Maisur Narasimhachar Srinivas, pp.
          56–72. Oxford University Press, Delhi.
Talbot, Cynthia
  2001   *Precolonial India in Practice: Society, Region, and Identity in Medieval
          Andhra*. Oxford, New Delhi.
Thapar, Romila
  2002   *Early India: From the Origins to AD 1300*. University of California
          Press, Berkeley.
Trainor, Kevin
  1997   *Relics, Ritual, and Representation: Rematerializing the Sri Lankan
          Theravada Tradition*. Cambridge University Press, Cambridge.
Trautmann, Thomas R.
  1997   *Aryans and British India*. University of California Press, Berkeley.
Trautmann, Thomas R., and Carla M. Sinopoli
  2002   In the beginning was the Word: Excavating the relations between
          history and archaeology in South Asia. *Journal of the Economic and
          Social History of the Orient* 45 (4):492–523.
Van Dyke, Ruth M., and Susan E. Alcock (editors)
  2003   *Archaeologies of Memory*. Blackwell, Malden.
Wheeler, Mortimer
  1954   *Rome beyond the Imperial Frontiers*. George Bell and Sons, London.
  1968   *The Indus Civilization*. Cambridge University Press, Cambridge.
Wiser, William H., and Wiser, Charlotte V.
  1969   *Behind Mud Walls: 1930–1960*. University of California Press,
          Berkeley and Los Angeles.

4.

RETHINKING RITUAL

Joyce Marcus

Ritual and religion have been central themes in anthropology since the nineteenth century. Any social anthropologist who observes a ritual ceremony receives a rich sensory experience that can include chanting, music, dancing, the burning of incense, and so on. Since archaeologists cannot experience these behaviors directly, they have had to develop a set of strategies to reconstruct them. In this chapter, I discuss the need to isolate patterns aimed at helping us discover specific principles that characterized one ethnic group or time period and general principles that characterized all of Mesoamerica over long periods of time. Rather than continuing to regard every rite or temple as unique (and relevant only to "religion"), we need to make the study of ritual a scientific endeavor, one that allows us to discover the interconnections among religion, economics, society, and politics.

Ancient ritual is a fascinating topic. Unfortunately, it is also one in which speculation tends to outstrip solid archaeological data (Marcus 1999:67). Progress is being made, however, by implementing numerous strategies: (1) collecting ritual data from more meaningful contexts; (2) documenting the diverse roles played by ritual; (3) explaining the fit (or lack of fit) between ethnohistoric and archaeological data on ritual; and (4) using residue analyses to determine the perishable contents of ritual vessels, caches, offering boxes, and tombs (Bell et al. 2004; Bozarth and Guderjan 2003; Hurst et al. 2002; Powis et al. 2002). In addition, the increasing commitment to extensive horizontal exposures should lead to the recovery of more in situ materials on the floors of buildings and patios as well as the recovery of more caches and activity areas.

MAKING THE STUDY OF RITUAL MORE RIGOROUS

Because so many aspects of ritual can be counterintuitive, we should try to avoid imposing modern, "commonsense" views on the past. In general, we should be more concerned with producing results that can be replicated by others than with creating unique and speculative interpretations. If we can situate ritual behavior in its sociopolitical and economic contexts, we might have some success in uncovering the principles by which ritual coevolved with sociopolitical organization. Although these goals sound reasonable, many of our colleagues persist in speculating. Clearly, it is easier to guess than to recover artifacts in meaningful contexts.

Some scholars would like to employ the "direct historical approach" (Parker 1922; Wedel 1938) but cannot because relevant data—whether hieroglyphic, ethnohistoric, or ethnographic—are lacking. Still others simply do not believe that we need to provide frameworks in which plausible alternative functions and/or meanings can be tested and eliminated. A frequent challenge for archaeologists lies in trying to explain a ritual whose characteristics seem unique, making it impossible to assign it to a class of phenomena. In such cases, one productive strategy may be to derive the ritual's "key principles," as I will suggest below.

In Part I of this chapter, I discuss a few definitions and components of ritual. In Part II, I isolate key principles. In Part III, I look at specific examples that illustrate how these key principles may be manifested in the archaeological record. In Part IV, I look at regularities and patterns in ritual.

PART I: DEFINING RITUAL

The word "ritual" has been used in many ways. Many social anthropologists believe that all ritual is embedded in religion, imbued with religious symbolism, and intended to reach deities or superhuman beings. Spiro (1973:97), for example, defined "ritual" as a symbolic action system that is culturally patterned and intended to address superhuman beings. Spiro emphasized that ritual activities and meanings are shared by members of a group with a common heritage whose goal is to speak to superhuman beings. Some, like Durkheim (1961), have thought of ritual as "abnormal," because it brings about a temporary shift from normal, profane time to abnormal, sacred time. Leach (1961) also saw ritual as creating moments of sacred time that interrupted the continuum of profane time.

Still other scholars, rather than dividing ritual into profane and sacred, divide it into time-dependent vs. ad hoc ritual, or calendric vs. non-calendric ritual. In the Chinese language, for example, such a distinction already exists: the term *ch'ang* refers to recurrent ritual, while *fei ch'ang* refers to ad hoc ritual.

Calendric rites are those performed year after year on fixed dates. Familiar calendric rites in our culture include Halloween and Christmas, two holidays that can be anticipated because they occur at the same time every year. Non-calendric rites are situational and often depend on unexpected events, such as winning a battle or mourning the sudden death of a president. Over time, however, the anniversaries of those unexpected events can become calendric rituals that are commemorated on the same day every year (U.S. examples would be the attack on Pearl Harbor and the shooting of President Kennedy).

Two examples of calendric (though not annual) ritual among the Aztec of Mexico were (1) the New Fire rites, celebrated every 52 years, in which all hearth fires were extinguished and many possessions destroyed; and (2) the "Eating of Water-Soaked Tamales," a rite held every eight years. The New Fire ceremony was sometimes commemorated by the carving of monumental stones, the discard of household pottery and figurines, and the burning of incense. Elson and Smith (2001) have made a good case that archaeological materials discarded at Chiconautla in the Basin of Mexico and at Cuexcomate in Morelos were the aftermath of New Fire ceremonies.

Though we might intuitively expect annual festivals to leave more archaeological evidence than less frequent events, such is not always the case. For example, many annual rites of the Aztec were dedicated to agriculture and involved perishable items such as flowers, tamales, tobacco, liquids, paper streamers, amaranth dough made into effigies, and copal resin made into cones or spheres. Such items do not preserve well and thus are known in greatest detail from documents.

When non-calendric rites are made calendric, our chances of recovering archaeological evidence for them may be increased. This is especially true if (1) the rites were conducted in or near nonperishable structures; (2) they involved the creation of caches, tombs, or large middens; and (3) they were associated with major feasts, funerals, and building dedications.

There are, of course, other definitions of ritual than those already presented, and some of them may be even more useful to archaeologists. Definitions that do not require all ritual to be religious are of particular utility. Indeed, some anthropologists use "ritual" as a generic noun that they modify, as in the expressions "religious ritual," "military ritual," "political ritual," "marriage ritual," "inauguration ritual," "secular ritual," "royal ritual," "commoner ritual," and so forth. In such usage, "ritual" simply refers to a set of behaviors enacted according to specific protocol. One scholar who viewed ritual in precisely this way was Rappaport (1999:25), who emphasized that not all ritual was religious, nor were all religious acts ritual.

Rappaport's (1999:24) definition of ritual is *"the performance of more or less invariant sequences of formal acts and utterances not entirely encoded by the performers*" (italics in original). His focus on "performance" and on "sequences of formal acts" is particularly useful to archaeology, since repeated performances can result in activity areas or features accompanied by certain artifacts (for example, caches or offering boxes). Rappaport's awareness that sequences and formal acts may be traditional, yet subject to change, is also extremely useful to archaeologists. Indeed, some acts and utterances may be traditional in form and content, but during performances they can be altered in unintentional ways.

From an archaeological perspective, it is the repetition of formal acts that increases the likelihood that physical evidence will be left. Even though there may be changes in ritual over time (for example, in location, content, meaning, and performance), the performers of such rituals would have felt pressure to conduct the ritual the same way every time. In fact, one goal of ritual is to maintain the appearance of unchanging tradition in the face of upheaval and change.

Since ritual must be performed over and over in prescribed ways to be effective, these repetitive performances can bring about patterning in the archaeological record. Archaeologists therefore need to locate the places where rituals were performed; draw inferences about why those places were considered appropriate for ritual; determine which nonperishable artifacts should be discarded there; and consider which perishable artifacts might also have been used, even when their recovery is unlikely.

Although we cannot directly observe ancient rituals, we can find the places where rites were performed and recover the paraphernalia discarded after the performance. For example, Mesoamerican archaeologists often find ritual paraphernalia in caches and offering boxes below ancient temples, as well as evidence for the dedication of buildings and the burning of incense in portable braziers (Marcus and Flannery 1994, 1996; Mock 1998). Since repetitive performances can produce patterning in the archaeological record, we should be able to find places repeatedly chosen for the deposition of artifacts used in ritual performances. The archaeological record may even allow us to observe changes in ritual over time.

There are both advantages and limitations in the recovery of ritual data. One advantage is that ritual sometimes has an invariant sequence of actions, a kind of "script" guiding the performer so that the rite can be repeated the same way each time. Without such order and repetition, archaeologists would have less hope of determining the pattern. A potential limitation, however, is that the paraphernalia used in a given ritual may be so conservative that we fail to detect that other aspects of the ritual, such as content and meaning, have changed. Even in those cases

FIGURE 4.1. To honor the mountains surrounding the Basin of Mexico, the Aztec made miniature replicas or effigies. (*a*) Examples of the effigies made during the month of Tepeilhuitl; at the top is Mount Tlaloc, with his characteristic teeth shown at the base of the hill. The four anthropomorphized mountains were offered incense, tamales, and meat in a ceremony called *calonoac*. (*b*) The effigy mountains (*Tepictoton*), made from amaranth and maize dough, represent Iztaccihuatl and Popocatepetl, among others. (Redrawn by K. Clahassey from Broda 1971: Figures 12, 14)

where changes in ritual practices may be almost imperceptible, we should never forget that every aspect of society, including ritual, can change.

A perennial problem in the study of ritual, at least from the perspective of archaeology, is that many rites involved perishable offerings such as flowers, paper, plants, cloth, food, and beverages. For example, during Tepeilhuitl (which corresponds to October 12–31), the Aztec honored the mountains ringing the Basin of Mexico by making effigy mountains (*ixiptla tepetl*) from maize dough mixed with amaranth (figure 4.1) and by making effigy lightning bolts by covering tree branches with amaranth paste.[1] After singing a different song to every mountain, the Aztec gave tamales to each (Sahagún 1997:64). Such rites would be virtually impossible to learn about without documents.

The Components of Ritual

Ritual has at least eight components, with some more likely to leave archaeologically recoverable traces than others. In the following list, I have drawn all my concrete examples from Mesoamerica because a world-wide list would require a much longer chapter.

1. One or more performers

2. An audience (humans, deities, ancestors)

3. A location (temple, field, patio, stairway, cave, top of an altar)

4. A purpose (to communicate with ancestors, to sanctify a new temple)

5. Meaning, subject matter, and content

6. Temporal span (hour, day, week)

7. Actions (chanting, singing, playing music, dancing, wearing masks and costumes, burning incense, bloodletting, sacrificing humans or animals, smoking, making pilgrimages to caves or mountaintops)

8. Foods and paraphernalia (stingray spines, obsidian blades, cones and spheres of copal incense, balls of rubber, paper streamers, beverages, meats, tamales) used in the performance of rites

Obviously, the components more likely to be recovered are locations (for example, caves, hilltops, fields, temples, plazas, palaces, and patios of houses) and paraphernalia (for example, obsidian blades, stingray spines, incense burners). Much less likely to be recovered are meanings, songs, dances, flowers, paper offerings, effigy dough figures, and so forth.

PART II: IDENTIFYING KEY PRINCIPLES

To advance the study of ritual in any part of the ancient world, we need to identify the key principles that structured ritual performance and gave it meaning. In Mesoamerica, such underlying principles operated on multiple levels: conceptual, structural, and hierarchical. Similar rites could be replicated in different cultural domains (for example, in the domestic and non-domestic spheres); at increasingly larger scales within a single settlement (in a house, in a residential ward, and in the settlement's main plaza); or at different villages or towns in a political hierarchy (at a third-tier site, at a second-tier site, and at the capital).

For example, a twentieth-century highland Maya ritual was treated by Vogt (1965) as a set of behaviors that were replicated on several levels. He defined *structural* replication, in which certain ritual behaviors were replicated at various levels of society, and *conceptual* replication, in which certain concepts were replicated in several domains of culture.

It is as if the Zinacantecos have constructed a model for ritual behavior and for conceptualization of the natural and cultural world which functions like a kind of computer that prints out rules for appropriate behavior at each organizational level of the society and for the appropriate conceptualizing of phenomena in the different domains of the culture. [Vogt 1965:342]

Vogt's focus on replication—especially structural replication—is of practical use to archaeologists because it is likely to leave traces in the archaeological record. As an example of structural replication, Vogt (1965:345) discussed a rite replicated at three levels: by one family in its house compound, by clusters of family compounds, and by entire hamlets. Seven rules had to be met to make a meal a *ritual* meal:

Rule 1: The meal must be served on a wooden rectangular table (see figure 4.2).

Rule 2: The table must be oriented with the long axis running east–west.

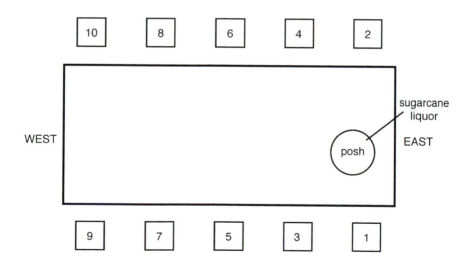

FIGURE 4.2. Seating at a highland Maya ritual meal is determined by rank. At the east end of the table sit the most highly ranked (1–4), while the lowest ranked (7–10) sit at the west end. (Redrawn from Vogt 1965:346)

Rule 3: The table must be covered with a pink and white striped cloth.

Rule 4: A bottle of *posh* (an alcoholic beverage) must be placed in the center of the east end of the table.

Rule 5: The participants must sit in small wooden chairs at the table in strict rank order.

Rule 6: The meal consists of posh, maize tortillas, chicken cooked in broth with chile, coffee, and bread.

Rule 7: The eating of the meal must follow a strictly prescribed sequence which consists of 11 basic steps describing which food is eaten first, who eats first, and so on.

Although many of Vogt's rules would leave few archaeological traces, knowing about them prepares us to look for certain clues in the archaeological record. Once we recognize a recurring attribute (for example, the tendency for a rite to occur in a rectangular space, with the paraphernalia used in that rite deposited at the corners of a room or building), we can excavate looking for such evidence.

The generation of ancient rules can also explain why a particular rite was conducted on a mountaintop, or why it might be replicated in rectangular spaces of different dimensions. Recognition of the rules helps us see connections between ritual localities within a single site as well as between sites.

In addition to looking for structural and conceptual replication in a single culture area or community, archaeologists can work to compare key principles utilized by societies at different levels of sociopolitical complexity within the same language family. Within the Uto-Aztecan language family, for example, there were hunter-gatherers, egalitarian village societies, chiefdoms, and states. All believed in a rectangular universe divided into four quadrants, each associated with a different color. This cosmological principle can always be seen, whatever the complexity of the Uto-Aztecan society.

PART III: KEY PRINCIPLES AND STRUCTURAL REPLICATION AMONG THE AZTEC OF MEXICO

Some archaeologists find structural replication easiest to detect when they take the "bottom-up" view, proceeding from the smallest to the largest unit—for example, from the activity area to the house, to the residential ward, to the main plaza. An alternative strategy is to take the "top-down" view, beginning at the capital and proceeding down to second- and third-tier sites. Both approaches are useful and complementary.

Because of their rich ethnohistoric documentation, the Aztec of the Basin of Mexico can be used to illustrate both approaches. I will select three interrelated cosmological principles and show how they manifest themselves on several levels. Those principles are (1) the universe is alive; (2) the universe is divided into four world quadrants; and (3) the supernatural forces that animate the world can be approached by humans who dress in appropriate attire and/or impersonate those forces. As I will make clear, the Aztec were not the only Mesoamerican group who held these views. Few other groups, however, had their beliefs recorded in as much detail by the conquering Spaniards of the sixteenth century.

Principle I. The universe is alive.

The indigenous populations of Mesoamerica perceived life not only in plants and animals, but also in objects that we consider inanimate (Marcus 1978, 1983a; Thompson 1970). In this view, called *animatism*, the earth, hills, mountains, caves, stalactites, rocks, streams, lightning, wind, the sun, the moon, water, and many more things were all considered to be alive (Lowie 1924; Tylor 1873). Many of them possessed an inner vital force, which the Zapotec called *pèe*, the Maya *ik*, the Mixtec *ini*, and the Aztec *teotl*. Mesoamerican people interacted with these living things by showing them respect, making offerings to them, and forming pacts with them which required reciprocal obligations (Marcus 1978). Mankind could only approach certain sacred hills, mountains, caves, and lightning by following appropriate behavior and wearing appropriate attire. This attribution of life to inanimate features of the landscape affected man–land relations and should therefore affect how we interpret Mesoamerican ritual (Marcus 2006).

As an example of how the system worked, we will look at how indigenous groups formed relationships with certain mountains, and see how understanding that relationship can be used to retrieve ritual data in meaningful contexts. Mesoamerican groups considered many mountains to be sacred and alive, transforming them into "activity areas" where ritual performances were conducted and offerings deposited or discarded.[2] Archaeologists should thus be able to document ritual performances there. For example, a prehispanic worshiper might climb a mountain to sacrifice a child, to burn incense, to burn paper spattered with drops of rubber or sacrificial blood, or to leave food, drink, and other objects as offerings. In return for this act of generosity, the petitioner hoped that a request would be answered—for example, that rain would come on time or that the harvest would be abundant. Humans made the first move and waited for the request to be answered. Meantime, their offerings became part of a ritual activity area.

The Basin of Mexico, where we have both ethnohistoric documents and archaeological data, provides good examples of such processes (figure 4.3). We will begin with the ethnohistoric data, which provide us with a model, and then proceed to the archaeology.

Throughout the October to May dry season, the Aztec performed a series of rites to ask for rain; several of these involved the sacrifice of children (Broda 1971: Table 1; Sahagún 1981:8). One of these rites was the festival Huey Tozoztli, led by members of the Aztec royalty accompanied by other nobles. Rulers from the cities of Tenochtitlan, Texcoco, Xochimilco, and Tlacopan ascended Mount Tlaloc to make offerings on the 4100-m summit. This location affords a marvelous view of the snow-capped volcanoes Iztaccihuatl (White Woman) and Popocatepetl (Smoke Mountain).[3] According to the sixteenth-century friar Diego Durán (1971: 156–157), the kings of these four cities made their annual pilgrimage to Mount Tlaloc at the height of the dry season, usually on April 29 or 30. There they called forth rain from the mountain's interior so that planting could begin.

To ensure that the rains would arrive on time, these rulers sacrificed children on the summit of Mount Tlaloc.[4] These rites took place in a per-ishable structure in front of a stone statue of Tlaloc,[5] the lightning/rain deity, whose name meant "something lying on the surface of the earth" (Arnold 1999; Klein 1980; Sullivan 1974). The name Tlaloc was an allu-sion to the fact that rain clouds often appeared to be lying atop Mount Tlaloc[6] (Townsend 1992:114). It was believed that *Tlalocan*, the domain of this deity, was a watery underworld situated inside the mountain[7] (Charnay 1887:84; López Austin 1994). Requests for rain could be made at the base or the summit, but the most important pilgrims, including the humans who impersonated the mountain deity, ascended to the summit (Broda 1971:281).

Another sixteenth-century source describes a white stone statue of Tlaloc, in human form, on the top of the mountain; on this statue's head was said to be a receptacle filled with liquid rubber (Pomar 1941:15). Into that receptacle the pilgrims placed kernels of corn—white, black, red, and yellow—as well as different varieties of beans, chiles, chía or *Salvia* (sage), and *huauhtli* or amaranth. The sacrificed children were reported to have

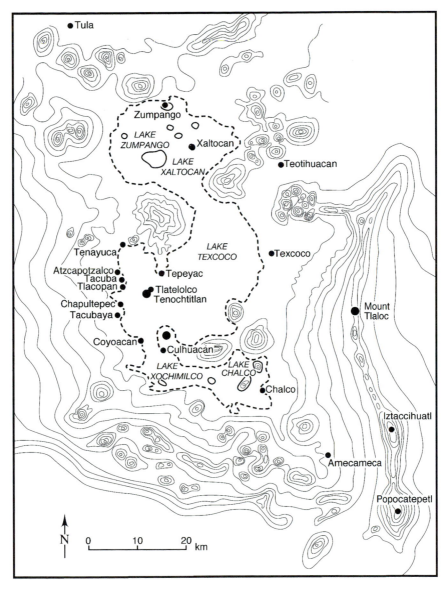

FIGURE 4.3. Map showing the location of sacred mountains—Mount Tlaloc, Iztaccihuatl, and Popocatepetl—to the east of the Aztec capital of Tenochtitlan. (Drawn by K. Clahassey)

been thrown in a cavern, "a dark and deep natural opening," near the statue of Tlaloc (Pomar 1941:18). These young victims stayed inside the hill, stored as maize kernels until the end of the rainy season; they played an active role in the growth of the corncobs and returned from Mount Tlaloc to the earth at harvest time[8] (Broda 2001:299; Torquemada 1969, II:151).

Now let us look at the archaeological data from Mount Tlaloc (Iwaniszewski 1994; Rickards 1929; Townsend 1991; Wicke and Horcasitas 1957). Although excavation there has been limited, mapping has yielded new data from the summit. There Richard Townsend and Felipe Solís found a narrow, 150-m-long processional corridor which required pilgrims to walk single file until they reached a rectangular stone enclosure or precinct (figure 4.4). The walls of the corridor are 3 m high and 2.3 m thick, while those of the outer rectangular enclosure are 2.35 m thick (Iwaniszewski 1994:161). There is a pit cut into bedrock, situated between the inner and outer enclosure walls, which may correspond to the "dark opening" where sacrificed children were thrown (Broda 1971:275; Iwaniszewski 1994:162). Townsend (1992:133) describes this pit as a 3-m-deep shaft surrounded by four large basalt boulders, each situated at an intercardinal direction; there was also a centrally placed boulder inside.

> This cosmological geometry recalls a famous page from the Codex Borgia, depicting Tlaloque standing at the intercardinal points and another, vertical Tlaloc in the central panel of the page. . . . We believe that the top of the mountain was modified in antiquity to remove other rock formations that might have interrupted the cosmological symmetry. [Townsend 1991:28]

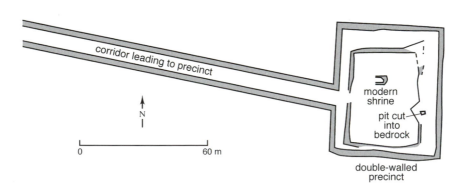

FIGURE 4.4. Stone constructions on the summit of Mount Tlaloc, east of the Basin of Mexico and north of Iztaccihuatl and Popocatepetl. A long corridor led pilgrims to the precinct where a statue of Tlaloc and his *tlaloque* once stood. (Redrawn by K. Clahassey from Iwaniszewski 1994: Figure 3)

Using Durán's (1971) description, Townsend (1992:136) suggests that Aztec royalty entered the corridor and enclosure bearing gifts, "following strict rank order, and then proceeded to dress the stone idols in Tlaloc's splendid regalia." They left offerings of food and sacrificed one or more children.[9] Although the Tlaloc statue photographed in the twentieth century is no longer present, Townsend and Solís did find obsidian blades, jadeite beads, pyrite mirror fragments, turquoise mosaic fragments, mold-made figurines, and broken pottery vessels.

There is no question that without Durán's and Pomar's accounts, we would have found it difficult to learn certain details about the ritual. For example, although we might have guessed that some participants were important people, we would not have realized that four of them were kings from four different Aztec cities. Given the presence of a pit cut into bedrock, we might have guessed that offerings or ritual paraphernalia were discarded there, but we would not have known that this dark place was the receptacle for the sacrificed children. (This function, known from the ethnohistoric sources, could be confirmed or dismissed, if this shaft were to be excavated.) Since the foods used as offerings were perishable, we would not have known that corn of four different colors was used to represent the four world directions of the Mesoamerican cosmos (see below). And, since paper, cloth, and feathers do not preserve well, we might not have realized that Tlaloc and the other stone statues were dressed in them by the kings who ascended the summit.

To learn more about Tlaloc, we can turn to the sixteenth-century friar Bernardino de Sahagún, who says:

> To him was attributed the rain; for he made it, he caused it to come down, he scattered the rain like seed, and also the hail. He caused to sprout, to blossom, to leaf out, to bloom, to ripen, the trees, the plants, our food. And also by him were made floods of water and thunder-bolts.

> And he was thus decorated: his face was thickly painted black, his face was painted with liquid rubber; it was anointed with black; his face was spattered with a paste of amaranth seeds. [Sahagún 1950:2]

What kinds of offerings would such a storm/lightning god want? Our evidence suggests that Tlaloc wanted

1. columns of smoke from burning incense and from burning paper spattered with drops of blood or rubber

2. caches of obsidian blades

3. items that were the color of water, such as blue-green beads and turquoise mosaics

4. sacrificed infants and children to serve as his assistants, his *tlaloque*

5. effigies of mountains made from corn dough and/or amaranth seeds

6. representations of Tlaloc in pottery or stone

7. wooden staffs shaped like lightning bolts, an obvious metaphor for the storms that bring rain

Let us look at these seven categories and see what kinds of traces they are likely to leave.

1. Although we might not recover paper, blood, rubber, or incense, we should be able to recover ceramic incense burners. These are abundant in Aztec debris, especially at ritual venues. In special circumstances, we might even recover copal incense (Altamira 1972:43; Montero García 2001:33); for example, spheres and cones of copal have been found at the bottom of the Lake of the Moon in the crater of the volcano of Toluca (figure 4.5). Although human or animal blood is difficult to recover, the implements used for bloodletting can be recovered: maguey spines and obsidian lancets, blades, or knives (Guilliem Arroyo et al. 1998; Iwaniszewski and Montero García 2001:106; Montero García 2001:32; Townsend 1991:29). As for the effigy figures of copal and rubber mentioned in sixteenth-century documents, they have been found in well-preserved contexts below the Templo Mayor in the Aztec capital of Tenochtitlan; at least 58

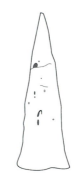

FIGURE 4.5. Offerings to Tlaloc included copal cones and spheres, such as these recovered from the Lakes of the Sun and Moon on the Toluca Volcano. (Drawn by K. Clahassey from photos in Montero García 2001: Figure 6)

separate offerings found there included copal gum or resin that had been formed into anthropomorphic figures, cylinders, balls, or other shapes (Guilliem Arroyo et al. 1998: Figure 10; López Luján 1994:477).

2. Ritual caches may contain offerings, gifts, or discarded paraphernalia associated with bloodletting and sacrifice. For example, obsidian lancets and knives are often discarded at the scene of the rite, and even maguey spines may be recovered (Montero García 2001:32).

3. There is iconographic evidence and ethnohistoric documentation suggesting that greenstone (jadeite) beads symbolized raindrops and corn kernels, both of which were closely associated with Tlaloc and his assistants. Four or five blue-green beads are sometimes found inside water jars depicting Tlaloc, and such jars have been found below the Templo Mayor of Tenochtitlan (figure 4.6). It is likely that the four beads represented the

FIGURE 4.6. Below the Templo Mayor of Tenochtitlan were stone offering boxes dedicated to Tlaloc. In this offering box (No. 48), we see several Tlaloc jars. (Redrawn by K. Clahassey from López Luján 1994: Figure 76)

four world directions, while the fifth (when present) represented the center of the universe (López Luján 1994). The color blue was closely associated with Tlaloc, and thus offerings to him are likely to be blue or blue-green (for example, jade, jadeite, turquoise, as well as ceramic, wooden, and stone items that were painted blue; see figure 4.7).

4. The skeletons of sacrificed children may be recovered. These small victims served as *tlaloque* or assistants to Tlaloc; their job was twofold: to take charge of the maize kernels, and to be ready to pour water from jars. In return for the blood of sacrificed children, Tlaloc supplied mankind with another precious liquid, water. Children were sacrificed to pay a debt to Tlaloc and were regarded as a down payment. Indeed, the Aztec term *nextlahualli*—"debt paid" or "debt payment"—is the most frequently used metaphor for the sacrifice of a person (Arnold 1999; Aveni 1991:71; Broda 1971:272–276; D. Carrasco 1991; López Austin 1988, Vol. 2: 292). As Broda (1991:84) has said, "human sacrifice, which formed one of the basic structural elements of ritual, was conceived as a magical act of reciproci-

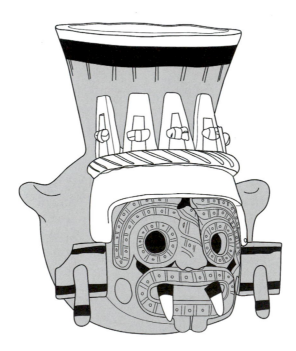

FIGURE 4.7. Painted Tlaloc vessel from Templo Mayor, Tenochtitlan. The white areas are painted white; the darkest areas are painted red; the predominant color of the vessel, including the face, is a bright blue (except for the red and white teeth protruding from the mouth). (Drawn by K. Clahassey from a photo in Matos Moctezuma 1984:86)

ty according to the principle of *do ut des* ('give that you may receive')."
Children sacrificed to Tlaloc were decapitated, just as the effigy dough
hills lost their miniature human heads (figure 4.1).

Tlaloc's sanctuary, one of the twin temples of the Templo Mayor, is
appropriately shown with water jars on its roof (see Durán 1994: Plate
30). Some of the paraphernalia commonly associated with Tlaloc were
deposited in that temple's offering boxes. One such offering box contained the bones of at least 42 children between the ages of 2 and 7
(Broda 1987a, 1987b; López Luján 1994:347; Román Berrelleza 1987).
Two of the children had wooden pectorals with turquoise mosaics similar to the mosaic fragments recovered on the top of Mount Tlaloc by
Townsend and Solís. Other children had necklaces of tiny greenstone
beads; five children had a bead in the mouth, evidently substituting for a
corn kernel. Finally, some children's bones bore traces of blue paint, the
color associated with Tlaloc and his assistants. Above the skeletal remains
of the 42 children were 11 stone sculptures, representing water jars with
Tlaloc faces on them; all the jars were intentionally placed on their sides,
tipped over to simulate the act of pouring water (López Luján 1994:199).

5. Effigies of mountains made from dough (whether maize or amaranth) are not likely to be recovered archaeologically. Judging from the
documents, the making of such dough figures was quite common (figure
4.1a, b), but to understand fully the role of *tzoalli* mountains, we are
dependent on ethnohistoric documents.

6. Representations of Tlaloc in pottery and stone have been found on
Mount Ajusco, on Mount Tlaloc, and in offering boxes dedicated to Tlaloc
under the Templo Mayor of Tenochtitlan (Charnay 1887:83–85, 169;
López Luján 1994; Montero García 2001:34). Some depictions show him
with blue paint on his face, large circles around his eyes, and surrounded
by raindrops, corn stalks, and/or blue-green beads (figures 4.7, 4.8).

7. Wooden staffs carved to represent lightning bolts ("rayos de
madera") have been found at 4,700 m in the Lakes of the Sun and the
Moon in the crater of the Toluca Volcano (Altamira 1972); on the summit
of Mount Iztaccihuatl at 5,000 m; and in the Templo Mayor of Tlatelolco
(Espejo 1945; Iwaniszewski and Montero García 2001; see figure 4.9).
The wood used for these objects has been identified as pine (*Pinus* sp.).
When such carved staffs have been found preserved in cists or offering
boxes, as at Tlatelolco, they often retain blue paint, characteristic of
Tlaloc (Guilliem Arroyo et al. 1998:112, Figures 13A, B). Stone staffs in the
shape of thunderbolts have been found beneath the Pyramid of the Moon
at Teotihuacan (Sugiyama and Cabrera Castro 2004) and in offering boxes

FIGURE 4.8. This Tlaloc deity or impersonator, with its characteristic goggle-eyed mask and prominent teeth, is surrounded by blue raindrops and/or blue beads called *chalchihuites*. (Redrawn from Broda 1971:249)

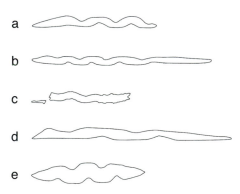

FIGURE 4.9. Lightning bolts made of wood or stone were held by Tlaloc impersonators (*a–d* are wood; *e* is stone). (*a*) 47 cm long, from the Lake of the Moon, Toluca Volcano; (*b*) 68 cm long, from the peak of Iztaccihuatl; (*c*) from excavations at the Templo Mayor, Tlatelolco; (*d*) 75.3 cm long, from the peak of Iztaccihuatl; (*e*) 42.9 cm long, from the Pyramid of the Moon, Teotihuacan. (*a–d*, Iwaniszewski and Montero García 2001: Figure 5; *e*, Sugiyama and Cabrera Castro 2004: Figure 86)

(for example, Offering H) beneath the Templo Mayor at Tenochtitlan (Broda 1987a: Figure 18; López Luján 1994).

Various depictions of Tlaloc show him holding a staff shaped like a lightning bolt (figure 4.10a–e). Durán (1971:155) describes Tlaloc and the staff as follows: "In his right hand Tlaloc carried a purplish wooden thunderbolt, curved like the lightning which falls from the clouds, wriggling like a snake toward the earth." Thus, ethnohistoric, iconographic, and archaeological evidence link Tlaloc to lightning and lightning bolts, not at all surprising since both are closely associated with thunder, rain, hail, and mountains among other Mesoamerican groups.

Principle II. The earth is divided into four quadrants.

Another widespread Mesoamerican principle is the view that the world was divided into four quarters, each associated with a specific color, tree, wind, or other attribute (Thompson 1934; Marcus 1983a:356). This principle was

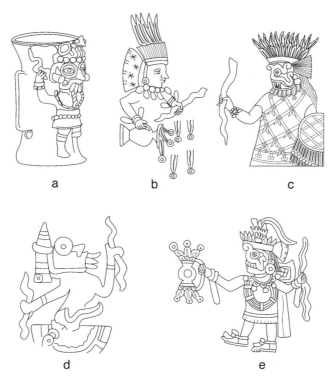

FIGURE 4.10. Tlaloc, shown holding a lightning bolt. (Redrawn from (*a*) Charnay 1887:83; (*b*) Kubler and Gibson 1951: Plate 12; (*c*) Iwaniszewski and Montero García 2001:107; (*d*) Seler 1963: Figure 252; (*e*) Caso 1936: Figure 14)

so ancient that by the time the Aztec displayed it, as we shall see, it had already been used by countless earlier Mesoamerican cultures.

As far back as 1100 B.C., we find examples of the "four-world-direction" motif on Formative-period celts and pottery (Covarrubias 1957: Figure 32). While some of these motifs display the usual four elements, others show five, forming what is called the *quincunx*—a center surrounded by four dots (Marcus 1999: Figure 6c–e). The most elaborate depictions may show re-dundancy—that is, multiple "four-direction" motifs, multiple Earth's head clefts, or multiple nested versions (Niederberger 1987: Figure 439). Such replication helps the viewer to understand what is being depicted.

A Formative household unit from San José Mogote, Oaxaca, has yield-ed what may be early evidence for the association of colors with world directions (Marcus 1998:13–15). In the dooryard of the unit were two cir-cular basins. One basin was 1.2 m in diameter, recessed 5 cm into the earth, lime-plastered and painted red. A similar basin 3 m to the south was paint-ed yellow. We suspect that the dooryard may originally have contained four such basins, each painted a different color. Unfortunately, a nearby arroyo had removed part of the dooryard, and it was not clear in what direction we would need to expand in order to search for other basins.

One clue to the function of these basins was that they had been water-proofed with lime plaster. They may thus have been used as the kind of ritual basin in which Zapotec women are known to have performed "div-ination on water" or *tiniyaaya niça* (Marcus 1998:12–13, 1999:80). Such divination involved tossing items like kernels of maize onto the surface of a water-filled basin, to see whether an odd number or even number of them floated. The results were used to make family decisions and answer questions with the aid of supernatural guidance.

Another ritual associated with four world directions comes from the same village of San José Mogote. At the dedication of Structure 28, a whitewashed temple built in roughly 600 B.C., offerings were placed at each of the four corners of its recessed floor. Buried in each corner was a serving vessel—brown vessels in the northeast and southwest corners and gray vessels in the northwest and southeast corners (Marcus and Flannery 2004: Figure 5). These were probably serving bowls that held food for celebrants during the building dedication and then buried after use.

Another Zapotec example comes from the mountaintop city of Monte Albán. The South Platform, a truncated pyramid supporting tem-ples, was dedicated by placing offerings at its corners. The offerings, dat-ing to roughly A.D. 300, were buried in stone boxes at the corners of the platform. Each box contained 5 large spiny oyster shells, 5 small spiny oyster shells, 10 tent olive shells, and 7 jade beads (Acosta 1958–1959:27; Marcus 1983b:176, 179; Marcus and Flannery 1996: 220–221).

This Mesoamerican *principle of quadripartition*—the division of the world into four quarters—was replicated at the level of the individual household, the corners of a major temple, and at an even higher level, the divisions of a territorial state. For example, in the Maya region there is a hieroglyphic text that associates the four world directions with four lords and four capital cities; a passage dating to A.D. 731 (on Stela A at the Honduran city of Copán) refers to four types of skies and heavens, then to four world directions, and then to four hereditary lords who ruled four different cities (Copán, Tikal, Calakmul, and Palenque) (Marcus 1993).

It is no surprise, therefore, that by the time of the Aztec, such principles were widespread. The Aztec divided their capital, Tenochtitlan, into four quadrants (*nauhcampa*), each associated with a color and a patron deity. The main plaza at Tenochtitlan was considered to be the center or navel (*tlalxico*) of the empire (like the central element of the earlier quincunx), with four quadrants radiating out from it.

Many Aztec rituals required that each item be offered to each of the four world directions and to the center.[10] Such rites could be replicated on several levels: in offering boxes, houses, temples, and the main plaza of a city. For example, copal was placed in each corner and in the center of an offering box at Tlatelolco (Guilliem Arroyo et al. 1998:111). Deities like Tlaloc, as well as his assistants, occurred in groups of four (or even five). One of the Tlalocs, in fact, was known as *Nappa Tecuhtli* or "Lord of the Four World Directions" (Sahagún 1950:21, 44). To honor Tlaloc and prepare for the sacrifice of a female child, the Aztec created an artificial forest of trees and shrubs in front of the temple of Tlaloc; in the center of the plaza they placed a huge tree and around it four small trees to complete a quincunx (Durán 1971:162). A depiction of a quincunx can be seen in figure 4.11, where four Tlalocs surround a blue center. This quadrupling (and quintupling) of Lightning and Rain supernaturals was characteristic of the Aztec, Zapotec, and Maya, as well as other Mesoamerican groups (López Austin and López Luján 2004; Marcus 1978:187; Marcus et al. 1983:39, Pijoán 1964; Thompson 1934).

Principle III. Supernatural forces and sacred items that are animate can be approached only by those wearing the appropriate attire and carrying the appropriate objects.

A third key principle in ancient Mesoamerica was that supernatural forces and deities, frightening and unapproachable under secular conditions, could

FIGURE 4.11. The Aztec painted four *tlalocs* surrounding a center on the underside of this lid from a stone offering box from Tizapán, Mexico. Each *tlaloc* is painted a different color. The shaded areas are painted blue. (Drawn by K. Clahassey from color painting in Pijoán 1964: Lámina I)

be approached by ritual impersonators. Such impersonators could be living humans, either adults or children; they could be stone or dough statues; they could even be the impersonator's costume, hanging from a wooden frame.

Petitioners could impersonate supernatural forces by wearing masks, headdresses, ornaments, and costumes, and by carrying appropriate paraphernalia. The strategy of wearing masks and costumes to approach the supernatural probably has deep roots in Mesoamerica but cannot be documented archaeologically until after 1400 B.C. At that time, early villagers were making pottery masks, ornaments, and costumes incorporating iron ore mirrors, mica, shell, feathers, animal teeth, and other body parts (Flannery and Marcus 2005). Figurines of the period 1150 to 850 B.C. often depict humans in elaborate masks and costumes (Marcus 1998; Niederberger 1987).

Now let us look in detail at Aztec ritual impersonation. In the language of the Aztec, the key word was *teixiptla*. This term could refer to living humans who wore a costume; to effigies of stone, wood, or dough; or to a ritual costume arranged on a wooden frame that included a mask (Hvidtfeldt 1958; Townsend 1992). Impersonators (*in ixiptla in teteo*) could represent deities, animals, maize, lightning, or other living things containing the vital force. Impersonators included both the priests who performed a sacrifice and the victims to be sacrificed. At one ritual, Durán (1964:111) says:

> The priests who were to perform the sacrifice stood in a long row, according to their rank. Each one of them was disguised as a god.

Even the dead might be costumed as impersonators. Speaking of the wooden statue of a dead Aztec king, Durán (1964:176) says:

> Over this garb he was dressed with the garments of the divinity Tlaloc so that he represented that deity. Upon his head was a crown of mixed white and green plumes. In one hand he held a shield of fine quality and in the other a stick carved in the form of lightning, like that of Tlaloc, since he was the god of thunderbolts and rain.

The Aztec frequently trained war captives destined to be sacrificed how to impersonate the deity Tezcatlipoca, "The Smoking Mirror." The Tezcatlipoca impersonator was supposed to be thin, handsome, fair, and blemish-free. For a year he would be treated as a god, enjoying luxury, fine food, and beautiful music. The impersonator was taught to speak more eloquently, to talk graciously with commoners whom he met during processions, and to play the flute (figure 4.12a). He might even be adorned with flowers and finery by the Aztec ruler himself. All this "living in the lap of luxury," however, ended after one year of living like a deity.

Twenty days before his sacrifice, the captive impersonator had his hair cut so that he would once again look like a warrior[11] (Sahagún 1981:70). During his final 20 days, he was given four women as wives, each dressed as a goddess impersonator, and each to be impregnated. The four goddesses being impersonated—Uixtocihuatl, Xilonen, Xochiquetzal, and Atlatonan—were associated with salt, maize, flowers, and water, respectively. During his final few days, the Tezcatlipoca impersonator and his four goddess companions traveled to different Aztec cities and handed out gifts. Their tour ended at a temple called Tlacochcalco. Sahagún (1981: 71) tells us that the captive impersonator ascended the temple steps of his own free will, breaking and discarding a series of flutes and whistles as he ascended (figure 4.12b). At the top, he was seized by the sacrificial priests, who stretched him over a stone and cut out his heart. His skull was later

a   b

FIGURE 4.12 The Aztec selected a fair, blemish-free lad to impersonate Tezcatlipoca for a year before he was sacrificed. (*a*) shows this impersonator (*ixiptla*) playing a flute (Sahagún 1981: Figure 15); (*b*) shows this impersonator being sacrificed; the flutes he discarded can be seen lying on the temple steps and at the base of the temple (Sahagún 1981: Figure 19).

removed and placed on a skull rack along with those of previous victims. Heyden (1991:200) interprets this sacrifice as follows:

> [T]he sacrifice of Tezcatlipoca signifies the end of the dry season. Tezcatlipoca's smoke is replaced with water from the sky, the dry gives way to the wet. . . . And the four symbols of agricultural abundance [four impregnated goddess impersonators] are free to bear fruit.

According to Sahagún (1981:66, 68), a Tezcatlipoca impersonator was sacrificed during an annual festival, and as soon as he was sacrificed, a new impersonator was chosen to represent Tezcatlipoca during the next year.[12] This rite was not an isolated request for abundance and life-giving rains, but part of a series of rites that involved the pilgrimages and child sacrifice on Mount Tlaloc and other summits as well as lakes. These rituals were intended to end the dry season and inaugurate a new agricultural cycle (Broda 1971; P. Carrasco 1976; Heyden 1991).

We have seen a series of Aztec rituals in which our three fundamental principles are brought together. Pilgrims traveled to the summit of a living mountain where children costumed as Tlaloc were sacrificed, where four colors of corn were offered, and where four boulders represented the world directions. Later, a captive who had impersonated Tezcatlipoca for a year (and impregnated four goddess impersonators) was himself sacrificed to end the dry season and inaugurate the planting season.

PART IV: DISCOVERING REGULARITIES AND RITUAL PATTERNS

In their desire to discover meaningful patterns in ritual, archaeologists often emphasize similarities at the expense of differences. Mesoamericanists are aware that variation exists among houses, wards, communities, sites, and regions, and among people of different status, occupation, and stratum, but there is a tendency to characterize Mesoamerica as a whole. We need to work harder to determine which patterns are specific to each ethnic group, and which are pan-Mesoamerican.

Mesoamericanists are aware that ethnohistoric texts have a major role to play in archaeological interpretation, but we sometimes forget that archaeology plays a crucial role in establishing the time depth of certain Contact-period rituals. We need to remember that ethnohistory tends to be biased in the direction of royal and noble ritual, and that to retrieve data on the much more numerous group of commoners, we must turn to the archaeological record. It is commonplace to see Contact-period noble ritual known from ethnohistory projected back onto much earlier, commoner ritual known from the archaeological record, but such projections could preclude our discovery of important differences between commoner and noble ritual performances.

A common misconception is that religious behavior was so conservative that it did not change over time in meaning, function, or practice. Ethnologists like Rappaport, however, make clear that each performance of a ritual can effect change in it, albeit inadvertent change. The performers conducting the rite may believe that they are following tradition, yet bring about almost imperceptible changes that are cumulative. Even when the archaeologically recoverable paraphernalia of a rite persist over thousands of years, the meaning and function of a rite may be gradually changing along with an evolving society.

Finally, let us turn to the most difficult question for any archaeologist: the meaning and purposes of ritual. We are familiar with all the usual anthropological explanations: ritual exists to maintain the religious and sociopolitical order, to convert secular space to sacred space, to promote social cohesion in times of disaster and uncertainty, to explain the cosmos and its natural forces, to communicate with ancestors or deities, to petition for help from benevolent supernaturals or appease malevolent ones, or to cure illness and ease anxiety. Yet an identification of meaning and purpose based on archaeological evidence is hard to make convincing. For periods and cultures without texts we are at a distinct disadvantage. Even when written records are at hand, one hesitates to push them too far into the past. Thus, archaeology must play the dominant role in documenting and explaining ritual activities and performances for early societies (Bell et al. 2004; Marcus and Flannery 1994, 1996, 2004; Mock 1998; Plunket 2002; Renfrew 1982, 1985; Renfrew and Zubrow 1994).

When we look at the artifacts left behind, we suspect that they hold the secret of the ritual; discarded artifacts, however, may convey only part of the story. The other part is the act of conducting the ritual, behaviors that we never witnessed. Only those who attended the performance heard the associated words, chants, or songs that supplied the meaning.

Working in the archaeologist's favor, however, is the fact that most ritual performances are repeated over and over. Repetition increases our sample and makes it more likely that we will deduce the underlying principles. As we have seen in our Mesoamerican examples, principles such as quadripartition, conceptual replication, and structural replication are likely to show up in plaza and city layouts, building dedications, stone sculptures, temple offering boxes, and even mountaintop shrines. Despite all the differences in artifacts, participants, and ritual venues, the underlying organizational principles may still be there for the most persistent archaeologist to discover.

NOTES

*   I thank the organizer, Evangelos Kyriakidis, for inviting me to participate in this important volume, and the Cotsen Institute and its Director, Charles Stanish, for sponsoring it.

1.   The Aztec used the term *tepictoton* for the miniature hills they made from *tzoalli*, an amaranth and corn dough. These small mountains were considered *tlaloque*, assistants to Tlaloc, the large mountain. Four tlaloque were assigned to the corners of the world, each controlling a different type of rain (Durán 1994:591–592). The day after having made offerings to Tlaloc and the tlaloque, participants removed the human heads atop the miniature hills ("they slew them, like sacrificial quail, twisting their necks") and delivered the dough figures to the priests' house (Sahagún 1950:21–22). (The Zapotec version of Tlaloc was also aided by four assistants; the Zapotec *Cociyo* and his assistants were depicted in a scene placed beneath a temple at ca. A.D. 20; see Marcus and Flannery 1996: Figure 219).

2.   "For they considered mountains to be gods; wherefore they fashioned [figures to represent] the mountains. And these images they named Tepictoton. . . And when they had these images, then they laid offerings before them, they sang before them, they did many things in their presence. Thus they paid them honor. Greatly were they in error, they who offered offerings to those who were only besotted. And indeed [the observance] is not now completely uprooted; even now some pay their debts [to them] on mountain tops. . . . Behold also how the ancient ones paid honors to the mountains. They called them Tepicme: [they said they

were] like men. Hence they placed masks upon them. And this the *tlamacazque*, the priests of the Tlalocs, did. And when they made these, the common men, those who had made vows, laid offerings before them; they ate, drank, and danced in their presence. And when their feast-day came, they cut up and divided the Tepicme, and they ate them" (Sahagún 1950:44–45).

3. Stone effigy shrines dedicated to the volcano Popocatepetl were used in the patios of most residences at Tetimpa, Puebla, an early village located on the northeastern flank of that volcano. Plunket and Uruñuela (2002:31) state: "The patio with its central shrine is an image that recalls the Aztec conception of the central direction as the navel from which the 'four quadrants extend out to the four directions' (Nicholson 1971:403)." Their excavations show that the occupants of Tetimpa were placing incense burners in front of volcano effigies 1,500 years before the Aztec did so.

4. "Just after dawn these kings and lords with their followers left [their shelters]. They took a child of six or seven years and placed him within an enclosed litter so that he would not be seen. This was placed on the shoulders of the leaders. All in order, they went in the form of a procession to the courtyard, which was called Tetzacualco. When they arrived before the image of the god Tlaloc, the men slew the child within the litter hidden [from those present]. He was slain by this god's own priests, to the sound of many trumpets, conch shells, and flutes. The child dead, King Motecuzoma, together with all his great men and chieftains, approached [the idol] and presented finery and a rich garment for the god. They entered the place where the image stood, and [Motecuzoma] with his own hands placed a headdress of fine feathers on its head. He then covered it with the most costly, splendid mantle to be had, exquisitely worked in feathers and done in designs of snakes. [The idol] was also girded with a great and ample breechclout, as splendid as the mantle. They threw about its neck valuable stones and golden jewels. Rich earrings of gold and stones were placed upon him, and on his ankles also. [The king] adorned all the smaller idols who stood next [to Tlaloc] in a similar fashion. After Motecuzoma had dressed the idol and had offered it many splendid things, Nezahualpilli, king of Tetzcoco, entered. . . . The idol and the smaller images had now been dressed in the manner described. Then was brought forth the sumptuous food which had been prepared for each king. . . . When the food had been put in its place, the priests who had slit the throat of the child came in with his blood in a small basin. The high priest . . . sprinkled the blood on the idol and on all the offerings and food. And if any blood was left, he went to the idol Tlaloc and bathed its face and body with it, together with all the companion idols, and the floor" (Durán 1971:157–159).

5. "On the summit of the mountain stood a great square courtyard surrounded by a finely built wall about eight feet high, crowned with a series of merlons and plastered with stucco. It could be seen from a distance of many leagues. On one side of the courtyard was a wooden chamber neither large nor small, with a flat roof. It was stuccoed within and without and possessed a beautifully worked and handsome [castellated] crown. In the middle of this room, upon a small platform, stood the stone idol Tlaloc, in the same manner in which Huitzilopochtli was kept in the temple [of Mexico]. Around Tlaloc were a number of small idols, but he stood in the center as their supreme lord. These little idols represented the other hills and cliffs which surrounded this great mountain. Each one of them was named according to the hill he stood for. These names still exist, for there is

no hill lacking its proper designation. Thus the small idols which stood around the great god Tlaloc had their own names, just like the hills which encircle the great mountain" (Durán 1971:156).

6. Sahagún (1997:121) says of Tlaloc: "He rains; he thunders; he strikes [with lightning]." Tlaloc represents and embodies lightning, thunder, hail, and rain.

7. "Tlaloc, according to Torquemada, was the oldest deity known, for when the Acolhuans, who followed the Chichimecs, arrived in the country, he was found on the highest summit of the Texcucan mountain. His paradise, called *Tlalocan*, was a place of delight, an Eden full of flowers and verdure; whilst the surrounding hills were called 'Tlaloc mounts.' He was emphatically the god of many places, of many names, and numerous personifications; as Popocatepetl he presided over the formation of clouds and rain, he was the 'world fertiliser,' the 'source of favourable weather,' sometimes represented dark in colour, his face running with water to signify a rich yielding soil; he carried a thunderbolt in his right hand, a sign of thunder and lightning; whilst his left held a tuft of variegated feathers, emblem of the different hues of our globe; his tunic was blue hemmed with gold, like the heavens after rain. His wife, *Chalchiuhtlicue*, goddess of waters, was represented wearing a blue petticoat, the colour of the mountain Iztaccihuatl when seen at a distance, which was sacred to her" (Charnay 1887:84).

8. Broda (2001:299) says that "Los niños, en cierta manera, eran el maíz. Los niños muertos jugaban un papel activo en el proceso de maduración de las mazorcas y, desde los cerros (es decir, el Tlalocan), regresaban a la tierra en el momento de la cosecha, al término de la estación de lluvias, cuando el maíz ya estaba maduro (¡los niños eran las mazorcas!)."

9. "And it is said that if the blood of that child was not sufficient, one or two other children were killed to complete the ceremony and compensate what had been lacking" (Durán 1971:159).

10. "Then they raised the incense ladle in dedication to the four directions. Thus they offered incense. And when they had raised it in dedication to the four directions, then they threw [the incense and the coals] into the brazier. Then the copal was smoking" (Sahagún 1981:194). Similarly, *pulque* was offered to the four quadrants (*nauhcampa*) (Sahagún 1981:196).

11 "His hair was shorn; he was provided a tuft of hair upon his forehead, like that of a seasoned warrior. They bound it; they wound it round and round. . . . And his forked heron ornament with a quetzal feather spray they bound to his warrior's hairdressing" (Sahagún 1981:70).

12. "In the time of Toxcatl there was Tezcatlipoca's great festival. At that time he was given human form; at that time he was set up. Wherefore died his impersonator, who for one year had lived as Tezcatlipoca. And at that time was appointed his new impersonator, who would again live as Tezcatlipoca for a year" (Sahagún 1981:66).

REFERENCES CITED

Acosta, Jorge R.
1958–59 Exploraciones arqueológicas en Monte Albán, XVIII temporada. *Revista Mexicana de Estudios Antropológicos* 15:7–50.
Altamira G., Armando
1972   *Alpinismo Mexicano*. Editorial ECLALSA, México.

Arnold, Philip P.
1999   *Eating Landscape: Aztec and European Occupation of Tlalocan.*
        University Press of Colorado, Niwot.

Aveni, Anthony F.
1991   Mapping the ritual landscape: Debt payment to Tlaloc during
        the month of Atlcahualo. In *To Change Place: Aztec Ceremonial
        Landscapes*, edited by Davíd Carrasco, pp. 58–73. University Press
        of Colorado, Niwot. (Paperback edition, 1999)

Bell, Ellen, Marcello A. Canuto, and Robert J. Sharer (editors)
2004   *Understanding Early Classic Copan.* University Museum Press,
        University of Pennsylvania, Philadelphia.

Bozarth, Steven R., and Thomas H. Guderjan
2003   Biosilicate analysis of residue in Maya dedicatory cache vessels
        from Blue Creek, Belize. *Journal of Archaeological Science*
        31:205–215.

Broda, Johanna
1971   Las fiestas aztecas de los dioses de la lluvia: Una reconstrucción
        según las fuentes del siglo XVI. *Revista Española de Antropología
        Americana* 6:245–327.

1987a   Templo Mayor as ritual space. In *The Great Temple of Tenochtitlan*,
        edited by Johanna Broda, Davíd Carrasco, and Eduardo Matos
        Moctezuma, pp. 61–123. University of California Press,
        Berkeley.

1987b   The provenience of the offerings: Tribute and cosmovision. In
        The Aztec Templo Mayor, edited by Elizabeth H. Boone, pp.
        211–256. Dumbarton Oaks, Washington, DC.

1991   The sacred landscape of Aztec calendar festivals: Myth, nature,
        and society. In *To Change Place: Aztec Ceremonial Landscapes*, edited
        by Davíd Carrasco, pp. 74–120. University Press of Colorado,
        Niwot. (Paperback edition, 1999)

2001   Ritos mexicas en los cerros de la cuenca: Los sacrificios de niños.
        In *La montaña en el paisaje ritual*, edited by Johanna Broda,
        Stanislaw Iwaniszewski, and Ismael Arturo Montero García, pp.
        295–317. Conaculta e INAH, México.

Carrasco, Davíd
1991   The sacrifice of Tezcatlipoca: To change place. In *To Change Place:
        Aztec Ceremonial Landscapes*, edited by Davíd Carrasco, pp. 31–57.
        University Press of Colorado, Niwot. (Paperback edition, 1999)

Carrasco, Pedro
1976   La sociedad mexicana antes de la conquista. In *Historia General de
        México*, vol. 1, edited by Bernardo García Martínez, José Luis
        Lorenzo, Ignacio Bernal, and Pedro Carrasco, pp. 165–286. El
        Colegio de México, México, D.F.

Caso, Alfonso
1936   *La Religión de los Aztecas.* Imprenta Mundial, México.

Charnay, Désiré
1887   *The Ancient Cities of the New World: Voyages and Explorations in Mexico and Central America from 1857–1882*. Harper and Brothers, New York.
Covarrubias, Miguel
1957   *Indian Art of Mexico and Central America*. Alfred A. Knopf, New York.
Durán, Diego
1964   *The Aztecs*. Translated by Doris Heyden and Fernando Horcasitas. Orion Press, New York.
1971   *Book of the Gods and Rites and the Ancient Calendar*. Translated and edited by Fernando Horcasitas and Doris Heyden. University of Oklahoma Press, Norman.
1994   *The History of the Indies of New Spain*. Translated, annotated, and with an introduction by Doris Heyden. University of Oklahoma Press, Norman.
Durkheim, Émile
1961   *The Elementary Forms of the Religious Life*. Translated by Joseph Ward Swain. Collier Books, New York.
Elson, Christina M., and Michael E. Smith
2001   Archaeological deposits from the Aztec New Fire Ceremony. *Ancient Mesoamerica* 12 (2):157–174.
Espejo, Antonieta
1945   Las ofrendas halladas en Tlatelolco. In *Tlatelolco a través de los tiempos* 5:15–29. Memorias de la Academia Mexicana de la Historia, México.
Flannery, Kent V., and Joyce Marcus
2005   *Excavations at San José Mogote 1: The Household Archaeology*. Memoir 40, Museum of Anthropology, University of Michigan. Museum of Anthropology, Ann Arbor.
Guilliem Arroyo, Salvador, Saturnino Vallejo Zamora, and Ángeles Medina Pérez
1998   Ofrenda en el Templo Mayor de México-Tlatelolco. *Arqueología* 19:101–117. INAH, México.
Heyden, Doris
1991   Dryness before the rains: Toxcatl and Tezcatlipoca. In *To Change Place: Aztec Ceremonial Landscapes*, edited by Davíd Carrasco, pp. 188–202. University Press of Colorado, Niwot. (Paperback edition, 1999)
Hurst, W. J., S. M. Tarka, T. G. Powis, F. Valdez, Jr., and T. R. Hester
2002   Cacao usage by the earliest Maya civilization. *Nature* 418:289–290.
Hvidtfeldt, Arild
1958   *Teotl and Ixiptlati: Some Central Concepts in Ancient Mexican Religion*. Munksgaard, Copenhagen.
Iwaniszewski, Stanislaw
1994   Archaeology and archaeoastronomy of Mount Tlaloc, Mexico: A reconsideration. *Latin American Antiquity* 5 (2):158–176.

Iwaniszewski, Stanislaw, and Ismael Arturo Montero García
2001   La sagrada cumbre de Iztaccihuatl. In *La montaña en el paisaje ritual*, edited by Johanna Broda, Stanislaw Iwaniszewski, and Ismael Arturo Montero García, pp. 95–111. Conaculta e INAH, México.

Klein, Cecelia F.
1980   Who was Tlaloc? *Journal of Latin American Lore* 6 (2):155–204. University of California, Los Angeles.

Kubler, George, and Charles Gibson
1951   The Tovar Calendar. *Memoirs of the Connecticut Academy of Arts & Sciences*, Vol. XI. Yale University Press, New Haven.

Leach, Edmund R.
1961   *Rethinking Anthropology*. The Athlone Press, London.

López Austin, Alfredo
1988   *The Human Body and Ideology: Concepts of the Ancient Nahuas*. Translated by Thelma Ortiz de Montellano and Bernard Ortiz de Montellano. 2 vols. University of Utah Press, Salt Lake City.
1994   *Tamoanchan y Tlalocan*. Fondo de Cultura Económica, México.

López Austin, Alfredo, and Leonardo López Luján
2004   El Templo Mayor de Tenochtitlan, el Tonacatépetl y el mito del robo del maíz. *Acercarse y mirar: Homenaje a Beatriz de la Fuente*, edited by M. T. Uriarte and L. Staines Cicero, pp. 403–455. Universidad Nacional Autónoma de México, México.

López Luján, Leonardo
1994   *The Offerings of the Templo Mayor of Tenochtitlan*. Translated by Bernard R. Ortiz de Montellano and Thelma Ortiz de Montellano. University Press of Colorado, Niwot.

Lowie, Robert H.
1924   *Primitive Religion*. Boni and Liveright, London.

Marcus, Joyce
1978   Archaeology and religion: A comparison of the Zapotec and Maya. *World Archaeology* 10 (2):172–191.
1983a   A synthesis of the cultural evolution of the Zapotec and Mixtec. In *The Cloud People: Divergent Evolution of the Zapotec and Mixtec Civilizations*, edited by K. V. Flannery and J. Marcus, pp. 355–360. Academic Press, San Diego.
1983b   Teotihuacan visitors on Monte Albán monuments and murals. In *The Cloud People: Divergent Evolution of the Zapotec and Mixtec Civilizations*, edited by K. V. Flannery and J. Marcus, pp. 175–181. Academic Press, San Diego.
1993   Ancient Maya political organization. In *Lowland Maya Civilization in the Eighth Century A.D.*, edited by Jeremy A. Sabloff and John S. Henderson, pp. 111–183. Dumbarton Oaks, Washington, DC.
1998   *Women's Ritual in Formative Oaxaca: Figurine-making, Divination, Death and the Ancestors*. Memoir 33, Museum of Anthropology, University of Michigan. Museum of Anthropology, Ann Arbor.

1999   Men's and women's ritual in Formative Oaxaca. In *Social Patterns in Pre-Classic Mesoamerica*, edited by David C. Grove and Rosemary A. Joyce, pp. 67–96. Dumbarton Oaks, Washington, DC.

2006   The roles of ritual and technology in Mesoamerican water management. In *Agricultural Strategies*, edited by Joyce Marcus and Charles Stanish, pp. 221–254. Monograph 50. Cotsen Institute of Archaeology, University of California, Los Angeles.

Marcus, Joyce, and Kent V. Flannery

1994   Ancient Zapotec ritual and religion: An application of the direct historical approach. In *The Ancient Mind*, edited by Colin Renfrew and Ezra B. W. Zubrow, pp. 55–74. Cambridge University Press, Cambridge.

1996   *Zapotec Civilization*. Thames and Hudson, London and New York.

2004   The coevolution of ritual and society: New ^{14}C dates from ancient Mexico. *Proceedings of the National Academy of Sciences* 101 (52):18257–18261.

Marcus, Joyce, Kent V. Flannery, and Ronald Spores

1983   The cultural legacy of the Oaxacan Preceramic. In *The Cloud People: Divergent Evolution of the Zapotec and Mixtec Civilizations*, edited by K. V. Flannery and J. Marcus, pp. 36–39. Academic Press, San Diego.

Matos Moctezuma, Eduardo

1984   The Great Temple of Tenochtitlan. *Scientific American* 251 (2):80–89.

Mock, Shirley B. (editor)

1998   *Sowing and the Dawning: Termination, Dedication, and Transformation in the Archaeological and Ethnographic Record of Mesoamerica*. University of New Mexico Press, Albuquerque.

Montero García, Ismael Arturo

2001   Buscando a los dioses de la montaña: Una propuesta de clasificación ritual. In *La montaña en el paisaje ritual*, edited by Johanna Broda, Stanislaw Iwaniszewski, and Ismael Arturo Montero García, pp. 23–47. Conaculta e INAH, México.

Nicholson, Henry B.

1971   Religion in pre-hispanic central Mexico. In *Handbook of Middle American Indians*, Vol. 10, edited by Gordon F. Ekholm and Ignacio Bernal, pp. 395–446. University of Texas Press, Austin.

Niederberger, Christine

1987   *Paléopaysages et archéologie pré-urbaine du Bassin de Mexique*. Etudes Mésoamericaines 11. Centre d'Etudes Mexicaines et Centramericaines, Mexico.

Parker, Arthur Caswell

1922   The archaeological history of New York. *New York State Museum Bulletin* 235–238. The University of the State of New York, Albany.

Pijoán, José
    1964   *Summa Artis: Historia General del Arte* 10. 4th ed. Espasa-Calpe,
            Madrid.
Plunket, Patricia (editor)
    2002   *Domestic Ritual in Ancient Mesoamerica*. Monograph 46. Cotsen
            Institute of Archaeology, University of California, Los Angeles.
Plunket, Patricia, and Gabriela Uruñuela
    2002   Shrines, ancestors, and the volcanic landscape at Tetimpa, Puebla.
            In *Domestic Ritual in Ancient Mesoamerica*, edited by Patricia
            Plunket, pp. 31–42. Monograph 46. Cotsen Institute of
            Archaeology, University of California, Los Angeles.
Pomar, Juan Bautista
    1941   *Relación de Tezcoco*. In *Nueva Colección de Documentos para la
            Historia de México: Relaciones de Texcoco y de la Nueva España*.
            Salvador Chávez Hayhoe, México, D.F.
Powis, T. G., F. Valdez, Jr., T. R. Hester, W. J. Hurst, and S. M. Tarka
    2002   Spouted vessels and cacao use among the Preclassic Maya. *Latin
            American Antiquity* 13 (1):85–106.
Rappaport, Roy A.
    1999   *Ritual and Religion in the Making of Humanity*. Cambridge
            University Press, Cambridge.
Renfrew, Colin
    1982   *Towards an Archaeology of Mind*. Cambridge University Press,
            Cambridge.
    1985   *The Archaeology of Cult*. Thames and Hudson, London.
Renfrew, Colin, and Ezra B. W. Zubrow (editors)
    1994   *The Ancient Mind*. Cambridge University Press, Cambridge.
Rickards, Constantine G.
    1929   The ruins of Tlaloc, state of Mexico. *Journal de la Société des
            Américanistes* 21:197–199.
Román Berrelleza, Juan Alberto
    1987   Offering 48 of the Templo Mayor: A case of child sacrifice. In
            The Aztec Templo Mayor, edited by Elizabeth H. Boone, pp.
            131–144. Dumbarton Oaks, Washington, DC.
Sahagún, Bernardino de
    1950   *Florentine Codex*. Book 1—*The Gods*. Translated by Arthur J. O.
            Anderson and Charles E. Dibble. Monographs of the School of
            American Research No. 14, Part II. School of American Research,
            Santa Fe, NM, and the University of Utah, Salt Lake City.
    1981   *Florentine Codex*. Book 2—*The Ceremonies*. Translated by Arthur J.
            O. Anderson and Charles E. Dibble. Monographs of the School of
            American Research No. 14, Part III. School of American Research,
            Santa Fe, NM, and the University of Utah, Salt Lake City.
    1997   *Primeros Memoriales*. University of Oklahoma Press, Norman.

Seler, Eduard
  1963   *Comentarios al Códice Borgia*. Fondo de Cultura Económica,
            México.
Spiro, Melford E.
  1973   Religion: Problems of definition and explanation. In *Anthropological
            Approaches to the Study of Religion*, edited by Michael Banton, pp.
            85–126. A.S.A. Monographs (Association of Social Anthropologists
            of the Commonwealth). Tavistock Publications.
Sugiyama, Saburo, and Rubén Cabrera Castro
  2004   *Voyage to the Center of the Moon Pyramid: Recent Discoveries in
            Teotihuacan*. Conaculta, INAH, México, and Arizona State
            University, Tempe.
Sullivan, Thelma D.
  1974   Tlaloc: A new etymological interpretation of the god's name and
            what it reveals of his essence and nature. In *Atti del XL Congreso
            Internationale degli Americanisti* (Rome-Genoa 1972), Vol. 2, pp.
            213–219. Tilgher, Genoa, Italy.
Thompson, John Eric Sidney
  1934   *Skybearers, Colors, and Directions in Maya and Mexican Religion*.
            Carnegie Institution of Washington Publication 436, Contribution
            10. Carnegie Institution of Washington, Washington, DC.
  1970   *Maya History and Religion*. University of Oklahoma Press,
            Norman.
Torquemada, Juan de
  1969 [1723] *Monarquía indiana*. 2 vols. Editorial Porrúa, México.
Townsend, Richard F.
  1991   The Mt. Tlaloc Project. In *To Change Place: Aztec Ceremonial
            Landscapes*, edited by Davíd Carrasco, pp. 26–30. University Press
            of Colorado, Niwot. (Paperback edition, 1999)
  1992   *The Aztecs*. Thames and Hudson, London.
Tylor, Edward B.
  1873   *Primitive Culture*. 2 vols. 2nd ed. John Murray, London.
Vogt, Evon Z.
  1965   Structural and conceptual replication in Zinacantan culture.
            American Anthropologist 67 (2):342–353.
Wedel, Waldo R.
  1938   The direct-historical approach in Pawnee archaeology.
            Smithsonian Miscellaneous Collections, Vol. 97, No. 7. Smithsonian
            Institution, Washington, DC.
Wicke, Charles, and Fernando Horcasitas
  1957   Archaeological investigations on Mount Tlaloc. *Mesoamerican
            Notes* 5:83–96.

5.

ARCHAEOLOGICAL ANDEAN RITUALS: PERFORMANCE, LITURGY, AND MEANING

Christine A. Hastorf

In many ways, the Andes of South America are still known today for their rituals. Hiking the Inka trails through breathtaking scenery or flying over the Nasca lines suggest how ritual processions marked the landscape, as they still do today in many parts of the highlands. These ethnographic links have helped archaeologists to infer such past ritual events as they blinker their views of other pasts. Most archaeological ritual discussions tend to focus on the political impact of the architecture and the remains. Less tied to the present yet very powerful in the archaeological Andean ritual discussion is the nested structural enclosure, found in both the highland and the coastal traditions. Ritual constructions are the earliest permanent architecture in the highlands. Their early evidence suggests a communal orientation of inclusion that shifts toward increasingly layered secrecy for select members over time. Enclosures and mountain-like mounds dominate the Andean ritual architecture, informing us of the ritual values gained from the landscape. Feasting evidence from plants, faunal remains, and ceramics have been linked to community rituals in more recent discussions. These interpretations have opened up the discussion to include a small-scale communality in conjunction with a long-lived memory. While presenting some of the ritual evidence in the Andean region, I will suggest how rituals might have participated in that area through their powers of inclusion and exclusion.

> Symbolic boundaries are necessary for the private organizing of experience. But public rituals that perform this function are also necessary to organize society. For only a ritual structure makes possible a wordless channel of communication that is not entirely incoherent. [Douglas 1973:74]

To ignore the importance of Andean ritual is to engage in a stunning oversight. But just as the worship of ancestors created certain patterns of Andean ritual architecture, the presence of oracular shrines was expressed in specific built environments. [Moore 1996:128]

Today in the highlands of Bolivia, Chile, Peru, and Ecuador, one encounters many rituals both daily and seasonally, demonstrating to even the most secularly oriented scholar that Andean life is imbued with ritual significance. Myths, meanings, and daily practices are linked to mountain peaks, rocks, caves, streams, and lakes, but also to field boundaries, canals, and houses, making the landscape as well as the built environment a place of potency beyond resource potentials. These are the places of the ancestors. The landscape is animated through interactions with the living, due to the ancestral spirits that have dominion over the earth. In the words of Catherine Bell (1992), the Andean landscape is "ritually dense." The activities linked to these supernaturals extend the impact of rituals throughout society. Due to this ubiquity, most Andean archaeologists assume that rituals were also significant in past Andean societies, but the evidence varies greatly across the region, reflecting a range of meanings within past political and social settings. How did the different forms of ceremony communicate meaning in Andean societies, and what meanings were being communicated? Were such events the locus of societal power and authority, and if so, how were these political meanings played out? These are difficult questions to answer in large part because the traces of ritual seem to be invisible. Archaeologists have thus veered away from investigating rituals directly, assuming the search for ritual meaning is too speculative. Yet societal formation is tied to meanings generated at ritual events and thus must be part of our goals in studying the past.

We cannot see these past rituals nor link those events to the social world of the actors (Insoll 2004). We need to incorporate what people were trying to communicate in our study of the past (Lewis 1980:6). Humphrey and Laidlaw (1994:vii) make it clear that associated meanings of ritual are not fixed but are reconstituted within the minds of the participants in each specific recurrence. In fact, ritual is one of the meaningful links (signification) between things and people, between the physical and the symbolic. As Connerton notes (1989), social memory is conveyed in ritual acts, forming the link between act and thing. We do not want to fall prey, however, to Goody's (1977) slippery slope of boundary-less notions, and so in this paper, I assume rituals to be activities linked to collective beliefs, regardless of how these beliefs are experienced by the participants. Archaeologists privilege the material object, yet we know that meanings can fluctuate around a thing, not only by context but also by their usage. This is the conundrum of and the impetus for our project.

In this chapter, I investigate the role rituals played in Andean societies and try to trace how these events created and maintained specific societies in the past. I propose that within marked spaces and prescribed sequences of actions, rituals constructed a kind of society whose events were remembered and referred to later in daily and domestic contexts, extending the place of ritual throughout society.

That is to say, rituals, while separate from daily activities, had an impact on the participants outside of ceremonial time and space, influencing the shape of society. These meanings reverberated through the rest of the year. Thus, the form of community created in ritual events would be referred to in other aspects of life. The evidence I present here comes from two Andean ritual situations: one that seems to have created an ambience of community and inclusion, allowing all who attended the ceremonies to gain a sense of membership from the event; and a second one that was more overtly hierarchical, suggesting levels of exclusion and social control that affected all who joined the society. Through architectural forms, boundaries, and images, we can get a glimpse of these societies and at least some of the meanings that were being disseminated to the populace.

THE PLACE OF RITUAL IN SOCIAL LIFE

In 1992, Catherine Bell told us that whatever else ritual is, it is value laden, strategic, and imagined. Ritual, in fact, is one of the main links between things and people, between the physical and the symbolic. People use memories of previous ritual experiences to create new enactments of rites which help restructure society. Repetition is an important ingredient in ritual and helps us see the links between material and meaning. Rituals are formed of a conservatism that gives them strength through tradition. But they also have an innovative potential that recalibrates them in each new setting (Kertzer 1988:12). Bell (1988) points out that ritual is codified by "textualization" or referring back to ritual texts—Atkinson's liturgical ritual (1989). Prescribed sequences must be adhered to in order to have a successful ritual. There is a right and a wrong ritual prescription (Humphrey and Laidlaw 1994:11). As repetition occurs, a stock of images and ideas is built up in association with previous ritual acts, reinforcing past relationships and values and carrying them into the future. These become mnemonics for future rituals as they reverberate significance. Because we can say that the Pre-Columbian Andes did not have writing or texts in the strict sense, such "textualization" must be derived from the signified architecture and associated material—that is, from the objects used in symbolic and ritual "textual" interpretation (see, for example, Conklin 1985; Aguero Piwonka et al. 2003; Paul and Turpin 1986). We can also look to the performance side of ritual. Performance rituals involve supernaturals, requiring transformative acts by individual ritual leaders (Turner 1974). Song, playing instruments, costumes, processions, ingestion of hallucinogens, voices, and dance all create a theater that allows participants to enter another world (Atkinson 1989). A set of ritual actions and associated objects are available to ritual performers to be used within each ritual setting, promoting the performers' qualifications and authenticity with each use (Atkinson 1989:15). These rituals require an audience, where mundane perspective is suspended, as the ritual leaders hope to convince the viewers of their authenticity. The participants are to believe, or at least act as if they believe, the transformation that is occurring before them.

The construction of society through the form and content of these liturgies can tell us something about the shape that society has taken (Geertz 1980; Ortner 1978). For example, rituals can be inclusionary or exclusionary, with differing concepts of participation and community that speak to the social realities of the time. These participatory shapes inform us about the shape and goals of society, and through that we can learn about general social structures. If rituals produce wordless channels of communication, as Mary Douglas (1973) points out, they are open to interpretation on many levels, both verbally and nonverbally (Lewis 1980:19). Lewis reminds us that we must continue to focus on what people were trying to communicate in those actions—the ideal meaning, as it were—rather than worry about capturing all of the many and different nuances (Lewis 1980:6).

Based on the tenet that ideas are crucial for rejuvenating and renewing a society, we can explore the notion that rituals, expressly reaffirming and reforming meanings, are important in social action. Atkinson notes that rituals cannot be seen as reflecting all social relations. Rather, rituals help *constitute* (and reconstitute) social relations. Time and again, new political (and religious) systems borrow legitimacy from the past by resurrecting liturgies, architecture, and symbols. Thus, ritual performances can become a political arena for crafting new societal directions (Humphrey and Laidlaw 1994:10). Rituals can influence and direct political change through their historical resonances. We can assume that rituals were essential in social group maintenance, but they also participated in change. By tracking a sequence of ritual activities in the Andes, we can surmise how memories associated with these events colored the experiences and the meanings that formed and maintained Andean societies (Kertzer 1988:12).

Archaeologists have had a rough time with ritual. Cultural historians have tended to use rituals as a dump heap for anything they could not understand. Processual archaeologists have claimed that rituals were merely politically expedient activities (Binford 1972; Flannery 1976). Post-processualists, postmodernists, feminists, and recent social theorists engage more with ritual, recognizing the active participation of ideas and meanings in the past (see Barrett 1994; Bender 1998; Hodder 1992a, 1992b; Thomas 1991). One aspect of materiality that we have gained from social archaeology is a more active linking between things and meanings, drawing upon social anthropology (Gell 1988; Miller 2005). This has allowed us to realize that objects can have different meanings in different contexts but also can maintain certain meanings over a long time. Such tenets allow us to think about the place of the object in ritual (Humphrey and Laidlaw 1994).

Another dimension of ritual experience is focused in community maintenance and neutralzing political difference. *Communitas* entails a reaffirmation of the group and its membership through transformation, consumption, and group membership (Turner 1969). These relationships are highlighted in performance rituals, through strong physical sensations, including eating and drinking, the loud sound of musical instruments, singing, calling, hearing stories, drumming, smelling pungent smells of incense and food (Bell 1992:81). All of these actions convey a sense of shared group experience. At the other end of the ritual spectrum, by contrast, ritual actors create distance from the audience and demonstrate layered separations of knowledge and overt power. This end of the spectrum is seen when ritual leaders have special knowledge that others do not and experiences in the ritual program convey their differences from the membership. These two opposite forces can come together in specific rituals, one masking the other. Take, for example, Russian Orthodox Easter church services, where there is much incense and priestly singing behind the screens. These activities maintain a highly charged yet stratified ritual setting. At the same time, everyone can kiss the icons and chant together, and at one point in the ceremony, the priests walk through the standing audience, waving the incense burners and creating a parade behind the icons around the church, as the whole community performs the transformation of Easter.

ANDEAN RITUAL

In the Andean archaeological literature, "religious traditions," as they are labeled, have become a frame within which ritual is often discussed. These traditions are described by specific, highly charged traits that slowly develop and then co-occur within large swatches of time and across space (see Burger and Burger-Salazar 1980; Chávez 1988; Conrad and Demerest 1984; Izumi and Sono 1963). These traditions must have developed through the slow addition of iconic traits shared across a broad region, but in general they are presented in the literature with little attempt to reconcile the meaning structures and societal forces that these traits were brought together by, let alone why these clusters of traits co-occurred when they did. Another Andean interpretation is built upon a Marxist, materialist, ideologically grounded tradition, which sees ritual primarily as useful in political and economic control linked to state formation (D'Altroy 1992; Murra 1980; Stanish 2003). Large-scale ceremonialism has dominated the coastal discussions, especially by Conklin (1985), Donnan (1985), and the Pozorskis (1986, 1987) concerning architectural ritual evidence, and by the Topics (1992), Conklin (1991), Bauer and Stanish (2001), and McEwan (1998) regarding highland sites. The recent historical stance weaves meanings gained from historical documents and ethnographies to interpret a more nuanced world of ritual (Abercrombie 1998; Spaulding 1984; Salomon 1995). These ethnohistoric authors discuss smaller-scale village rituals and their political ramifications. Archaeologically, we find such evidence in the Initial-Formative period rituals (see Bonnier 1997; Bonnier and Rozenberg 1988; Burger and Burger-Salazar 1980, 1985; Chávez 1988; Donnan 1985; Hastorf 1999, 2003).

Andean ethnographies discuss the nature of religion, ritual, and personhood (Abercrombie 1998; Allen 1988; Arnold 1991; Astvaldsson 1994; Bastien 1978; Dransart 2002; Gose 1994; Harris 2000; Platt 1987; Sallnow 1987; Urton 1981). These publications track ritual in a world that is animated and filled with meaning, built upon cultural memories that link individual humans to the spirits of the landscape, earth, water, and sky through remembered rituals. We see reflections of civic-ceremonial rituals in the standing buildings and sacred locations (huacas: burial chambers, caves, hearths, standing stones). These spirits initiate people in a cycle of life and death where the dead inhabit the world of the living through the loci of interaction, land, animals, and water. These rituals concern small groups, on the scale of the community.

There is a disjuncture between then and now, due to the Spanish conquest and the cognitive ruptures that resulted, separating thought from thing—the mind-body Cartesian division—while obliterating many cultural traditions. This conquest persists today, as the Western global society as well as the Catholic and evangelical religions continue to impact Andean traditions. When scholars criticize the application of modern concepts in the past, they are reminding us of the Spanish filter on the past history as it diminishes the prehispanic rituals (see Isbell 1997).

I present ritual examples in the Andean sequence to illustrate some of the roles of ritual in the past (figure 5.1). One type reflects long-term

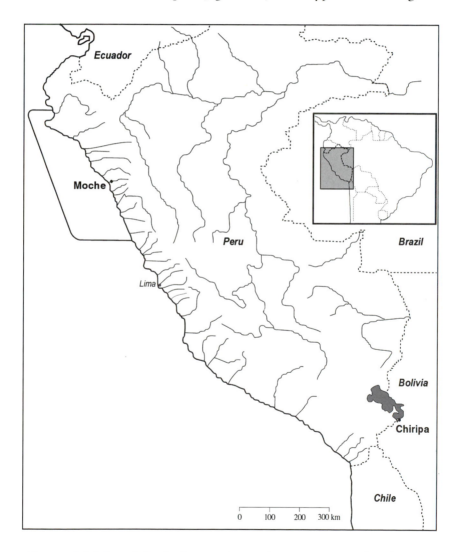

FIGURE 5.1. Map of the Andean region, with areas mentioned in the text. (By William Whitehead)

social maintenance through the use of inclusionary principles, highlighting the role of performance and participation in the construction of community life. Another displays the role of exclusion: more overt power is evident in the architecture in which some cannot see or participate. This form maintains a hierarchical society.

Much of the highland and early coastal ritual data suggest rites of communion and communitas. Open spaces, burials, and cave-like rooms are part of this early communal-oriented ritual, most likely built upon family rituals of the dead. Domestic rituals have rarely been sought in Andean research, as they are hard to identify. These rituals have been specifically discussed by Dean and Kojan at Chiripa, however (Kojan and Dean 1999; Dean and Kojan 2001). Burial studies by Alva (2001), Alva and Donnan (1993), Castillo (2000), Isbell (1997), and Hastorf (2003) focus on rituals surrounding the dead that allow us to see memory construction through ritual. Cave-like enclosures on top of mountain-like mounds or within buildings make up the early ritual architecture. These rooms within rooms remind us of the mountain caves that are filled with burials throughout the Andes, giving these dark spaces ritual value by their association with ancestral stores (figure 5.2).

These sites often have open spaces for large gatherings that hold evidence for eating and drinking. The important role of drinking in such places links community rituals with family rituals. Feasting evidence has been identified archaeologically across the Andes in botanical, faunal, and ceramic analysis: in Gero and Lau's Early Intermediate Callejon de Huaylas examples (Gero 1992; Lau 2002); Jerry Moore's beer production evidence at the Late Intermediate site of Manchan on the central coast (1981); Hastorf and Johannessen's (1993) Late Intermediate Mantaro Valley material; and Tamara Bray's (2003) chicha use by the Inka. All of these groups placed maize beer consumption at the core of social communitas building. The processing of fermented beer—and then its consumption—epitomize the importance of transformation. Beer's transformative qualities mimic the transformation of ancestral spirits, with their power to produce and transform the fruits of the earth, animating the crop as well as nourishing the people who consume it (Arnold 2000). These traits are transferred to the drinkers such that they feed themselves as well as the ancestors through these transformations (Allen 1988). Drinking opens up links between beings and brings people closer to the world of the dead and thus is a ritual act (Harvey 1994:227).

We find evidence for small gatherings within early ceremonial architecture. Non-domestic "ritual" constructions are the earliest permanent

FIGURE 5.2. Ritual cave from Guaman Poma with *wakas* inside.
(From Guaman Poma de Ayala 1980 [1613])

architecture in highland archaeology. The early evidence consists of broad, bounded plazas with patterned, if sparse distributions of artifacts, suggesting a communal orientation to the events within this inclusive space. Asana is the earliest example we have of this in the south-central high mountains, dating to around 3000–2400 B.C. (Aldenderfer 1991). The site has postholes that mark a series of walled enclosures sitting to one side of a plastered surface, along with basins, hearths, ash lenses, platforms, and stone circles. Aldenderfer calls this precinct "ceremonial" and suggests that this non-domestic sector was used as a "ritual space to integrate the group" through feasting and dancing (1990, 1991).

Early architectural evidence on the coast, as in the highlands, begins with evidence of a space to gather in. The essential ingredients of these ritual sites include large demarcated spaces with accompanying small, enclosed spaces. Much like caves on the mountain slopes, multiple small, separate chambers are built upon mounds. The small enclosures, about 4 × 4 m, often have a prepared floor and a hearth (Moore 1996:132). The site of Caral, in the Supe Valley, provides some of the earliest evidence for platform mounds with plazas (Shady 1997; Shady et al. 2001). Many of these rooms are associated with bodies or body parts, especially crania. This architectural expression suggests small, specific group gatherings that somehow dovetail with larger, flexible groups associated with the large, open spaces. This dual component of small enclosures with large auditorium-like space continues in many settings for over three thousand years across the region.

Richard Burger and Lucy Salazar-Burger uncovered the earliest and most essential of the so-called Kotosh religious tradition: individual chambers at the site of Huaricoto in the Callejon de Huaylas (1980, 1985, 1986). From this site they defined this ritual tradition as a "performance of burning offerings in hearths within enclosed spaces, both on the coast and highlands" (Burger and Salazar-Burger 1980:28). Bonnier and Rozenberg (1988) also discussed this tradition; they focused on the importance of sitting in these rooms with a small group and being immersed in smoke and offerings. The archaeological evidence strongly suggests a focus on transformation via small group communitas performance rituals; strong smells in smoky, enclosed spaces; and rites of initiation and myth telling, as in the sweathouses and kivas of the North American Southwest. There is evidence of closure and curation, as well as of replastering and rebuilding. People came to these locations, replastered the rooms, convened in rooms with fires, and consumed and burned food offerings—chili peppers, meat, fish, marine shell, all special items found in these hearths. The hearths were then sealed off, guarding sacred ritual items (Grieder et al. 1988). This tradition's evidence suggests periodic small-scale offerings, small family gatherings, or shamanistic meetings. The hearth was clearly the focal point in these rooms. Later, mounds were built up with multiple rooms on top, allowing events to occur but in restricted, selective secrecy within these small chambers.

The elaboration of this Huaricoto style of early ritual structures in the northern highlands began around 2400 B.C., first labeled by Izumi and Sono (1963; Izumi and Terada 1972), who excavated at Kotosh in the 1960s. This so-called Kotosh religious tradition has also been referred to as the "Mito tradition," based on one architectural phase at Kotosh (Bonnier 1997). Kotosh and La Galgada are made up of small plastered chambers, built sequentially upon twin mounds. Each building phase contained small 4 × 4 m chambers with sunken hearths and ventilation shafts surrounded by a bench and niches. Other variants were found at Buena Vista in the Chillón Valley and even at early Chavín de Huantar (Rick et al. 1998; Vega-Centeno 2006). Although very little has been recovered from these chambers, there is evidence that human bodies and their curation were linked, as seen in the burials at La Galgada, crania found in a pit at Asia, and plastered representations of bodies at Kotosh. Venerating the dead, ritual feasting, and other inspirational shamanistic rituals within enclosed spaces are evident.

The Burgers' (Burger and Salazar-Burger 1986) interpretation of these structures applies ethnohistorical analogies of ranked, nested ritual centers to suggest that these early Formative (Initial) highland sites were part of a network of shared ideas and materializations of a common ritual belief. They assume that such ritual sites, like Huaricoto, were probably only used several days a year, as some shrines are today. This is an example of the "empty ritual center" phenomenon that surfaces in Andean ritual discussions, based on the lack of dense domestic refuse uncovered at these ceremonial sites (Silverman 1993). Such a model suggests that people did not live in and around these "Kotosh-like" mound centers, but moved into ritual time physically when they went in procession to the sites. However, there are stone-walled rooms at the base of La Galgada and Kotosh that have rubbish surrounding them, suggesting that people did live next to these ritual edifices. All sites that have been sampled beyond the mounds have contained rubbish, suggesting that in fact these places did have year-round residents. Unfortunately, we lack the detailed, provenanced recording and fine screening at these sites that would allow us to say more specifically what events went on in these chambers as well as in the landscape surrounding these structures.

A similar ritual tradition has been outlined for slightly later sites to the south in the Titicaca Basin, beginning around 900 B.C. This has been called the "Yayamama religious tradition" by Karen M. Chávez (1988), "Chiripa" by Ponce Sangines (1989), and the "Pa-Ajano tradition" by Max Portugal Ortíz (1981). The material traits of these early settled

"Formative" societies are trapezoidal, semi-subterranean enclosures with restricted access and supernatural figures carved on upright stone stelae that are often standing within sunken enclosures (Ponce Sanginés 1990; figure 5.3). These stone pillars are placed within spaces that can hold about 50 people, suggesting that supernatural beings were called upon during the gatherings that occurred in these enclosed, unroofed spaces.

FIGURE 5.3. An upright stone at Chi'si. (Photograph by the author)

These semi-human images developed out of what David Browman (1972) and the Chávezes (1976) see as a shift in the imagery from water-loving creatures into surreal animals, culminating in humans, most often in pairs of one male and one female. The earlier stone images are small and portable, whereas the larger and later ones are placed within ritual precincts, suggesting a marking of place. Most of these stones are not dated. This primarily descriptive approach has not led to social discussions of these highly symbolic items. The contemporaneous surreal human images also seen to the north, in the Callejon de Huaylas region, suggests some sharing of ceremonial styles, with an early emphasis on performance, spatial enclosure, supernatural interaction, and inclusion.

To better understand the community-constituting rituals that could have occurred within these structures, I turn to the site of Chiripa, where our project team, as well as other archaeologists, have worked since the 1930s, asking a series of related questions of the settlement (Bennett 1936; Kidder 1956; Browman 1978; Hastorf 1999). We can look more closely at the artifactual distributions to see if we can learn more about the types of rituals and other accompanying activities that could have occurred within these sunken enclosures, associated with the carved stones.

CHIRIPA

Since I began working at Chiripa in 1992 with the Taraco Archaeological Project (TAP), every year, before we begin fieldwork, we hold a codified ceremony to propitiate the earth spirits that we are about to interact with. We hire a local shaman (*yatiri*) to throw coca leaves and determine the best time for this ceremony. At the appointed time, we gather at a chosen place, directed by the yatiris of the community, to ask for acceptance and blessing, so that the excavations will go well both in the ground and in the community. All participants gather in the evening for this ritual, as the yatiri and his assistants lay out the offerings we have gathered. By throwing the leaves and chanting, the yatiris look for a propitious blessing. Certain objects are collected together, representing a range of life forms and regions. These items are laid out in a sequence with accompanying prayers and incantations. Throughout, much drinking and libating occurs. The transformation of the ritual leaders, as well as of the participants, is important and takes place through the coca chewing and alcohol drinking (Allen 1988). Coca leaves are thrown regularly in order to see if there will be good fortune in the upcoming events and for each person involved. Once all participants have been included and all offerings made, the deposition of these things into the earth receives great consideration.

This is the climax of the ceremony. Again the leaves are thrown, and the spirit of mother earth, *Pachamama*, is requested to suggest a time and place for this sacred deposition. Once the appointed hour has come, the whole group walks to the selected spot with the offerings on a blanket. This location is often on the archaeological mound, still a locus of spirit and ritual. A pit is dug, wood is collected, and individuals are chosen to light the fire, which then receives the items. The objects are laid in the pit in a special sequence, as incense is placed on the offerings. It is particularly important for the earth spirits to smell and see the fire, so much discussion occurs about how the incense is thrown onto the fire. Once these offerings have been completed, everyone in the group makes an incantation and departs. It is important at that point in the ritual not to turn and look at the fire, nor to see the flames again. It is being consumed by mother earth. If you do turn around, you run the risk of being consumed into the earth along with the offering. This is a performance-centered ritual for a small group of people. Everyone needs to be convinced that the spirits heard our request and accepted our offerings. We also need to see that the local inhabitants learn that the earth has accepted us working there, so that they can allow also us to excavate. This ritual now has become our main recourse when things seem to be difficult in the community. How far back does such performative social glue extend?

This ritual "tradition" and what such rituals might mean can be explored at the site of Chiripa, where TAP has been working for 15 years, tracking the early sequence of ceremonial construction over 2,000 years (Hastorf 1999, 2003; Roddick 2002). The Taraco Archaeological Project defines the early and middle "Formative" occupation of the Chiripa site in three phases—Early, Middle, and Late Chiripa—from 1500 to 200 B.C. These phases are based on changes in the ceramic assemblage, and on accompanying radiocarbon dates that anchor the sequence in time. The site is made of three culturally contoured terraces, rising up from the lake.

Chiripa was founded around 1500 B.C., 600 years before the Yayamama religious tradition traits were in full association across the Titicaca Basin. The settlement at that time was about 4 ha in size. What does the excavated material tell us about the possible ritual actions at the site? I propose that the rituals were inclusive at Chiripa, as they are today. From the start, the architectural and artifactual evidence suggests a focus on community gatherings to worship the ancestors. The evidence begins with several walled plazas enclosing pit interments, where women were the central figures of multiple burials (Hastorf 2003). Some of the burials included extra large cooking pots, as if the dead were buried with their feasting utensils. This

area, excavated in 1992 and 1996 by the TAP, has evidence of feast preparation and presentation, including fish, quinoa, potatoes, large cooking vessels,
and decorated pottery. Later, around 1000 B.C., this plaza burial ground
gained a sunken trapezoidal enclosure with one niche (figure 5.4).

The sunken enclosures at Chiripa have down-sloping drainage
canals emanating from their surfaces, perhaps to collect libations and
rainfall for water flow within rituals at specified times. Across the floors
of these enclosures, we uncovered fragments of large, decorated ceramic
bowls, fragments of clay trumpets with mottled camelid heads, and
incised braziers, suggesting that incense smoke, music, and feasting were
the essence of the group ritual within these walled, but open-to-the-
heavens enclosures. The enclosed spaces (14 × 11 m) could accommodate

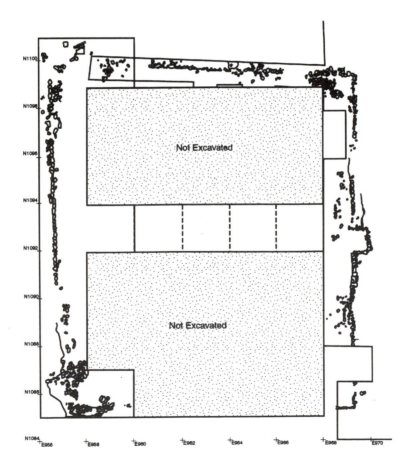

FIGURE 5.4. *Choquehuanca* in plan. (By William Whitehead)

gatherings of about 50 people, removed from daily life with a view up to the heavens. Ritual storage of the ancestors was important and visible, giving a sense of democratic ritual access. A niche at one end of the Choquehuanca enclosure can be compared with later niches in the sunken enclosures at the later, Early Intermediate Period site of Pukara, where Kidder found a human mandible (K. Chávez 1988; S. Chávez 1992) and at Viracochapampa where the Topics found a secondary human burial (Topic and Topic 1983). Another example of niches for the visible curation of the dead and related remembrance icons was uncovered at Pukara, in the small niches of a pre-Pukara rectangular structure in sector BG. While two of the niches were empty, the other two held a painted stone head and a stone human figure (Wheeler and Mujica 1981: 29). McEwan's excavations at the Middle Horizon site of Pikillacta also suggest that the niched halls were likely for ancestor worship (1998:80). If we assume that the residents of Chiripa periodically placed significant items in this niche at Choquehuanca—as people did slightly later at Pukara, and later still at Tiwanaku and Wari—we can suggest that this Choquehuanca niche is early evidence of ancestral presentation and veneration at Chiripa, dating to between 1000 and 800 B.C.

The evidence at these enclosures suggests communal rituals, perhaps with processions in and out of the enclosures, as food and drink were prepared and consumed around them (Steadman 2003). The enclosure floors were relatively clean compared with the exterior surfaces, which were rich with artifactual deposits, suggesting that the enclosures were used less regularly than the surrounding ground surfaces. One can envision music and song as people processed into the walled space, feasted, sacrificed, propitiated, and then processed out. The size of the enclosure suggests that these communal performance rituals could have been accessible to all the participants, reaffirming lineage as well as community identities. These traits suggest rituals of inclusion, as any and all could at least watch the events occurring within the enclosures. This single, fairly large space would allow for many families to join in the audience, pulling in folks from surrounding communities to the festival.

Between 800 and 500 B.C., a shift in ceremonial architecture and in associated ritual occurred in the region. During this time, the Chiripa inhabitants constructed dual ritual spaces—a platform and a sunken enclosure—following a trend that continues for 2,000 years across the central Andean region until the end of the Middle Horizon (Kolata 1993; Stanish 1997). On the middle terrace at Chiripa, a platform was built on top of an enclosure that contained a series of small, cobble-walled rooms. Over time, these were periodically burned and then replastered with yellow clay. Our dates for the new plasterings and subsequent firings show that this occurred every 30 years, suggesting generational renewal of these structures. The only clear evidence we have of activities in these early rooms comes from small hearths that burned herbs (Moore and Hastorf 2000). These small, visually restricted chambers suggest that they were primarily for curation and ceremonial preparation. The mound, with structures around a sunken enclosure, was designed for controlling access. This architectural construction—with the platform standing above ground within the settlement—suggests a notion of selective visual access to the mountains and special knowledge. There are surreal stone images (both human and geometric) associated with the mound, suggesting multiple manifestations of the spirits and/or ancestors. By contrast, the sunken enclosures that continued to be built were more democratic, like the earlier ones, harkening back to earlier times. They provided a more flexible, open space in which the whole community could participate and watch. The ceramic evidence suggests that there was feasting and incense burning within these spaces, as well as food processing (Steadman 1999, 2003; Logan 2006). The larger interior spaces were gathering points for a group to participate in sensory, communal performances of music, trumpets (sound), incense (smell), and food (taste), whereas the small chambers suggest secrecy and exclusion of a more liturgical nature (Atkinson 1989).

At about 500 B.C., the whole Chiripa platform was remodeled, with regular, well-crafted chambers built on an ever-higher platform (figure 5.5) (Whitehead 1999). This is the time that the Yayamama religious tradition coalesced—when stones were etched into highly charged symbolic images, and festival artifacts such as tubes for hallucinogenic plant snuffing, incense burners, and drinking vessels became widespread. Surreal human-like images became the typical image, suggesting ancestral powers (figure 5.6). Two entrances led up into the mound, into a 26 × 26 m encircled sunken plaza. Groups could move around and congregate within this central plaza. Opening off the plaza now were 14 well-constructed and standardized rooms. These small, fully planned rectangular rooms offer inner niches and chambers, much like caves, that could have stored sacred items both large and small. The first archaeologists working on the mound, Bennett (1936) and Kidder (1956), thought that these chambers were houses, homes for the elite. Chávez reoriented this idea to one of centralized storage, like a bank, for lineages (1988). A further interpretation is that each structure was more like a family cave, used for curation, not so much for food stores but for ritual storage of important lineage items that memorialize and help re-

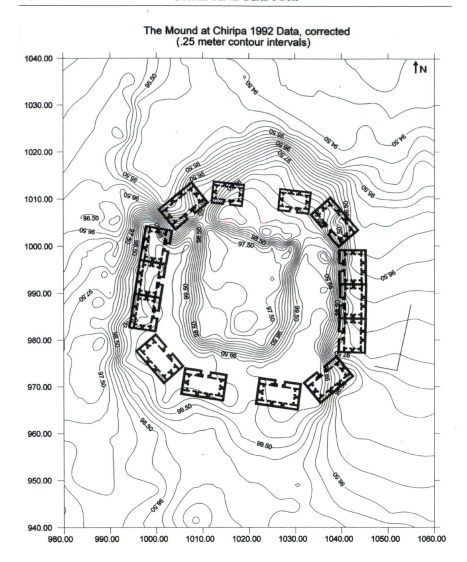

FIGURE 5.5. The Chiripa mound upper structures. (By William Whitehead)

create the lineages in larger ceremonies (Hastorf 2003). These structures
have burials under the floors, as well as small, nested openings within the
chambers, allowing for the storage of important ritual items, including
wrapped mummy bundles, ceramic trumpets, drinking bowls, jugs, textiles,
and carved stones (Arriaga 1968 [1621]:19). Evidence in one of the structures excavated by Kidder's team in the 1950s suggests that these chambers
were for mummy bundle curation and veneration; there was little wear on

FIGURE 5.6. Yayamama stone head carving.

the sills of these sub-chamber rooms ("bins"). The mound seems to have been an ancestral shrine; the 14 contemporaneous, identical structures located around the single plaza may have been for smaller, private rituals.

Large processions of up to 200 people could have walked onto the mound and into the inner courtyard; it was still a human-sized meeting space, accommodating flexible activities and interactions, such as dancing and propitiating (the gathering estimate was made using 3.6 m^2/person, from Moore 1996:149). The same types of activities could have occurred within the interior plaza as occurred in the sunken enclosures, but here they would not be visible to those outside of the mound. The mound chambers could have held sacred items, such as ancestor bundles. This ritual evidence highlights the importance of lineage and community on the landscape. This one mound, like many others across the Andes, suggests both the inclusionary performance rituals of a large plaza and the smaller, exclusionary ceremonies of the small chambers.

The rooms on the mound strongly suggest a two-tiered level of ritual activity at Chiripa (Moore 1996). Evidence of a shift from collectivity to selective authority at Chiripa is seen in the repetitive rooms' entrances (Pauketat 2000). These chambers have openings with slots for sliding woven or wooden doors. The sealing off of these spaces is unusual in the Andes, suggesting not only restricted access but restricted knowledge. The entrances reflect social control as well as sacred authority, both part of liturgical ritual. The difference in size between the small rooms and the inner courtyard also supports the notion of inequality in access to the ancestors and their memories. There were those who could go into the rooms and be with the sacred, but the majority participated and/or watched in the plaza, perhaps only listening from off the mound.

Off-mound enclosures continued to be constructed throughout this time (500–200 B.C.). The artifacts found on the surface of these sunken enclosures suggest that performances occurred there as well. Decorated ceramics were the most common artifact, including fragments of ceramic trumpets with mottled camelid heads (Steadman 1999: Figure 27d). It is thought that these trumpets were used in ceremonies, like the large marine *Strombus* shells portrayed in Moche iconography and found at Chavín de Huantar (Lumbreras 1989). Such trumpets or other noisemakers would have called people, both alive and dead, to the ceremony, designating ritual time as well as space. I think that these trumpets might have been used for consuming hallucinogenic plants, replaced by the smaller tubes, which became more common over time (Berenguer Rodriguez 1987). Ongoing analysis will determine if this is so. Fragments of incense burners were uncovered on the floors as well. Smoke is a universal sacred element used to cleanse and call the deities (Groom 1981). Special presentation and consumption vessels suggest feasting (Steadman 1999).

The Middle Formative mound and sunken enclosures reflect performance rituals that called upon most of the senses: the communal feasting brought people together through acts involving special foods (taste), incense burning (smell), and trumpet blasts (hearing); and the procession into demarcated spaces, removed from daily use areas, brought them closer to the ancestors (sight). The central enclosures reflect a spatial flexibility, channeling audiences into the arena but leaving them undirected once there. The smaller chambers connote more specific, codified actions. These ritual spaces both defined and maintained the social structures within the long-lived Chiripa community. This sequence gives a sense of how the Chiripa residents used ceremony to renew their collective memory, building cohesion within and between the kin groups and beyond, through inclusion and sharing of ceremonies and memories. By the same token, in later times, these same nested structures became a locus for maneuvering the political claims of the descent groups, perhaps with some individuals becoming more powerful, through exclusionary rituals and restricted access to certain memories (Atkinson 1989; Hendon 2000).

The sunken enclosures would have allowed many to participate or view sacred acts and items within the niches. On the mound, most people would have watched and listened in the interior plaza as the sacred objects were brought out to view—more like icons in liturgical events than an event in inspirational shamanic performances. The mound chambers suggest a shift toward liturgically oriented rituals, as secrecy and difference became increasingly present with the more elaborate ritual icons of the Yayamama religious tradition. The ritual propitiations and remembrances in the enclosure performances would have been gradually replaced with the more restrictive and restricting secretive liturgical actions within the small chambers, brought out to the larger group only occasionally (Humphrey and Laidlaw 1994:11).

This example of one settlement's ritual history allows us to see the growth of a ritually dense world where ritual remained fluid through the reconstitution within the minds of the participants. The ritual events brought home to everyone their place within the world, both on the landscape and within society. As the social world shifted from democratic inclusiveness to increasing selectivity, we see the growth of political differences that resulted in the creation of a larger, ceremonial center, 15 km to the southwest of Chiripa some years later.

SUMMARY

From these brief examples of Andean ritual evidence, we learn how a range of ritual events can be discussed with some clarity. The Andes is rich with ritual evidence that ranges from small familial ancestor worship to the animation of and transformation into superhuman powers by political leaders. Andean ritual is materialized in architecture, suggesting procession and pilgrimage, and in hearths and ceramics, informing us about smell, taste, hearing, touch, and sight—and thus about smoke and alcoholic transformation, marking the shift from real to ritual time and demonstrating the powers of the telluric ancestors and the life-giving forces of the dead. Several theoretical approaches to ritual exist within the Andean literature, but there is much that can still be studied with these rich data sets that illustrate a range of rituals.

Social meanings are often discussed in current Andean ethnographic research, but these subtleties rarely carry over into archaeology. The ethnographic and ethnohistorical material can be effective fodder for model building within and beyond the Andean discussions, but the theoretical ritual literature is still underutilized. Ritual is laden with contextual ramifications of transformation and animation, of performance, selective knowledge and memorializing, of activating meaning in architecture and object, and of transference into daily life. The archaeological evidence informs us that rituals have been key to every sedentary Andean group. Yet few archaeologists expressly bring ritual into their discussion of past social life, despite its clear importance in the amount of time people spent building structures and in the visibility of these on the landscape, let alone in the preparation that must have occurred for the periodic ceremonies. Feasting at burial locations conveys a sense of feeding and sharing with the dead while animating and empowering the living. Recursive Andean rituals are built upon memory, sacrifice, and belief in the sacredness of earthly power, described by Descola (1996), Fausto (1999), and Beth Conklin (1995) for the Amazon.

Some rituals, marked on the landscape, were transformational and inclusive, as seen in the large coastal sites with many platform mounds and huge plazas, providing us with a sense of movement through nested states of liminality, from normal time and normal personhood to sacred supernatural communication. These events require an audience that must believe in, or at least must act as though they believe in, these deities (Atkinson 1989; Humphrey and Laidlaw 1994). Much ritual work is geared to convince people to believe in things that are not always held in common, or to sense the long-term value of certain attitudes. Given that today we have no real knowledge of the original meanings of the ritual artifacts we come across, we have to assume that this same kind of intentional persuasion was operating in the past. No such underlying meanings are inherent in the artifacts, but ritual actions confer them. People attempt to counteract the meaninglessness of ritual by imposing religious meanings onto places and things, urged on by memory and situated significance. Active reengagement of the community is an ongoing issue in every group, calling up rituals of one form or another to move people into belief or action.

Tension helps to concentrate the force and power of ritual and heighten the memories. The mixing of things brings about energy and an awareness of greater powers. Certain life-force images, like the Yayamama religious tradition's images, allowed different groups to build dynamic yet ambiguous rituals to gain access to ancestral powers, while becoming connected through mutual usage. Liminal spaces and transgressions become important, such as the sacrifice of an animal or the loss of daily norms (Turner 1969). Throughout the Andes, the focus on life forces has remained prominent. This animated force reverberates through the stone images and the ceramics, recalling how the resources, animals, fields, lakes, streams, and land are owned by the ancestors, if on loan to the living. Delimited sacred ritual space is an important materialization of the Andean past, seen at every site from the earliest material manifestations. A concept of elevation linked ritual leaders, ancestors, and deities to mountains, imagined through restricted and nested access; small openings contained wrapped and curated things. Through these objects and their placement we can draw inferences about boundaries—of ritual and daily practice—and about the power of ritual authority, the belief in ritual constructs, and the resonance of images through time and space.

While there are many themes left unaddressed in this chapter on Andean ritual, I have tried to take one theme—the dynamic between inclusion and exclusion in ritual—and track it through an example drawn from the archaeological record. This allows us to see how communal events could bring people into the group through transformation, and how these could, in turn, be transformed into more hierarchical rituals, which could lead to other powers within the social world. Both of these ritual types create meanings different from those achievable in everyday reality. Thus, even foods consumed during ritual time are different from the same dish consumed in daily life.

ACKNOWLEDGMENTS

My thanks to Evangelos Kyriakidis, Carol Leyba, Chip Stanish and the Cotsen Institute, and the people of Peru and Bolivia.

REFERENCES CITED

Abercrombie, Thomas A.
  1998   *Pathways of Memory and Power: Ethnography and History among an Andean People*. University of Wisconsin Press, Madison.
Aguero Piwonka, Carolina, Maricio Uribe Rodríguez, and Jose Berenguer Rodríguez
  2003   La iconografía Tiwanaku: El caso de la escultura lítica. *Textos Antropológicos* 14 (2):47–82.

Aldenderfer, Mark
  1990   Late Preceramic ceremonial architecture at Asana, southern
           Peru. *Antiquity* 64:479–493.
  1991   Continuity and change in ceremonial structures at late Preceramic
           Asana, southern Peru. *Latin American Antiquity* 2 (3):227–258.
Allen, Catherine J.
  1988   *The Hold Life Has, Coca and Cultural Identity in an Andean
           Community.* Smithsonian Institution Press, Washington, DC.
Alva, Walter
  2001   The royal tombs of Sipan: Art and power in Moche society. In
           Moche Art and Archaeology in Ancient Peru, edited by Joan
           Pillsbury, pp. 233–246. Yale University Press, New Haven.
Alva, Walter, and Christopher B. Donnan
  1993   *Royal Tombs of Sipán.* Fowler Museum of Cultural History,
           University of California, Los Angeles.
Arnold, Denise Y.
  1991   The house of earth-bricks and Inka-stones: Gender, memory
           and cosmos in ayllu Qaqachhaka. *Journal of Latin American Lore*
           17:3–69.
  2000   "Convertirse en persona" el tejido: La terminología aymara de un
           cuerpo textil. In *Actas de la 1 Jornada Internacional sobre Textiles
           Precolombinos*, pp. 9–28. Edited by Victòria Solanilla Demestre.
           Servei de Publicacions de la UAB, Barcelona.
Arriaga, Pablo Jose de
  1968 [1621] *The Extirpation of Idolatry in Peru.* Translated by Clark
           Keating. University of Kentucky Press, Lexington.
Astvaldsson, Astvaldur
  1994   Wak'a: An Andean religious concept in the context of Aymara
           social and political life. Ph.D. dissertation, Department of
           Spanish and Spanish American Studies, School of Humanities,
           King's College London, University of London.
Atkinson, Jane
  1989   *The Art and Politics of Wana Shamanship.* University of California
           Press, Berkeley.
Bauer, Brian, and Charles Stanish
  2001   *Ritual and Pilgrimage in the Ancient Andes.* University of Texas
           Press, Austin.
Barrett, John
  1994   *Fragments from Antiquity.* Blackwell, Oxford.
Bastien, Joseph
  1978   *Mountain of the Condor: Metaphor and Ritual in an Andean Ayllu.*
           American Ethnological Society: Monograph 64. West Publishing
           Co., St. Paul.

Bell, Catherine
    1988   Ritualization of texts and textualization of ritual in the codifica-
            tion of Taoist Liturgy. *History of Religions* 27 (4):366–392.
    1992   *Ritual Theory, Ritual Practice*. Oxford University Press, Oxford.
Bender, Barbara
    1998   *Stonehenge: Making Space*. Berg, New York.
Bennett, Wendell C.
    1936   Excavations in Bolivia. *Anthropological Papers of the American
            Museum of Natural History* 35 (4):331–505.
Berenguer Rodriguez, J.
    1987   Consumo nasal de alucinogenos en Tiwanaku: Una aproximación
            iconográfica. *Boletin del Museo Chileño de Arte Precolombino* 2:33–53.
Binford, Lewis R.
    1972   Introduction and some comments on historical versus processual
            archaeology. In *An Archaeological Perspective*, edited by L. Binford,
            pp. 1–19, 114–121. Seminar Press, New York.
Bonnier, Elizabeth
    1997   Perceramic architecture in the Andes: The Mito tradition. In
            *Archaeologica Peruana 2—Prehispanic Architecture and Civilization in
            the Andes*, edited by Elizabeth Bonnier and Henning Bischof, pp.
            120–144. Reiss-Museum, Mannheim.
Bonnier, Elizabeth, and Catherine Rozenberg
    1988   Del Santuario al Caserio: Acerca de la neolitización en la
            cordillera de las Andes Centrales. *Boletin del Instituto Frances de
            Estudios Andinos* 17 (2):23–40.
Burger, Richard, and Lucy Burger-Salazar
    1980   Ritual and religion at Huaricoto. *Archaeology* 33:26–32.
    1985   The early ceremonial center of Huaricoto. In *Early Ceremonial
            Architecture in the Andes*, edited by Christopher Donnan, pp.
            111–138. Dumbarton Oaks, Washington, DC.
    1986   Early organizational diversity in the Peruvian highlands:
            Huaricoto and Kotosh. In *Andean Archaeology*, edited by Ramiro
            Matos Mendieta and Solveig Turpin, pp. 65–82. UCLA Institute
            of Archaeology, Los Angeles.
Bray, Tamara L.
    2003   Inca pottery as culinary equipment: Food, feasting and gender in
            imperial state design. *Latin American Antiquity* 14:3–28.
Browman, David L.
    1972   Asiruni, Pukara-Pokotia and Pajano: Pre-Tiahuanaco southern
            Andean monolithic stone styles. (Forthcoming in *Haffenveffer
            Museum of Anthropology Journal* 2.)
    1978   The temple of Chiripa (Lake Titicaca, Bolivia). In *El hombre y la
            cultura andina*, edited by Ramiro Matos Mendieta, III Congreso
            Peruano, pp. 807–813. Editora Lasontay, Lima.

Castillo, Luis Jaime
  2000   *La ceremonia del sacrificío: Batallas y muerte en el arte mochica*. AFP
          Integra, Museio Arqueolóico Rafael Larco Herrera.
Chávez, Karen L. Mohr
  1988   The significance of Chiripa in Lake Titicaca Basin developments.
          Expedition 30 (3):17–26.
Chávez, Sergio
  1992   The conventionalized rules in Pucara pottery technology and
          iconography: Implications for socio-political developments in the
          Northern Lake Titicaca Basin. Ph.D. dissertation, Department of
          Anthropology, Michigan State University.
Chávez, Sergio, and Karen Mohr Chávez
  1976   A carved stela from Taraco Peru, and the definition of an early
          style of stone sculpture form the altiplano of Peru and Bolivia.
          Ñawpa Pacha 13:45–83.
Conklin, Beth A.
  1995   "Thus are our bodies, thus was our custom": Mortuary cannibal-
          ism in an Amazonian society. *American Ethnologist* 22 (1):75–101.
Conklin, William
  1985   The architecture of Huaca de los Reyes. In *Early Ceremonial
          Architecture in the Andes*, edited by Christopher Donnan, pp.
          139–164. Dumbarton Oaks, Washington, DC.
  1991   Tiahuanaco and Huari: Architectural comparison and interpreta-
          tions. In *Huari Administrative Structure*, edited by William H.
          Isbell and Gordon McEwan, pp. 281–291. Dumbarton Oaks,
          Washington, DC.
Connerton, Paul
  1989   *How Societies Remember*. Cambridge University Press, Cambridge.
Conrad, Geoffery and Arthur Demarest
  1984   *Religion and Empire: The Dynamics of Aztec and Inca Expansionism*.
          Cambridge University Press, Cambridge.
D'Altroy, Terence N.
  1992   *Provincial Power in the Inka Empire*. Smithsonian Institution Press,
          Washington, DC.
Dean, Emily, and David Kojan
  2001   Ceremonial households and domestic temples: "Fuzzy" defini-
          tions in the Andean Formative. In *Past Ritual and the Everyday*,
          edited by Christine A. Hastorf, pp. 109–135. Kroeber
          Anthropology Society, Department of Anthropology, University
          of California, Berkeley.
Descola, Phillipe
  1996   *In the Society of Nature*. Cambridge University Press, Cambridge.
Donnan, Christopher (editor)
  1985   *Early Ceremonial Architecture in the Andes*. Dumbarton Oaks,
          Washington, DC.

Douglas, Mary.
1973   *Natural Symbols*. Random House, New York.
Dransart, Penelope Z.
2002   *Earth, Water, Fleece and Fabric, An Ethnography and Archaeology of Andean Camelid Herding*. Routledge, London and New York.
Fausto, Carlos
1999   Of enemies and pets: Warfare and shamanism in Amazonia. *American Ethnologist* 26 (4):933–956.
Flannery, Kent V.
1976   *The Early Mesoamerican Village*. Adacemic Press, New York.
Geertz, Clifford
1980   *Negara: The Theatre State in Nineteenth-Century Bali*. Princeton University Press, Princeton, NJ.
Gell, Alfred
1988   *Art and Agency: An Anthropological Theory*. Oxford Clarendon Press, Oxford.
Gero, Joan M.
1992   Feasts and females: Gender ideology and political meals in the Andes. *Norwegian Archaeological Review* 25 (1):15–30.
Goody, Jack
1977   Against ritual: Loosely structured thoughts on a loosely defined topic. In *Secular Ritual*, edited by Sally F. Moore and Barbara Meyerhoff, pp. 25–35. Van Gorcum, Amsterdam.
Gose, Peter
1994   *Deathly Waters and Hungry Mountains: Agrarian Ritual and Class Formation in an Andean Town*. University of Toronto Press, Toronto.
Groom, Nigel
1981   *Frankincense and Myrrh: A Study of the Arabian Incense Trade*. Longman, New York.
Grieder, Terence, Alberto Bueno Mendoza, C. Earle Smith, and Robert Malina
1988   La Galgada in the world of its time. In *La Galgada, Peru: A Preceramic Culture in Transition*, pp. 192–203. University of Texas Press, Lubbock.
Guaman Poma de Ayala, Felipe
1980 [1613]   *La primera nueva cronica y buen gobniero, Historia grafica del Peru*, edited by John Murra, Rolena Adorno, and Jorge Urioste. Siglo Veintiuno, México.
Harris, Olivia
2000   *To Make the Earth Bear Fruit: Essays on Fertility, Work and Gender in Highland Bolivia*. Institute of Latin American Studies, London.
Harvey, Penny
1994   Gender, community and confrontation: power relations in drunkenness in Ocongate (southern Peru). In *Gender, Drink and Drugs*, edited by Maryon McDonald, pp. 209–233. Berg Publishers, New York.

Hastorf, Christine A. (editor)
    1999   *Early Settlement in Chiripa, Bolivia: Research of the Taraco
            Archaeological Project.* Contributions, Archaeological Research
            Facility Monograph Publications, No. 57, University of
            California, Berkeley.
    2003   Community with the ancestors: Ceremonies and social memory
            in the Middle Formative at Chiripa, Bolivia. *Journal of
            Anthropological Archaeology* 22:305–332.
Hastorf, Christine A., and Sissel Johannessen
    1993   Pre-Hispanic political change and the role of maize in the central
            Andes of Peru. *American Anthropologist* 95 (1):115–138.
Hendon, Julia
    2000   Having and holding: Storage, memory, knowledge and social
            relations. *American Anthropologist* 102 (1):42–53.
Hodder, Ian
    1992a   *Theory and Practice in Archaeology.* Routledge. London.
    1992b   Material practice, symbolism and ideology. In *Theory and Practice
            in Archaeology*, edited by Thomas C. Patterson, pp. 201–212.
            Routledge, London.
Humphrey, Caroline, and James Laidlaw
    1994   *The Archetypal Actions of Ritual.* Oxford Clarendon Press, Oxford.
Insoll, Timothy
    2004   *Archaeology, Ritual, Religion.* Routledge, London.
Isbell, William
    1997   *Mummies and Mortuary Monuments: Post Processual Prehistory of
            Central Andean Social Organization.* University of Texas Press, Austin.
Izumi, Seiichi, and Toshihko Sono
    1963   *Andes 2, Excavations at Kotosh, Peru, 1960.* Kadokawa Publishing,
            Tokyo.
Izumi, Seiichi, and K. Terada
    1972   *Andes 4: Excavations at Kotosh, 1963 and 1966.* University of Tokyo
            Press, Tokyo.
Kertzer, David
    1988   *Ritual, Politics and Power.* Yale University Press, New Haven.
Kidder, Alfred
    1956   Digging in the Titicaca Basin. *University Museum Bulletin* 20 (3):
            16–29.
Kojan, David, and Emily Dean
    1999   *Early Settlement at Chiripa, Bolivia: Research of the Taraco
            Archaeological Project.* Contributions, University of California
            Archaeological Research Facility, edited by Christine Hastorf,
            No. 57, pp. 37–41. University of California, Berkeley.
Kolata, Alan
    1993   *The Tiwanaku.* Basil Blackwell, Oxford.

Lau, George F.
2002   Feasting and ancestor veneration at Chinchawas, North Highlands
        of Ancash, Peru. *Latin American Antiquity* 13 (3):279–304.
Lewis, Gilbert
1980   *Day of Shining Red*. Cambridge University Press, Cambridge.
Logan, Amanda L.
2006   The application of phytolith and starch grain analysis to under-
        standing Formative Period subsistence, trade, and ritual on the
        Taraco Peninsula, Highland Bolivia. M.A. thesis, University of
        Missouri, Columbia.
Lumbreras, Luis
1989   *Chavín de Huantar en el naciemiento de la civilización andina*.
        Instituto Andino de Estudios Arqueología, Lima.
McEwan, Gordon
1998   The function of niched halls in Wari architecture. *Latin American
        Antiquity* 9 (1):68–86.
Miller, Daniel (editor)
2005   *Materiality*. Routledge Publishers, London.
Moore, Jerry D.
1981   Chimu socio-economic organization: Preliminary data from
        Manchan, Casma Valley, Peru. *Ñawpa Pacha* 19:115–128.
1996   *Architecture and Power in the Ancient Andes*. Cambridge University
        Press, Cambridge.
Moore, Katherine, and Christine A. Hastorf
2000   The re-interpretation of cultural context in excavation and
        analysis of archaeobiological samples from Chiripa, Bolivia.
        Paper presented at the Symposium Integrating Plants, Animals
        and People in Archaeological Interpretation, organized by
        Naomi Miller and Kate Moore, at the 65th Annual Meetings of
        the Society for American Archaeology, April 7, 2000.
        Philadelphia, PA.
Murra, John
1980   *The Economic Organization of the Inca State*. Contemporary Studies
        in Economic and Financial Analysis. JAI Press, Greenwich, CT,
        and London.
Ortner, Sherry
1978   *Sherpas through their Rituals*. Cambridge University Press,
        Cambridge.
Pauketat, Timothy
2000   The tragedy of the commoners. In *Agency in Archaeology*, edited
        by Marcia-Anne Dobres and John Robb, pp. 113–129. Routledge,
        London.
Paul, Anne, and Solvieg A. Turpin
1986   The ecstatic shaman theme of Paracas textiles. *Archaeology*
        39:20–26.

Platt, Tristan
    1987   Entre ch'axwa y muxca. Para una historia del pensamiento políti-
            co Aymara. In *Tres reflexiones sobre el pansamiento andino*, edited by
            Thérèse Bouysse-Cassagne, pp. 61–132. Hisbol, La Paz.
Ponce Sangines, Carlos
    1989   Estilo escultórico Chiripa en al Peninsula de Santiago de Huata.
            Textos Antropológicos 1 (1):45–78.
    1990   *Descripción sumaria del templete semisubterráneo de Tiwanaku.*
            Juventud, La Paz.
Portugal Ortíz, M.
    1981   Expansión del estilo excultórico Pa-Ajanu. *Arte y Arqueología*
            7:149–159.
Pozorski, Shelia, and Thomas Pozorski
    1986   Recent excavations at Pampa de las Llamas-Moxeke, a complex
            Initial Period site in Peru. *Journal of Field Archaeology* 13:381–401.
    1987   *Early Settlement and Subsistence in the Casma Valley.* University of
            Iowa Press, Iowa City.
Rick, John W., Silvia Rodríguez Kembel, Rosa Mendoza Rick, and John A. Kembel
    1998   La arquitectura del complejo ceremonial de Chavín de Huántar:
            Documentación tridimensional y sus implicancias. *Boletín de
            Arqueología PUCP* (2): 181–214.
Roddick, Andrew P.
    2002   Archaeological approaches to ritual in the Andes: A ceramic
            analysis of ceremonial space at the Formative Period site of
            Chiripa, Bolivia. M.A. thesis, Department of Anthropology and
            Sociology, University of British Columbia.
Sallnow, Michael J.
    1987   *Pilgrims of the Andes.* Smithsonian Institution Press, Washington, DC.
Salomon, Frank
    1995   The beautiful grandparents: Andean ancestor shrines and mortu-
            ary ritual as seen through colonial records. In *Tombs for the
            Living: Andean Mortuary Practices*, edited by Tom D. Dillehay, pp.
            315–353. Dumbarton Oaks, Washington, DC.
Shady, Ruth
    1997   *La ciudad sagrada de Cara.* Universidad Nacional Mayor de San
            Marcos, Lima.
Shady, Ruth, Jonathon Haas, and Winifred Creamer
    2001   Dating Caral, a Preceramic site in the Supe Valley on the central
            coast of Peru. *Science* 292:723–726.
Silverman, Helaine
    1993   *Cahuachi in the Ancient Nasca World.* University of Iowa Press,
            Iowa City.
Spalding, Karen
    1984   *Huarochiri, An Andean Society under Inca and Spanish Rule.*
            Stanford University Press, Stanford.

Stanish, Charles
   1997   The settlement history of the southwestern Titicaca Basin. In
            *Archaeological Survey in the Juli-Desaguadero Region of Lake Titicaca
            Basin, Southern Peru*, pp. 113–119. Fieldiana Anthropology New
            Series No. 29. Field Museum of Natural History, Chicago.
   2003   *Ancient Titicaca: The Evolution of Complex Society in Southern Peru
            and Northern Bolivia*. University of California Press, Berkeley.

Steadman, Lee
   1999   The Ceramics. In *Early Settlement at Chiripa, Bolivia: Research of
            the Taraco Archaeological Project*, edited by Christine A. Hastorf.
            Contributions, University of California Archaeological Research
            Facility, No. 57, pp. 61–72. University of California, Berkeley.
   2003   Ceramic Analysis. In Taraco Archaeological Project Report on
            2003 Excavations at Kala Uyuni. Report submitted to the Unidad
            Nacional de Arqueología de Bolivia, pp. 60–79. http://andean.
            kulture.org/bandy/TAP-2003-informe-english.pdf, accessed
            Feburary 5, 2007.

Thomas, J,
   1991   *Rethinking the Neolithic*. Cambridge University Press, Cambridge.

Topic, John R., and Teresa L. Topic
   1983   *The Huamanchucho Project: Preliminary Report of the Second Season,
            June–August 1982*. Department of Anthropology, Trent
            University, Peterborough, Ontario.

Turner, Victor
   1969   *The Ritual Process: Structure and Anti-Structure*. Aldine, Chicago.
   1974   *Dramas, Fields and Metaphors: Symbolic Action in Human Society*.
            Cornell University Press, Ithaca.

Urton, Gary
   1981   *At the Crossroads of the Earth and the Sky: An Andean Cosmology*.
            University of Texas Press, Austin.

Vega-Centeno, Rafael
   2006   Construction, labor organization, and feasting during the late
            Archaic Period in the Central Andes. *Journal of Anthropological
            Archaeology* 15 (1):61–88.

Whitehead, William
   1999   Radiocarbon dating. In *Early Settlement at Chiripa, Bolivia:
            Research of the Taraco Archaeological Project*, edited by Christine A.
            Hastorf, pp. 17–21.Contributions, University of California
            Archaeological Research Facility, No. 57. University of
            California, Berkeley.

Wheeler, Jane, and Elías Mujica
   1981   Prehistoric pastoralism in the Lake Titicaca Basin, Peru,
            1979–1980 field season. Report submitted to National Science
            Foundation, Washington, DC.

6.

THE ARCHAEOLOGY OF RITUAL, OF CULT, AND OF RELIGION

Colin Renfrew

Archaeologists have frequently considered the archaeology of ritual as one aspect of the archaeology of cult, and recent approaches in inferring religious practice from archaeological evidence are briefly reviewed. Many kinds of repeated perfor-mative action occur, however, in contexts other than those directly associated with cult. Some of these are civic rituals, often reinforcing the authority and practice of power. Others are more mundane, validating what have been called "institu-tional facts"—shared beliefs and values within a society. Ritual in this sense often creates meaning. The study of ritual may thus be regarded as one of the approach-es toward a more general cognitive archaeology, without necessarily seeking to dis-tinguish or emphasize the practice of cult.

The Cotsen symposium for which the first draft of this paper was gen-erated proved for me a very informative experience. My own approach to questions of ritual, and of the indications of the practice of ritual that may be preserved in the archaeological record, arose initially from the consideration of the archaeology of cult practice, and thus of the archaeology of religion. In particular, it came about from the experience of excavating, at the site of Phylakopi on the Aegean island of Melos (fig-ures 6.1, 6.2), a series of small rooms containing finds which led me to suggest that the complex unearthed was a shrine or sanctuary, dating back to the Mycenaean period, to the later centuries of the second millennium B.C. (Renfrew 1985). Such considerations can lead in several directions. For instance, they beckon toward a large field that might be designated the "archaeology of religion" (Insoll 2004). They raise questions also about our approach to the thoughts and beliefs (or belief systems) of ear-lier times, as inferred from the archaeological record, and thus to what may be termed "cognitive archaeology" (Renfrew 1994).

Ritual is very soon implicated in such discussion, since most, perhaps even all, religions involve cult practices: practices that are time-struc-tured and involve performance, with the repetition of words and actions

FIGURE 6.1. The sanctuary area at Phylakopi on Melos seen from the west.
(From Renfrew 1985: Plate 8)

in formalized ways. Anyone discussing the practices associated with early religions will soon also be considering ritual.

Already in 2002, Kyriakidis (2002) had emphasized, in his doctoral dissertation, that consideration of the so-called open-air sanctuaries of Minoan Crete could usefully focus on the practice of ritual, and indeed upon the institutionalization of ritual, without necessarily setting these things in an explicitly religious context. The discussions at the Cotsen symposium developed this theme very much further. The papers asserted and exemplified various points about ritual, about its definition and about its meaning, which showed clearly how wrong it would be in general to regard ritual as simply a practice ancillary to religion. While in general the practice of religion does indeed involve ritual, the converse is simply not necessarily the case. Discussion of the matter is not helped by the difficulty in finding an acceptable definition of ritual. The interesting arguments put forward by Bell (1997; this volume) against seeking to define ritual too closely, reveal how widespread and pervasive ritual behavior is, and how difficult indeed it is to generalize about it. Moreover, I find first disconcerting and then illuminating the view of Humphrey (Humphrey and Laidlaw 1994) that both the practice and the form of a ritual may take definitive shape before the

FIGURE 6.2. Reconstruction in perspective, showing the West Shrine at Phylakopi in use during Phase Ib. (From Renfrew 1985: Figure 9.6)

verbal formulation of the meaning or interpretation that is (subsequently) ascribed to it. This viewpoint opens up a perspective that situates practice and performance at the center, leaving the development of an interpretive framework as sometimes a secondary consideration.

In what follows, some aspects of the approach developed earlier toward the archaeology of religion are set out in relation to these observations. In the last section they are reconsidered, giving due weight to the potentially autonomous status of the practice of ritual, as so informatively developed by some of the other contributors to the symposium

THE ARCHAEOLOGY OF RELIGION:
MOTIVATION OF THE ARCHAEOLOGIST

The anthropologist or historian who is interested in culture change over the long term must take account of what might be described (perhaps in rather idealist language) as the "motivating forces" within society, which seem to contribute in some cases to the foundations of the social order. In many cases, these forces may be described as religious, or at least they have a religious dimension. Sometimes there is little evidence as to an explicit belief system that might with confidence be recognized as a "religion," yet there is clear documentation of very considerable investment of labor and of effort, often over extended periods, toward symbolic goals. For such cases, where considerable investment of labor has gone into the establishment of a specific place as a symbolic focus, the term "location of high devotional expression" has been proposed, with specific reference to the complex of structures at Chaco Canyon in the American Southwest (Renfrew 2001c). A visit to such monumentally impressive ceremonial centers at Teotihuacan in the Valley of Mexico or to Karnak in Egypt illustrates the scale of the outlay both of labor and of symbolic investment that can be involved, although the boundary between religious and social at these centers would be difficult to determine. In such instances, the social order and the religious order of society are often mutually reinforcing. But in both of these two cases, there is an amply sufficient imagery of deities or of supernatural creatures to indicate the strong presence of the sacred or divine, so that the designation as "religious" can be documented and justified. When such iconography is lacking, as at Chaco Canyon, the arguments are less decisive, although they may still be felt to be persuasive. The same would apply to some of the great prehistoric monuments of northwestern Europe—for instance, at Stonehenge or Carnac in Brittany—where there is no explicit iconography to aid our own interpretation.

Clearly such motivating forces are founded upon belief systems that may be difficult of access for the archaeologist. In general, in the absence of written records, the approach to belief in a vanished society can only be through behavior (such as will leave some trace in the material record), although in favorable cases, iconography may also offer a positive line of access. The notion of "ritual" certainly encompasses much religious behavior, but, as I have noted above, the concept extends more widely to categories of activity that are not specifically predicated upon religious belief or the practice of cult. The question remains to be answered, in relation to any specific ritual practice, whether it is indeed directed toward the powerful motivating forces suggested above, and whether those forces are correctly to be regarded as "religious" rather than "secular." Clearly, the religious/secular dichotomy itself presents problems, which merit further consideration.

DEFINING RELIGION

While it might be pedantic to spend too much time in the formulation of definitions, it is perhaps helpful to establish more clearly what we are talking about. The range of behaviors that might be described as ritual was, of course, much discussed at the seminar. The definition of "ritual" by Rappaport (1999:24) as "the performance of more or less invariant sequences of formal acts and utterances not entirely encoded by the performers" was introduced into the discussion at the symposium by Joyce Marcus. It will suffice at this point, and the matter is further discussed below. As she noted, Rappaport emphasized that not all ritual is religious, nor are all religious acts ritual.

Definitions of religion vary widely; if we start with the *Shorter Oxford English Dictionary* (Onions 1973:1978), we find: "Action or conduct indicating a belief in, reverence for and desire to please, a divine ruling power [...]: Recognition on the part of man of some higher unseen power as having control of his destiny, and as being entitled to obedience, reverence and worship." The essence of religion is some framework of beliefs. Nor are these simply philosophical beliefs about the world, or even about its origin. They must relate to forces that go beyond it, transcend it. These forces, while immanent, must also—to warrant the term "religion" (in the view of most commentators)—be transcendental, or supernatural, or at least superhuman (Spiro 1966:91). In the words of the *Shorter Oxford English Dictionary* once again (Onions 1973:2193) on the concept "supernatural": "that is above nature, transcending the powers of the ordinary course of nature."

Some scholars, however, minimize or reject the distinction drawn here between natural and supernatural, on the grounds that some religions do not themselves make this distinction. They have generally stressed the institution, the church, from which, according to Durkheim, religion is inseparable: "A religion is a unified system of beliefs and practices relating to sacred things, that is to say things set apart and forbidden—beliefs and practices which unite into one single moral community called a Church, all those who adhere to them" (Durkheim 1965:47). Geertz (1966:4) offers a definition of religion that manages to avoid both the concept of the supernatural and of a church or institution: "a system of symbols which acts to establish powerful, pervasive and long-lasting moods and motivations in men by formulating conceptions of a general order of existence, and clothing these conceptions with such an aura of factuality that the moods and motivations seem uniquely realistic." Such a definition, however, might apply to a number of the "institutional facts" recognized by Searle (1995), of which the most obvious would be money. The system of coinage (including paper money) by which the world's economic system works today could be described in very much these terms. But the injunction to "render unto

Caesar that which is Caesar's" (that is, the coin bearing the image of Caesar) makes an explicit distinction between the divine and the mundane world, with money definitively assigned to the latter.

One has the impression here that Durkheim and Geertz are expressly seeking to avoid the notion of the supernatural. Of course, definition is a matter of choice. But the notion of religious experience and of the numinous (Otto 1923) can be a helpful one, emphasizing that religion is a matter of feeling as well as reason. The definition offered by Spiro (1966:96) seems here convenient: "an institution consisting of culturally patterned interaction with culturally postulated superhuman beings."

That definition is adopted here, and can be used in the discussion as to which practices or rituals might be described as religious and which are not. That distinction would be very much more difficult to draw were the definitions of religion offered by Durkheim or by Geertz to be adopted.

ARCHAEOLOGICAL CORRELATES
FOR RITUAL AND FOR RELIGION

It is probably fair to say that most considerations of the archaeological correlates for religion or for religious ritual have not made sufficient distinctions between evidence of ritual practice in general and that of specifically religious ritual practice. That criticism certainly applies to my own discussion "Archaeological correlates: The deductive system" in *The Archaeology of Cult* (Renfrew 1985:18–21), as noted earlier. It seems true also for the recent important paper by Marcus and Flannery (2004), "The coevolution of ritual and society," where they make no explicit separation between religious ritual and other kinds of ritual, although as researchers influenced by Rappaport, they are very conscious of the distinction (Marcus, this volume). In their valuable survey, they trace the evidence for ritual behavior in Oaxaca. Ritual features are seen as far back as the Archaic and Early Formative periods, but it is not until the "Period of Rank Society" (3100 to 2450 B.P.) that temples appear along with indication of ritual sacrifice. With the succeeding emergence of the Zapotec state, two-roomed temples appear and two calendars (260 days and 365 day) are documented. Such a paper, focusing upon chronology, was not the place for a detailed discussion, and the subtleties involved in such a consideration are well brought out in Marcus's consideration of Zapotec urns (Marcus 1983). There it is argued that many of these effigy vessels previously regarded as representing deities are, in fact, representations of ancestors, often showing attributes associated with great supernatural forces, such as lightning. A comparable point arises from her treatment of the figurines of the Formative period in Oaxaca (Marcus 1998), which she interprets as representing ancestors and believes were used in rituals relating to ancestors (but which are not correctly described as "ancestor worship"). Other scholars have sometimes interpreted these figurines as representing deities. These issues have a significant bearing upon the consideration as to whether their use constituted a religious ritual—particularly if our use of the word "religion" depends on the involvement of the transcendental or the supernatural. It is at this point that definitions begin to break down (as Bell suggests with reference to ritual), and that categories such as "religious" and "secular" become somewhat fuzzy.

In *The Archaeology of Cult*, I first considered aspects of sacred ritual and identified four aspects of religious ritual, which then allowed me to develop a list of 18 correlates thought to be of relevance. The correlates were potential indications in the archaeological record that might be taken to suggest cult practice. The four main points were:

1. Attention focusing

2. Special aspects of the liminal zone

3. Presence of the transcendent and its symbolic focus

4. Participation and offering.

Of these, it may be noted that points 2 and 3 relate particularly to the sacred and transcendent, while 1 and 4 could be characteristic of a range of rituals, including secular rituals. This is not the place to discuss each point, or each of the 18 correlates, in detail. But it is indeed clear that many of them would apply as much to a secular as to a religious ritual. Moreover, it is bound to be a rare case that has convincing evidence of a ritual being performed specifically with respect to a supernatural being or force. Here iconographic representation may be crucial. But it is precisely there that interpretations may differ—as in the case of the Zapotec urns.

THE POWER OF RITUAL: RITUAL CREATES MEANING

Although I accept the wisdom behind Bell's assertion that it is not prudent to define "ritual" too closely, it may not be inappropriate at this point to discuss further what I think we are talking about. Ritual may involve many things, and among these will be structured and repeated performative action. Not all those present at the performance need be actors in it, nor act in the same way. Others may be looking at the performance with close attention, and in so doing, become, in a sense, participants. In many cases, ritual can imply a considerable number of participants, who may gather together for the purpose. Places where ritual is performed may thus also be places of assembly.

In practice, ritual observances are time-structured in at least two senses. In the first place, they are carried out periodically, at specific times, which may themselves be of significance. And since the two principal terrestrial systems for measuring time are based upon the daily and annual terrestrial rotations, many rituals are diurnal or annual, frequently governed by (or associated with) seasonality. Others are governed by the life cycle of the individual—birth, incorporation into the social group (as by baptism), coming of age, marriage, professional recognition (as by guild membership), retirement, death. Secondly, rituals are in themselves internally time-structured, with well-determined sequences of actions, with prescribed repetitions and assigned durations.

Furthermore, ritual actions involve movements and utterances that are themselves kinetic and thus also time-structured. The movements can involve processions, dances, genuflections, and gestures of considerable variety, which are often rhythmic and some of which may be repeated. The utterances likewise require repetition and rhythm. Both movement and utterance may involve musical accompaniments, and the utterances maybe chanted or sung.

Since one of the lessons of the symposium was, for me, to appreciate more fully the pervasive nature of rituals that may be regarded as secular rather than religious, it may be germane to consider briefly the annual ceremony of the Trooping of the Colour as an example of a ceremony or ritual that is largely secular in nature. It takes place annually near Whitehall, in London, on the Horseguards Parade, in the presence of the sovereign. It is one of those ceremonies where the symbolism, being obsolete, has lost a little of its force—a circumstance that serves only to reveal more clearly the significance of other aspects of the procedure. The "color" in question is the standard or flag of a specific regiment, one regiment in particular being chosen for the honor in that particular year. Before the days of tanks and armored vehicles, the regimental standard had an active role in warfare, being taken into battle at the head of the regiment and serving as a rallying point for foot soldiers as well as for cavalry.

Traditionally, the sovereign herself attends the ceremony, on horseback. There is a whole sequence of formal marching and parading, while the bands play: the drill takes place with cavalry as well as with foot soldiers. The procedures are, of course, strictly defined and very well rehearsed. All of those involved are military personnel, so that the occasion is primarily a military one. But the spectators are of course civilians, and the parade, as well as being watched by many spectators (including members of the government), is televised. So there are various elements of symbolism involved. One clear symbolic element is the paying of respect by the military personnel present, representing the armed forces, to the head of state in full view of the nation. The head of state is likewise seen paying respect to the symbols of the military.

It seems appropriate to mention this example of ritual, taken from the modern world, since it exemplifies to a considerable extent one aspect of the view put forward by Humphrey, that the meaning of the ritual need not be something that could be defined prior to its enactment. Of course, here the specific, original meaning—namely, that of the formal recognition (by the queen, representing the nation) of the "color" (as the symbol of military loyalty and bravery)—is still intelligible as one of the underlying functions of the ceremony. But today, colors no longer have a significant role in military life other than on this particular day, and the flag in question is no longer carried into battle. Instead, the ceremony itself, the ritual, *is* the point. The ceremony has its own rules and conventions which have built up over the years. Simply by taking part, the queen is doing her job, just as the military personnel are doing theirs.

From the purely archaeological point of view, of course, such performative actions as these leave little trace. In other contexts, however, one might expect feasting and ceremonial drinking on such an occasion, which might well leave material indications in the record. The artifacts used—the military dress, the colors themselves, the harness of the horses, the instruments of the band—would be highly diagnostic, opening the way when noted to some account of the ceremony. In the British royal calendar, there are other state occasions such as this that serve both to symbolize and to enact, and hence renew, essential features of the state. The state opening of Parliament is one of these, again being structured on an annual basis. The coronation of the monarch is another such, but this time predicated on the life cycle of the monarch himself.

It is not difficult to find parallels for such occasions in many state societies—for instance, in the ceremonies associated with the Egyptian pharaoh, or with the Maya rulers, as recorded in their stelae. In ancient Greece, where kingship was not common, most cities had civic rather than royal festivals, like the great Panathenaia of classical Athens. In many cases, such ceremonies have a religious as well as a civic dimension. The great horse race, the Palio, at Siena, for example, a medieval ritual still practiced, is ostensibly held so that the horse and rider of one contrada (district) of the city may win honor before the Palio, the banner of the Blessed Virgin Mary. But as a ritual, the horse race is essentially secular. In both the Athenian and Sienese cases, the ritual goes back to the time when the city was an independent political entity. Its performance has much to do with celebrating and perpetuating that independence.

Elsewhere (Renfrew 2001a, 2006) I have written of the importance within societies of what John Searle (1995) terms "institutional facts," those shared understandings by which societies operate. Kingship—the existence and the conditions of existence of the office of monarch—would be one of these, or indeed the "social contract" by which any system of government operates. In many cases, the existence and the notional "truth" of these institutional facts is affirmed by the practice of rituals. Such civic rituals often involve, through their enactment, the social relationships that establish the system of governance, and by displaying these in operation, they reinforce them. Indeed, ritual is very good at affirmation, at reasserting the status quo. But it is very good, also, at stabilizing and reinforcing a new social configuration.

In discussing the monuments of Neolithic Britain, including the long barrows and the henges, I have suggested (Renfrew 2001b) that their construction was not so much a reflection or representation of the social units involved (often territorially based units), as actually constitutive of them. That is to say that, when the local residents who constructed a long barrow as a burial monument came together to do so, the very activity of working together, the reality of completing the work, and the subsequent experience of using it communally for ceremonies of burial of the local population, in effect produced the new social unit. The ritual dimension associated with the construction and use of such monuments can readily be imagined. It can also be documented.

It is a common feature the world over that the disposal of the dead involves rituals, just as is commonly the case with the social contract of marriage. When the burial procedure is one of collective burial, those are rituals that occur, time after time, at the place appointed. And when that place is a monument, formed and built by communally shared labor, one can well see that the rituals are likely to become well established.

Such procedures are in fact documented in some cases, notably at some of the megalithic tombs of Denmark. There, assemblages of ceramic vessels are frequently found at the entrance, interpreted by the excavators as documenting feasting held in relation to the dead.

Although it is easy to imagine that such feasting will also have had religious connotations, since death and the world beyond are often situated within a religious belief system, it is not necessary for us to consider them in that light. To take an example, I hope not a misleading one, from contemporary Western society, it is common after a funeral for the relatives of the deceased to offer alcoholic refreshment to the mourners attending, after the funeral. That may certainly be termed a ritual, since it forms a strong convention. Often those who do not habitually drink alcohol will do so on such an occasion. But there is no suggestion that this formalized drinking has a religious connotation, even if the funeral itself may have one.

RITUAL AND INSTITUTIONAL FACTS

The active role of ritual in society, as a mechanism by which institutional facts may be brought into being and then repeatedly affirmed, has not yet been discussed by archaeologists in quite those terms. Searle has noted:

> One of the most fascinating features of institutional facts is that a very large number, although by no means all of them, can be created by performative utterances [...]. In declarations the state of affairs represented by the propositional content of the speech act is brought into existence by the successful performance of that very speech act. [Searle 1995:34]

He offers such examples as "The meeting is adjourned" and "War is hereby declared." But, when the content is of considerable importance, the simple verbal statement may seem insufficient. For the performative utterance to carry great weight, the performative element will often be of considerable importance. For, as Rappaport (1979:193) has argued, a ritual does not only establish social convention, it establishes acceptance. By taking part in a ritual, the participants tell themselves and others that they are willing to go along with it. Going along with the ritual implies public acceptance of the conventions established by the ritual. Acceptance in turn brings with it the obligations entailed by the convention. Thus, many performative utterances will be accompanied by appropriate rituals.

As we have seen, however, with the Trooping of the Colour, many rituals that establish or reinforce institutional facts do not involve any spoken words at all. And as Rappaport (1979:193) indicates, by performing a ritual the participant "indicates to himself and to others that he accepts" the ritual.

From this perspective, ritual can play a crucial role in establishing and maintaining many aspects of the social order. It solemnizes and affirms.

And it can do so without necessarily appealing to a religious dimension. Yet, since it is often the role of ritual to solemnize, it will often do so by reference to central aspects of the prevailing belief system. When there is a coherent and prevailing system of religious beliefs, elements of that system are likely to be invoked, even when the relationships and the structures that the ritual is affirming are in essence secular. Thus, for many legal purposes in society today, it is considered necessary to swear an oath. And although this can be done by the mechanism of solemn affirmation, without reference to any religious system, where such systems exist it is usual to invoke them. Thus, in a Christian society, oaths are in many cases sworn upon the Holy Bible. In degree-giving ceremonies in British universities, the degree is generally conferred in the name of the Holy Trinity, unless the recipient is agnostic or of another faith and requests a different formula.

These considerations are relevant to the archaeological record, for they remind us of the various roles that ritual can play. The discovery of evidence of ritual behavior in the archaeological record is thus not necessarily to be taken as indicative of cult practice. It may indicate the affirmation of institutional facts that are of significance to society. It is therefore appropriate to seek an explanation or an interpretation that need not necessarily appeal to religious beliefs.

THE DISTINCTION OF RITUAL FROM RELIGION

Any reader with knowledge of current anthropology is likely to be unsurprised at the direction this paper has taken. It is simply recognizing that, in the archaeological record, there are likely to be many cases of ritual practices that we need not situate in a context of religious belief or practice. It is nonetheless useful to be explicit on this point, since archaeologists have in the past, as we have noted, sometimes tended to conflate the two areas of activity.

The current emphasis in the archaeological literature upon feasting (for exampke, Dietler and Hayden 2001; Wright 2004) points perhaps in a new direction, recognizing some of the autonomous functions of ritual practice when quite separate from religious observance. For, while feasting may indeed take place in a religious context, and many religious festivals do involve formulaic eating and drinking, a religious context need not be assumed.

But what of the major works of early societies, discussed earlier in this paper? What of the plazas and ball courts of Mesoamerica? What of the henge monuments of Neolithic Britain? What of the temples of Malta?

The labor input in these cases was so large that I find it difficult not to imagine some more holistic belief system, in which religious belief must have been at least one component of the motivation, that led to these prodigious works. One can imagine a Stonehenge where the ritual center had an essentially social or "civic" dimension. The rituals could involve feasting and even a sporting competition, as a prehistoric precursor to the periodic games of early Greece. But we have seen earlier that there is no necessary separation between religious and secular in most societies. And when one begins to incorporate the cosmos within the equation—as is implied by the alignment upon the midsummer sunrise at Stonehenge— I would argue that there must have been an encounter with a holistic worldview that we must designate as a religion.

So while, as archaeologists, we should emancipate ritual from an automatic association with religion, there may still be the temptation to associate the two when dealing with projects operating upon so prodigious a scale.

REFERENCES CITED

Bell, Catherine
   1997   *Ritual: Perspectives and Dimensions*. Oxford University Press, Oxford.
Dietler, Michael, and Brian Hayden (editors)
   2001   *Feasts: Archaeological and Ethnological Perspectives on Food, Politics and Power*. Smithsonian Institution Press, Washington, DC.
Durkheim, Emile
   1965 [1912] *The Elementary Forms of Religious Life*. Translated by J. W. Swain. Free Press, New York.
Geertz, Clifford
   1966   Religion as a cultural system. In *Anthropological Approaches to the Study of Religion*, edited by Michael Banton, pp. 1–46. A.S.A. Monographs 3. Tavistock, London.
Humphrey, Caroline, and James Laidlaw
   1994   *The Archetypal Actions of Ritual*. Clarendon Press, Oxford.
Insoll, Timothy
   2004   *Archaeology, Ritual and Religion*. Routledge, London.
Kyriakidis, Evangelos
   2002   The ritual and its establishment: The case of some open air Minoan rituals. Ph.D. dissertation, University of Cambridge.
Marcus, Joyce
   1983   Rethinking the Zapotec urn. In *The Cloud People: Divergent Evolution of the Zapotec and Mixtec Civilizations*, edited by Kent V. Flannery and Joyce Marcus, pp. 144–148. Academic Press, New York.

1998   *Women's Ritual in Formative Oaxaca*. Memoirs of the Museum of
        Anthropology, University of Michigan 33. University of
        Michigan, Ann Arbor.

Marcus, Joyce, and Kent V. Flannery
2004   The coevolution of ritual and society: New ^{14}C dates from
        ancient Mexico. In *Proceedings of the National Academy of Sciences of
        the USA* 101 (52):18257–18261.

Onions, Charles Talbut (editor)
1973   *The Shorter Oxford English Dictionary*. Clarendon Press, Oxford.

Otto, Rudolf
1923   *The Idea of the Holy*. Oxford University Press, Oxford.

Rappaport, Roy A.
1979   *Ecology, Meaning and Religion*. North Atlantic Books, Berkeley.
1999   *Ritual and Religion in the Making of Humanity*. Cambridge
        University Press, Cambridge.

Renfrew, Colin
1985   *The Archaeology of Cult, the Sanctuary at Phylakopi*. Thames and
        Hudson, London.
1994   Towards a cognitive archaeology. In *The Ancient Mind, Elements of
        Cognitive Archaeology*, edited by Colin Renfrew and Ezra B.W.
        Zubrow, pp. 3–12. Cambridge University Press, Cambridge.
2001a   Symbol before concept: Material engagement and the early
        development of society. In *Archaeological Theory Today*, edited by
        Ian Hodder, pp. 122–140. Polity Press, Cambridge.
2001b   Commodification and institution in group-oriented and individu-
        alizing societies. In *The Origin of Human Social Institutions*, edited
        by W. Garry Runciman, pp. 93–118. Oxford University Press,
        Oxford.
2001c   Production and consumption in a sacred economy: The material
        correlates of high devotional expression at Chaco Canyon.
        American Antiquity 66 (1):14–25.
2006   Becoming human, the archaeological challenge. *Proceedings of the
        British Academy* 139:217–238.

Searle, John R.
1995   *The Construction of Social Reality*. Allen Lane, Harmondsworth.

Spiro, Melford E.
1966   Religion: Problems of definition and explanation. In
        Anthropological Approaches to the Study of Religion, edited by
        Michael Blanton, pp. 85–126. A.S.A. Monographs 3. Tavistock,
        London.

Wright, James (editor)
2004   *The Mycenaean Feast*. American School of Classical Studies at
        Athens, Princeton.

7.

LIVING RITUAL AND INDIGENOUS ARCHAEOLOGY: THE CASE OF ZIMBABWE

Terence Ranger

Drawing on material from contemporary Zimbabwe, this chapter argues that it is possible and useful to turn on its head one of the major questions addressed in this book. Instead of asking how we can know whether an excavated site was a shrine, we can ask whether a modern site that is undoubtedly a shrine will leave a significant archaeological record. The chapter focuses particularly on the oracular caves of the High God cult in the Matopos Mountains of southwestern Zimbabwe. It discusses the caves themselves, from which the voice of God emerges through a possessed menopausal woman and is interpreted by a custodian priest or priestess. These are sites of intense religious experience, visited each year by thousands of pilgrims. Yet each cave is supposed to be as close to a state of nature as possible. Nothing is constructed in it save a screen of wooden slats at the entrance which is designed to decay. There have been reports of "ritual" objects said to have been removed from the caves, but these seem to have been no more than pots indistinguishable from remains associated with human occupation in thousands of other caves in the Matopos. The sacredness of the site as a shrine might have to be reconstructed on the basis of certain natural phenomena in or near the caves, particularly pools, and from ethnographic data on the relationship of the cave to its surrounding landscape. The chapter goes on to discuss other sites associated with the oracular caves, such as "villages" where priests live and pilgrims are received and where, at the least, evidence of an unusually large settlement should exist. The chapter ends with a brief discussion of Great Zimbabwe as a sacred site. Included in this discussion is reference to recent work that argues that likewise at Great Zimbabwe, it is not so much the layout of the stone remains that gives us the best understanding of its sacrality, but the relationship of the monument to its natural and human environment. The focus of archaeologists on the origins and the preservation of the site itself, it is argued, obscures an understanding of its ritual character.

With its mixture of places, periods, and disciplines, the third Cotsen Advanced Seminar at UCLA was a daring enterprise from the beginning. But perhaps the greatest risk was taken in the invitation extended to me to speak at the end of the proceedings. I am neither an archaeologist nor an ethnographer. I am a historian—and one, what is more, whose books have all been about the last hundred years. I might have viewed the proceedings as an outsider and spoken of them either admiringly or mockingly. But, in fact, I think that as a contemporary historian I have something to offer on the topic of archaeology and ritual. My chapter is not a commentary on the proceedings, except indirectly and by analogy. It is a contribution to them.

On the program of the seminar, I was described as of "Oxford and Zimbabwe." We heard so much about Cambridge rituals during the discussions that it might be thought my own presentation would emerge from comparisons with Oxford's invented traditions. But it is the Zimbabwe half of my experience on which I want to draw. I first went to southern Rhodesia in 1957; I have taught at the University of Zimbabwe for two periods, one of six years and another of four. Since 1980, I have visited Zimbabwe every year. I have written seven books about its modern history. It is in Zimbabwe that I have encountered archaeology, anthropology, and ritual.

As a Zimbabweanist, I want to make two points. The first is that a historian of Africa, even of modern Africa, is bound to have promiscuous relations with archaeology and anthropology. When I went to southern Rhodesia in 1957, I had been appointed to teach late medieval and early modern European and British history. During my six years in Oxford, I had heard Africa mentioned once. I was eager to turn myself into an Africanist and began to do so at once. This meant learning from the disciplines that knew Africa. There was virtually no historical writing on Africa in 1957. There was, however, plenty of archaeology and anthropology. Thus, I can claim that I took part in Roger Summers's excavations at Great Zimbabwe in 1958 (Summers and Robinson 1961). I can claim that I shared a common-room in what was then University College of Rhodesia and Nyasaland (UCRN) with the great urban sociologist Clyde Mitchell and the formidable anthropologist Jaap Van Velsen. My relationships with these disciplines, however, were very deferential. I literally sat—or knelt—at their feet. In the 1958 Great Zimbabwe excavations, my task was to sift soil from the midden and to run with anything I found to Roger Summers's tent so that he could assess and, if not too busy, explain. (I do not think I found anything that could have been described as a ritual object.) In the UCRN common-room, I listened silently to the often voiced wisdom of Mitchell and Van Velsen. As they sometimes pointed out, it did not seem likely that historians would ever match the understanding of Africa attained by their discipline.

Forty-five years have passed and things have changed. There is an abundance of historical writing on Africa, much of it based on oral field-work, some of it my own. With the benefit of hindsight, I can see clearly the limitations of Roger Summers's theoretical position and the limitations of Manchester School anthropology. I have even written a book to provide a historian's riposte to Clyde Mitchell's classic sociological study of an African urban dance (Mitchell 1956; Ranger 1975). In the context of this workshop, though in no other, it is permissible for me to boast that my intellectual influence is acknowledged both in Innocent Pikirayi's brilliant recent survey of the archaeology of the Zimbabwe culture (Pikirayi 2001) and in Professor Wendy James's extraordinary "new portrait of anthropology" (James 2003). So as a Zimbabweanist, I have had an intense relationship with archaeology and anthropology.

But the second point I want to make is that, as a Zimbabweanist, I have encountered living ritual. Many of the "ancient" phenomena we discussed at this seminar can be found in contemporary Zimbabwe. I have myself heard the voice of God articulated by possessed women speaking beside pools in caves in the extraordinary granitic Matopos hills (Ranger 1999). There are five oracular shrines in the Matopos, set in a sacred landscape (Nyathi 2003). The African peoples who live around Great Zimbabwe demand access to the monument in order to perform rituals there. Archaeologists, as curators and guardians of the monument, have to respond to these ritual initiatives (Fontein 2003). During the guerrilla wars of the 1970s, young armed strangers, bearing war nicknames and rifles, were inducted into the patriarchal culture of Shona kinship by means of rituals performed by spirit mediums (Lan 1985). Scholars of Zimbabwe, whether archaeologists, anthropologists, or historians, have had to try to analyze the significance of these modern rituals, as well as those invented since 1980 by the nationalist state (Kriger 1995; Werbner 1998). Many of the questions posed at the seminar have contemporary Zimbabwean analogies: how to define a shrine; how to interpret an oracular cult; how to "read" the symbolic layout of a monument and to discern the rituals performed there; how to reconstruct a sacred landscape; how to understand myths of origin; how to understand epigraphy at an "imperial" site; how to tell whether a dance, now being performed on public television as government propaganda is really "traditional." All these questions and more arise in Zimbabwe. And the point is that they arise in combination. The archaeological and ethnographic record of the ancient world is all too often piecemeal and fragmented. Students of Zimbabwe can see everything going on at once and everything interacting with everything else. The Zimbabwean reality reminds us how complex and contested ritual and monument can be.

In what follows I want to explore this Zimbabwean reality. But first I'd like to take advantage of the reference to me in the acknowledgments in Wendy James's *The Ceremonial Animal*. I do so in order to make a point about which ritual-related questions make sense and which do not.

WENDY JAMES AND THE CEREMONIAL

In her study of anthropology as it is practiced today, James takes her inspiration from a comment by Wittgenstein:

> One could begin a book on anthropology by saying: When one examines the life and behavior of humankind throughout the world, one sees that, except for what might be called animal activities, such as ingestion etc., etc., etc., human beings also perform actions which bear a characteristic peculiar to themselves, and these could be called ritualistic actions. [Wittgenstein 1993]

Yet James prefers Wittgenstein's second thoughts that we should instead view the human species as "the ceremonial animal" on the grounds that "ceremonial" is more inclusive than "ritual" and lacks its liturgical connotations (Bouveresse 1982; Clack 1999; Collins 1996). James quotes Rodney Needham to the effect that "ritual is a kind of activity—like speech or dancing—that man as a ceremonial animal happens naturally to perform"(quoted in Needham 1985:177). Yet she differs from both Wittgenstein and Needham, making "ceremonial" yet more fundamental than either. Commenting on Wittgenstein, she remarks that human eating cannot be called an "animal activity" since it is always so patterned, structured, and meaningful. By contrast to Needham, she thinks that ceremonial behavior preceded speech. "There is so much going on in life besides language. . . . language is something [that] emerged from dance. . . . ordinary language [is] a specialised distillation out of song" (James 2003:4, 74).

In a foreword to her book, Michael Lambek remarks how "persons are socially formed in the series of rituals and attention directed at them from conception" (Lambek 2003:xix); how for James "ceremony cannot reflect or represent 'society' because it is intrinsic to what we mean by society" (Lambek 2003:xx); and how she sees "ceremoniousness as possibly a more profound characteristic of humanity than rationality itself" (Lambek 2003:xxi). Lambek sums up: "Our ceremoniousness, the manifestation of mindful bodies and embodied minds, is not to be reduced to biology, economics or psychology" (Lambek 2003:xxii–xxiii).

James's work seems to me to be relevant to the discussions at the seminar. Throughout the seminar, Colin Renfrew demanded that "ritual" be defined as something clearly distinct from other forms of human behavior. James's answer would be that such a definition is impossible because ritual, or ceremonial, "is intrinsic to what we mean by humanity" (James 2003:7). During the last discussion at the seminar, there was a suggestion that archaeologists seek to identify the origins of ritual. James would think this an impossible task, certainly for an archaeologist, though she does cite work that speculates on the origins of the ceremonial, sometimes by analogy with contemporary southern African societies (Dunbar et al. 1999; Knight 1991). Of Renfrew's two main questions, James would find, as I did, that one—What is ritual?—is essentially unanswerable; on the other hand, the other—How can I know whether what I have found is a shrine?—is perfectly sensible and answerable.

In short, the question of the origins and development of particular forms of ritual or ceremonial, and of the sites at which they take place, is perfectly suited to archaeological or ethnographic or, indeed, historical inquiry. If humanity is defined by ceremonial, then a historian's task will largely be to trace the patterns thrown up by the ceremonial animal's requirement for meaning in any given time or place. James tells us that human beings always "give shape to space" and "give shape to time." These shapes change and differ, and it is up to us to trace and map these differences and transformations; to reconstruct a series of "ritual landscapes"; and to trace those "spiritual 'investments' in the forms of the land itself, which can exert an influence far into a future without any link with former pragmatic land use" (James 2003:215; see also Morphy 1991; Hastrup 1998). Like several presentations at the Cotsen seminar, James draws attention to "ceremonial centres on the landscape"; to "pattern across the landscape"; and to "socially defined cycles" of time (James 2003:65–68). She writes:

> Anthropologists have often concerned themselves with "cosmological" space. In comparison to geographers they have lifted their eyes off the surface of the earth, and sought to understand the fundamental spatial scheme and formulae which organise the whole. Archaeologists too have always been alert to aspects of "organised" orientation in the construction of settlements and buildings, especially religious buildings, and have often speculated about the

ideas of ancient peoples on the basis of this external cultural deposit. [James 2003:67]

Southern African geographers, at least, would claim that they too have "lifted their eyes off the surface of the earth" and sought to understand the "fundamental spatial scheme" (Lester 2003; Beinart and McGregor 2003:4). But in general, James has much to offer those who seek to understand contemporary southern Africa. She knows that it is not only the "ideas of ancient peoples" that must be analyzed in terms of the organization of space and time. And she makes a direct connection with the work many of us have been doing when she comments, "I have relied very much on background in history . . . especially the efforts of historians to understand the turbulence of past and current events in Africa" (James 2003:298; see also Alexander et al. 2001).

In short, James enables me to bridge the millennia between the emergence of the "ceremonial animal" and the practices of contemporary Zimbabwe. I want it to be clearly understood that I am not saying that Zimbabweans are still doing age-old—still less, "primitive"—ceremonials. What they are doing is organizing space and time in their own ways, all of them recent in historical terms and some of them very recent. Zimbabwean sacred landscapes and oracular cults are neither the same as nor continuous from those of the ancient Mediterranean. What one sees in Zimbabwe are not "survivals" but living systems and practices of meaning. Nevertheless, they are similar to and can be used to raise questions about the other cases explored in this book.

SACRED LANDSCAPES AND ORACULAR SHRINES: THE CASE OF THE MATOPOS

The Matopos Mountains lie an hour's drive to the southwest of Zimbabwe's second city, Bulawayo. Late in 2003, they were declared a World Heritage site under UNESCO's recent concept of the "cultural landscape" (Munjeri et al. 1995). The Matopos lack any "monument" save for the grave of Cecil John Rhodes and the obelisk erected there for the men of the Allen Wilson patrol who died in December 1893 in pursuit of the Ndebele king, Lobengula. Nor has there been any Iron Age archaeological investigation in the Matopos. The hills were the birthplace of an indigenous Rhodesian archaeology, which was for a long time the colony's main claim to scientific distinction, but this was directed to Stone Age sites in caves and rock overhangs. As Roger Summers has noted, "the prehistory of southern Rhodesia has been written almost entirely as a result of archaeological studies in the Matopos" (Summers 1963; see also Jones 1949; Walker 1995). Matopos Stone Age remains in themselves, however, do not constitute much of an argument for World Heritage status, except as a proof of the antiquity of human occupation of the hills. But many of the caves excavated contained fine examples of the rock art for which the Matopos are famous and which spectacularly announce the arrival of the ceremonial animal. These paintings—and the hundreds of thousands of others scattered around the hills—certainly begin to make a case for an internationally significant landscape (Garlake 1987, 1995; Walker 1996). They have always featured largely in the guidebooks to the Matopos (Nobbs 1924; Tredgold 1956).

With the development of UNESCO's concept of cultural landscape, however, some caves in particular have become critically important. These are the caves in which oracular rain shrines operate. The first global strategy meeting for the African Cultural Heritage and World Heritage Convention met in Harare in October 1995. It had five working groups. The Working Group on Archaeological Heritage noted that among the cultural properties currently on the World Heritage list in sub-Saharan Africa, "there were no cultural landscapes or sites with specified religious significance"; it recommended that investigation be made into the Matopos "for its cultural as well as natural landscape." The Working Group on Human Settlements recommended the Matopos as an example of "living heritage." The Working Group on Religious and Spiritual Heritage laid emphasis on "trance, rituals, ceremonies, rites of passage, . . . natural features and landscapes, e.g., mountains, lakes and pools, trees, forests, rocks." It recommended the Matopos as a key rain-making area, "significant not only to Zimbabwe but also to the people of Northern Botswana and Transvaal" (Munjeri et al. 1995:104–109).

When it came to compiling the Zimbabwean dossier on which the successful bid for World Heritage was based, great stress was laid on the continuous and current operation of the cave shrines. Lynette Nyathi summarizes the dossier's propositions. The Matopos were a very complex natural system, it said, distinguished from other granite landforms "because of its unique juxtaposition of rocks, [its] range of inhabitants [and its] physically intricate ecology" (Nyathi 2003: 8). Human beings have always lived in small, scattered groups in the innumerable valleys. "It is the rain shrines that provide the most far-reaching bond between the villages. . . . It is no wonder to anyone that the spirits chose to reside in such a unique and magnificent place" (Nyathi 2003:8). Nyathi, summarizing the Nomination Dossier, explains:

The diverse cultural heritage in the area spans a period of more than five hundred thousand years, with continual settlement over at least one hundred thousand years from early Iron Age to the present, a cultural time depth and variety not represented anywhere else in the country and possibly in the region. The diversity of the cultural patrimony in the Matobo Hills area bears testimony to the intertwined relationship between man and the natural environment. In fact a symbolic relationship still exists between the local communities and the hills. The existence of religious shrines all over the Matobo Hills area [is] a clear testimony that the cultural landscape has maintained and sustained its religious status for the greater part of its human occupation. [Nyathi 2003:11]

There can be no doubt, then, that we are dealing with shrines. Much research has been done on the organization of particular shrines; on their relationship to each other; on their "constituencies"; and on their management of pilgrims coming from all over southern Africa (Daneel 1998; Nthoi 1995; Nyathi 2003; Ranger 1999; Schoffeleers and Mwanza 1978; Werbner 1989). There can be no doubt, either, that many of these cave shrines have been, and that some still are, oracular. There are innumerable individual testimonies and press reports to the Voice of the High God emanating from the interior of the caves, uttered in archaic language by possessed priestesses crouched by pools, and interpreted to petitioners by priests. The Tswana anthropologist Leslie Nthoi has made an interesting analysis of the difference between ritual procedures at shrines that receive pilgrims but do not possess the Voice and shrines where petitioners can converse directly with the divine. He has also recorded many oral accounts of oracular answers to questions and the signs that accompany them (Nthoi 1995). The missiologist-anthropologist Martinus Daneel, who has been visiting the shrines of the eastern Matopos since the 1950s, reproduces in his latest book transcripts of "carefully recorded oracular sessions [which] capture the actual discourse taking place during a cave ceremony" (Daneel 1998:170). One such session took place at Bembe shrine on 10 January 1989, where "the entranced female Voice of the oracle transmitted from the cave depths" (Daneel 1998:170). That same night he recorded a longer session at the nearby Dzilo cave where a different female Voice spoke with his delegation (Daneel 1998:173–178). Daneel has a large collection of such taped transcripts which he proposes in future to publish and analyze from a theological perspective.

The question for us here, then, is the reverse of the one asked by Colin Renfrew in his presentation to the seminar. He had excavated an edifice that contained probable ritual material which made him think it might be a shrine. How could he tell whether it was? Our quandary is to imagine how archaeologists will be able to identify Matopos oracular shrines in an unforeseeable future when they have ceased to operate. We have what are unmistakably shrines, but we have no archaeological material relating to them whatever. Recently a survey of Iron Age sites was undertaken in the Matopos, but few sites have been excavated. Stone Age excavations have, of course, been carried out over a long period, but none of these have taken place in caves that are now, or are said to have been, shrines of the High God Mwali. The case is little better with ethnographic evidence. Suppliants do not enter the oracular caves—indeed, on the two occasions tape-recorded by Daneel, suppliants sat with their backs to the cave entrance and could see nothing at all inside the cave. Cave entrances are screened with rough wooden palisades, but beyond that we have only fragmentary evidence on how they are laid out and what ritual objects, if any, they contain. From time to time—indeed frequently—there have been reports of "desecration" of a shrine, and recently the senior shrine, Njelele, was set on fire. Sometimes desecration has been alleged to have taken the form of looting or removal of cult objects. Thus, a military intelligence report for 1918 recorded that Trooper Atfield, a white policeman, had entered Njelele cave, "the headquarters of these natives," and removed some of the sacred objects. "Six months later he died. Natives are convinced that his death resulted from this act" (Ranger 1999:53). There was no description in this, or similar reports, of the nature of the sacred objects. So far as I know, no Zimbabwean museum collections contain objects that can be reliably linked with the rituals of the Mwali cult (Ellert 1984). Offerings were—and are—certainly made, but any that have been described are common or transitory, like the "wire bracelets, beads and wisps of woven grass, some twigs or the like" left by Africans in the early 1920s at Silozwane cave (Nobbs 1924:191).

The Matopos shrines present us with the same combination of spiritual power and "pokiness" that ancient historians described during the seminar. A clue here may be given in David Coplan's account of the great cave shrine of Badimong on the South African /Lesotho border. Like the Matopos shrines, Badimong today attracts thousands of pilgrims from many distant places; unlike them, it does not articulate the Voice of God but represents the spiritual force of a multitude of ancestors. It is very different physically as well. It is not so much a cave as a huge overhang;

pilgrims do not sit respectfully at its entrance but perambulate along its whole length. Yet Coplan's description of it makes several points crucial for the Matopos shrines:

> The way of the pilgrims takes visitors along a central path. . . . On the left, one soon passes the low, swampy pool of khanyapa, the tutelary spirits of Basotho diviners, which takes the shape of a snake with the breasts of a woman, and instructs spirit mediums as to their ritual dress and other matters in dreams. On the right, a short distance above the path, is an altar decorated with flags of different primary and secondary colours, tended to by a female dance healer, who arranges them, as she said, "to direct you to that location within the caves where your ancestors wish to find you". From here paths lead up the steep incline to the right and left sides of the valley, where on both slopes are small, attractive enclosures for dwelling, ritual and convalescence. The [white] farmers [on whose land the cave shrine is located] try to forbid the building of permanent structures at the shrine, and pilgrims too observe strictures against modifications to the natural environment that might offend the ancestors whose home this is. Interestingly, the makeshift shelters built into the long cave wall reflect a spiritualised vernacular architecture designed in dreams, and bear only an underlying, not a decorative, resemblance to indigenous African housing. Some enclosures are inhabited for weeks by those that the ancestors have "arrested". . . . Others are used for services on special celebration and feast occasions and by a range of healers, diviners, prophets and churches. [Coplan 2003:982]

There is much more going on inside Badimong cave than in any of the Matopos shrine caves. Coplan describes how ancestors prescribe to pilgrims in dreams "the specific section along the lines of cave walls, clearings and pools and streams where they wish to find one." The Badimong shrine contains San "paintings left on the walls of cliff overhangs"; "the two contrasting cultural landscapes" of white farmers and black pilgrims overlay "the ancient hunting trails of the San foragers." Contemporary pilgrims to Badimong inscribe their names on the cave walls like graffiti, saying: "It is like the Bushmen; you draw for remembrance" (Coplan 2003:984–985). The idea of "makeshift shelters" within the caves, however temporary, or of graffiti scribbled on the cave walls, is unthinkable at the Matopos oracular shrines, as is the invocation within them of any spiritual power other than that of Mwali. Nthoi presents an oral account by a cult official at Njelele of the great disaster that befell the priestly Mbikwa clan, custodians of Njele in the nineteenth century. Some of the Mbikwa began to use "a talking calabash which was believed to have some strong potency to rejuvenate the old. The use of this new source of mystical power within the Njelele shrine offended Mwali. Consequently the Voice at Njelele ordered the annihilation of the whole Mbikwa house" (Nthoi 1995:372). Talking calabashes would cheerfully be added to the assemblage at Badimong.

Nevertheless, Coplan's two main points apply to the Matopos oracular shrines. Most of the ritual sites at an oracular shrine are natural rather than constructed. And whatever is constructed is provisional and temporary so as to avoid "modifications to the natural environment that might offend" (Coplan 2003:982) divinity. Thus, for Njelele (the senior Matopos shrine), Nthoi tells us that "there is a fountain or pool on top of the Njelele hill itself, from which the priest was expected to draw water, which he would later pass on to messengers at the rain ceremony normally held in September" (Nthoi 1995:167). He also tells us that each messenger is allowed to "draw water from a little pool near the shrine to carry home. The seeds which they have brought from home are blessed, treated with some substance and given back to them to take home" (Nthoi 1995:184). A natural area of flat ground, close to the cave, was used for performances by the Mwali adepts, who in the manner of Wendy James's analysis, danced to Mwali before they spoke to Him/Her.

The contesting guardians at Njelele in the early 1990s—Sitwanyana Ncube and his ex-wife Gogo Ngcatu—claimed to derive their authority directly from their encounter with nature at the shrine. Sitwanyana claimed to have spent "three months living with a lion, leopard, baboon, snake in Sihazabana cave . . . where I was taught the traditions of the shrine. I was talking directly to a snake which is the one which showed me all the caves" (Ranger 1999:23). Ngcatu "claimed to have dived into deep and hazardous rivers [among] crocodiles and water snakes and to have emerged unscathed. . . . she claims to have spent five hours under water having conferences with the ancestors who pledged their support for reforms at the shrine" (Mafu 1995:295).

But if key ritual sites are natural rather than constructed, the local congregation around an oracular shrine is expected to do some work to maintain it and will suffer misfortune if they do not. The congregation has to clear the mouth of the shrine and to construct at its entrance a barrier of roughly tied logs. Nthoi tells us that when Nkobamwe Mbikwa arrived at Njelele in 1947, after a period during which the oracle had been silent, he found that the shrine was unkempt; the mouth of the cave was choked with tall grass; the logs used as a barrier had long ago rotted away or been destroyed by termites. He appointed a "sweeper" to restore the shrine to its proper condition (Nthoi 1995:373). Yet even these interventions avoid interference with nature as much as possible. Cult adepts "sweep" the shrine with their hands and not with brooms; stone tools are used to cut the grass rather than metal ones; the logs used to construct the entrance barrier are deliberately chosen from wood subject to decay. The point lies in the impermanence: humans have constantly to serve the shrine and never to impose themselves upon it (Ranger 1999:23).

These cave shrines, in short, with their possessed female oracles, have resisted the change from nature to culture to civilization which took place at Delphi. There seems little for an archaeologist to detect. Maybe there will prove to be some regularities in the layout of the caves themselves; no anthropologist has walked a route in the Mwali caves as Coplan has done at Badimong, and we possess no account of what lies inside them. The closest we have is a description by the young Zimbabwean scholar Oliver Zvabva, of an oracular cave in northeastern Zimbabwe, in the mountainous frontier between Zimbabwe and Mozambique. At this Nyachiranga shrine, the Voice of Dzivaguru, eastern Zimbabwe's High God, is heard. The structures inside the cave are very symbolic and have a bearing on agricultural fertility. In the cave there is a stream which has its source in the cave, which flows into a ninga, or bottomless pit; a baobab tree; a dome-shaped pillar; mipfura trees with beehives; and two expansive rock dwalas, one close to the entrance and the other at the back of the cave. In the cave, the scenery is attractive, full of life: biological as well as social (Zvabva 1988). This notion of a landscape internal to the shrine cave is a fascinating one. Perhaps when we have more such descriptions, some sort of pattern will emerge that will help us understand why some caves are chosen as shrines rather than others, and perhaps will even help future archaeologists to determine whether a cave is likely to have been a shrine or not. But although the cave itself becomes "the holy of holies" when the Voice speaks from within it, it is not sensible to equate the cave with the shrine. Each Matopos shrine uses several caves simultaneously; old caves are abandoned and new ones developed. To meet this difficulty, Schoffeleers and Mwanza, in their organizational model of the interaction of the shrines, write that "the term 'shrine' is used here to indicate the local organizational unit consisting of an acknowledged officialdom which controls the oracular activities at one or adjacent caves" (Schoffeleers and

Mwanza 1978:305). A shrine thus includes not only the inner cave, but also the outer apparatus: the village of the priestly family; the receptions and preparation rooms for pilgrims; and the quarters of the dancers and other performers. These externals can be seen and studied quite easily.

Leslie Nthoi, for instance, though not allowed to visit the Njelele caves nor attend any ceremony on the mountain, was able to live for several weeks in the village of one of the competing high priests, David Ndlovu, and was permitted to observe the arrival of pilgrims and to talk with them about their purposes. Even then he faced many frustrations: "most of the pilgrims who came to Njelele were spirit mediums [and] when I tried to talk to them about any issue, they often told me that they were simple vessels and therefore knew nothing. The moral pressure of me to submit to learn by being there, rather than by asking questions, was overwhelming" (Nthoi 1995:20). Still, since the Njelele caves were officially closed during his visit, even if used in secret, much of the work of the cult went on in David's village itself. For the supplicants, the climax of their pilgrimage came in morning sessions in the great hut in David's village where they "poured out their hearts to the deity and ancestral spirits." Nthoi slept in a small hut so close to the large one that "I was able to eavesdrop on the proceedings in the shrine without leaving my bed" (Nthoi 1995:20).

The family of Lynette Nyathi, a University of Zimbabwe historian, actually lives near Dzilo shrine in the eastern Matopos. She is very familiar with the external structures on the shrine, although she has not yet been able to make a promised dawn visit to the "original" oracular cave in which there is said to be a representation of the woman founder to which drinking water is offered even today during conditions of severe drought. Leslie Nthoi's problem was that he was a "foreigner" from Botswana; Lynette's is that she is a potentially sexually active young woman. But foreigners and girls and anthropologists and archaeologists are able to visit the Chokoto priestly village at Dzilo and to photograph it—there are many pictures of it in books. Unfortunately, these are not very revealing of its structure and layout. But it is clear that the external structures associated with management of an oracular shrine are both numerous and differentiated.

A successful shrine priest disposes of a great deal of wealth: gifts of cattle to Mwali; gifts of maize and meat to make beer, feed the pilgrims, and propitiate the god; gifts of money. Richard Werbner thus describes the wealth of Ntogwa, priest of an oracular shrine in northeastern Botswana, as ten wives, herdsmen, hundreds of head of cattle, sacks of grain, and a bank account (Werbner 1989:272). The village of such a successful priest needs to be as large as that of any other polygamous entrepreneur—of whom there are very few in the Matopos.

Sitwanyana Ncube's village at Njelele, though burned by his enemies at least twice, is once again a large and bustling settlement. And to his own hut and those of his wives, one has to add the accommodation for pilgrims and structures for specialist dancers and performers. We have a description of one of the least well-known shrines, Manyangwa in southeast Zimbabwe. It was visited in September 1994 by Reverend Hezekiel Mafu. It was the time of the annual rain ceremony, and the keeper's village was thronged with community representatives bringing gifts and with female wosana dancers. In the proper spirit of the ceremonial animal, proceedings began with dance:

> The dancing was done in front of the shrine [i.e., the cave] itself. They danced in the open air with no shoes on or cover in the scorching sun. . . . [When] they became chained by the spirits in the process of dancing they fell to the ground [and] on the ground they either rolled or writhed from side, but always in line with the rhythm and beating of the drums. (Mafu 1995: 299–300)

But there was also provision for other types of ceremonies. Manyangwa had invited government officials and other dignitaries (none of whom showed up) and erected a platform for them and a special room "reserved for guests." This was packed to capacity with elders and with a high table at one end where Manyangwa sat with a young lady secretary who recorded the names, district, and chief of those present. Later Mafu was given "a conducted tour" of the Wosana village located half a kilometer away and used twice a year when the dancers came for rain and first fruits ceremonies. The village itself was a conglomeration of more than 75 grass-thatched huts whose walls of poles were not plastered and were without doors. In the center of the village was a grass-thatched hut whose yard was cemented with a special mortar. It was a sacred hut, the abode of Ubabamkulu, the most revered and feared hut in that community. No one entered its yard with shoes on. Manyangwa "clapped for entry." Inside the hut "was a big calabash filled to capacity with bubbling beer," enough for the coming ceremonies. In this village there were two dancing places, one for day dancing and the other for night. No kindling of fire was allowed in the Wosana village; no spilling of water; no lights or lamps; no urination; no sexual intercourse; and no killing of any creature (Mafu 1995).

This Wosana village was clearly erected on the same principles of provisionality and built-in obsolescence as the log barriers at the oracular caves or the shelters at Badimong. And despite the relative size and elaboration of priests' villages themselves, these too are constrained by a cult ideology of simplicity and naturalness. Immediately after Zimbabwean independence in 1980, there was a cultural nationalist attempt to modernize Njelele and the other shrines. Joshua Nkomo, leader of the Zimbabwe African Peoples Union, had seen national shrines both in Britain—Westminister Abbey—and in other parts of Africa, such as the tombs of the kings of Buganda. Nkomo thought of himself as the "owner" of the Mwali shrines; he visited them regularly to speak with the Voice and derived a great deal of influence in western Zimbabwe through myths of the divine favors bestowed upon him at Njelele and Dula caves. But he thought they should be "improved." His close associate in such matters, Tenjiwe Lesabe, told me of Nkomo's injunction to his followers: "I, as Joshua, would have loved to see you people respect Njelele like the old people did, number one. Number two, I'd like you people to make improvements to that place, it's shabby, there's no accommodation. You should have toilets in that area, and have water, and at least have houses, so that every chief in this country, Zimbabwe as Zimbabwe, should have a house" (Ranger 1999:255).

At his political rallies, Nkomo urged all his supporters to go on pilgrimage to Njelele. The district administration budgeted for buildings at the shrine; a hotel was planned; there would be clusters of houses for chiefs, along with an impressive permanent residence for the shrine priest and flush toilets for pilgrims. A modest Zimbabwean version of the transition of the Delphic oracle from natural site to templed town would get underway. But Nkomo's plan ran into total opposition from the chiefs, priests, and people of the Matopos. It was much too far away from taboos on fire and sex and urination! (Ranger 1999:255–261). Njelele remains defiantly "shabby" to this day.

Despite the absence of elaboration, there probably would be enough data for future archaeologists to deduce and locate shrines—a concentration of caves and perennial pools, adjacent to polygamous villages with large meeting houses and to "ritual" settlements with much less permanent structures. But in addition, it would be necessary for them to set such sites in a ritual landscape. Indeed, this is the direction in which contemporary Zimbabwean archaeology is moving. As Innocent Pikirayi writes in his recent account of southern Zambezian states: "I find it convenient to comprehend the cultural ecology of folk I am investigating, to comprehend the physical environment and cultural adaptation—to understand

the manner by which people and their cultures are fit into a landscape"
(Pikirayi 2001:33).

The most ambitious attempt to map the landscape into which Mwali
adepts "fit" has been made by the anthropologist Richard Werbner in an
account of the total shrine system. "The shrines are many," say his informants, "God is one" (Werbner 1989:251). Werbner describes interaction
between local, interlocal, regional, and "cardinal" shrines:

> Every oracle of Mwali is the centre of a considerable and ever-
> changing part of the cult. It is consulted and speaks about the moral
> condition of the land and the people in land shrine communities
> distributed over thousands of square miles. For each oracle there is
> a regional network of sacred central places, the oracle being at the
> heart of the network or region. Such a region develops across eth-
> nic, district and even international boundaries. [Werbner 1989:254]

Werbner produces maps of part of this huge sacred landscape, including a map of congregations and shrine flows in northeastern Botswana; a
map of "interlocal shrines and bands of adepts"; another of "territorial
divisions of north-eastern Botswana"; and a final one of "congregations of
South-Western Region, Botswana and Zimbabwe" (Werbner 1989:267,
273). This last map includes the "cardinal" shrines of the Matopos,
"placed symbolically and ecologically above the rest. Being innermost,
they are located within an enclaved zone in the Matopo Hills. Their sites
are moved the least of all" (Werbner 1989:279). Werbner constructed his
maps on the basis of ethnographic data. Unlike the Nasca lines and the
"ritual processions marking the landscape" in the Andes, the boundaries
shown on Werbner's maps have left no mark on the ground. This sacred
landscape is on too vast a scale to be useful to archaeologists. More
restricted explorations of Matopos shrine landscapes, however, could be
as helpful as they have proved in the case of Thotlakonda. One of
Pikirayi's honor students, Lynette Nyathi, has produced very suggestive
work on the landscape around the Dzilo shrine in the eastern Matopos.
She establishes local names for the shrine itself—its "real" name is
Zhame, the breast—and for adjoining mountains, sacred forests, pools,
and the like. There are, in fact, many contesting names, reflecting the
complex history of memory and layers of occupation in the Matopos.
Here one can construct ritual landscapes for many successive periods.
Nyathi is also concerned to trace landscape interactions among the
Matopos shrines—for instance, the still-preserved sacred groves that

mark the passage of the male Mwali manifestation at Dula shrine to join his female manifestation at Dzilo/Zhame. In a landscape of innumerable caves and pools, the oracular shrines are distinguished and located cosmologically even more than geographically. Nyathi sets out to discern "the territorial division of the landscape" between the shrines of eastern Matopos and their "traditional co-ordination" on the basis of a "geographic continuity which allowed for intensive concentration and pooling of information." She describes an "ecological religion" in which, within a massively overpopulated communal area, there are nevertheless "areas that are considered sacred and not to be tampered with in any way," and she shows how enforced changes to the landscape, such as dams, are brought into the ideology of the cult. She finds that while "locals" who live around the shrines are uniformly cynical about the priesthood and even the Voice, "sacred places seem to be more significant in their lives" (Nyathi 2003:65–66). Priests are corrupted by wealth and their manipulation of the pilgrims who come to the shrines from afar. The eastern Matopos sacred landscape is a matter for locals themselves.

> They go to such places to consult the spirits and to gain inspiration for their day to day activities. Over and over again, these places are connected with or have what the western world classes as "natural" features . . . such as mountain peaks, springs, rivers, woods and caves. . . . In the Matobo Hills indigenous traditional religious beliefs were and still are instrumental in the preservation of the tangible heritage through a system of taboos and cultural norms. . . . The need to keep the hills as a venerated landscape is inculcated into the local communities at the ceremonial gatherings that take place annually at the Mwali shrines. [Nyathi 2003:66]

Nyathi reveals a gendered landscape: near to Njelele there is an area called Denjalila, "inhabited by female spirits operating at the Njelele shrine." Male contenders for the priesthood, penetrating an area reserved for female spirituality in order to brew beer and "perform their ceremonies," were so afflicted by the Denjalila spirits that they fled to the city of Bulawayo. She also reveals a dangerous landscape. One inhabitant of Zhame "cleared a piece of land believed to be owned by the great amalinda spirits for settlement purposes and was attacked by a mysterious illness that subsequently led to his death"; another went hunting with his dogs on Kangaru Mountain, on which there was once a Mwali shrine. He disturbed a leopard in a cave and "a strong current of air siphoned him into the cave where he spent the whole day and night before being rescued." Yet another local discovered "a belt of gold in one of the mountains in the area." He began to drill the mountain, and "in retaliation molten lava oozed out of the solid granite mountain until the man and his party abandoned their tools and fled to Bulawayo" (Nyathi 2003:67–73). The point is that the male and female elders who tell these stories can walk Lynette around these sites and would continue to be able to do so even if a particular shrine were to fall into disuse. At the same time, the point is that the past existence of that shrine would continue to be reflected in these readings of the sacred landscape.

So far, I have focused very much on the oracular caves, the shrine village complex, and the levels of sacred landscape in which they are set. But the fact that they all operate in the present day enables us to see not only cult dynamics in all their complexity, but also their integration and interaction with wider social, economic, and political processes. An individual shrine cannot be separated from the whole cult dynamic, but neither can it be separated from local and national politics.

What emerges most strongly is the intense competition and conflict that characterizes both the shrines and their relationship to "symbolic" and "secular" politics. The whole range of authorities I have cited attest to this. My own study of the modern history of the Matopos, *Voices from the Rocks*, seeks to include the history of the shrines over the past hundred years as part of a total narrative of conquest, dispossession, nationalism, war, party political strife, clashes of environmental narratives, and the like (Ranger 1999). Here I present a description rather than illustrate the multiple levels of conflict:

These begin with the idea that the human custodians of the shrines always live in extreme danger. They are chosen—if their tenure is legitimate—by the Voice or by the rocks; they are continually subject to personal and family disaster if they offend divinity. The oral history of each shrine family is replete with flights, accidents, incests and blasphemies, epidemics and retributive punishment. Control of a shrine is a very dangerous activity but it is also a highly rewarding one. So there are contests within each shrine—between male priests and female mediums; between brothers; between competing clan claimants. Then there are contests between the cardinal shrines, as each vies to extend its region and to claim more pilgrims. Many of these contests are expressed in terms of ritual breaches—one competing priest or shrine will accuse another of not understanding or of deliberately flouting proper ceremonial traditions. It is, in fact, impossible to establish what "proper" ceremonies and rites are or were (Nthoi 1995; Ranger 1999; Werbner 1989).

These contests are extended, of course, to other forms of religious use of the Matopos landscape. There are mission churches and schools sited closed to every oracular shrine; missionaries and their converts in the past used to enter and thus pollute the oracular caves. Today the main conflicts are with African-initiated prophetic churches, which share belief in the creative agency of the Voice and the power of holy places but claim a monopoly of the Voice and place for themselves (Mafu 1995; Nyathi 2003). Other ideological conflicts have arisen over the doctrines of "scientific" conservationists. Conservation "experts" have long sought to impose methods of cultivation and land use sharply contrasting with those ordained by the shrines. Both in Rhodesian times and since independence, they have demanded the total evacuation of human beings from the Matopos in order to restore a "natural" landscape.

The shrines have become involved in and endangered by war—in 1896 and in the 1970s and 1980s. Administrators of both the Rhodesian minority- and the Zimbabwean majority-rule governments have wanted to suppress the shrines; they have arrested priests and spied on their interaction with pilgrims. The shrines have also become involved in and endangered by party politics, with Joshua Nkomo's ZAPU (Zimbabwe African People's Union) using them as a source of legitimacy, and Robert Mugabe's government trying to wrest control of them for more reliable "Shona" priests and priestesses. *Voices from the Rocks* illustrates what kind of symbolic discourse, cultic narrative, and ceremonial practice emerge from this admixture of shrine and national politics. Every kind of indigenous conservationist movement has sought authority from Dzilo/Zhame, and all have received benediction from the Voice (Daneel 1998; Wilson and Mawere 1995). Today the cardinal shrines are involved once again in the politics of heritage, as the implications of UNESCO's doctrine of cultural landscape play themselves out on the ground.

I am not quite sure how it advantages an archaeologist of ritual to know all this—even a Zimbabwean archaeologist of ritual, let alone one working on ancient societies. But perhaps this question can be clarified by looking more briefly at my second Zimbabwean case, the archaeology and politics of the Great Zimbabwe monument.

RITUAL AND THE SILENCE OF GREAT ZIMBABWE

Like the Matopos shrines, Great Zimbabwe has been, and still is, the subject of intense contestation. Like the whole Matopos area, Great

Zimbabwe is a UNESCO World Heritage site, though as a monument rather than as a cultural landscape. But it is the differences between the two rather than the similarities that I wish to explore. The Matopos shrines offer us an abundance of ritual and no archaeology. Great Zimbabwe, as it stands at present, offers us an abundance of archaeology and no ritual.

It is true that when whites first saw Great Zimbabwe (Burke 1969; Mauch 1874, 1876), they invoked visions of fantasy rituals. Gazing at the ruins in 1871, Carl Mauch concluded that "the ruin on the hill is a copy of Solomon's temple on Mount Moriah and the building on the plan a copy of the palace where the Queen of Sheba lived during her visit to Solomon" (quoted in Summers 1963:19). These extraordinary but influential conclusions were partly based on what Mauch had learned about contemporary Karanga sacrifices, which he thought identical to the sacrifices of "the Israelites." Thereafter, until deep into the Rhodesian period, white imaginations were intoxicated with thoughts of sensual Sheban ceremonies. Rhodesian spiritualist Percy Fletcher, reacting fiercely against archaeological theories of the medieval date of Great Zimbabwe, went so far as to hold a seance in the elliptical building then known as the Temple, in which he summoned up the spirit of Sheba herself to confirm her ownership of Great Zimbabwe.

But if Rhodesians were happy to imagine biblical orgies taking place there, they did not seek to use Great Zimbabwe for their own ceremonial purposes. There was, admittedly, a moment when the monument attracted the attention of that great inventor of symbol and ceremony, Cecil Rhodes. Rhodes thought of Great Zimbabwe as evidence for a long vanished white civilization which he was going to restore. He toyed with the idea that he should be buried on what the Rhodesians called the "Acropolis," the royal hill at Great Zimbabwe. When the Allen Wilson patrol was wiped out by the Ndebele in December 1893, Rhodes had their bones gathered up from the battlefield and buried outside the "Temple" at Great Zimbabwe in an area he thought might become a Rhodesian Valhalla. It is interesting, if alarming, to imagine that Rhodes's grave and the Allen Wilson patrol might have been commemorated at Great Zimbabwe by massive classical monoliths designed by Rhodes's favorite architect, Herbert Baker. In any event, however, Rhodes saw Mzilikazi's grave in the Matopos in 1896 and decided to move the center of the Rhodesian symbolic universe into the hills. The bones of the Wilson patrol were excavated yet again, under cover of night so as not to anger the settlers of Fort Victoria, and carried off to be buried at World's View in the Matopos under their Baker monolith. Only a metal plaque survived until after Zimbabwean independence to remind visitors to Great Zimbabwe of its connection with the settler occupation of the country.

Thereafter, the successive keepers of Great Zimbabwe were interested first in loot and then in an increasingly responsible custodianship of the monument—mapping, maintaining, rebuilding. The first white custodians recorded the little wars of local African chieftaincies and something about their ethnography, rituals, and traditions. But these were thought to have no possible connection with the monument since it was clear that the local peoples had arrived in the area long after its building and, indeed, abandonment. The main connection between the locals and Great Zimbabwe was their use, first as coerced and then as low-paid labor, in clearing the site, in building walls, and so on. Great Zimbabwe was, of course, a major attraction for white tourists. The most important symbolic appropriation that took place was the construction of a golf course, which involved blocking a sacred pool and inconveniencing, at the least, the njuzu water spirits who dwelled in it. Tourists were presented with the monument as a very ancient stage set, long emptied of actors. Local people, meanwhile, were denied access to Great Zimbabwe to stage their own ceremonies (Fontein 2003).

The crucial activities in this empty theater—certainly not without drama themselves—were the excavations by a sequence of archaeologists (Caton-Thompson 1931; Fontein 2006; Garlake 1973; Hall, 1905, 1909; MacIver 1906; Summers and Robinson 1961; Willoughby 1893). Hence, by the 1970s there was an abundance of archaeology but no ritual at Great Zimbabwe.

None of these archaeologists, though differing fiercely with one another, had been chiefly concerned with studying what Wendy James calls "giving shape to space" (James 2003:65) or "giving shape to time" (James 2003:68). They were concerned primarily with origins (and with decline) and, after that, with building styles and sequences. In the 1970s, admittedly, attention was given to the environmental context of Great Zimbabwe. Its abandonment began to be explained in terms of the ecological concept of "carrying capacity".

Some archaeologists believe that Great Zimbabwe was abandoned abruptly about A.D. 1450. They explain this in terms of the intolerable pressure of Great Zimbabawe's 18,000 inhabitants on the local resources (Huffman 1987; Pikarayi, 2001). But this environmental determinism remained a long way from Pikirayi's ambition "to comprehend the cultural ideology of folk . . . the manner by which people and their cultures are fitted into a landscape" (Pilirayi 2001).

In the early 1980s, two developments occurred which, in quite different ways, lent sophistication to our understanding of Great Zimbabwe's position in space. One was the development at Uppsala University of computerized maps of Zimbabwean archaeological site "clusters within a constellation of points using a modified form of nearest neighbour analysis," revealing "the relative density of site distributions." For the Great Zimbabwe period, stated here as ca. A.D. 1250 to 1450, "the maps show that the Zimbabwe State was organised as (at least) a three tier structure and therefore satisfies in this regard one of the important archaeological criteria for comprising a true state" (Sinclair and Lundmark 1984:15).

This "spatial analysis" tried to obtain at least political meaning from the patterned relationship of Zimbabwean sites to one another. After further "correspondence analysis" and "multi-dimensional scaling," the project hoped "to develop a general model of the cycle of state formation on the Zimbabwean plateau" (Sinclair and Lundmark 1984:19).

But this Uppsala work did not appear to yield much real understanding of the archaeology of ritual and ceremony. Another attempt at decoding spatial patterns, however, addressed precisely these issues. This time the focus was inward, on the layout and decoration of Great Zimbabwe itself. Thomas Huffman was convinced that the monument must represent something more than the labor-intensive showpiece of an African state. It had been given importance not only by its size but by the rituals and ceremonials performed there and by the symbolic statements made by its wall patterns. As he asserts, "since spatial order organises people, spatial and social organisations are different expressions of the same thing, and the underlying structure must be part of a society's worldview" (Huffman 1996:6). In his book *Snakes and Crocodiles*, he seeks to work from the ethnography into the archaeology and then back to the ethnography again, hoping in this way both to interpret the symbols and layout of the monument and to demonstrate cultural change.

HUFFMAN BRINGS SACRED NATURE
RIGHT INTO THE MONUMENT

The court and palace were the hub of political activity and the physical focus of sacred leadership. According to Huffman, both places were imbued with mountain and pool symbolism, and the striking wall designs expressed various aspects of leadership through this idiom. The "crocodile" (the check mark in the designs) in its pool (dark line) was dominant, while the "snake in the water" (cord) and "snake of the mountain" (chevron) reflected the related themes of control over fertility and rain, respectively.

He also sees Great Zimbabwe as a site of repeated and crucially important ritual. In his model, a ritual royal sister makes rain at a special site; kings are buried on mountaintops; caves are the center of "national rain-making rituals." Above all—and this is his most controversial and disputed assertion—he draws on Venda ethnography to argue that the great elliptical building was designed for female initiation ceremonies and dances (Huffman 1996:6, 103).

Huffman's work has been hotly contested (Beach et al. 1997; Beach et al. 1998). His Shona ethnography is arbitrary and limited; the Venda parallels are not legitimate; as Pikirayi remarks, "it seems highly unlikely that they would invest so extravagantly in a prestigious monumental structure such as this one for the purpose of initiation" (Pikirayi 2001:137). Nevertheless, Pikirayi himself is attracted by cognitive archaeology; Great Zimbabwe, he writes, "was built to express a society. Its very layout illustrated their world view" by means of "binary symbolic divisions" (Pikirayi 2001:134). In an important article commenting on the work of both Huffman and of the late oral historian, David Beach, Pikirayi remarks that neither "were fluent in the Shona language and therefore had to omit certain aspects of Shona cosmology . . . for example the many rituals surrounding the Shona courts. I suggest the need to focus research on the study of cultural landscapes" (Pikirayi 1999:141).

Pikirayi's own survey of the Zimbabwe culture has a chapter entitled *The Landscapes of Southern Zambezia*. Yet the scale of his book is perhaps too wide to allow him to set Great Zimbabwe in the context of its own landscape. One not only needs to bring "nature" inside the monument, as Huffman does (Huffman 1996), but to relate the monument to its own natural setting. Pikirayi notes that archaeologists have not yet done this. "The plateau is a great patchwork of micro-environments," he writes. "Archaeologists, however, have tended to spend their time at the major zimbabwes," thus interacting only with "the testimony of the long dead" (Pikirayi 1999:246).

Fortunately, however, a doctoral thesis completed in 2003 allows us to hear the testimony of the living. The anthropologist Joost Fontein spent two years living among the people of the chiefly dynasties situated close to Great Zimbabwe. He also worked in the record office of National Museums at the monument itself; in the National Archives in Harare; and at the UNESCO Heritage office in Paris. Fontein was thus able to bring together the imaginative landscape of the local people with the perspectives of Zimbabwean archaeologists and of the international heritage industry. Fontein's thesis is entitled *The Silence of Great Zimbabwe*. The silence is constituted by an abundance of archaeology and an absence of ritual.

The ancestors of the peoples who live around Great Zimbabwe arrived in the area only in the seventeenth and eighteenth centuries, well after the complex had been abandoned. Consequently, they have never been of interest to archaeologists of the monument, who have been obsessed with origins. The Rhodesian archaeologists took it for granted that local traditions and rituals were irrelevant; Zimbabwean archaeologists, who wanted to claim an African origin for Great Zimbabwe, also ignored the local peoples. They assumed that only the oral traditions of the Mutapa Empire of the northeast could throw light on the origins, function, and symbolic significance of the monument.

Yet, as Fontein shows, even if the local peoples did not build or occupy Great Zimbabwe, they used it, both practically and imaginatively. One group—Mugabe's people—buried their dead chiefs among the ruins; another group—Nemwana's people—held their rain-making rituals there. Both groups narrated myths about Great Zimbabwe's interaction with the local landscape—with hills and caves and pools. As Fontein writes:

> Sacred places in the landscape act as "vehicles" through which the social and sacred worlds meet. Not only are these liminal places on the landscape marked by specific customs, taboos and rules . . . it is through these practices themselves that their sacredness is achieved. A place is not sacred unless treated as such. [Fontein 2003:142–143]

Powerful spirit female mediums construct histories that connect the monument to both ancient and recent history. Guerrilla veterans claim that they derived power from visiting it during the liberation war. All these interests press in upon Great Zimbabwe, applying to perform rituals there. The Mugabe want to honor their dead chiefs, even if their bodies have been ejected from the monument; the Nemwana want to resume their rain rituals; the guerrillas want to bring back the heroic dead from mass graves in Mozambique and to rebury them at Great Zimbabwe (just as Rhodes buried the Allen Wilson patrol there). The great mediums want to turn the monument into a national spiritual power point. Ambuya VaZarira, senior medium of the Mugabe people, has close links with the Zhame shrine in the Matopos. She describes herself as "custodian" of Great Zimbabwe and plans to restore its holiness by bringing mediums from all over the country to perform rituals to "make our mountain sacred" (Fontein 2003:60).

Yet none of these interests have been allowed access to the monument; no rituals have been performed there. International and national rather than local interests have been invoked by the archaeological custodians in order to keep the ruins sanitized. When guerrillas wanted to rebury their Mozambican dead at Great Zimbabwe on Independence Day in 1981, Cran Cooke, Keeper of the monument, noted that "over a public holiday, such ceremonies would cause havoc and give great annoyance to tourists. It would undoubtedly get out of hand" (Fontein 2003:245). In October 2000, Chief Mugabe asked to perform a rite to honor the war dead. The Zimbabwean Museums representative, Dawson Munjeri, refused.

> Great Zimbabwe is not only a national monument but it is also a UNESCO World Heritage Site which must abide by the provisions of the United Nations World Heritage Convention. One of these rules is that a World Heritage Site shall not be used for purposes that may bring disrepute to the Convention. [Fontein 2003:183]

Even now, as Zimbabwe's "revolutionary" Third Chimurenga, spear-headed by the war veterans, is challenging the authority of the educated, the archaeologists are still able to guard Great Zimbabwe. On May 10 2003, a male spirit medium appeared at the monument accompanied by chiefs, officials, and war agents. He proclaimed that he had come to "unlock the mystery"; to "perform a ritual ceremony" to "open up the underground [where] lie structures in which people lived and lie hidden treasures." But even this formidable delegation was turned away by "officials from the Department of Museums and Monuments [who] felt that the self-proclaimed spirit mediums would tamper with physical structures at the national shrine" (Ranger 2004; *Daily News*, June 13 and 14, 2003).

This total prohibition on their attempts to carry out ritual means that the local people regard the monument as "desecrated"—in their words, the Voice that used to speak there is silent. Great Zimbabwe is available to Robert Mugabe's government for the performance of ceremonies: in May 2003, a nationally televised rite was held there to celebrate the reuniting of two halves of one of the Zimbabwe birds. This ceremony achieved the agenda both of the Zimbabwe government and of the current archaeological keeper of the monument, Edward Matenga. As Matenga writes:

> The determination by the Zimbabwean Government to reclaim the birds stemmed from a desire to rehabilitate Great Zimbabwe as

a cultural symbol of the African people. The desire was inspired by
the belief that the potency of Great Zimbabwe as the guardian spirits of the nation lies in its possession of sacred artefacts. . . . It was
imperative to bring back the bird emblems in order to re-equip and
revive the shrine of Great Zimbabwe. [Matenga 1998:57]

But Fontein insists that the presence of the Zimbabwe birds in the
site's museum is not enough to "revive the shrine." Only the performance
of rituals can give the monument back its voice, and only the local mediums and chiefs can carry out or organize such rituals.

CONCLUSION

I hope that this discussion of the Matopos shrines and of Great
Zimbabwe has demonstrated the dynamism of ritual and the complexity
of its relationship with archaeology and archaeologists. In Zimbabwe,
both ritual and archaeological sites are contested and mobile. The
attempt by Great Zimbabwe's curators to keep the monument "as it was"
is doomed to failure. The landscape around the Matopos shrines or
Great Zimbabwe is also contested—one meaning given to it by the
shrines, another by "scientific" agricultural experts, another by nationalist ideology (Ranger 1999). Robert Mugabe told the UNESCO Heritage
conference at Victoria Falls in October 2003 that its objectives "were
synonymous with Zimbabwe's philosophy" and that "now that land has
been returned to the people [in Zimbabwe's fast-track redistribution pro-
gram] they were able once more to enjoy the physical and spiritual communion that was once theirs" (Ranger 2004; *Herald*, October 30, 2003).
But this remains mere rhetoric unless local sacred landscapes are understood and respected.

Both ritual and indigenous archaeology are more alive in Zimbabwe
than they are elsewhere in southern Africa. Nevertheless, the same questions arise, for instance, in the current archaeology of South Africa. The
archaeologist Nick Shepherd has recently published a review of "the state
of the discipline" in South Africa, which he sees as balanced among the
demands of "science, culture and identity" (Shepherd 2003). In particular,
he offers some splendid examples of global and local impacts on South
African archaeology.

On 1 September 2002, the leaders of the World Earth Summit, meeting in Johannesburg, journeyed to Sterkfontein cave "to pay Homage to
their Human Ancestors." Sterkfontein is renowned for its hominid
remains and is a World Heritage Site. The leaders were addressed by

Philip Tobias, doyen of South African human origins studies. President Thabo Mbeki declared that "we have to scratch not just the collective mind of historians, but also, most importantly, the hard surface of the African continent." Then the United Nations Secretary-General, Kofi Annan, and Mbeki himself performed an earth ritual. They imprinted their bared left feet in a tray of wet cement. Their footprints will be on permanent display at Sterkfontein, together with a message from Annan: "[W]hile the footprints [of our distant ancestors] on nature were small, ours have become dangerously large" (Shepherd 2003:824).

This inventive ceremony was welcomed by Tobias. But Shepherd gives an example of local claims upon a South African monument which had an altogether different reception from archaeologists. The main precursor site to Great Zimbabwe, Mapungubwe, lies within the South African border. On Heritage Day, September 24, 2000, an exhibition of gold "ceremonial treasure" from the Limpopo Valley sites opened in Cape Town. It was named after the Venda word for gold, Musuku; at its opening there was an address from "a passionate Venda nationalist." He read a poem about the early Venda leaving their footprints in the "still soft-hot" rock. It was as if an exhibition of ceremonial objects from Great Zimbabwe were to open in Harare with an address by the senior spirit medium of Mugabe or Nemwana. Some South African archaeologists reacted as Fontein would predict. Two members of the University of Cape Town Archaeology Department wrote to the exhibition organizers to protest. The Venda had developed as an ethnicity long after the building of Mapungubwe; they had nothing to do with its origins; and, as for the "still soft-hot" rocks, "science and creation narratives cannot be mixed in this way" (Shepherd 2003:824–825).

The concluding sentences of Shepherd's article follow:

> The challenge is to have something to say to the complexity and complicity of contemporary circumstances. It means finding in Christopher Neluvhalani's account of Venda pre-history not only evidence of geological absurdity and historical distortion, but a deep-seated need for archaeologists to mediate between folk and academic archaeologies, a desire for archaeology to engage with issues of culture and identity, and the signs of a poetic sensibility thinking deeply through the past. [Shepherd 2003:844]

This makes an excellent way to conclude these reflections on archaeology and ritual in contemporary Zimbabwe.

REFERENCES CITED

Alexander, Jocelyn, Joanne McGregor, and Terence Ranger
  2002   *Violence and Memory*. James Currey, Oxford.
Beach, David, Michael F. C. Bourdillon, James Denbow, Martin Hall, Paul
          Lane, Innocent Pikirayi, and Gilbert Pwiti
  1997   Reviews of Huffman, *Snakes and Crocodiles: Power and Symbolism
          in Ancient Zimbabwe. South African Archaeological Bulletin* 52:
          125–138.
Beach, David, Michael F. C. Bourdillon, James Denbow, Gerhard
          Liesegang, Johannes Loubser, Innocent Pikirayi, David
          Schoenbrun, Robert Soper, and Ann Brower Stahl
  1998   Cognitive archaeology and imaginary history at Great
          Zimbabwe. *Current Anthropology* 39 (1):47–72.
Beinart, William, and Joanne McGregor
  2003   *Social History of African Environments*. James Currey, Oxford.
Bouveresse, Jacques
  1982   *L'Animal Cérémoniel: Wittgenstein et l'Anthropologie*. Editions l'Age
          d'Homme, Paris.
Burke, Eric Edward
  1969   *The Journals of Carl Mauch*. National Archives, Salisbury.
Caton-Thompson, Gertrude
  1931   *The Zimbabwe Culture*. Oxford University Press, Oxford.
Clack, Brian
  1999   *Wittgenstein, Frazer and Religion*. Cambridge University Press,
          Cambridge.
Collins, Elizabeth
  1996   A ceremonial animal. *Journal of Ritual Studies* 10:59–84.
Coplan, David
  2003   Land from the ancestors: Popular religious pilgrimage along the
          South African–Lesotho Border. *Journal of Southern African Studies*
          29 (4):977–993.
Daneel, Marthinus
  1998   *African Earthkeepers*. Pretoria, Unisa.
Dunbar, Robin, Chris Knight, and Camilla Power
  1999   *The Evolution of Culture*. Edinburgh University Press,
          Edinburgh.
Ellert, Henrik
  1984   *The Material Culture of Zimbabwe*. Longman, Harare.
Fontein, Joost
  2003   The silences of Great Zimbabwe: Contested landscapes and the
          power of heritage. Ph.D. dissertation, University of Edinburgh.
  2006   *The Silence of Great Zimbabwe: Contested Landscapes and the Power
          of Heritage*. UCL, London.

Garlake, Peter
    1973   *Great Zimbabwe*. Thames and Hudson, London.
    1987   *The Painted Caves. An Introduction to the Prehistoric Art of Zimbabwe*. Modus, Harare.
    1995   *The Hunter's Vision. The Prehistoric Art of Zimbabwe*. British Museum Press, London.

Hall, Richard Nicklin
    1905   *Great Zimbabwe*. Methuen, London
    1909   *Prehistoric Rhodesia*. Unwin, London.

Hastrup, K. Kirsten
    1998   *A Place Apart: An Anthropological Study of the Icelandic World*. Clarendon Press, Oxford.

Huffman, Thomas N.
    1987   *Symbols in Stone, Unravelling the Mystery of Great Zimbabwe*. Wits University Press, Johannesburg.
    1996   *Snakes and Crocodiles. Power and Symbolism in Ancient Zimbabwe*. Wits University Press, Johannesburg.

James, Wendy
    2003   *The Ceremonial Animal. A New Portrait of Anthropology*. Oxford University Press, Oxford.

Jones, Neville
    1949   *The Prehistory of Southern Rhodesia*. Museum Memoirs. Cambridge University Press, Cambridge.

Knight, Chris
    1995   *Blood Relations: Menstruation and the Origins of Culture*. Yale University Press, New Haven.

Kriger, Norma J.
    1995   The politics of creating national heroes: The search for political legitimacy and national identity. In *Soldiers in Zimbabwe's Liberation War*, edited by Ngwabe Bhebe and Terence Ranger, pp. 139–162. James Currey, Oxford.

Lambeck, Michael
    2003   Foreword. In *The Ceremonial Animal. A New Portrait of Anthropology*, by Wendy James. Oxford University Press, Oxford.

Lan, David
    1985   *Guns and Rain. Guerrillas and Spirit Mediums in Zimbabwe*. James Currey, Oxford.

Lester, Alan
    2003   Introduction: Historical geographies of Southern Africa. *Journal of Southern African Studies* 23 (3):595–613.

MacIver, David R.
    1906   *Mediaeval Rhodesia*. Macmillan, London.

Mafu, Hezekiel
    1995   The 1991–92 Zimbabwean drought and some religious reactions. *Journal of Religion in Africa* 25(3):288–308.

Matenga, Edward
    1998   *The Soapstone Birds of Great Zimbabwe. Symbols of a Nation.* African
            Publishing Group, Harare.
Mauch, Karl
    1874   *Reisen im Inneren von Sud Africa, 1965–72.* Justus Perthes, Gotha.
    1876   Vorlaufige Notiz uber die Ruinen von Zimbabye. *Zeitschrift für
            Ethnologie* 8:186–189.
Mitchell, Clyde
    1956   *The Kalela Dance. Aspects of Social Relationships among Urban Africans
            in Northern Rhodesia.* Rhodes-Livingstone Papers, Manchester.
Morphy, Howard
    1991   *Ancestral Connections: Art and an Aboriginal System of Knowledge,*
            edited by D. Munjeri et al. University Chicago Press, Chicago.
    1995   *African Cultural Heritage and the World Heritage Convention.*
            National Museums and Monuments, Harare.
Needham, Rodney
    1985   Remarks on Wittgenstein and Ritual. In *Exemplars,* by Rodney
            Needham. University of California Press, Berkeley.
Nobbs, Eric
    1924   *Guide to the Matopos.* Maskew Miller, Cape Town.
Nthoi, Leslie
    1995   Perspectives of religion. A study of the Mwali cult of Southern
            Africa. Ph.D. dissertation, University of Manchester.
Nyathi, Lynette
    2003   The Matopo Hills shrines: A comparative study of the Dula,
            Njelele and Zhame shrines and their influence on the surround-
            ing communities. History Honours dissertation, University of
            Zimbabwe.
Pikirayi, Innocent
    1999   David Beach, history and the archaeology of Zimbabwe.
            Zambezia 26 (2):135–144.
    2001   *The Zimbabwe Culture. Origins and Decline in Southern Zambezian
            States.* Altamira, Oxford.
Schoffeleers, J. M. and R. Mwanza
    1978   An Organisational Model of the Mwari Shrines. In *Guardians of
            the Land,* edited by J.M. Schoffeleers. Mambo, Gweru.
Shepherd, Nick
    2003   State of the discipline: Science, culture and identity in South African
            archaeology. *Journal of South African Studies* 24 (4):823–844.
Sinclair, Paul J., and Hans Lundmark
    1984   A spatial analysis of archaeological sites from Zimbabwe. In
            Frontiers: Southern African Archaeology Today, edited by Martin
            Hall et al. Monographs in African Archaeology 10, BAR
            International Series 207. BAR, Oxford.

Summers, Roger
  1963   *Zimbabwe. A Rhodesian Mystery*. Nelson, London.
Summers, Roger, and Kenneth R. Robinson
  1961   *Zimbabwe Excavations 1958*. Cambridge University Press, Cambridge.
Ranger, Terence O.
  1975   *Dance and Society in Eastern Africa*. Heinemann, London.
  1999   *Voices from the Rocks. Nature, Culture and History in the Matopos Hills of Zimbabwe*. James Currey, Oxford.
  2004   Nationalist historiography, patriotic history and the history of the nation: The struggle over the past in Zimbabwe. *Journal of Southern African Studies* 30 (2):215–234.
Tredgold, Robert
  1956   *The Matopos*. Federal Department of Printing, Salisbury.
Walker, Nicholas
  1995   *Later Pleistocene and Holocene Hunter-Gatherers of the Matopos*. Studies in African Archaeology 10. Uppsala.
  1996   *The Painted Hills. Rock Art of the Matopos*. Mambo, Gweru.
Werbner, Richard
  1989   Regional cult of God Above. Achieving and defending the macro-cosm. In *Ritual Passage. Sacred Journey*, edited by Robert Werbner, pp. 245–298. Smithsonian Institution, Washington, DC.
  1998   Smoke from the barrel of a gun: Postwars of the dead, memory and reinscription in Zimbabwe. In *Memory and the Postcolony*, edited by Robert Werbner, pp. 71–99. Zed, London.
  1993   Remarks on Frazer's *Golden Bough*. In *Philosophical Occasions 1921–1951*, edited by James Klagge and Alfred Nordmann, pp. 115–155, 511–512. Hackett, Indianapolis.
Willoughby, .J
  1893   *A Narrative of Further Excavations at Zimbabwe*. George Philip, London.
Wilson, Ken, and Abraham Mawere
  1995   Socio-religious movements, the state and community change: Some reflections on the Ambuya Juliana cult of Southern Zimbabwe. *Journal of Religion in Africa* 25:3.
Zvabva, Oliver
  1988   Nyachiranga Regional Cult. B.A. Honours thesis, Religious Studies, University of Zimbabwe.

8.

THE REINVENTION OF ODISSI
CLASSICAL DANCE AS A TEMPLE RITUAL

Alessandra Lopez y Royo

The great myth of much Indian classical dance is that it was a temple ritual, per-
formed by a special class of women known as devadasis. *This is how Odissi dance,*
a classical form from eastern India (re)created in the 1940s/1950s, is often
described.

This paper questions the reinvention of Odissi classical dance as an age-old
temple ritual. Odissi is a reconstruction produced in post-independence India, an
archaeological project of restoration and reinvention. To make the dance recogniz-
able and to validate it and give it status, continuities were sought with dancing
activities going back to the pre-Christian era, with reference to temple sculpture
found in Hindu, Buddhist, and Jain cave temples. The ritualistic dimension of
the dance has been exaggerated in all accounts, underplaying its entertainment
value and its earlier connection with twentieth-century theater. Archaeology has
been instrumental in the creation of this Odissi myth. Through such endorse-
ments, Odissi dance has been exoticized to an extreme.

All human activities can, to some extent, be classified as ritual or ritualistic,
and thus a ritual dimension to Odissi is not being denied. However, the exclusive
attribution of ritual value to the dance needs to be questioned, as this is most rel-
evant to its contemporary context.

I would like to begin with a series of passages, from various sources, that
explain Odissi, a genre of Indian classical dance (also known as Orissi,
depending on the spelling given to the transliteration of the word from
the Oriya language) to the non-adept:

> Like other forms of Indian classical dance, the Odissi style traces
> its origins back to antiquity. Dancers are found depicted in bas-
> relief in the hills of Udaygiri (near Bhubaneshwar) dating back to
> the 1st century BC. The Natya Shastra speaks of the dance from
> this region and refers to it as Odra-Magadhi. [www.indoclassical
> .com, accessed October 2003]

155

The first record of dance in Orissa is found in the manuscripts
pertaining to the rituals of Lord Jagannath at his world famous
temple at Puri. Dance as a ritual finds mention in Utkala Khanda
of Skanda Purana, Niladri Mahodaya, Madala Panji etc. besides
many other texts. There it was extensively practised by Devadasis
or temple dancers (only females) as an ongoing ritual for the
pleasure of the Lord. The Devadasi dance at the temple of Lord
Jagannath at Puri was also known as the Mahari dance. The
Devadasis were called Maharis, which literally means, according
to some, one who is deeply in love with the Lord. Dancing has
remained a very important and indispensable item in the daily rituals (seva) of Lord Jagannath since the time of Ganga rulers of
Utkal. . . . We also find dancing as a ritual in the temple of Lord
Jagannath mentioned in Agni Purana, Vishnu Purana, Srimad
Bhagavatam, Padma Purana, and Vamadeva Samhita. [Rahul
Acharya, Odissi dancer, www.narthaki.com, accessed October
2003]

Of them all, it was the temple dancers (sic) who shone brightest.
The Bharatnatyam of Malaviki (sic) Sarukkai was flawless, her
divine performance as intricate as lace. Dressed in orange, she
brought elephants and birds to life in her hands. The Odissi
dancer Madhavi Mudgal moved with easy precision, red-painted
fingers and flashing eyes sculpting her stories, while the white
and gold skirts of Bharati Shivaji and her disciple-daughter
flowed harmoniously in the undulating circles of Mohiniattam,
the most sensual of the styles. It was a graceful end to an enlight-
ening trip. [Alice Baines, Review of Edinburgh Festival, *The
Guardian*, August 28, 2002]

Odissi dance is considered one of the oldest based on archeological evidence. The present day Odissi is however a culmination of
a process of reconstruction from various dance traditions of
Orissa like the Maharis, the Goptuas (sic) and the Bhandanrutya
traditions. Maharis are equivalent to the Devadasis of the South.
Goptuas (sic) are basically men who dressed themselves like
female dancers and danced like the Maharis. Jayadeva's
Gitagovinda has enriched the content and style of this form of
dance. . . . Odissi is not merely a dance form. It is a synthesis of

beauty, grace, rhythm, melody, spirituality and devotion. It provides a feast for the eyes, music for the ears and succor for the
soul. Through this dance, the danseuse pays obeisance to the
Lord in all his myriad manifestations. In essence this unique
dance form is a tribute to divinity. [Ramendra Kumar, *The Hindu*,
March 9, 2001]

Ratna's sole mission now is to reconstruct the mahari dance tradition in Orissi (in spirit, form, depiction of female characters and
choreography) and both create a research institute as well as perform and promote the cause of the women's (mahari) tradition
that was effectively silenced and given only a nodding acknowledgment during the years of reconstruction of the neo-classical
Orissi dance, in the post-colonial nationalistic fervor of the 40's
and 50's. Since then the principal gurus of Orissi dance have
revived and recreated the gotipua (male) tradition of Orissi dance
and brought it to international acclaim as "the" style of Orissi classical dance. [Odissi dancer and academic Dr. Ratna Roy's home-
page,   http://www.olywa.net/ratna-david/ratna.htm,   accessed
October 2003]

These are only a few examples of contemporary writing about Odissi.
The review in *The Guardian*, a well-known British broadsheet, typifies the
misconceptions and the aura of exoticism that surround Odissi and, more
generally, Indian dance in the Western world. In a breathtaking manipulation of history, contemporary performers are identified as temple
dancers; the brightness of their costume and makeup become the only
feature of the dance being commented upon, and images of sensuous,
exotic rituals are conjured up through the use of carefully selected words
such as "divine performance," "flashing eyes," and "white and gold skirts."
    Kumar's comments make it clear that in this construction of Odissi,
archaeology has had a role to play: specifically, there has been a deliberate emphasis on certain archaeological evidence and on narratives woven
around this evidence and its interpretation. Odissi has been thus reconstructed, re-created, restored—a metaphorical ancient temple rearranged
and re-erected on new grounds—and the value of age-old ritual is
ascribed to its performance, regardless of the fact that it takes place on
the contemporary urban proscenium. Its contemporary performance is
perceived as a ritual reenactment, and its supposed ritual origin fills it
with mystique.

Ratna Roy's mission statement is self-explanatory. Dr. Roy's feminist cause is admirable, but in the way she states it, she gives new life to the *mahari* dance myth, creating a polarity between male dance teachers and an original group of female rightful owners of the dance.

Much has been written on ritual, ritual practices, and ritual and (theatrical) performance. Ritual has been variously defined. "Ritual generally refers to human experience and perception in forms which are complicated by the imagination, making reality more complex and unnatural than more mundane instrumental spheres of human experience assume," writes Hughes-Freeland (1998:2). Already in 1993, when Richard Schechner rewrote his essay *The Future of Ritual*, writings on ritual were, by his own admission, "voluminous," so much so that "even to say it in one word, ritual, is asking for trouble. Ritual has been so variously defined—as concept, praxis, ideology, yearning, experience, function—that it means very little because it means too much" (Schechner 1993:228). If that were the case in 1993, it is even more so now, 13 years on. Catherine Bell's influential reframing of ritual (Bell 1992, 1997) opened the way to a rethinking of ritual as a category. Ritual and the performative seem to overlap: indeed, a number of writers no longer maintain that ritual is a performance genre but look at performance as a series of ritual practices and ritualization (Hughes-Freeland 1998:6).

I do not disagree that an Odissi performance, or indeed a classical ballet performance (see Wulff 1998), can be seen as a kind of ritual; ritual is, moreover, a particularly apt frame for viewing certain types of performance in which ritual is referenced (Lopez y Royo 2003a). In an Odissi performance, ritual is not just referenced, it is evoked. Indeed, I would suggest that, in a sense, an Odissi performance is a modern ritual performed on stage to celebrate a reinvented tradition and heritage. Here I am mindful of what Hobsbawn wrote in 1983 about recent traditions that strive to establish continuity with the past (Hobsbawn 1983:1–14).

The reinvention of Odissi as the reenactment of an ancient temple ritual is problematic, however, and I intend to question this construction. It raises several issues, which connect with one of the main themes of the Cotsen symposium: the overemphasis on and the exoticization of ritual, which in this case turns into an exoticization and "othering" of Odissi dance and its performers. It is this overemphasis on its ancient ritual value that distorts contemporary Odissi performance practice; yet this distortion also constitutes the mystique and appeal of contemporary Odissi. The overemphasis on ritual embraces the sacred, the extraordinary, and the exotic, as the domain of ritual, seen through Western eyes, and turns

Odissi into an alluring and mysterious art, situated in ancient Orissan temples through a myth sustained by archaeological narratives. This myth of origin is also an instrument of control and even censorship within the practice of the dance, and thus at times it actually hinders the growth of Odissi as a contemporary artistic form.

SIXTY YEARS OF ODISSI

Most current historical narratives of Odissi seek to establish neat continuities and, skillfully, to avoid ruptures, differences, and ambiguities. Their main objective is to establish the antiquity of Odissi, in an effort to give a lineage to the dance of today. They begin, quite predictably, with the Rani Gumpha caves of the pre-Christian era and their reliefs of dancing scenes; they move on to the *alasa kanyas* (indolent maidens) of the Rajarani temple in Bhubaneshwar and the voluptuous Konarak stone dancers of the Sun temple (figure 8.1); and then linger on the Jagannath temple in Puri (figure 8.2). The sacred *maharis* (Oriya *devadasis* or temple dancers) and their "erotic" rituals[1] for the entertainment of the god

FIGURE 8.1. One of the wheels of the Sun temple at Konarak, Orissa.
(Photo by A. Lopez)

enshrined in the temple, Lord Jagannath, are central to such narratives, even though the *maharis'* actual input into Odissi dance is hard to determine. Next in this kind of narrative come the *gotipuas*, young male street dancers who mimic the sacred rituals of the maharis, dressing up like

FIGURE 8.2. The sacred city of Puri, Orissa. (Photo by A. Lopez)

them and performing acrobatics (figures 8.3, 8.4).[2] Finally, enter the gurus, mostly former *gotipua* dancers, initially young men at loose ends in search of gainful employment, seriously affected by the transition from colonial rule to independence and by the tremendous changes in the system of patronage.

This is the point where the narrative verges on the lyrical: the gurus realized that the "sacred art" of the *maharis* might disappear forever unless they acted fast and in concert. Never mind about the *maharis* themselves (here Ratna Roy certainly has a point)—out of the temple, poverty had corrupted them and they were seen as no better than prostitutes. But their art was sublime. Thus, the gurus began to work on the dance in earnest, teaching girls from respectable families, some of whom went on to become dancers of international repute. Working together with scholars, they refined and redefined their craft, found a name for it—Odissi—and turned it into one of the classical styles (or genres) of Indian dance, fighting off some initial resistance from the Bharatanatyam reformers who would rather see Odissi as an offshoot of Bharatanatyam.[3] This whole endeavor was inscribed in the artistic revival, reconstruction, and rhetoric

FIGURE 8.3. *Gotipua* party, Raghurajpur, Orissa. (Photo by A. Lopez)

FIGURE 8.4. Grille from Mukteshwar temple, Orissa, showing a group of male dancers. (Photo by A. Lopez)

of post-independence India, where each region's creative arts were being rediscovered and brought to attention, nationally and internationally.

It is a story with a happy ending, at least for some of the people involved who acquired wealth and status in the process. There are, of course, variations in the narrative. Sometimes, instead of beginning with Rani Gumpha, the story starts with the Indus Valley; and the Harappan bronze statuette of a bejeweled woman in a proto-*tribhanga*[4] is presented as evidence that Odissi is very ancient, pre-Vedic, and wholly indigenous. Sometimes there is some confusion over the relationship between *gotipuas* and *maharis*, and it is never wholly clear what exactly the dance of the *maharis* looked like, despite a number of claims (see Roy's comments, above). Sometimes the rivalries between the gurus are downplayed or highlighted, depending on the circumstances. Some of the gurus became successful, others did not, and this inevitably caused bitterness, jealousy, and accusations of inauthenticity. And then there were the scholars: unearthing manuscripts (and occasionally attributing to them greater antiquity than warranted),[5] finding references that might apply to the

Odissi technique in old Sanskrit manuals (resulting in an attempted Sanskritization of the dance, though never as successful as that of the Southern Bharatanatyam), and helping to connect temple sculptures with dance movements—in sum, following the agenda of rewriting a suitable history of the dance. This archaeological investigation of Odissi led, in other words, to an Odissi constituted by its narrative (cf. Joyce 2002). In this narrative, Odissi and ritual are intertwined and almost interchangeable: Odissi is seen first and foremost as a banned temple ritual. This is central to its mystique, and it contributes to the way Odissi has been marketed on the urban and international performance circuit.

The actual history of Odissi is more interesting than its myth. The dance was born in the theaters of the city of Cuttack, in Orissa, in the mid-1940s (Citaristi 2001; Pani 2000). Until then, there had been no Odissi, and it would take at least another 15 years before the name Odissi began to acquire some currency. A number of musicians, former street dancers, and actors began working together. These were people who had been exposed to dance from outside Orissa—such as the dance of pioneer modern dancer Uday Shankar at Almora—and who were fully aware of the resurgence of Bharatanatyam in the South. They were receptive to the major changes that were sweeping across the country. Dance numbers were added, for entertainment, to the plays that were being performed in the Cuttack theaters. Among the people involved in the Cuttack theater movement—the Jayantika group led by Kalicharan Patnaik—were Pankaj Charan Das, Kelucharan Mahapatra and his wife Laxmipriya, Durllav Chandra Singh, Hariharan Rout, and a number of others. It was in the Cuttack theaters that the Odissi compositions that later became important repertoire pieces were actually created. Among them was the *Dashavatar* (The Ten Incarnations of Vishnu), the performance of which has now become *de rigueur* in most Odissi recitals and which has subsequently been choreographed and rechoreographed by a number of dance masters (Citaristi 2001:71–73).

Kelucharan Mahapatra went on to become the most famous and the best established guru of Odissi, honored by the government of India, the Orissa state government, and a number of international learned bodies and organizations and acclaimed on his tours to Europe and the United States. He has trained thousands of dancers, including the late Sanjukta Panigrahi, acknowledged as one of the greatest Odissi exponents and dancers of our time. Kelucharan Mahapatra, best known as Kelu Babu, came from a low-caste family with no musical or dance background, from Raghurajpur, a village near Puri inhabited primarily by *citrakaras* or makers of *patacitra* paintings. Kelu Babu danced as a *gotipua* when he was a boy and learned to play the *mardala* drum and the *tabla*, which later became a great asset for him as a composer and choreographer of Odissi.

Another name on the list of important Cuttack theater group members is Pankaj Charan Das, also a famous guru of Odissi, though never as successful as Kelu Babu, whom he initially taught (or so the story goes). Pankaj Charan Das came from a *mahari* family, and it is often said that he taught the *mahari* style of Odissi. No doubt Pankaj Charan Das knew songs and tunes that traditionally belonged to the *maharis'* repertoire, but it is also true that he choreographed and rechoreographed dance pieces from scratch, emphasizing male dancing and creating several new dances for himself (he was an outstanding performer with tremendous stage presence) and for others. Some of his dazzling choreography found its way into the repertoire of dancers who never learned directly from him: his choreography is so well known that it has "traveled." In a sense, Pankaj Charan Das taught the "Pankaj Charan Das" style of Odissi, just like Kelu Babu taught his own. So did Deba Prasad Das, whose background was again mixed; he had been an *akhada pila*, *akhadas* being places in Puri where young men, some of them *gotipuas*, trained in combat, practiced body-building techniques, played the *mardala*, took *bhang*, danced, and sang in the evenings to entertain one another.[6] All these styles of Odissi are very much a modern creation, a way for the gurus to differentiate their own work while still keeping to a set of rules they established, more or less collectively, as they went along. In some ways, it has been difficult to maintain the dance form: some performers are happy to change the rules, despite the efforts made by the Odissi dance establishment in Orissa to maintain distinctions and to create an Odissi dance canon, and more generally, to police the form, making sure that the rules of the newly established classicism are not transgressed.

Even more interesting, in this respect, was the refashioning of Odissi at the hands of Guru Surendranath Jena, now in his early 80s (figure 8.5). Based in Delhi but from Orissa, Sura Babu re-created Odissi throughout the 1960s, deriving movements almost entirely from the Konarak sculptures and choreographing dance pieces that made no attempt to conform with the general rules laid down by the other masters. His work was rejected by the Odissi dance establishment in Orissa but was recognized by national bodies such as the Sangita Natak Akademi and acclaimed by India's foremost dance scholar, Kapila Vatsyayan, for the plasticity of the compositions, born out of long-standing research in sculpture and Orissan iconography. To this day, his Odissi (figures 8.6–8.8) remains con-

FIGURE 8.5. Shrimati Pratibha Jena, daughter of Guru Surendranath Jena.
(Photo by A. Lopez)

troversial. On a recent trip to Orissa I was told, rather melodramatically, by a known Odissi dancer in Bhubaneshwar that Sura Babu "should be jailed" for what he did to Odissi, as he has broken all "the age-old rules" of this tradition of dance. In saying this, she was clearly taking sides in internal rivalries within the Odissi dance world, invoking "tradition" which she presented to me as immutable and perennial.

The history of Odissi is inscribed in the broader project of modernization and classicization (in Euro-American terms) of Indian dance (Meduri 1996; Lopez y Royo 2003b). The dance has been shaped by the different dance discourses in the subcontinent and their entanglement with political power. For example, when "appropriation" was raised as an issue, in the late 1970s and 1980s, in the context of Bharatanatyam—that is, as the dance that rightfully belonged to the *devadasis* of the South was appropriated by middle-class Brahmin women such as Rukmini Devi Arundale, the founder of the Kalakshetra school (Allen 1997)—the history of Odissi also began to be written in terms of appropriation, with dispossessed *maharis* looming large in the picture. *Maharis* were indeed dispossessed but not exactly of

FIGURES 8.6. and 8.7. Jaya Chattopadhyai, disciple of Guru Pratibha Jena, in
Odissi *tribhangi* and *cauka*. (Photos by A. Lopez)

FIGURE 8.8. Jaya Chattopadhyai, disciple of Guru Pratibha Jena, in another Odissi *tribhangi*. (Photo by A. Lopez)

their dance, as there was very little left of it. Even scholars who had been actively involved earlier in the search for a *mahari* lineage of the dance later began to invoke some caution: "[T]he idea that Odissi evolved and was nurtured in the temple of Lord Jagannath at Puri is partially incorrect," writes Jiwan Pani, an Oriya expert of Odissi music and dance; "what was being danced in the temples, including that of Lord Jagannath at Puri, was basically ritualistic in character" (Pani 2000:147). But *maharis* have become symbols of Odissi, and Odissi has been refashioned in their image, reimagined as a *mahari* ritual—and this remains true regardless of claims arising from time to time that the Odissi one sees today is entirely based on the *gotipua* imitation of the dance of the *mahari* and is thus inauthentic.

MAHARIS AND CONTEMPORARY ODISSI PERFORMANCE

Maharis were women in the service of the temple of Jagannath, in Puri. Dedicated to the temple from a young age, they were married to the god. Their main duty was to sing and dance to the god at specific times of the day and evening. Whereas in Southern India the *devadasis* were banned from the temples in 1947, as they were perceived to be associated with prostitution, in Puri they continued until the 1960s to perform their *seva* (service) in the temple. The practice died of its own accord because of the enormous political, economic, and social changes that took place and the pressure on *maharis* to discontinue their *seva*: "[T]he view of the devadasis as morally degenerate women and of the royal courts and the kings as the instruments of this degeneration solved a contradiction for the nationalist elite who were concerned with the 'revival' of Indian arts. . . . The attitude of revivalists in Orissa had a definite effect on the devadasis of Puri" (Marglin 1985:29).

Marglin's *Wives of the God-King* (1985), based on her research in Puri in the late 1970s, marked an important moment in reappraising the *mahari*. Until then, *maharis* had been regarded with a sense of embarrassment by the nationalist Odissi reformers. Marglin trained in Odissi with Guru Surendranath Jena and had a successful career as a performer. She later went to Puri to find out more about the *maharis* and their lifestyle. Through her work, the role of the *maharis* as ritual specialists of traditional Orissa was clarified, with a new emphasis placed on their sexuality and its auspiciousness, connecting *maharis* with tantric practices. Though married to Jagannath, the *maharis* were closely involved with the king, who was the earthly representative of their husband. They were associated with palace rituals as well as temple rituals. Marglin identified the *maharis* as "the auspicious married women"[7] and views them from the perspective of the "values of auspiciousness and inauspiciousness" from which "women are seen in a very different light. They are creators and the maintainers of life, the sources of prosperity, well-being and pleasure" (Marglin 1985:300). This she contrasts with the earlier "exclusive binary opposition" of purity/impurity which until then had dominated most work on Indian ritual practices.

Marglin's (1985) study was timely and significant. However, her reappraisal of *maharis* was not meant to restore Odissi to the *maharis*. In fact, what one gleans from Marglin's account is that modern Odissi and *maharis* do not belong to each other. Marglin lived among (admittedly elderly) *maharis* for long periods; they told her that in the old days, dances were performed as part of the various rituals in the temple and at court (Marglin 1985:171–175). One of the *maharis* apparently also taught her a couple of dances, which, unfortunately, are not described in her book. What is clear, though, from Marglin's writings is that *maharis* sang together with their dancing.[8] It seems that the dancing itself was primarily of the *abhinaya* type—a term roughly translated as performing mime, or performing *bhav*, as the *maharis* would say (Marglin 1990:220)—referring to an emotional and intellectual state rendered through gesture and glance.

Odissi was being created anew as an imagined *mahari* ritual, but the *maharis* were apparently excluded from this process, though at least one or two maharis were active participants in the revivalist movement (Marglin 1985:30–31). Whether this should be construed as an act of appropriation is arguable; the situation is more complex than this notion of appropriation would entail. Leaving aside the issue of the stigma attached to maharis, which caused a number of them to change status and sever links with Puri even before the Odissi reconstruction was in full swing (the 1955 census reports only 30 *devadasis* in the Jagannath temple; Marglin 1985:25), it is worth considering some of the practicalities involved. As Odissi was a new invention, old *maharis* making up the rules of what was essentially a new form unknown to them could have caused problems. *Maharis* did not have a "dance" (as in stage dance) repertoire as such; they mostly knew *abhinaya* songs and, it would seem, some pure dance pieces, whose rhythmic complexity cannot be ascertained. Their *abhinaya* was delivered in a style that did not suit the proscenium stage. *Maharis* had no theatrical experience, and Odissi, the new dance, had been born out of the theaters and was meant for the stage, not for the temple; the gurus, including Pankaj Charan Das, were reinventing it, keeping an eye on other dance developments at a pan-Indian level and emphasizing the theatricality of the new form.

Conversations I had in Bhubaneshwar with several Odissi teachers, including Guru Gajendra Panda (figures 8.9, 8.10), all pointed to this: the space available for dancing in the temple was only a small chamber; the *maharis* could not perform a very elaborate *nrtta* within such constraints; thus, it was most unlikely they would have had complex *nrtta* items in their repertoire that could be used outside the temple. The *gotipuas* and the *akha-da pila*, on the other hand, had had rigorous body training that could be adapted to the new dance. Citaristi has endeavored to describe the training of the *maharis*, using as sources Harapriya Devi and Kokila Prabha *Mahari*, interviewed when still alive, as well as information taken from older textual sources, such as the *Madala Panji* (of uncertain date but perhaps earlier than the eighteenth century; Kulke 2001:8) and an eighteenth-century manuscript by Lavania Mahari (Citaristi 2002:15–23). Thus, while it is not clear which period of training she is characterizing, Citaristi describes the rituals involved in establishing a relationship with the dance master[9] and the rules of propriety a mahari should follow. Descriptions of dances are minimal—for example: "[when the midday meal started] the performance

Figure 8.9. Guru Gajendra Panda. (Photo by A. Lopez)

usually consisted of *nrtta* (rhythmic dance) accompanied by the sound of the *pakhawaj* (percussive instrument) without any melody or song. . . . the dancer would at the beginning execute a triple turn to be able to offer a triple obeisance to both God and King. The devotees present would stand and watch from the two sides" (Citaristi 2002:17–18). This passage tells us only that the maharis danced to the *pakhawaj* but does not convey anything specific about the dance. Citaristi goes on to discuss the singing of the *maharis* and their costume and ornaments.[10]

FIGURE 8.10. Guru Gajendra Panda. (Photo by A. Lopez)

We thus have the very interesting phenomenon of a secular dance, whose sources are varied, being classicized and refashioned to reflect a reimagined temple ritual, with the dancer taking on the persona of a temple dancer. The set repertoire of an Odissi performance is made up of dances of offering, *nrtta* pieces built around complex cross-rhythms, *abhinaya* pieces composed on the verses of the *Gita Govinda*, an erotic devotional poem about the divine lovemaking of Radha and Krishna, Oriya devotional poems, and a final piece called *Moksha* ("liberation"), a *nrtta* which in its cadences attempts to convey the movement to soul liberation and serenity. Temple songs—the *Gita Govinda* itself was decreed as the only source for *mahari* singing at the Jagannath temple by King Prataparudradeva in the sixteenth century—street dancing, sculpturesque poses inspired by the rich imagery of Orissan temples, and folk songs and tunes all found their way into today's Odissi, alongside aesthetic developments inspired by other Indian classical dances.[11] Nevertheless, the Odissi/*mahari* equation still holds strong, despite being intrinsically contradictory.

Why Odissi should have been reinvented as a temple ritual is not easy to say. It worked at the time, it gave status to the dance, it gave an element of mystique to its performance. It is also true to say that Odissi embodies Oriya sensibilities and reflects Oriya nationalism and Oriya identity. An interesting co-development of Odissi was the research focused on Jagannath by the Oriya School of the 1970s, with its work centered on the culture of Puri and its attempts to go beyond the local to participate in a pan-Indian discourse. These newer studies on Jagannath "seem to have evolved into a full fledged project with Jagannath as a metaphor of Orissa's multifaceted culture" (Kulke 2001:12). The Odissi dance culture, with its emphasis on Jagannath, seems to partake of this.

Odissi as the dance of the *mahari* of Lord Jagannath continues to play on the ambiguity and ambivalence of a ritual and exotic spectacle when performed out of its Oriya home. In Orissa itself, there is no substantial theater-going audience, and Odissi is either performed at state functions, tagging along at the end of so-called cultural programs, or it is performed at international festivals such as the winter event at Konarak or at five-star hotels to audiences of non-Oriya visitors. Marketed as a dance modeled on the image of a temple ritual dance, Odissi is labeled as a "Hindu" dance and is thus inscribed in a Hinduizing discourse that has been sweeping through contemporary India with renewed impetus; even if a dancer is not herself Hindu, she acquires a Hindu identity by turning into an imaginary *mahari*.[12] Reflecting on this process, which was very visible in the Indian dance of the 1970s and was later to be ruptured by the "contemporary dance movement," Coorlawala writes:

> Invariably in the classical dance forms the "tradition" meant Hindu rituals, mythology and culture, with occasionally token appreciation of internationally recognised artists as Allah Rakha and Akbar Ali Khan. Muslim monuments, . . . art, manners of dress, dance and music were gradually marginalised as were other non-Hindu performers and their art. . . . While a third century aesthetic was being

nostalgically recovered and touted as the aesthetic of the dance of India, it resulted in confused conflations of Western ideologies with indigenous values. [Coorlawala 1994:202]

In the past 20 years, there has been a formidable movement within Indian dance that has attempted to subvert the dominant notion of dance classicism and has tried to go beyond the parameters set by traditionalists. This is not the right context to review this vibrant and very influential work. But it is relevant to note that from the 1980s onward, there has been a sustained attempt, originating in the cities, at breaking regional boundaries in terms of dance forms (for example, Bharatanatyam, usually seen as southern and hence to be performed by southerners, is now performed by non-southerners) and working with the classical dance vocabulary, going beyond traditional themes, no longer upholding a notion of tradition as static and immutable.

This movement, very strong in the context of Bharatanatyam and Kathak, has only just begun to touch Odissi. There are now a number of dance dramas being choreographed, in an attempt to create group dancing rather than the solo form. Tentatively, some non-Oriya Odissi dancers are working creatively within the classical format, moving away from the *mahari*-inspired "ritualistic" Odissi but retaining its aesthetic conventions.[13] I should make it clear, at this juncture, that I am in no way condemning what has now become, in the course of six decades, "traditional" Odissi. It is a breathtakingly beautiful dance form, rich and complex. I am a great admirer of the work of the Odissi gurus, who made this richness and complexity possible; and on the few occasions when I had the opportunity to see both Kelu Babu and the great Sanjukta perform, I was deeply touched and spellbound, to paraphrase Wulff, in an "Odissi revelation" (Wulff 1998:117). But my enchantment with Odissi does not stem from a fascination for an exotic temple ritual performed by an exotic dancer (Curda 2003). What appeals to me is the perfection of its formal structure as a dance and its immense, still largely untapped creative potential, beyond the imagined ritual fiction. To a great extent, the myth of the age-old temple ritual actually becomes more interesting when it is revealed to be a fiction; dancers can continue to invoke Krishna and turn themselves into heroines longing for their lord's cooling touch, and the audience can continue to revel in the melody of the Odissi tunes. The magic of the performance will not be lost if the audience knows that Odissi was never danced by *maharis* but was instead born out of the concerted effort of a group of very creative men and women, in the cities of Orissa and beyond.

CONCLUSION

A theater in New Delhi, London, New York, Singapore. . . . To the beat of the *mardala* drum, the dancer, her back to the audience, enters stage left, flowers in her cupped hands, her feet tracing small arcs as she steps forward, her torso rhythmically and subtly moving, walking languidly toward the center of the stage. She turns around herself in the *cauka* (square) position, stops center stage facing the audience, and begins to perform her *Bhumi Pranam* (Salutation to the Earth) and *Mangalacharan* (Invocation), at the end of which flowers will be scattered on the stage as an offering to the god. On her left, at the front of the stage, there is an image of Lord Jagannath, garlanded with flowers, with coconut and incense offerings. On her right, the musicians and singers are seated. In the background, there may be a cloth from Pipli village, famous for its appliqué work, or there may be a large photograph of one of the Bhubaneshwar temples.[14] She wears a costume modeled on the attire of a *mahari*, cut of a raw or white silk sari with typical Orissan patterns. She wears only silver jewelry, and her makeup includes heavily kohled eyes, an elaborate *tilaka*, and a series of white dots all around her forehead and her eyes, down to her cheeks. She is, as far as her audience is concerned, the re-embodiment of a *mahari*; the whole performance will play on this ambivalence. From time to time the dancer will speak to her audience, moving to the side of the stage and using a microphone, explaining what she is about to do, translating Oriya and Sanskrit poetry into English, giving an indication of what the gestures mean, those same gestures she will use in the piece she is going to dance.[15] Throughout, Jagannath will dominate the proceedings from his seat, and the smell of sandalwood joss sticks will be all-pervasive. The stage has been turned into a temple; the dancer beckons her audience to follow her in her worship.

Whereas Odissi is not and never was a ritual temple dance, there is nevertheless a convergence between ritual and Odissi performance, found in the performativity of both. This, however, raises another order of questions, which would be more properly dealt with in a different paper: "[T]he central issue of performativity," warns Schieffelin (1998:205), "whether in ritual performance, theatrical entertainment or the social articulation of ordinary human situations is the imaginative creation of a human world. The creation of human realities entails ontological issues."

Odissi has been, and can be, viewed through different frames: as a reinvented ritual temple dance, as a theatrical performance about ritual, as a layer of framed illusions, as theater art firmly situated in the present. Throughout this paper, I have endeavored to strip Odissi of its mystique, revealing the fiction of its origin myth, which has been sustained through manipulation of archæological and anthropological evidence. Though it never began as a ritual, Odissi performance does make reference to ritual, and its theater audience pretends to be witnessing a temple ritual. In Western terms, we would say that as the performer establishes a relationship with the audience throughout the performance, the audience "suspends its disbelief" and is drawn in, participating in an illusionary ritual of spiritual worship (see Meyerhoff 1990), which will be more effective and "real" depending on the skill of the performer. Here, however, we need to discard this entirely Western frame, as it does not allow us to fully grasp the dynamics involved: "Asian performance is founded on the assumption that the world constituted in performance is not separate from the world outside performance" (Zarrilli 1990:146). What happens here is a more complex process of active performer–audience interaction which taps into a different aesthetic—known in the relevant literature as the *rasa* theory—and which is shared by Odissi and other dance and theatrical forms of India.[16] Zarrilli has analyzed the mechanics of this process at length, suggesting that "the actor and spectator co-create the figure embodied in the actor as "other.". . . That dynamic figure exists between audience and actor, transcending both, pointing beyond itself" (Zarrilli 1990:144).[17]

The case of Odissi is instructive. I am not interested in defining either ritual or (theatrical) performance in essentializing terms, nor do I think that establishing firm boundaries between ritual and performance is truly useful (Humphrey and Laidlaw 1994). There are times when ritual and performance converge and conflate; there are times when they do not. This may involve exactly the same practices: it is the relationship between participant and spectator and between performer and ritual specialist that seems to be crucial to this fluidity of conflation/separation and its reconfiguration. Balinese trance dancers perform for tourists in Batubulan, near the capital Denpasar, in a theater setting and enact a trance dance using their theatrical skills; the same performers in a different situation—an Odalan (temple festival), for example, an occasion where the relationship with their audience will involve a different set of loyalties and expectations—will go into a deep trance and will need the use of various paraphernalia, such as the sprinkling of holy water by a priest, to come out of the trance. One is interpreted as a theatrical performance—a tourist performance, at that[18]—the other as a ritual, but their outward appearances, even the dynamics, are the same. Or are they? "Theories and contexts," warns Bell (1997:267), "affect what is seen as ritual and by whom, while those activities deemed to be ritual in turn have theoretical and contextual consequences." This fluidity is something that ought to be taken into greater account in interpretations, anthropological, archaeological, and otherwise, of ritual and its contexts.

GLOSSARY

NOTE: Throughout the paper and in this glossary, I have tried to follow the conventional transliteration system of South Asian languages but without using diacritical marks. So *c* stands for the sound "ch," and *s* stands either for sibilant *s* or for "sh" (an accent above the *s* or a dot below it would more properly denote the latter). However, some terms are now commonly known in their phonetic rendering—for example, *mangalacharan* or *choko*. I have given this alternative spelling in brackets. In all quotations, I have followed the spelling chosen by the author.

abhinaya: The expressive part of an Odissi dance

abhinaya candrika: An Oriya treatise on dance and music

akhada: Gymnasia where the young men of Puri trained in combat

alasa kanya: In Hindu temple iconography, these are languorous maidens

bhang: A drink whose main ingredient is *cannabis indica*

bhav: The Oriya name for *abhinaya*

bhumi pranam: An invocatory dance in Odissi (lit. "salutation to the earth")

carya nritya: A Buddhist dance from Nepal

cauka: A position of Odissi with the legs fully bent at the knees and pointing sideways, forming a square

citrakara: A painter of *patacitras*

dasavatar: The ten incarnations of the Hindu god Vishnu (*dashavatar*)

devadasi: Temple dancer, especially from Southern India

gotipua: Young boys who performed as street dancers, dressed as women and portraying stories of the divine pair Radha and Krishna

mahari: Devadasi employed in the service of the Puri temple of Lord Jagannath

maithuna: An iconographic motif appearing on Hindu temple walls, showing a couple indulging in sexual practices

Mangalacaran (mangalacharan): Part of the *bhumi pranam*, this is the invocatory portion of the dance

mardala: A drum used in Odissi music

moksa: According to Hindu belief, this is the final liberation of the soul from the cycle of birth and rebirth

mudra: Symbolic hand gestures (as opposed to *hasta*, a term denoting hand gestures in general)

Nataraja: Siva, lord of the dance

nrtta: A rhythmic dance without *abhinaya*

odalan: A Balinese temple festival

pakhavaj (or *pakhawaj*): A drum, also called *mardala* in Odissi

Pancakanya (*panchakanya*): Five female characters from the Mahabharata epic, including Draupadi, the wife of the Pandava brothers

patacitra: Oriya paintings made on silk cloth

pila: A boy

rasa: According to Indian aesthetic theories, *rasa* is the sentiment evoked by dramatic performance. There are altogether nine *rasas*.

sakhi bhava: A conventional theme in dance, depicting a friend (a *sakhi*) of the lovelorn heroine, usually Radha, who tries to give her emotional support and advice.

sevayat: Someone who performs a *seva* or ritual obligation for Jagannath

tilaka: A red mark applied on the forehead with *kumkum* powder

tribhanga (or *tribhangi*): A posture involving three bends or, more properly, three shifts along the vertical axis of the body, at the neck, at the waist, and at the knee

NOTES

1. The dance of the *maharis*, interpreted in a tantric way, was symbolic of sexual intercourse: "the association between dance and sex is very strong . . . the dance ritual is also known to stand for the last 'm' in the five 'm' offerings of the tantric *sakta* ritual. This last 'm' is *maithuna*: sexual intercourse" (Marglin 1985:95).

2. Marglin has commented that a form of male dancing must have been performed in temples, perhaps only Siva temples, because one can see reliefs of male dancers sculpted on the Bhubaneshwar Saiva temples (figure 8.4). However, the custom of young men dancing dressed like women seems to have been introduced by the vaishnavites in the sixteenth century, worshipping Krishna in a *sakhi bhava* fashion—as a female friend of Radha's (*sakhi*). The *gotipuas* were young boys linked with the *akhadas* where they practiced combat and similar activities, and on festival days in Puri they danced the Radha/Krishna story dressed like *maharis* (Marglin 1985:317; Kothari 1968:32).

3. It took much effort and imagination to establish Odissi as a classical dance throughout the 1950s and 1960s. Initially, it was viewed by purists as a hybridized Bharatanatyam; Rukmini Devi, the Bharatanatyam reformer, founder of the famous Kalakshetra school in present-day Chennai, was reported to have frowned on the "vulgarity" of the Odissi repertoire when she first saw it (Citaristi 2001:119).

4. The *tribhanga*, or triple bend, is one of the basic postures of Odissi dance, together with the *cauka* (pronounced "choko") or square.

5. The case of the *Abhinaya Candrika*, a manuscript discovered by D. N. Patnaik, is notorious. Patnaik originally fixed its date to the twelfth century (Patnaik 1958:10), but later dated it to the seventeenth century in a new edition of the same work. More recently, Das has given the date of the *Candrika* as 1750 (Das 2001:x)

6. The *akhadas* are part of the traditional culture of Puri which revolves around the temple of Jagannath. The majority of Puri's inhabitants are *sevayats*, people who perform a *seva* (service) at the temple. *Bhang*, a drink made out of a concoction of cannabis and milk, is freely available in Puri, one of the holiest cities of India. It is said that cannabis is dear to Lord Shiva, and *sadhus* (holy men) are known to be great consumers of *thandai* (a drink similar to *bhang*). Puri, as a holy city, is full of itinerant sadhus, who have contributed to the development of a "bhang culture."

7. See also Kersemboom-Story's *Nityasumangali* (1987) on the *devadasis* of Tiruvarur, in Tamilnadu.

8. Marglin (1985) gives the subdivisions among devadasis as *bhitara gauni* and *bhahara gauni*, also called *nacuni* (dancers). See also Acharya 2002.

9. It is interesting to note here that *maharis* were also taught by male teachers. Patnaik reports that the late Mohan Mahapatra was known as a guru of *maharis* (1971: 61).

10. Dancer and scholar Uttara Asha Coorlawala, with whom I discussed this issue, agrees that Odissi and *mahari* dance are not the same. However, on the basis of her first-hand knowledge of the dance and of Odissi dancers in the 1970s, Coorlawala believes that there definitely was a *mahari* dance and that we can see glimpses of it in "the style codes and movement grammars, inherited from his mother" that Pankaj Babu taught and in the *panchakanya* series of dances that Ritha Devi, a known disciple of Pankaj Babu, used to dance and which exhibit a female quality "that other Odissi does not have" (Coorlawala, personal communication 2004). Nevertheless, I remain convinced that Guru Pankaj Das relied on more than his knowledge of the *mahari* tradition, instead drawing on his own creativity, through which that knowledge was filtered. I have never seen the *panchakanya* choreography, so I cannot comment on it, but it seems clear that it was adapted by Pankaj Babu for the stage and that Devi further nuanced her interpretation of the piece. The female quality "that other Odissi does not have" may well be an interpretation through a contemporary feminist sensibility rather than an inherent quality of the dance. I fully respect Coorlawala's knowledge and scholarship; but I am nevertheless wary of claims, which continue today, that the *mahari* dance can be retrieved and restored. From time to time there are dancers who boldly claim to have unearthed and revived *mahari* choreography, but to me this sounds like a rehearsal of the argument that there is an ancient golden past. I must emphasize here, as it may not be evident from the above, that Coorlawala does not argue for any retrieval or restoration; in fact, she believes that whatever *mahari* dance there was, it is now lost and there is no going back.

11. Some Odissi gurus, such as Mayadhar Rout, trained in Kathakali and in Bharatanatyam at the famous Kalakshetra school in Madras (Chennai); Sanjukta Panigrahi was also Bharatanatyam trained.

12. Nowadays there are also male dancers. They do not perform dressed as women, but they do take on a feminine persona when dancing Odissi.

13. Minneapolis-based Odissi dancer and scholar Ananya Chatterjea should be mentioned here for her emotionally powerful work, coming out of her investigation of Odissi classicism.

14. Meduri has explored the formation of the temple stage in the work of Rukmini Devi, for Bharatanatyam and its significance (Meduri 2006). The temple stage devised by Devi has been transferred to all the other solo forms of Indian classical dance, and hence to Odissi, but substituting the Nataraja icon with that of Jagannath.

15. O'Shea has recently made the controversial suggestion, with reference to Bharatanatyam—and thus, by extension, applicable to other Indian classical genres—that this practice reflects an orientalist attitude to the dance: "This kind of pre-performance synopsis lines up two thought-systems: an English verbal framework and a South Indian choreographic one. The explanation of mudras in succession interprets the 'Eastern' choreography through the 'Western' linguistic system." She concedes, however, that "although verbal interlocution reiterates an orientalist problematic, the factors that foster the appearance of interlocution unsettle orientalist notions of a static tradition" (O'Shea 2003).

16. I am aware of Ahmed's critique of Zarrilli's reliance on the Hindu upanishadic world view in his articulation of what becoming the character means in Indian performing traditions. However, for Odissi, this Hindu assumption is appropriate. Ahmed, in his rebuttal of Zarrilli's thesis, refers to *carya nritya* of Nepal, an expression of Vajrayana Buddhism, and warns us not to fall into the trap of equating Indian with Hindu (Ahmed 2003:2)

17. *Rasa* is, according to the Indian aesthetic tradition, a sentiment, distinct from emotion: the actor/dancer manipulates emotions that exist in him or herself and these turn into sentiments for the spectator (Kothari 2003:147).

18. Schechner asks, when does a tourist show turn into "theatrical art" (Schechner as quoted in Ahmed 2003:19), and Ahmed suggests that to answer the question, one has "to investigate the economic pressures and cultural redundancy that many South Asian performers face in a 'globalized' world threatening to erode cultural plurality" (Ahmed 2003:19).

REFERENCES CITED

Acharya, Rahul
  2002   *Mahari—The Divine Damsels.* http://www.boloji.com/dances/00116.htm.
Ahmed, Syed Jamil
  2003   Carya Nritya of Nepal. When "becoming the character" in Asian performance is nonduality in "Quintessence of Void." *The Drama Review, Journal of Performance Studies* 47 (3):1–24.
Allen, Matthew
  1997   Rewriting the script for South Indian Dance. *The Drama Review, Journal of Performance Studies* 41 (3):63–100.
Baines, Alice
  2002   Review of Edinburgh Festival. *The Guardian*, August 28, 2002.
Bell, Catherine
  1992   *Ritual Theory, Ritual Practice.* Oxford University Press, Oxford and New York.
  1997   *Ritual: Perspectives and Dimensions.* Oxford University Press, Oxford and New York.
Citaristi, Ileana
  2001   *The Making of a Guru: Kelucharan Mahapatra, His Life and Times.* Manohar, Dehli.
  2002   Devadasis of the Jagannath temple: Precursors of Odissi music and dance. In *Dance as Intangible Heritage*, edited by L. Kirastis. International Organisation of Folk Art, Corfu.

Coorlawala, Uttara
   1994   Classical and contemporary Indian dance: Overview, criteria and a
             choreographic analysis. Ph.D. dissertation, New York University.
Curda, Barbara
   2003   'Oh…To dance like an Oriya girl!. *Pulse*, Autumn: 40.
Das, Maya
   2001   *Abhinaya Candrika and Odissi Dance.* Eastern Books Linkers, Delhi.
Hobsbawm, Eric
   1983   Introduction: Inventing traditions. In *The Invention of Tradition*,
             edited by Eric Hobsbawm and Terence Ranger, pp. 1–14.
             Cambridge University Press, Cambridge.
Hughes-Freeland, Felicia
   1998   Introduction. In. *Ritual, Performance, Media*, edited by Felicia
             Hughes-Freeland, pp. 1–28. Routledge, London.
Humphrey, Caroline, and James Laidlaw
   1994   *The Archetypal Actions of Ritual. A Theory to Ritual Illustrated by the
             Jain Rite of Worship.* Clarendon Press, Oxford.
Joyce, Rosemary
   2002   *The Languages of Archaeology.* Blackwell Publishers, Oxford.
Kersenboom-Story, Saskia C.
   1987   *Nityasumangali: Devadasi Tradition in South India.* Motilal
             Banarsidass, Delhi.
Kothari, Sunil
   1968   Gotipua dancers. *Sangeet Natak* 8:32–34.
   2003   *Saundarya* and *Sancharibhavas* in dance. *Evam, Forum on Indian
             Representations* 2:146–150.
Kulke, Herman, and Burkhard Schnepel
   2001   Jagannath and Orissan studies: Accomplishments and prospects.
             In *Jagannath Revisited. Studying Society, Religion and the State in
             Orissa*, edited by Hermann Kulke and Burkhard Schnepel, pp.
             1–24. Manohar, New Delhi.
Kumar, Ramendra
   2001   In *The Hindu*, March 9, 2001.
Lopez y Royo, Alessandra
   2003a   Translating Buddhism through dance performance: The Rock
             Corridor. Paper presented at Translation and Recreation, a work-
             shop exploring the interrelation of dance and other art forms,
             Queen's College Old Kitchen, Cambridge, May 2003,
             http://www.cam.ac.uk/societies/dance/.
   2003b   Classicism, post-classicism and Ranjabati Sircar's work: Re-defin-
             ing the terms of Indian contemporary dance discourses. *South
             Asia Research* 23 (1):153–169.
Marglin, Appfel Frederique
   1985   *Wives of the God-King. The Rituals of the Devadasis of Puri.* Oxford
             University Press, Delhi, Oxford, and New York.

1990   Refining the body: Transformative emotion in ritual dance. In
           Divine Passions: The Social Construction of Emotion in India, edited
           by Owen M. Lynch, pp. 220–226. University of California Press,
           Berkeley.
Meduri, Avanthi
   1996   Nation.Woman. Representation. The sutured history of the
           devadasi and her dance. Ph.D. dissertation, New York University.
   2006   Interculturalism, temple-stage and modernism in Bharatanatyam.
           Paper presented at the symposium Identités Culturelles, Identités
           Artistique, Centre National de la Danse, Paris, 15 January 2006.
Meyerhoff, Barbara
   1990   The transformation of consciousness in ritual performances:
           Some thoughts and questions. In *By Means of Performance*:
           Intercultural Studies of Theatre and Ritual, edited by Richard
           Schechner and Willa Appel, pp. 245–249. Cambridge University
           Press, Cambridge.
O'Shea, Janet
   2003   At home in the world? The Bharatanatyam dancer as transna-
           tional interpreter. *The Drama Review, Journal of Performance
           Studies* 47 (1):176–186.
Pani, Jiwan
   2000   Odissi. In *Indian Dance: The Ultimate Metaphor*, edited by Shanta
           Serbjeet Singh, pp. 147–162. Ravi Kumar Publisher, Bookwise,
           New Delhi.
Patnaik, Dhirendranath
   1971   *Odissi Dance*. Orissa Sangeeta Natak Akademi, Bhubaneshwar.
Schechner, Richard
   1993   *The Future of Ritual. Writings on Culture and Performance.*
           Routledge, London and New York.
Schieffelin, L. Edward
   1998   Problematizing performance. In *Ritual, Performance, Media*, edited
           by Felicia Hughes-Freeland, pp. 194–207. Routledge, London.
Wulff, Helena
   1998   Perspectives towards ballet performance: Exploring, repairing
           and maintaining frames. In *Ritual, Performance, Media*, edited by
           Felicia Hughes-Freeland, pp. 104–120. Routledge, London.
Zarrilli, Phillip
   1990   What does it mean to "become the character": Power, presence,
           and transcendence in Asian in-body disciplines of practice. In *By
           Means of Performance, Intercultural Studies of Theatre and Ritual*,
           edited by Richard Schechner and Willa Appel, pp. 131–148.
           Cambridge University Press, Cambridge.

9.

RITUALIZED TECHNOLOGIES IN THE AEGEAN NEOLITHIC? THE CRAFTS OF ADORNMENT

Marianna Nikolaidou

This paper considers prehistoric technology as a promising field of ritually encoded action, open to archaeological exploration. I focus on the rich record of craft production in the Late and Final Neolithic communities of the Aegean, with special emphasis on adornment. In the absence of stratified hierarchies and rigidly codified belief systems from these societies, I propose that social and cultural knowledge was inscribed into the manufacture and use of important artifacts, and that such practices might have been elevated to ritual status. The archaeological record suggests that the contexts of technical performance were imbued with symbolism to become arenas of negotiation for power and identity.

The human need and potential for ritual emerged vividly through the diverse case studies presented at the Cotsen seminar. We followed different expressions of this urge across space and time, among members of the same culture or even in the experiences of the individual. From conspicuous public performances to exclusive rites of select groups or private observances, there seem to be inexhaustible occasions for the ritualization of human actions (Bell 1992 and this volume), that is, their elevation to a rank of priority over other practices. For ritual is not so much about conveying ideas that are to be understood unequivocally. Rather, it is the very participation, body and soul, in an act valued higher than the mundane order, that enables realization of fundamental symbolic knowledge and imparts to those involved a sense of superiority and of belonging (Eliade 1959; Geertz 1973; Turner 1974; Vidal 1985). The more flexible the conceptual framework, the greater the opportunity for an act to become meaningful and empowering in the context of "what it echoes, what it subverts, what it alludes, what it negates" (Bell 1992:220; compare Lewis 1980).

Such evaluations extend beyond the domains of religious cult or official ceremony, to include behaviors that are traditionally classified "practical" or "profane" (Eliade 1959). This paper considers prehistoric technology as such a promising field of ritually encoded action, open to archaeological exploration. I focus on the rich and evocative record of craft production in the Late and Final Neolithic communities of the Aegean, with special emphasis on adornment. Discussion is informed by social, stylistic, and cognitive approaches to technology; archaeological analyses of ritual; and the current interest in identity and corporeality in prehistory.

RITUALIZING TECHNOLOGY

In archaeology, technology has been studied mainly in its tangible, material qualities: experimental reproductions examine how things are made and how they work; processual and Marxist analyses are concerned with the logistics and systemic operations of production and consumption. Despite their valuable contributions, such approaches have, nevertheless, often missed an essential point: that technology is not only, or even primarily, about the human influence on matter or the physical constraints of material upon human action. Above all, it has to do with ideas about the surrounding physical world and man's place in it (Heidegger 1978:180; Lechtman 1977; Lemonnier 1986, 1992a, 1992b). As has been aptly remarked, "in learning how to use tools we are secretly learning how to use ourselves" (Wagner 1975:77); tools objectify our skills not only to act upon the environment, but also to invest it with cultural value and life (compare Chapman 1998).

Cognitive and cultural approaches to technology, advocated in the seminal works of Leroi-Gourhan decades ago (Leroi-Gourhan 1943, 1945, 1964, 1965), have recently been attracting wider attention among archaeologists. As we realize that "not nature but culture is the main constraint of technique" (van der Leeuw 1992:241), paradigms are shifting to the study of technology in its totality of material, social, and symbolic associations (Dobres and Hoffman 1994:211–258; Pfaffenberger 1988, 1992). Technological choices are structured selections among valid functional alternatives (Lechtman 1977; Sackett 1977, 1990) in a broad field of interaction where material culture is planned, produced, used, repaired, and discarded (Lemonnier 1992a, 1992b). Conversely, artifacts acquire meaning and symbolism as they are being crafted and used (Graves-Brown 1995): they establish conceptual connections and organize experience; they create typologies and narratives of events. Hence, our perception of *homo faber* should be expanded to recognize producers as "facilitators in larger processes of natural reproduction in which magic and ritual play a preponderant part" (Rowlands 1993:148). Numerous examples around the world show how ritual and symbolism become embedded in the *technai* of everyday life (for example, Eliade 1959); indeed they are indispensable links in the *chaînes opératoires* (compare Schlanger 1994) through which the world is perceived and transformed.

Could we then ritualize technology in archaeological thinking? A good starting point would be to employ analytical tools that have been developed for better-explored fields of ritual behavior, such as cult. Renfrew (1985:1–25; 1994; also this volume) lists a number of indicators that, he argues, should have cross-cultural validity for the archaeological identification of ritual phenomena. Several of these indicators seem relevant to the technological process:

1. Symbolism of the raw materials, including prestige values bestowed on imported or exotic resources (Helms 1993) and cosmological meanings and taboos differentiating substances from one another (D. Miller 1985).

2. An empowering sense of wisdom, felt by those possessing the geographical knowledge to procure and/or technical expertise to process resources (Helms 1993).

3. Social skills, necessary to organize production and consumption (Dobres and Hoffman 1994; Elster 1997 and in press).

4. Repetitive patterns, structuring craft activity. These are especially important in societies with cyclical concepts of time, based on the seasonal rhythms of production and marked by rituals of regeneration. Personal histories and cultural traditions are further condensed in the life cycles of portable artifacts as these change hands through heritage or exchange (Rowlands 1993).

5. Redundancy of symbols, evident in stylistic codes governing technical procedures, form, and/or function of the products (see contributions in Conkey and Hastorf 1990).

6. Display, sought in technical excellence and/or formal elaboration (Boas 1955; Layton 1991).

7. Feelings of *communitas* (Turner 1974:50–54, 272–298) among the practitioners of a craft and special bonds between mentor and apprentice (De Boer 1990). Learning and practicing are often circumscribed by initiations, mystic rites, and taboos which place, physically and symbolically, crafters in a liminal position between the community and forces beyond it (D. Miller 1985; Van Gennep 1960:101–158).

8. Liminality and mystique experienced in the interaction between craftsman and material, where the potential of the substance is explored to its limits, and the person's skill, patience, and transformative power are tested. Among Inuit carvers, for example, mastery upon the stone, perceived as a striving to release meaning and life in nature, is valued for its own merit more than for the resulting sculptures (which are often abandoned: Layton 1991:31–32). Motor habits, senses, natural surroundings, raw materials, tools, and methods of application, all physical and cognitive elements engaged in production (Karlin and Julien 1994) can play a "mystifying" (Pfaffenberger 1988: 250) role.

9. Ceremonial uses of the end products, including offering, festive breakage, and special deposition (Brück 1999; Chapman 1998, 2000).

TECHNOLOGIES OF RITUAL IN THE AEGEAN NEOLITHIC

The Late and Final Neolithic periods, roughly spanning the late sixth to early fourth millennium cal B.C. (for comprehensive summaries, see Papathanassopoulos 1996), are represented by communities of sedentary farmers-herders, actively involved in specialized craft and trade within regional and interregional networks. Man-made mounds, formed by successive habitation over centuries or millennia, are prominent in the settlement pattern—although there is increasing evidence for extensive flat sites and occupation of caves or naturally inaccessible high locations (Cullen 2001; Papathanassopoulos 1996). Society was apparently structured along family and kinship lines, without strong marks of the vertical ranking that we usually associate with political complexity (but see Halstead 1995); alternative lines of differentiation were very likely at work, based on age, gender, individual skills, or other factors that elude us (Nikolaidou 2003c; Perlès 2001; Perlès and Vitelli 1999). Neolithic sites lack conspicuous temples, ceremonial plazas, or even areas in the domestic space than can be safely recognized as shrines only (see Theocharis 1981). Instead of prominent cultic figures, small figurines are ubiquitous in a variety of contexts, a fact that defies a single, religious interpretation (Talalay 1993, with references).

What we do see, on the other hand, is a profusion of portable material culture: stone and bone tools, receptacles and mace heads of polished stone, ornaments, a variety of effigies, distinct pottery wares, and special ceramic utensils. There is a pervasive formal elaboration that exceeds practical requirements of function, as can be observed in the predilection for exotic substances, high-quality craftsmanship, and/or rich decoration of the artifacts. Many such goods circulated in transactions of a socioeconomic or symbolic nature, with resources and specialists probably also moving along (Perlès 1992; Perlès and Vitelli 1999). The archaeological record suggests that craft specialization, trade, and ceremony were primary contexts of social cohesion in the Neolithic of southeast Europe (Sherratt 1984), but they also provided fields of distinction for gifted individuals. For example, Vitelli's study of the ceramic technologies at Franchthi Cave in southeast Greece (Vitelli 1993, 1999) demonstrated that early pottery fulfilled primarily social and symbolic roles, with utilitarian applications following centuries later. Ceramic skills would have bestowed, according to Vitelli, a ritual (shamanistic?) status to the first women potters. In a synthesis of the Early Neolithic in Greece, Perlès (2001) likewise envisages a complementary operation of ritual and technical authorities, who guided decisions about habitat, subsistence, or resources for important technologies.

Ornament-making is one of the crafts characterized by firm technical traditions, systematic output of high symbolic value, and a special role in networks of trade and social interaction. One of the largest ornament assemblages in the Aegean was excavated at the Neolithic and Early Bronze Age tell settlement of Sitagroi, in the Drama plain of northeast Greece (Elster and Renfrew 2003; Renfrew et al. 1986) (figure 9.1). A comprehensive study of these artifacts (M. Miller 2003; Nikolaidou 2003a; Shackleton 2003) has allowed us to better understand technological patterns that were already emerging from more limited findings and reports at other, comparable sites. In what follows I summarize the results of our analysis and explore how ritual personae might have been constructed, in the context of producing and/or through the products of the *technai* of adornment. The Late and Final Neolithic horizons of occupation (Sitagroi phases II and III, 5400–3600 cal B.C.; Renfrew et al. 1986: 173, Table 7.3) represent the peak of activity at the site and in the wider region of the Drama plain (figure 9.2), as well as in other areas of Northern Greece (Andreou et al. 2001).

THE CRAFTS OF ADORNMENT AT SITAGROI

The site has yielded no less than 931 ornaments, thanks to the application of water-sieving which allowed for the retrieval of very small items. Beads and pendants (figure 9.3), bracelet/annulets (figure 9.4), and pins constitute

Figure 9.1. The site of Sitagroi on the map of southeast Europe. (Reprinted from Renfrew, Gimbutas, and Elster 1986: Figure 1.2, p. 7)

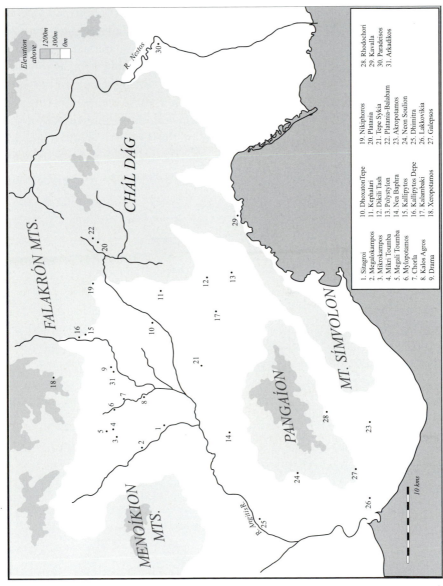

FIGURE 9.2. Sites of the Drama plain and surrounding region. (Reprinted from Elster and Renfrew 2003: Figure 1, p. xxvi)

an assemblage important in quantity and typological variability, and for its affinities to other groups from the Aegean and the Balkans. The artifacts were analyzed in terms of temporal distribution; raw materials; procedures of manufacture; chronology and typology; and possible uses, as inferred from the find contexts, archaeological *comparanda*, figurine iconography, and ethnographic support. Considered together, these parameters revealed purposeful selection of resources, processing techniques, practices for local consumption, and regional distribution of the finished goods (compare Elster and Nikolaidou 1995; Nikolaidou 1997). Crafters chose to work with local limestone, clays, and bone, as well as with imported shells

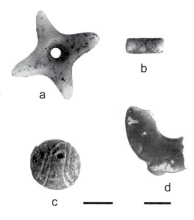

FIGURE 9.3. An assortment of elaborated beads (*a–c*) and a pendant (*d*) from Sitagroi, phases I–III. (Reprinted from Elster and Renfrew 2003: Plate 9.11.)

FIGURE 9.4. Shell bracelet/annulets of *Glycymeris,* phase III. (Reprinted from Elster and Renfrew 2003: Plate 9.6.)

(*Glycymeris* and *Spondylus gaederopus*) from the Aegean Sea 25–30 km away, metal from mines relatively close by in northern Greece or farther north in the Balkans (Renfrew and Slater 2003), and stones from west Macedonia and eastern Thrace (Dixon 2003). These sought-after materials were worked into standardized forms of beads and bracelets/annulets with closely controlled shapes and dimensions. Specific fashions for wearing are suggested by the recurrent combinations of different ornaments in excavated units and by similar ornamental patterns on figurines. And there were prescribed ways of manipulating the end products, involving intentional breakage of *Spondylus* bangles on-site and wide circulation of shell ornaments made of Aegean species over the Balkans and perhaps even farther north (Greenfield 1991; Renfrew 1973; Séfériades 2000; Willms 1985).

A complex set of cultural attitudes is reflected in the above choices. Regarding raw materials, intensive use of clay only in phase III appears in keeping with the overall prominence of ceramics in the symbolic apparatus of this period: figurines and miniatures, decorated pottery, vessels of elaborated form, and seals and other items of notation (see contributions in Renfrew et al. 1986; Elster and Renfrew 2003). Massive daub structures, of which several have been traced at Sitagroi, characterize Balkan architecture in the later Neolithic or Chalcolithic—"the age of clay," as it has been termed (Stevanovic 1997). Clay may well have offered an expedient local substitute for harder-to-obtain materials, in times of increased production demands (M. Miller 2003:381), but it could also have been invested with conceptual value. Other substances speak to a fascination with the distant and the new at the expense of the local and familiar: attractive marine shells were highly preferred over freshwater mussels easily available from the village river (Shackleton 2003); and the few copper and gold trinkets (figure 9.5) echo the encounter with the innovative metallurgies of the Balkans (Renfrew and Slater 2003). Aesthetics and symbolism must have urged people to take the risks to procure these desirable commodities (compare Elster, in press; Trubitt 2003), the extraction of which required planning, physical and technical skills, and appropriate tools and facilities (Tsuneki 1989). Whether Sitagroi groups themselves traveled to obtain the resources or these circulated down the line, it would have been necessary to forge affiliations in the region and farther afield (Perlès 1992:117). Differences in the geographical environment of participating communities—plains, coastal regions, and mountains (Andreou et al. 2001)—may also have resulted in social and conceptual differentiation (compare Broodbank 1993; Séfériades 2000), and moving across territories would have best been handled via ceremony and symbolism (Van Gennep

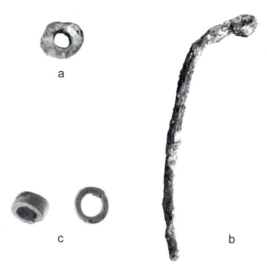

FIGURE 9.5. Copper (a–b) and gold (c) ornaments, Phases II and III.
(Reprinted from Elster and Renfrew 2003:
Plates 8.1.b: a, 8.2.a: b, 8.4: c, respectively)

1960:98). The whole enterprise of acquisition was possibly surrounded
with stories and myths, news from friends near and afar, and celebrations
of farewell and return bestowing an aura of prestige to those involved: daring travelers, traders, crafters, spiritual and social facilitators (compare
Elster, in press; Helms 1993).

Preforms found in various stages of manufacture (Elster and Renfrew
2003: Plates 9.3, 9.2.2) attest to on-site ornament production at Sitagroi.
Tools and installations were relatively uncomplicated, but the tasks did
require knowledge and dexterity, as we learn from experimental reproductions and technical study (Gardner 2003a, 2003b; M. Miller 2003; Renfrew
and Slater 2003). We have come to respect those ancient specialists who
patiently worked their materials into durable forms of beauty, preserving
the technical wisdom of millennia but also taking new steps of their own.
For example, the crafters in phase III systematically sought large valves of
the strong *Spondylus* for their bangles and larger beads, and reserved the
more delicate *Glycymeris* for easier-to-produce ornaments, whereas previously the two species were used interchangeably. But the methods of
smoothing and forming the mollusc remained unchanged over centuries
(M. Miller 2003; Shackleton 2003; compare Tsuneki 1989: Figures 6–7),
which indicates that technical performance was possibly invested with stylistic value (compare Sackett 1990). Expert stone-carvers produced a

demanding variety of fired steatite beads, group-strung and -ground ("*heishi*" fashion) for standardized results (figure 9.6). Clay beads and pendants would have posed no difficulty to the village's experienced potters, who took care to decorate some with motifs popular in the ceramic repertoire. Likewise, bone beads and pins would have been easily made by bone-workers producing various high-quality tools and implements (Elster 2003). There were also those skilled with metals, who shaped sheets and wires into beads and pins. An exceptional association of finds attesting to metallurgical activity came from the phase III Hearth and Debris levels, including a clay hearth with baked surface, many sherds or crucible fragments with copper deposits, and two copper ornaments: a roll-headed pin (figure 9.5b) and an awl (Renfrew and Slater 2003:305–309).

A community of knowledgeable crafters thus comes to life through the small handicrafts of adornment, and it is worth exploring how these people learned and practiced their art. It is possible that training started in childhood (compare Karlin and Julien 1994:162–163) as happens, for example, nowadays with bead production in traditional India (Possehl 1981). In such a case, could apprenticeship be experienced as initiation to a new social and ritual persona (compare Eliade 2001; Van Gennep 1960)? A clue may be offered by the miniatures and models found at Sitagroi and elsewhere; these effigies include tools, manufactured goods such as pots and furniture, and images of ornamented humans, all of which could have been craft-related symbols: charms, didactic devices, or social tokens (Nikolaidou 2003b; Marangou 1992; Talalay 1993). In the absence of securely identified ornament workshops (but see Tsuneki 1989), and considering the overall layout of Neolithic villages, we assume that goods were produced in domestic areas, with fine debris swept away afterward (M. Miller 2003:373). The aforementioned Hearth and Debris levels, for example, produced evidence not only for metalworking but also for spinning and

FIGURE 9.6. Fired steatite beads.
(Reprinted from Elster and Renfrew 2003: Plate 9.2.3)

weaving, along with a remarkable profusion of high-quality stone and bone tools, elaborate ceramics, figurines and miniatures, and seals and other items of notation (Nikolaidou and Elster 2003: 456–458, Table 12.3). It is interesting, then, to contemplate how technologies were woven into the fabric of household life: its routines, times of ceremony, and heritage (Elster 1997; Hendon 1996; Tringham 1991; Whittle 2006). Were the secrets of the *technai* well kept, a special source for family pride? Or were they shared among households and communities via marriage, partnership, and exchange? What rules dictated the allocation of tasks and craft-related authority? Were raw materials differently evaluated? An instructive ethnographic case of such classifications is seen in the bead industry of traditional India, which is organized according to endogamous structures, age- and gender-specific labor divisions, and levels of ritual purity (Kenoyer, Vidale, and Bahn 1991: 55–59; Possehl 1981).

Although the particular contexts of production in the prehistoric Aegean elude us, it is plausible to think that technical performance involved negotiations—of space, time, labor, knowledge, and values (compare Costin 1991; Dobres and Hoffman 1994). Ritualization of materials and roles was perhaps the strategy chosen to deal with conflicts, cultivating a communal ethos to ensure the smooth flow of production. It is indicative that the more demanding-to-produce artifacts are those that featured prominently in exchange networks. Within the Drama plain, shell ornaments possibly circulated in return for foodstuffs, textiles, or mats (Elster 1995; Yannouli 1997:123–125). In Thessaly, *Spondylus* from the coastal center of Dimini was forwarded to inland communities (Tsuneki 1989). Large quantities of *Spondylus* preforms and finished products were likewise found at the extensive flat site of Makrygialos, farther north along the Macedonian coast (Besios and Pappa 1996), and at the lake settlement of Dispilio in the mountainous regions of west Macedonia (Ifantidis 2006). Routes through the Balkan peninsula by river or mountain pass carried this valuable material far from its loci of extraction, to be incorporated into new cultural settings such as the rich assemblages at the cemetery of Varna (compare Willms 1985). It might well be that the experiences and ideas encoded in the productive strategy would in turn determine to an extent the importance of the end products (Kenoyer 1991: 82–84; Renfrew 1969).

The excavated ornaments, their find contexts, and figurine iconography document a vivid concern with adornment. At Sitagroi, recurrent combinations of artifacts in the archaeological record and similar arrangements on figurines reveal distinct ornamental styles (compare

Kenoyer 1991), with preference for colors, sizes, and shapes also echoing important classifications. A more subtle variation in artifact form and/or modes of wearing points to individual choices within a framework of long-standing principles. Just as training to the crafts of ornament-making may have involved important cultural perceptions, so also learning the arts of adornment, knowing how to appreciate and use them properly, could have been an important step toward personal and social maturity. The archaeological record evokes ritualized contexts for adornment, in diverse fields of experience.

Ornaments would have been used on different parts of the body, hair, garments, and accessories. Further embellishments perhaps included tattooing and painting, as evidenced by decorative motifs or red paint on figurines and by implements possibly used for ornamentation such as engraved cylinders and other stamp-like objects, lumps of ocher, color trays, and scarification (?) needles (Nikolaidou 2003a). Elaborate costumes are indicated by designs on figurines and fine pottery which probably imitate woven prototypes (Elster 1992; Gimbutas 1986). It is likely that Aegean textiles were beaded or decorated with bone and shell appliqués, a fashion amply attested for the Neolithic and Bronze Age in Europe and Anatolia (Barber 1991). At Sitagroi, several excavated contexts contained ornaments together with spinning and weaving equipment and with pattern-bearing figurines, thus reinforcing the hypothesis for a special connection between ornament and textile production (Nikolaidou and Elster 2003; compare Marangou 1997). Garments seem to have been especially ornate during the Late and Final Neolithic, when beads also exhibit their greatest variation of shape, color, and material, and cluster in attractive assortments. Perhaps many of these tiny beads were assembled together into string-skirts, a garment consisting of joined strands of material partially covering and partially revealing the lower body; impressions of such types of skirts on figurines come from many prehistoric sites, and they have been interpreted as emblematic of women's fertility and/or sexuality (Barber 1994). Given that most ornate Neolithic figurines can be recognized as female, it is conceivable that some at least are images of brides in their finery: work of their own hands, cherished heirloom, or special family acquisition displayed during these ceremonies of passage. A role of textiles in marital transactions has already been suggested for Neolithic communities (Elster 1995; Sheratt 1984), and we may extend the hypothesis to include items of adornment. If so, figurine imagery would have brought to focus notions of gender, age, status, mating availability, group affiliation, and family prestige.

Ornamentation could have started at an early age, as is indicated by the small diameter of most shell bracelet/annulets (figure 9.4) which, if indeed worn around the wrist or ankle (and not as pendants or hair ornaments; Marangou 1991), could only belong to children (Shackleton 2003; compare Karali-Yannacopoulos 1992:163). The possibility that at least some of these special items were reserved for young members of the community calls attention to the often neglected lives of children (Baxter 2004; Moore and Scott 1997), ranging from birth, coming of age, role play, learning about ideals of beauty and propriety, receiving of gifts, protection, affectionate treatment, to the rites of death. Alternatively, shell circlets may have been given to a child and then worn continuously through his/her adult years, as happens, for instance, with the lovely jade bangles given to Chinese girls as luck charms. Age- and gender-related symbolisms and benign functions are attested in the shell bangles from prehistoric Harappan and contemporary traditional cultures of the Indus Valley (Kenoyer 1991:96–97). Archaeological findings indicate a special association of these ornaments with adult women in prehistory. Nowadays Indian men and boys wear bangles for protection and to denote status and ethnicity; young maidens carry them during courtship; and for married women they ensure the well-being of the family. Being highly personalized, a woman's shell bangles are broken upon the husband's death.

Purposeful breakage has also been inferred for the fragmentary *Spondylus* bangles from the Aegean, where they greatly outnumber intact examples. At Sitagroi, careful examination of more than 160 pieces not only showed that broken surfaces were old, but also identified very few joints (M. Miller 2003). This points to intentional and consistent fragmentation prior to discard. At Dimini in Thessaly, a large concentration of broken and burnt bangles in one area of the settlement has been interpreted (Halstead 1993) as a strategy by "elite" families to restrict intrasite circulation of ornaments, which they would themselves accumulate and forward to peer groups inland in return for food, marital mates, and labor. Privileged manipulation might also be the case at Sitagroi, where clusters of broken *Spondylus* bangles (figure 9.7) were found in levels rich with high-quality tools and symbolic artifacts (Nikolaidou and Elster 2003). The motives underlying such concentrations need not be limited to social strife, however. As the aforementioned Indian examples indicate, group identities, family concerns, or personal attachment might have been at play as well (compare Chapman 2000). That shell ornaments were cherished possessions is suggested, among other things, by mending (?) perforations on some of the fragments (figure 9.8). Smashing such valuables could have involved the dynamics of inclusion/exclusion or protection/aversion, materialized in performances of consumption and display, offering and receiving, bonding or separating.

At Sitagroi, the picture we get from the excavated contexts throughout the mound sequence (Nikolaidou and Elster 2003) is one of different households participating in ornamentation, although conceivably in varying roles. Persistence in selected materials, crafting methods, forms, and fashions of adornment gives the impression of an aesthetic *koiné* shared by the villagers of Sitagroi, their neighbors in the Drama plain, and affiliated groups in other regions. Stylistic conformity perhaps materializes attempts to create an ideal "single social space" (Kotsakis 1996:170), as a counterbalance to antagonisms that would unavoidably arise among parties competing over the same material and symbolic resources (Sherratt 1984, 1993). Control of access to important knowledge and goods is an important source of power (Bender 1985), and those eager to secure it might have found in ritual an effective path of pursuit: inequalities briefly negated in the liminal milieu of "anti-structure," they would be eventually reaffirmed as the natural and legitimate order of society (Bloch 1980; Turner 1974). Communitas can be traced not only across space but also through time, as ornamental traditions show remarkable endurance throughout the Neolithic and into the Early Bronze Age (Nikolaidou 1997). These and other long-lived styles of material culture (such as figurines or polished stone tools) would have kept alive traditions and memories of generations past. The performance of crafts in habitation loci occupied successively over centuries or millennia bespeaks the power of the ancestral place in the construction of life histories, through remembrance and reenactment (compare Chapman 1998; Day and Wilson 2002; Kotsakis 1999).

FIGURE 9.7. Group of fragmentary *Spondylus* bangles, phase III. (Reprinted from Elster and Renfrew 2003: Plate 9.5.)

Items of adornment from Aegean Neolithic sites have often survived scantily or in fragments, ambiguous in their contextual associations. Nevertheless, they can be evaluated as key elements in socioeconomic networks, points of reference in the community's narratives and world views, vehicles for the transmission of important knowledge, links of social integration, but also marks of differentiation. The decorated human body thus emerges as a powerful symbol (Marcus 1993), in its many layers of corporeal and social existence (compare Hamilakis et al. 2002; Knapp and Meskell 1997; Nikolaidou 2002). Visibility, movement, texture, and touch would focus attention (compare Renfrew 1985:1–25) on the ritualized body, in the contexts of ornament manufacture and display. And there would be plenty of opportunity to perceive and to be perceived within villages tightly built on the limited space of a mound, such as at Sitagroi. The recovery of ornaments together with items of utility (tools, pots) and with symbolic products (such as figurines) perhaps indicates that people felt it necessary to be decorated for both work and celebration. Williams writes significantly that among the Turkana of Kenya, "to be without ornament is to be without identity" (Williams 1987:34).

FIGURE 9.8. Large segment of perforated *Spondylus* bangle, phase III. (Reprinted from Elster and Renfrew 2003: Plate 9.4.)

CONCLUSIONS

It has taken scholars a long time to appreciate the social and symbolic dimensions of technology. In Western experience, a dichotomy between mind and matter results in the categorization of practices as either "symbolic" or "functional." Such polarizing paradigms have made us inattentive to more integrated concepts of technique in nonindustrial cultures, where technical knowledge and action are woven into the symbolic fabric of existence. A variegated spectrum of craft production in the Aegean Neolithic highlights a primary role of technology in the structuring of social and ritual experience. In the absence of stratified hierarchies and rigidly codified belief systems, complex cultural knowledge would have been inscribed into the manufacture and use of important artifacts. The excavated assemblages suggest that the contexts of technical action also provided ritualized fields for multiple negotiations of power and identity (compare Conkey 1991). It is perhaps in ritual garments, faded though they may be after millennia, that prehistoric life appears at its most fascinating.

ACKNOWLEDGMENTS

The contributions at the Cotsen Advanced Seminar on Ritual, although not focused on technology, have inspired many ideas in this paper. I thank Evangelos Kyriakidis, who invited me to participate in the seminar as discussant and to this volume. Ernestine Elster and the Office of Publications at the Cotsen Institute of Archaeology at UCLA kindly gave permission to reproduce illustrations from the Sitagroi site reports, Volumes 1 and 2. I am further indebted to Ernestine for being willing to discuss my ideas, at various stages of formulation, and for her comments on an earlier draft. All omissions and errors remain mine.

REFERENCES CITED

Andreou, Stelios, Michael Fotiadis, and Kostas Kotsakis
    2001   Review of *Aegean Prehistory V: The Neolithic and Bronze Age of Northern Greece*. In *Aegean Prehistory: A Review*, edited by Tracey Cullen, pp. 259–327. Archaeological Institute of America, Boston.
Barber, Elizabeth Wayland
    1991   *Prehistoric Textiles: The Development of Cloth in the Neolithic and Bronze Ages with Special Reference to the Aegean*. Princeton University Press, Princeton.
    1994   *Women's Work: The First 20.000 Years*. W. W. Norton & Co., New York.
Baxter, J. Eva
    2004   *The Archaeology of Childhood: Children, Gender, and Material Culture*. AltaMira, Walnut Creek, CA.
Bell, Catherine
    1992   *Ritual Theory, Ritual Practice*. Oxford University Press, Oxford.
Bender, Barbara
    1985   Prehistoric developments in the American mid-continent and in Brittany, Northwest France. In *Prehistoric Hunter-Gatherers: The Emergence of Cultural Complexity*, edited by T. Douglas Price and James A. Brown, pp. 21–57. Academic Press, Orlando.
Besios, Manthos, and Maria Pappa
    1996   Neolithikos oikismos Makrygialou, 1993. *To Archaiologiko Ergo sti Makedonia kai Thraki* 7:215–222.
Bloch, Marc
    1980   Ritual and the non-representation of society. In *Symbol as Sense: New Approaches to the Analysis of Meaning*, edited by Mary Le Cron Foster and Stanley H. Brandes, pp. 93–102. Academic Press, New York.
Boas, Frank
    1955   *Primitive Art*. Dover Publications, New York.

Broodbank, Cyprian
   1993   Ulysses without sails: Trade, distance, knowledge, and power in
             the early Cyclades. *World Archaeology* 24 (3):315–331.
Brück, Joanna
   1999   Ritual and rationality: Some problems of interpretation in
             European archaeology. *Journal of European Archaeology* 2
             (3):313–44.
Chapman, John
   1998   Objectification, embodiment, and the value of places and things.
             In *The Archaeology of Value: Essays on Prestige and the Processes of
             Valuation*, edited by Douglass Bailey, pp. 106–130. BAR
             International Series 730. Oxford.
   2000   *Fragmentation in Archaeology: People, Places, and Broken Objects in
             the Prehistory of South Eastern Europe*. Routledge, London.
Conkey, Margaret
   1991   Contexts of action, contexts for power: Material culture and gen-
             der in the Magdalenian. In *Engendering Archaeology: Women and
             Prehistory*, edited by Joanne M. Gero and Margaret Conkey, pp.
             57–92. Basil Blackwell, Oxford.
Conkey, Margaret, and Christine Hastorf (editors)
   1990   *The Uses of Style in Archaeology*. New Directions in Archaeology.
             Cambridge University Press, Cambridge.
Costin, Cathy
   1991   Craft specialization: Issues in defining, documenting and explain-
             ing the organization of production. *Archaeological Method and
             Theory* 7:1–38.
Cullen, Tracey (editor)
   2001   *Aegean Prehistory: A Review*. Archaeological Institute of America,
             Boston.
Day, Peter M., and David Wilson
   2002   Landscapes of memory, craft, and power in Prepalatial and
             Protopalatial Knossos. In *Labyrinth Revisited: Rethinking "Minoan"
             Archaeology*, edited by Yannis Hamilakis, pp. 143–166. Oxbow
             Books, Oxford.
DeBoer, Warren R.
   1990   Interaction, imitation, and communication as expressed in style: The
             Ucayali experience. In *The Uses of Style in Archaeology*, edited by
             Margaret Conkey and Christine Hastorf, pp. 82–104. New
             Directions in Archaeology. Cambridge University Press, Cambridge.
Dixon, John
   2003   Petrological analysis. In *Prehistoric Sitagroi: Excavations in Northeast
             Greece, 1968–1970*, Vol. 2: *The Final Report*, edited by Ernestine S.
             Elster and Colin Renfrew, pp. 147–174. Monumenta Archaeologica
             20. Cotsen Institute of Archaeology at UCLA, Los Angeles.

Dobres, Marcie Anne, and Christopher R. Hoffman
    1994   Social agency and the dynamics of prehistoric technology. *Journal of Archaeological Method and Theory* 1 (3):211–258.
Eliade, Mircea
    1959   *Sacred and Profane: The Nature of Religion.* Translated from the French by Willard R. Trask. Harcourt and Brace Jovanovich, New York.
    2001   *Rites and Symbols of Initiation: The Mysteries of Birth and Rebirth.* Translated by W. R. Trask. Harper and Row, New York.
Elster, Ernestine S.
    1992   An archaeologist's perspective on prehistoric textile production: The case of Sitagroi. In *I Drama kai i periochi tis: Istoria kai politismos,* pp. 29–46. Praktika Epistimonikis Synantisis, Dimos Dramas.
    1995   Textile production at Sitagroi and beyond: Spinners and weavers, exchange and interchange. Paper presented at the panel "The archaeology of tools and technology: Craftsmen and craftswomen, producers and consumers," 97th Annual Meeting of the Archaeological Institute of America, San Diego.
    1997   Construction and use of the Early Bronze Age Burnt House at Sitagroi: Craft and technology. In *Techni: Craftsmen, Craftswomen, and Craftsmanship in the Aegean Bronze Age,* edited by Robert Laffineur and Philip P. Betancourt, pp. 19–36. Aegaeum 16. Université de Liège: Histoire de l' art et archéologie de la Grèce antique; University of Texas at Austin: Program in Aegean Scripts and Prehistory.
    2003   Bone tools and other artifacts. In *Prehistoric Sitagroi: Excavations in Northeast Greece, 1968–1970,* Vol. 2: *The Final Report,* edited by Ernestine S. Elster and Colin Renfrew, pp. 31–51. Monumenta Archaeologica 20. Cotsen Institute of Archaeology at UCLA, Los Angeles.
    In press Odysseus before Homer: Trade, travel, and adventure in prehistoric Greece. In *Epos: Reconsidering Greek Epic and Aegean Bronze Age Archaeology,* edited by Robert Laffineur, Kenneth Lappatin, and Sarah P. Morris. Université de Liège: Histoire de l' art et archéologie de la Grèce antique; University of Texas at Austin: Program in Aegean Scripts and Prehistory.
Elster, Ernestine, and Marianna Nikolaidou
    1995   Shell artifacts from Sitagroi, Northeast Greece: Symbolic implications of gathering in an early agricultural society. Paper presented at the conference "From the Jomon to Starr Carr: Prehistoric foragers of temperate Eurasia," Cambridge and Durham.
Elster, Ernestine S., and Colin Renfrew (editors)
    2003   *Prehistoric Sitagroi: Excavations in Northeast Greece, 1968–1970,* Vol. 2: *The Final Report.* Monumenta Archaeologica 20. Cotsen Institute of Archaeology at UCLA, Los Angeles.

Gardner, Elizabeth
  2003a   Technical analysis of the ceramics. In *Prehistoric Sitagroi:
           Excavations in Northeast Greece, 1968–1970*, Vol. 2: *The Final
           Report*, edited by Ernestine S. Elster and Colin Renfrew, pp.
           283–295. Monumenta Archaeologica 20. Cotsen Institute of
           Archaeology at UCLA, Los Angeles.
  2003b   Graphite painted pottery. In *Prehistoric Sitagroi: Excavations in Northeast
           Greece, 1968–1970*, Vol. 2: *The Final Report*, edited by Ernestine S.
           Elster and Colin Renfrew, pp. 296–298. Monumenta Archaeologica
           20. Cotsen Institute of Archaeology at UCLA, Los Angeles.
Geertz, Clifford
  1973   *The Interpretation of Cultures*. Basic Books, New York.
Gimbutas, Marija
  1986   Mythical imagery of the Sitagroi society. In *Excavations at
           Sitagroi, A Prehistoric Village in Northeast Greece*, Vol. 1, edited by
           Colin Renfrew, Marija Gimbutas, and Ernestine S. Elster, pp.
           225–301. Monumenta Archaeologica 13. UCLA Institute of
           Archaeology, Los Angeles.
Graves-Brown, Paul M.
  1995   Fearful symmetry. *World Archaeology* 27 (1):88–99.
Greenfield, Haskel J.
  1991   A *kula* ring in prehistoric Europe? A consideration of local and
           interregional exchange during the Late Neolithic of the Central
           Balkans. In *Between Bands and States*, edited by Susan A. Gregg,
           pp. 287–308. Southern Illinois University, Center for
           Archaeological Investigation, Occasional Paper 9. Southern
           Illinois University, Carbondale.
Halstead, Paul
  1993   *Spondylus* shell ornaments from Late Neolithic Dimini, Greece:
           Specialized manufacture or unequal accumulation? *Antiquity* 67:
           503–509.
  1995   From sharing to hoarding: The Neolithic foundations of Aegean
           Bronze Age society. In *Politeia: Society and State in the Aegean
           Bronze Age*, edited by Robert Laffineur and Wolf-Dietrich
           Niemeier, pp. 11–22. Aegaeum 13. Université de Liège: Histoire
           de l'art et archéologie de la Grèce antique; University of Texas at
           Austin: Program in Aegean Scripts and Prehistory.
Hamilakis, Yannis, Mark Pluciennik, and Sarah Tarlow (editors)
  2002   *Thinking through the Body: Archaeologies of Corporeality*. Kluwer
           Academic/Plenum, New York.
Heidegger, Martin
  1978   *Basic Writings*. Harper, San Francisco.
Helms, Mary
  1993   *Craft and the Kingly Ideal: Art, Trade, and Power*. University of
           Texas Press, Austin.

Hendon, Julia A.
  1996   Archaeological approaches to the organization of domestic labor:
          Household practice and domestic relations. *Annual Review of
          Anthropology* 25:45–61.
Ifantidis, Fotis
  2006   Ta kosmimata tou neolithikou oikismou Dispiliou Kastorias:
          Paragogi kai chrisi mias aisthitikis ergaleiothikis. M.A. thesis,
          Aristotle University of Thessaloniki.
Karali-Yannacopoulos, Lilian
  1992   La parure. In *Dikili Tash, Village préhistorique de Macédoine
          Orientale, I,* edited by René Treuil, pp.159–164. Bulletin de
          Correspondance Hellénique Supplément 24. École Française d'
          Athènes, Athens.
Karlin, Claudine, and Michèle Julien
  1994   Prehistoric technology: A cognitive science? In *The Ancient Mind:
          Elements of Cognitive Archaeology,* edited by Colin Renfrew and
          Ezra B. W. Zubrow, pp. 152–164. New Directions in
          Archaeology. Cambridge University Press, Cambridge.
Kenoyer, J. Mark
  1991   Ornament styles of the Indus Valley tradition: Evidence from
          recent excavations at Harappa, Pakistan. *Paléorient* 17 (2):79–98.
Kenoyer, J. Mark, Massimo Vidale, and Kuldeep K. Bahn
  1991   Contemporary stone bead making in Khambat, India: Patterns of
          craft specialization and organization of production as reflected in
          the archaeological record. *World Archaeology* 23 (1):44–63.
Knapp, A. Bernard, and Lynn Meskell
  1997   Bodies of evidence on prehistoric Cyprus. *Cambridge
          Archaeological Journal* 7 (2):73–104.
Kotsakis, Kostas
  1996   Exchanges and relations. In *Neolithic Culture in Greece,* edited by
          George A. Papathanassopoulos, pp. 168–170. Nicholas P.
          Goulandris Foundation, Museum of Cycladic Art, Athens.
  1999   What the tells can tell: Social space and settlement in the Greek
          Neolithic. In *Neolithic Society in Greece,* edited by Paul Halstead,
          pp. 66–76. Sheffield Studies in Aegean Archaeology 2. Sheffield
          Academic Press, Sheffield.
Layton, Robert
  1991   *Anthropology of Art.* Cambridge University Press, Cambridge.
Lechtman, Heather
  1977   Style in technology: Some early thoughts. In *Material Culture:
          Styles, Organization, and Dynamics of Technology,* edited by Heather
          Lechtman and Robert Merrill, pp. 3–20. West Publishing, St. Paul.
Lemonnier, Pierre
  1986   The study of material culture today: Toward an anthropology of
          technical systems. *Journal of Anthropological Archaeology* 5: 147–186.

1992a   Introduction. In *Technological Choices: Transformation in Material Cultures since the Neolithic*, edited by Pierre Lemonnier, pp. 1–35. Routledge, London and New York.

Lemonnier, Pierre (editor)
1992b   *Technological Choices: Transformation in Material Cultures since the Neolithic*. Routledge, London and New York.

Leroi-Gourhan, André
1943   *Évolution et techniques; L'homme et la matière*. A. Michel, Paris.
1945   *Évolution et techniques; Milieu et techniques*. A. Michel, Paris.
1964   *Le geste et la parole I: Technique et langage*. A. Michel, Paris.
1965   *Le geste et la parole II: La mémoire et les rythmes*. A. Michel, Paris.

Lewis, Gilbert
1980   *Day of Shining Red: An Essay in Understanding Ritual*. Cambridge Studies in Social Anthropology Vol. 27. Cambridge University Press, Cambridge.

Marangou, Christina
1991   Figurines Néolithiques parées de Macédoine Orientale (Néolithique Récent, Grèce du Nord). In *Actes du XIIe Congrès Internationale des Sciences Préhistoriques et Protohistoriques, Bratislava, 1–7 Septembre 1991*, Vol. 2, edited by Juraj Pavuk, pp. 327–334.
1992   *Eidolia: Figurines et miniatures du néolithique récent et du bronze ancien en Grèce*. British Archaeological Reports International Series 576, Oxford.
1997   Neolithic micrography; Miniature modelling at Dimitra. In *Neolithiki Makedonia, Meros I. Dimitra: Proistorikos oikismos konta stis Serres. I anaskafi ton eton 1978, 1979, 1980*, edited by Dimitrios Grammenos, pp. 227–265. Ypourgeio Politismou, Tameio Archaiologikon Poron, Athens.

Marcus, Michelle I.
1993   Incorporating the body: Adornment, gender, and social identity in ancient Iran. *Cambridge Archaeological Journal* 3 (2):157–178.

Miller, Daniel
1985   *Artefacts as Categories: A Study of Ceramic Variability in Central India*. Cambridge University Press, Cambridge.

Miller, Michele
2003   Technical aspects of ornament production at Sitagroi. In *Prehistoric Sitagroi: Excavations in Northeast Greece, 1968–1970*, Vol. 2: *The Final Report*, edited by Ernestine S. Elster and Colin Renfrew, pp. 369–382. Monumenta Archaeologica 20. Cotsen Institute of Archaeology at UCLA, Los Angeles.

Moore, Jenny, and Eleanor Scott (editors)
1997   *Invisible People and Processes: Writing Gender and Childhood into European Archaeology*. Leicester University Press, London and New York.

Nikolaidou, Marianna
 1997 Ornament production and use at Sitagroi, Northeast Greece: Symbolic and social implications of an Early Bronze Age technology. In *Techni: Craftsmen, Craftswomen, and Craftsmanship in the Aegean Bronze Age*, edited by Robert Laffineur and Philip P. Betancourt, pp. 177–196. Aegaeum 16. Université de Liège: Histoire de l'art et archéologie de la Grèce antique; University of Texas at Austin: Program in Aegean Scripts and Prehistory.

 2002 Palaces with faces in Minoan Crete: Looking for the people in the first Minoan states. In *Labyrinth Revisited: Rethinking "Minoan" Archaeology*, edited by Yannis Hamilakis, pp. 73–97. Oxbow Books, Oxford.

 2003a Items of adornment. In *Prehistoric Sitagroi: Excavations in Northeast Greece, 1968–1970*, Vol. 2: *The Final Report*, edited by Ernestine S. Elster and Colin Renfrew, pp. 331–360. Monumenta Archaeologica 20. Cotsen Institute of Archaeology at UCLA, Los Angeles.

 2003b Miniatures and models. In *Prehistoric Sitagroi: Excavations in Northeast Greece, 1968–1970*, Vol. 2: *The Final Report*, edited by Ernestine S. Elster and Colin Renfrew, pp. 431–442. Monumenta Archaeologica 20. Cotsen Institute of Archaeology at UCLA, Los Angeles.

 2003c Complexity in Late Neolithic and Bronze Age societies in Macedonia, Northern Aegean. Paper presented at the "Complex Society Group Meeting," Cotsen Institute of Archaeology at UCLA.

Nikolaidou, Marianna, and Ernestine S. Elster
 2003 Contextual commentary, Phases I–V. In *Prehistoric Sitagroi: Excavations in Northeast Greece, 1968–1970*, Vol. 2: *The Final Report*, edited by Ernestine S. Elster and Colin Renfrew, pp. 453–468. Monumenta Archaeologica 20. Cotsen Institute of Archaeology at UCLA, Los Angeles.

Papathanassopoulos, George A. (editor)
 1996 *Neolithic Culture in Greece*. N. P. Goulandris Foundation, Museum of Cycladic Art, Athens.

Perlès, Catherine
 1992 Systems of exchange and organization of production in Neolithic Greece. *Journal of Mediterranean Archaeology* 5 (2):115–164.

 2001 *The Early Neolithic in Greece: The First Farming Communities in Europe*. Cambridge University Press, Cambridge.

Perlès, Catherine, and Karen D. Vitelli
 1999 Craft specialization in the Neolithic of Greece. In *Neolithic Society in Greece*, edited by Paul Halstead, pp. 96–107. Sheffield Studies in Aegean Archaeology 2. Sheffield Academic Press, Sheffield.

Pfaffenberger, Bryan
    1988   Fetishised objects and humanised nature: Towards an anthropol-
            ogy of technology. *Man* (N.S) 23:236–252.
    1992   Social anthropology of technology. *Annual Review of Anthropology*
            21:491–516.
Possehl, Gregory L.
    1981   Cambay bead making: An ancient craft in modern India.
            Expedition 23 (4):39–47.
Renfrew, Colin
    1969   The autonomy of the South/East European Copper Age.
            Proceedings of the Prehistoric Society 35:12–47.
    1973   Trade and Craft Specialization. In *Neolithic Greece*, edited by
            Demetrios R. Theocharis, pp. 179–200. National Bank of Greece,
            Athens.
    1985   *The Archaeology of Cult: The Sanctuary at Phylakopi.* British School
            of Athens Supplementary Volume No. 18. Thames and Hudson,
            London.
    1994   Towards a cognitive archaeology. In *The Ancient Mind: Elements of
            Cognitive Archaeology*, edited by Colin Renfrew and Ezra B. W.
            Zubrow, pp. 3–12. New Directions in Archaeology. Cambridge
            University Press, Cambridge.
Renfrew, Colin, Marija Gimbutas, and Ernestine S. Elster (editors)
    1986   *Excavations at Sitagroi, A Prehistoric Village in Northeast Greece*, Vol.
            1. Monumenta Archaeologica 13. UCLA Institute of
            Archaeology, Los Angeles.
Renfrew, Colin, and Elizabeth Slater
    2003   Metal artifacts and metallurgy. In *Prehistoric Sitagroi: Excavations
            in Northeast Greece, 1968–1970*, Vol. 2: *The Final Report*, edited by
            Ernestine S. Elster and Colin Renfrew, pp. 301–322. Monumenta
            Archaeologica 20. Cotsen Institute of Archaeology at UCLA, Los
            Angeles.
Rowlands, Michael
    1993   The role of memory in the transmission of culture. *World
            Archaeology* 25 (2):141–151.
Sackett, James R.
    1977   The meaning of style in archaeology: A general model. *American
            Antiquity* 42 (3):369–80.
    1990   Style and ethnicity in archaeology: The case for isochretism. In
            The Uses of Style in Archaeology, edited by Margaret Conkey and
            Christine Hastorf, pp. 32–43. New Directions in Archaeology.
            Cambridge University Press, Cambridge.
Schlanger, Nathan
    1994   Mindful technology: Unleashing the *chaîne opératoire* for an
            archaeology of mind. In *The Ancient Mind: Elements of Cognitive
            Archaeology*, edited by Colin Renfrew and Ezra B.W. Zubrow, pp.

143–151. New Directions in Archaeology. Cambridge University Press, Cambridge.

Séfériades, Michel L.
2000   *Spondylus gaederopus*: Some observations on the earliest European long distance exchange system. In *Karanovo, Band III: Beiträge zum Neolithikum in Südosteuropa*, pp. 423–437. Phoibos Verlag, Vienna.

Shackleton, Nicholas
2003   Preliminary report on the molluscan remains from Sitagroi. In *Prehistoric Sitagroi: Excavations in Northeast Greece, 1968–1970*, Vol. 2: *The Final Report*, edited by Ernestine S. Elster and Colin Renfrew, pp. 361– 365. Monumenta Archaeologica 20. Cotsen Institute of Archaeology at UCLA, Los Angeles.

Sherratt, Andrew
1984   Social evolution: Europe in the Later Neolithic and Copper Ages. In *European Social Evolution: Archaeological Perspectives*, edited by John Bintliff, pp. 123–134. University of Bradford, Bradford.
1993   What would a Bronze Age world-system look like? Relations between temperate Europe and the Mediterranean in later prehistory. *Journal of European Archaeology* 1 (2):1–57.

Stevanovic, Mirjana
1997   The age of clay: The social dynamics of house construction. *Journal of Anthropological Archaeology* 16:334–395.

Talalay, Lauren
1993   *Deities, Dolls and Devices: Neolithic Figurines from Franchthi Cave, Greece*. Excavations at Franchthi Cave, Greece, Fascicle 9. Indiana University Press, Bloomington and Indianapolis.

Theocharis, Demetrios R.
1981   *Neolithikos politismos: Syntomi episkopisi tis Neolithikis ston elladiko choro*. National Bank of Greece, Athens.

Trubitt, Mary Beth
2003   The production and exchange of marine shell prestige goods. *Journal of Archaeological Research* 11 (3):243–277.

Tsuneki, Akira
1989   The manufacture of *Spondylus* shell objects at Neolithic Dimini, Greece. *Orient* 25:1–21.

Tringham, Ruth
1991   Households with faces: The challenge of gender in prehistoric architectural remains. In *Engendering Archaeology: Women and Prehistory*, edited by Joanne M. Gero and Margaret Conkey, pp. 93–131. Basil Blackwell, Oxford.

Turner, Victor
1974   *Dramas, Fields and Metaphors: Symbolic Action in Human Societies*. Cornell University Press, Ithaca.

Van der Leeuw, Sander
   1992   Giving the potter a choice: Conceptual aspects of pottery tech-
           niques. In *Technological Choices: Transformation in Material Cultures
           since the Neolithic*, edited by Pierre Lemonnier, pp. 238–288.
           London and New York, Routledge.
Van Gennep, A.
   1960   *The Rites of Passage*. Translated by Monika B. Vizedom and
           Gabrielle L. Caffee. University of Chicago Press, Chicago.
Vidal, Jean Marie
   1985   Symboles et symboliques. In *Le symbolisme dans le culte des grands
           religions*. Actes du Colloque de Louvain-la-Neuve, 4–5 Octobre
           1983, edited by Julien Ries. Homo Religiosus 11. Centre d'
           Histoire des Religions, Louvain-la-Neuve.
Vitelli, Karen D.
   1993   *Franchthi Neolithic Pottery*, Vol. 1: *Classification and Ceramic Phases
           1 and 2*. Excavations at Franchthi Cave, Greece, Fascicle 8.
           Indiana University Press, Bloomington and Indianapolis.
   1999   *Franchthi Neolithic Pottery*, Vol. 2: *The Later Neolithic Ceramic
           Phases 3 to 5*. Excavations at Franchthi Cave, Greece, Fascicle 10.
           Indiana University Press, Bloomington and Indianapolis.
Wagner, Roy
   1975   *The Invention of Culture*. Prentice Hall, Englewood Cliffs, NJ.
Whittle, Alasdair
   2006   *The Archaeology of People: Dimensions of Neolithic Life*. Routledge,
           London and New York.
Williams, Sarah
   1987   An "archaeology" of Turkana beads. In *The Archaeology of
           Contextual Meanings*, edited by Ian Hodder, pp. 31–38.
           Cambridge University Press, Cambridge.
Willms, Christoph
   1985   Neolithischer *Spondylus*schmuck: Hundert Jahre Forschung.
           Germania 63 (2):331–343.
Yannouli, Eftychia
   1997   Dimitra, a Neolithic and Early Bronze Age site in Northern
           Greece: The faunal remains. In *Neolithiki Makedonia*, Meros I.
           *Dimitra: Proistorikos oikismos konta stis Serres. I anaskafi ton eton
           1978, 1979, 1980*, edited by Dimitrios Grammenos, pp. 101–127.
           Ypourgeio Politismou, Tameio Archaiologikon Poron, Athens.

10.

COGNITION, RELIGIOUS RITUAL, AND ARCHAEOLOGY

Robert N. McCauley and E. Thomas Lawson

The emergence of cognitive science has stimulated new approaches to traditional problems and materials in well-established disciplines. Those approaches have generated new insights and reinvigorated aspirations for theories in the sociocultural sciences that are both more systematic and more accountable empirically than available alternatives. Projects in the cognitive science of religion and in cognitive archaeology seek to redress imbalances within those disciplines favoring the interpretive over the explanatory, without reviving any sort of scientistic or explanatory exclusivism. In both archaeology and religious studies, new subfields have begun to thrive, which take theoretical inspiration from cognitive science and sometimes deploy its findings and, in the case of the cognitive science of religion, even its methods in the course of testing their theories. This paper contains three sections. The first provides a framework for thinking about the constituents of culture as a means for situating ritual and for considering its accessibility to cognitive and archaeological analysis. The second outlines our theory of religious ritual competence and the ritual form hypothesis. The third reviews the theory's predictions about various properties of individual religious rituals and religious ritual systems and speculates about the theory's possible implications for some archaeological matters. At the end of the paper is a glossary of technical terms from our theory of religious ritual.

The emergence of cognitive science over the past thirty years has stimulated new approaches to traditional problems and materials in well-established disciplines. Those approaches have generated new insights and reinvigorated aspirations for theories in the sciences of the sociocultural (about the structures and uses of symbols and the cognitive processes underlying them) that are both more systematic and more accountable empirically than the recently available alternatives. Without rejecting interpretive proposals, projects in both the cognitive science of religion and in cognitive archaeology seek to redress imbalances within those disciplines favoring the interpretive over the explanatory (Lawson and McCauley 1990; Renfrew 1994a). Both projects aim to reinvigorate scientific aspirations without reviving any sort of scientistic or explanatory *exclusivism*. Both have arisen, in part, in response to the science-bashing crusades that have enjoyed such prominence in both disciplines over the past twenty years.

With the exception, perhaps, of linguistics, the influence of cognitive science has been as notable in archaeology and religious studies as it has been in any discipline in contemporary intellectual life. In both disciplines, new subfields have begun to thrive, which take theoretical inspiration from cognitive science and, at least sometimes, deploy its findings and, in the case of the cognitive science of religion, even its methods in the course of testing their theories.

This paper contains three sections. The first provides a framework for thinking about the constituents of culture as a means both for situating ritual and for considering its accessibility to cognitive and archaeological analysis. The second section outlines our theory of religious ritual competence and the ritual form hypothesis. The final section reviews the theory's predictions about an assortment of properties of both individual religious rituals and religious ritual systems. It includes occasional speculations about some of the theory's possible implications for some archaeological matters.

A word of caution before we begin: we are not archaeologists. Our knowledge of that field is slight. Speculating (anywhere other than, by invitation, here) about how any aspect of our theory might bear on archaeologists' positions or findings or activities (especially their activities in the field) would border on unbridled presumption. Because of a broad coincidence in our orientations, what comments we do offer look primarily at resonances and connections with work in cognitive archaeology.

THE CONSTITUENTS OF CULTURE

A central assumption of Dan Sperber's (1996) "epidemiological" approach to culture is that culture is constituted in part through distributions of beliefs in populations of human minds. Humans have all sorts of beliefs. Every human mind contains various idiosyncratic beliefs. Probably, human minds also automatically develop some intuitive beliefs in common. (Tooby and Cosmides [1992] have suggested that the range and variety of this kind of intuitive belief may be far greater than previously suspected.) Human minds also contain other beliefs, both intuitive and reflective, that seem to manifest striking similarities across individuals but have originated neither as a part of our built-in equipment nor as a standard development thereof, but rather on the basis of communication with other people in the course of humans making their ways in the world. Cultures change, in part, because the frequencies of those communicated beliefs change within populations of human minds.

That such regularities across individual minds should exist at all among these communicated beliefs is surprising at one level, according to Sperber (1996:106–112), in light of the vagueness and the vagaries of human communication and the tendencies of human minds to misunderstand, to misremember, and to play around with ideas. Sperber insists that communication usually does *not* result in the replication of beliefs, but rather in their alteration. Consequently, among other things, this new psychologically grounded account of culture must survey the cognitive variables that influence the shapes of these beliefs as well as their persistence, their proliferation, and their resulting distributions. The shift to the subpersonal, cognitive level is vital, however, since detecting such distributions of beliefs is not the same thing as explaining them. A central question concerns how cognitive processes constrain both the forms of these beliefs and their transmission.

Nonetheless, this position entails no drastic psychological reductionism. That is because, first of all, it is not out to explain everything about culture. Second, these widespread, enduring, communicated beliefs are by no means the whole story about culture. They are only a subset of the class of "cultural representations" (Sperber 1996:25). An epidemiological approach to culture highlights the causal interactions between these beliefs and a second sort of cultural representation, which Sperber (1996: 61–62) calls "public representations." Public representations of culture basically come in two forms: (1) artifacts (broadly construed to include structured environments as well as tools) and (2) practices.

It is with this addition of talk about these two sorts of public representations that a framework arises within which we can situate the central notions that this paper addresses. So, archaeologists study, among other things, the public representations of culture that are artifacts (again, broadly construed), primarily from past human groups. The public representations of culture that are practices include ritual. An archaeology of ritual focuses on the causal relations between ritual and artifacts as public representations of culture. Cognitive approaches in archaeology, cognitive approaches to ritual, and cognitive approaches to culture, generally, exploit, among other things, the theoretical, substantive, and methodological resources of the cognitive sciences in order to gain insights about the underlying psychological and cognitive constraints that shape these public representations and their connections. These approaches offer promise for such inquiries for at least two reasons. First, public representations of culture (whether artifacts or practices) occupy that status because human minds either do possess or have possessed (relevant) mental representations. Second, presumptions about conceptual relations between artifacts and practices providing clues about their causal relations reliably depend on assumptions that such conceptual relations are at least represented mentally, if not constituted and mediated mentally as well (figure 10.1). This calls for elaboration.

Virtually all of the public representations that are objects are artifacts.[1] These artifacts include everything from clothes, icons, and gardens to tools, texts, and temples. They are the parts of the natural world that humans have intentionally altered and structured to serve their own purposes. In and of themselves, these objects are not topics of direct psychological investigation, although, as cognitive archaeologists have stressed, human beings have plenty of states of mind and mental representations (that cognitive scientists may study in living human beings) pertaining to such objects. In fact, on Sperber's epidemiological account of culture, humans must have (or have had) these mental representations for these objects to exist as public representations of culture at all. As Sperber (1996:81) notes, public representations of culture "have meaning only through being associated with mental representations." Cognitive scientists are continuing to develop ever more sophisticated means for acquiring empirical evidence about the character of those mental representations. Cognitive archaeologists have made valuable contributions here by investigating the inferences that can be drawn about mental representations on the basis of the remnants of the material cultures available (Mithen 1996; Renfrew and Scarre 1998).

Typically, the mental representations and states of mind pertaining to artifacts are tied up with various practices associated with those objects. It

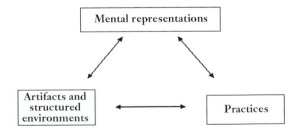

FIGURE 10.1. Causal relations among cultural representations.

is such bonds that enable archaeology to contribute to our understanding both of cultural practices and of the accompanying mental representations (Renfrew 1994b:51). Such practices concern language, education, agriculture, politics, religion, art, science, and more. The link between practices and mental representations is, perhaps, even more transparent than is the one between mental representations and artifacts. That practices are practices, and that they are the specific practices that they are, clearly depend at least as much upon people's mental representations as they do upon those practices' publicly available properties.[2]

This is particularly true about rituals. That the practices that constitute a wedding are the practices that constitute a wedding depends crucially upon the participants' beliefs about those practices. Our theory of religious ritual competence examines the underlying psychological and cognitive constraints that shape this particular type of cultural practice (Lawson and McCauley 1990; McCauley and Lawson 2002). The cognitive approach to the study of ritual concentrates (1) on the similarities among the mental representations that people possess about ritual actions, (2) on cognitive explanations of those similarities, and (3) on the implications of the cognitive theories behind those explanations for further explaining a variety of rituals and ritual systems' features.

The strategy of studying ritual by attending to the mental representations that accompany those cultural practices offers some significant advantages. Approaching ritual or any other cultural phenomenon in this way increases the prospects for testing hypotheses experimentally, since the cognitive sciences generally and psychology especially have developed far more extensive and sophisticated experimental means for testing theories than have the social sciences. Moreover, minds and brains (even more so) are both more discrete and more localized than cultural systems are. We do not wish to overplay this last point, though, since it touches directly on the relationship of the cognitive approach to ritual and cognitive archaeology. Let us explain.

The causal arrows in figure 10.1 are all bidirectional. No doubt, for many explanatory purposes, our skulls basically limn the contours of our cognitive systems. However, if for no other reasons than the pervasive and pivotal roles of perception and action for the human cognitive economy, for many other explanatory purposes cognitive analyses of culture will not only require the examination of the causal relationships between mental representations and public representations (both artifacts and practices); they will also often require the inclusion of both public representations and those causal relationships in their characterizations of the relevant cognitive processes. Cognizing—and cultural cognizing, in particular—is regularly situated cognizing (Hutchins 1994). Or, alternatively, if not our minds, then certainly our mentality constantly extends into the external environment, which is to say that it extends into the public representations of culture. Carrying out what may initially seem like thoroughly cognitive tasks commonly involves explanatory appeals to public representations. So, for example, I can "remember" what to take to the office each day by consulting a list I compile across the previous day that is left by the door to the carport. Remembering here employs an external tool that enables me to gather the items that I will need at considerable temporal remove from when they came to mind. My mnemonic skill in this case unequivocally depends on structures outside of my cranium that I have imposed on the environment.[3]

Cognitive scientists such as Merlin Donald (1991), William Bechtel (1996), and Andy Clark (1997) have underscored the vital role that external prosthetic devices often play in our cognitive accomplishments. Our species' development of language[4] (at least tens of thousands of years ago) and the technology of literacy (a few thousand years ago) have driven the most profound changes in our cognitive abilities. By imposing structures on our environments and especially by imposing coded, symbolic structures on them, we expand our cognitive horizons by according things in the world—from the books that fill our libraries to the World Wide Web—roles to play in our cognitive processing, transforming the materials in question into cognitive devices.

Human beings are often incapable of solving problems without such tools. Try multiplying two four-digit numbers without using one of these tools or another. As Matthew Day (2004a:107) notes, even "for . . . problems like this run-of-the-mill multiplication task, the solution is often unthinkable without the aid of these cognitive artifacts." An important debate within the contemporary cognitive science of religion concerns the extent to which religious cognition depends upon possessing such external cognitive artifacts.

Pascal Boyer (1994a, 2001) has tended to downplay the place of such external cognitive gadgetry in religious cognition. Boyer argues that religious cognition is the natural outcome of common variations across a constellation of internal, domain-specific, cognitive dispositions that have evolved in the human mind. In his view, religious representations readily arise in human minds, and once they do, they are particularly likely to persist and get transmitted to other minds. Religious representations are ideas that human minds find good to think. Religious artifacts play a prominent role only in the transmission of religious ideas (if even there). They may enhance the appeal of religious ideas, but for Boyer, those ideas originate and persist in human minds because of their intrinsic psychological appeal.

It should come as no surprise that cognitive archaeologists put greater emphasis on the role of external over internal cognitive equipment and on the role of such equipment in religious cognition, in particular. Their objects of study, after all, are the cognitive accessories that are outside of human heads. Cognitive archaeologists raise two pivotal issues, at least about cognition. The first concerns what kind of mind it takes to have created such artifacts. The second, which is the issue at hand, deals with what such artifacts enable these minds to do. When he claims that "we transform religious ideas into material form so that we can perform operations on them which are beyond the capacity of the mind," Steven Mithen (1997:72) falls short of adopting the strong position Day scouted above, since he does not hold that all religious ideas depend upon such artifacts for their creation. But he and other cognitive archaeologists argue, in effect, that accounts of religious cognition, let alone of religion, will prove needlessly impoverished and, at least some of the time, notably incomplete, if they ignore the contributions that public representations of culture play (Renfrew 1998:2).

We agree with Boyer that religious cognition, at least comparatively speaking, involves forms of thought that human beings find much easier and more natural to handle than they do many others (for example, many of the forms of thought necessary for doing science) (McCauley 1999a, 2000a). Furthermore, since we discover almost none of our tools in nature fully formed, it seems fairly clear that activities inside human heads bear the principal responsibility for getting this synergistic relationship between our mental states and aspects of the external environment rolling. This is why the fabrication of tools plays such a prominent role in the discussions of both archaeologists and primatologists (Mithen 1996; Boesch and Boesch 1993). But those observations do not diminish the importance of Day's argument (2004b) that those tools regularly provide a "scaffold" that is indispensable to many of our subsequent cognitive activities and achievements. The simple storage of information in texts, instead of in human memories, is probably the most obvious illustration and a topic to which we return at the end of this section.

When construing ritual as the outcome of situated cognition, exploring the connections between cognitive theorizing about ritual and the cognitive archaeology of ritual brings us to the crossroads of this debate. Ritual performances, no less than spoken words, are transitory public representations of culture (see n. 4). Ritual is neither the cognitive dispositions and representations that constitute ritual knowledge and inform ritual performance that our theory discusses, nor the artifacts and structured environments that are inevitably associated with performances that cognitive archaeologists study. These are, however, from the standpoint of this more liberal cognitive approach to culture, the two key variables (internal and external, respectively) that shape, constrain, and illuminate ritual performances.

Like any other archaeologists interested in ritual, cognitive archaeologists scrutinize artifacts in order to obtain evidence about rituals. However, cognitive archaeologists must also remain alert to the bearing of material culture on the guiding questions in their field—namely, what do artifacts show about the minds that created them, and what do those artifacts enable those minds to do? Cognitive archaeologists attend to the clues that artifacts offer about their creators' psychological states and cognitive accomplishments. Thus, they burden themselves with an extra problem, but they also enjoy an extra set of inferential opportunities. A culture's artifacts and its practices not only provide evidence about one another, they also constitute evidence about cultural participants' mental representations (Mithen 1996). Consistent with the comprehensive set of possibilities that figure 10.1 illustrates, though, the crucial point for our purposes here is that independent evidence from cognitive science about cultural participants' mental representations can offer insights about their public representations too. Our theory analyzes the links between participants' mental representations and their ritual practices. The hope here is that summarizing its major commitments in the next section will spur archaeologists' reflections on these matters in some useful way.

Whether our specific theory will prove helpful or not, the framework we have sketched suggests adding a fifth type to Colin Renfrew's (1985:12–13) list of four types of evidence available to anthropologists about cultural participants' mental representations pertaining to ritual. Renfrew cites:

1. verbal testimony (both oral and written),

2. direct observation of practices,

3. nonverbal records (e.g., depictions documenting beliefs and practices), and

4. material culture (both artifacts and structured environments).

To this list we propose adding cognitive and psychological evidence about the mental representations of religious ritual participants.

This evidence comes in two forms: ethnographic (Abbink 1995) and experimental (Malley and Barrett 2003). Behind the contention that experimental evidence from contemporary populations of subjects may have some bearing on archaeologists' proposals about past cultures stand assumptions about features of human minds that have persisted for dozens of millennia in the face of considerable cultural variability, as Boyer is wont to stress. This is hardly less true about the applicability of ethnographic evidence in an age in which scarcely a single place on earth that humans inhabit remains untouched by radio, air travel, television sets, T-shirts, and baseball caps. Wary of evolutionary psychologists' strong claims about fixed mental modules in contemporary human minds, Mithen (1996:164–167) argues for increasing "cognitive fluidity" between these domain-specific capacities over our genus's evolutionary course. Yet even he thinks that such cognitive fluidity results in recurring patterns of religious representations (such as totemism and anthropomorphism) throughout human groups, regardless of their material circumstances.

In contrast to the approaches that have dominated religious studies and the psychology of religion for the last hundred years, the cognitive science of religion looks primarily to cognitive constraints both on the forms of religious representations and on their transmission, rather than to religious experience, to explain these recurring patterns (McCauley 2000b). The two most important rationales that researchers cite are, first, that many participants in religious systems do not have anything that either they or those who study them are inclined to describe as uniquely religious experiences, and, second, that whatever role extraordinary experience may play in the generation of religious representations, those representations inevitably encounter selection pressures in the course of their transmission. Their successful transmission turns on their assuming forms that are, at least, recognizable, attention grabbing, memorable, motivating, and communicable. Boyer (1994b, 1999, 2001) has discussed the first three of these considerations at length and in detail. In our discussions of religious ritual, we have focused on the third and the fourth, that is, on memory and motivation (McCauley 1999b; McCauley and Lawson 2002).

In reflecting on the contributions of material culture to our cognitive accomplishments, we noted earlier that probably the most conspicuous example is how we use written materials, instead of our memories, to store information. Literacy can promote the preservation, propagation, and elaboration of religious representations, including rituals, just as it can with any other cultural form. This may well be why Renfrew lists verbal testimony, including written verbal testimony, first among the forms of evidence available to anthropologists (and archaeologists) interested in ritual (Whitehouse and Martin 2004).

Nonetheless, it is nonliterate (and overwhelmingly illiterate) societies that occasion the most interesting questions for a cognitive theory of ritual, for at least three reasons. First, our theory looks to recurrent features of the human mind to account for some of the recurrent features of religious ritual. It does not follow on our account that literacy does not matter, but it does follow that with respect to the recurrent features in question, it probably does not matter nearly as much as it does on other fronts. The forms the theory describes should be ones that all religious ritual systems manifest. Second, religion predates literacy. Religious representations first erupted and were transmitted among our ancestors before anyone had ever thought of written linguistic symbols. Third, without the aid of lasting public representations of linguistic symbols, the dynamics of human memory abetted only by non-linguistic artifacts disclose a clear cognitive core to these cultural questions. Without the aid of texts, the responsibility not only for remembering what rituals are about but for remembering the rituals themselves falls to individual human memories and their external, non-linguistic, cognitive contrivances.

We raise this point because human memory abetted only by non-linguistic artifacts is precisely the circumstance in which archaeology would seem particularly well suited to contribute to our knowledge about ritual. Relevant anthropological evidence indicates, however, that in small-scale societies at least, drawing inferences about either rituals or participants' mental representations in nonliterate societies, where the only lasting public representations are non-linguistic, is tricky business. If that is so, then presumably, any aid a cognitive theory of ritual might supply should be welcome.

The most orderly connections that Fredrik Barth (1975:207–231) finds among the Baktaman (a nonliterate, small-scale society in the highlands of New Guinea) are what he calls "analogic coding." Analogic coding exhibits neither any "logical closure" nor some "limited set of alternatives" (Barth 1975:208, 229). Each setting in which the Baktaman reuse a ritual artifact involves what are otherwise undisclosed symbolic nuances. As often as not, they invite new interpretations that introduce new values for these various artifacts (Barth 1987:76). "The medium is one of metaphor, as in the manipulation of sacred concrete objects and ritual acts to generate statements about fertility, dependence, etc." (Barth 1987:75). The underlying metaphors are "non-verbal" because the symbols are non-linguistic, concrete artifacts, and because the Baktaman are either unwilling to articulate these symbolic relations or are incapable of doing so.[5]

Barth (1987:76) holds that participants possess this analogically coded knowledge intuitively. The anthropologist cannot reduce such knowledge to unambiguous propositional form, but this does not entail that either its contents or, especially, its effects are utterly random. "The medium in which the knowledge is cast allows other and rich forms of understanding" (Barth 1987:76). The inevitable vagueness surrounding these artifacts and rituals' contents requires that an analysis of transmission highlights neither "the sayable" nor "[the] said" but only what is "received," "reactivated," and constantly re-created via those metaphors and idioms that "catch on and are re-used."

Two comments are in order here. First, Barth's more detailed comments about those other, rich forms of understanding that analogic coding facilitates concern the artifacts and rituals' effects (rather than any putative contents). The male initiations, on which Barth (1987:79) focuses, transform "a group of young persons into men" who possess "a general area of common sensibilities and intuitions" and "a range of understandings sufficient so its members can be moved by the same symbols and thoughts." Baktaman initiations instill in the initiate distinctive cognitive dispositions and sensibilities concerning self, cohort, society, and Nature, as opposed to any clear symbolic contents. Second, although he characterizes his specific approach as "generative," Barth's project can also be fairly described as "epidemiological." He (Barth 1987:28) maintains that "every person's mind is full of representations of cultural objects, which are handled by mental processes and in due course give shape to the person's acts." For Barth, like Sperber, the chief task is to delineate the causal variables that shape the distributions of cultural representations.

In the next section, we will, in addition to outlining our theory, briefly sketch, near the end, some of its implications for an epidemiological analysis of one salient cognitive variable that shapes religious rituals: memory. The necessary conditions for the successful transmission of cultural representations that we enumerated above dictate that remembering rituals and creating the sort of social psychological effects that Barth describes (particularly motivating participants to transmit the relevant mental representations to appropriate others) are key selection pressures shaping a religious system's rituals.[6] Although we have discussed both, we focus on the former here. We have argued that rituals' mnemonic effects are precisely ones that the experimental literature in cognitive psychology suggests make for enhanced accuracy. We have also argued, though, that whatever accuracy of recall is achieved is not to ensure the faithful transmission of contents so much as it is to increase the probability of a communal sense of continuity in the transmission of cultural materials and to decrease the probability of introducing socially divisive variations (McCauley 1999b; McCauley and Lawson, 2002).

THE THEORY OF RELIGIOUS RITUAL COMPETENCE

Theorizing about religious ritual systems from a cognitive viewpoint involves (1) modeling cognitive processes and their products and (2) demonstrating their influence on religious behavior. Particularly important for such an approach to the study of religious ritual is the modeling of participants' representations of ritual form.

The theory of religious ritual competence models the *tacit* knowledge that participants possess about their religious rituals. The principal evidence about that competence is the rich body of intuitions participants have about a variety of features concerning their rituals that pointed investigations can tap (McCauley and Lawson 2002:4–6).

The theory's most basic commitment is that the cognitive apparatus for the representation of religious ritual form is the same system deployed for the representation of action in general. The differences between everyday action and religious ritual action turn out to be fairly minor from the standpoint of their cognitive representation. This system for the representation of action includes representations of agents. Whether we focus on an everyday action, such as closing a door, or a ritual action, such as initiating a person into a religious group, our understanding of these forms of behavior as actions *at all* turns critically on recognizing agents.

The theory's second crucial commitment is that the roles of agents possessing counterintuitive properties (CI-agents[7] hereafter) in participants' representations of religious rituals will prove pivotal in accounting for a wide variety of those rituals' properties. "For effective ritual, the deity . . . must in some sense be present" (Renfrew 1985:18). By examining how ritual participants represent the "presence" of CI-agents in their rituals, the theory accounts systematically for a constellation of religious rituals' varying features.

The claim that this commitment to the existence of CI-agents is the most decisive recurrent feature of religion across cultures is controversial. With everything in mind from Theravada Buddhism to Marxism to football, some scholars maintain that presumptions about CI-agents are not critically important to religious phenomena. In this view, cheering at football games or marching on May Day are just as much religious rituals as sacrificing pigs to the ancestors. Perhaps, but in that case what we have, then, may not be a theory of religious ritual. Instead, it is only a theory about actions that individuals and groups repeatedly perform within organized communities of people who possess conceptual schemes that include presumptions about those actions' connections with the actions of agents who exhibit various counterintuitive properties. If that is not religion (and religious ritual), so be it, but we suspect that this description covers virtually every uncontroversial case that anyone would be inclined, at least pre-theoretically, to include as an instance of religion and very few of the cases they would be inclined to exclude.

Rituals often occasion an astonishingly wide range of interpretations from both participants and observers. The meanings associated with rituals may vary, but such variability typically has no effect on the stability of the rituals' underlying forms. Although they have brought nearly as many interpretations as the times and places from which they hail, pilgrims to Mecca continue to circumambulate the Ka'bah the same way year after year. Not only do other things matter besides meanings, for some explanatory purposes meanings may hardly matter. See, for example, Jason Slone's (2004) account of the absence of nuns in contemporary Theravada Buddhism. We think that much about religious rituals' forms are overwhelmingly independent of meanings. There is also a respect in which some very general features of ritual form are independent not only of meanings but even of specifically cultural details. In other words, these very general features of religious ritual form are independent of both semantic and cultural contents. Clarifying these general features of action is valuable for distinguishing the roles CI-agents can play in participants' representations of their religious rituals.

The action representation system humans possess imposes fundamental, though commonplace, constraints on ritual form. Attention to these constraints enables us to look beyond the variability of religious rituals' details to some of their most general underlying properties. The crucial point is that religious rituals (despite their various unusual qualities) are actions too. Postulating special machinery to account for the representation of religious rituals is unnecessary. The requisite cognitive equipment is already available. A wide range of evidence from developmental psychology indicates that from early infancy, human beings represent agents and the actions they perform very differently from the ways they represent other entities and events (Michotte 1963; Rochat 2001). Developmental psychologists have discovered that infants know (and therefore are capable of representing) the difference between the agent and the patient of an action as well as whether the patient is just an inanimate object or also an agent capable of acting too. This is to say that they distinguish the vital action roles from one another as well as the sorts of entities capable of filling each (Leslie 1995).

Humans pick out agents on the basis of a host of cues concerning such things as characteristic structures, motions, and behaviors. So, agents have faces and bodies with bilateral, vertical symmetry. They are self-moving, often with irregular but goal-directed motions, paths, and speeds, and they have particular facial and bodily motions that correlate with various emotional and intentional states. At as early as nine months, we seem capable not merely of recognizing agents but of attributing goals to them (Rochat 2001). By roughly the age of four, a child grasps that human agents' understanding of their world depends upon how their minds represent it (Perner et al. 1987; Wimmer and Perner 1983). Children recognize agents' intentionality—that is, they formulate mental representations of other people's mental representations. They come to understand that what people do (usually) depends upon how they represent their actions to themselves. By roughly school age, children have obtained all of the fundamental presumptions built into what developmental psychologists call a "theory of mind"—a theory that may undergo further elaboration but whose basic assumptions undergo no substantial change thereafter (Wellman 1990). This cognitive machinery for the representation of agency and action seems task specific, and it is (with only a few exceptions) ubiquitous among human beings (Baron Cohen 1995). The representation of religious rituals requires no special cognitive apparatus beyond this garden-variety cognitive machinery that all normal human beings possess.

Agents and their agency are clearly the pivotal concepts for the representation of action, but they are not the whole story. A basic representational framework for characterizing this special sort of event must also capture familiar presumptions about the internal structures and external relations of actions too. The action representation system captures basic action structures, which, among other things,

- ❑ include the roles (agents, acts, instruments, and patients) that distinguish actions (and rituals) from other events and happenings,

- ❑ take, as action (and ritual) elements, the various entities and acts, as well as their properties, qualities, and conditions, that can fulfill these roles in actions (and religious rituals),

- ❑ reflect the constraint that, although any item filling the role of the agent may also serve as a patient, not all items that serve as patients may also fill the agent role,

❑ reveal points of variability in the forms of actions such as whether they involve the use of instruments as a condition of the act, and

❑ accommodate the enabling relationships between actions, such as whether the performance of one act presupposes the performance of another.

Normal human beings have a ready intuitive grasp of all of these matters.

Since all religious rituals in our theory consist of agents acting upon patients, a description of a religious ritual's structure will include three ordered slots for representing a religious ritual's three fundamental roles: its agent, the act, and its patient. All of a ritual's details fall within the purview of one or the other of these three roles (figure 10.2).

Our claim that all religious rituals (as opposed to religious action more broadly construed) include an agent doing something to a patient departs from popular assumptions. Priests sacrifice goats, ritual partici-pants burn offerings, and pilgrims circle shrines, but people also pray, sing, chant, and kneel. Even though such religious activities may be parts of religious rituals, in and of themselves they do not qualify as religious rituals in our theory's technical sense. In our theory, all religious rituals are inevitably connected sooner or later with actions in which CI-agents putatively play a role *and* bring about some explicitly describable change

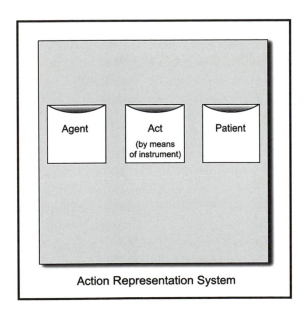

FIGURE 10.2. Action representation system.

in the religious world. So, initiations are religious rituals in this account. In participants' representations of initiations, CI-agents are ultimately responsible for the initiate's change in religious status. Sometimes those CI-agents participate directly. Frequently, initiations culminate in meeting the CI-agent face to face (Renfrew 1985:18). Often, though, this link to the actions of CI-agents is indirect. CI-agents can act through their ritually appointed intermediaries, such as an ordained priest.

We advance this restricted notion of religious rituals for four reasons. The first is that invariably, religious rituals, unlike mere religious acts, bring about changes in the religious world (temporary in some cases, permanent in others) by virtue of the fact that they involve transactions with CI-agents. Those interactions affect, on the basis of intersubjectively available information, to what or whom anyone can subsequently apply the religious category associated with this act, and that application does not turn on the participants' states of mind. So, for example, if the priest baptizes Paul, then henceforth the term "baptized" may be used to describe Paul, regardless of Paul's or the priest's state of mind when the ritual occurred. (What will matter is only that the priest qualifies as an appropriate ritual agent, which itself turns on the priest's own ritual history.) In short, religious rituals in our technical sense are religious acts that cannot be faked. This is not true about religious actions (such as prayer) that are not rituals in this more restricted sense.

Second, religious rituals are distinguishable on the basis of what we have called an "insider-outsider criterion." Although mere religious actions are typically open to outsiders, religious rituals are restricted in some way. (Who counts as an outsider may change over time.) A non-Catholic is welcome to pray with Catholics but not to take the Eucharist. Although anyone can practice yoga, only Brahman boys can be invested with the sacred thread (Penner 1975). Excepting "entry-level" rituals (for example, for juniors or new converts), those who are not participants in the religious system are not eligible to participate in that system's rituals. The third consideration is that rituals are invariably associated with other rituals. Other sorts of religious actions need not be. Again, excepting entry-level rituals, participating in religious rituals turns unwaveringly on having performed earlier religious rituals. A Jew must have gone through his bar mitzvah in order to qualify to become a rabbi, but that is not necessary for him to be eligible to pray. Below we develop this idea further in the discussion of the embedding of what we call "enabling" rituals within the representations of rituals. The fourth ground for employing our technical sense of the term "religious ritual" simply looks to the theory's explanatory success (and to the success of the resulting research program the theory inspires). If a theory is successful on many fronts, then that fact is relevant to the defense of any of its details.

The action representation system can represent ritually salient qualities and properties of the agents, actions, and patients. This includes specifying what makes the agent eligible to perform the action, what properties a particular act must possess, as well as the qualities of the patients that make them eligible to serve in that role. The conceptual schemes of particular religious systems will designate which qualities and properties matter. A cognitive representation of a religious ritual will include the formal features that determine participants' judgments about that ritual's status, efficacy, and relationships to other ritual acts.

Just as participants possess qualities and properties that may require specification, sometimes conditions on ritual actions do too. Rituals sometimes require fulfilling particular conditions for their execution; for example, carrying out some task may require particular instruments. Ritual agents often need specific tools in order to do their jobs properly. These tools can be anything the tradition permits: antelope bones for divining, sharp stones for circumcisions, red ocher for coloring corpses, or nettles for whipping initiates. Instruments, however, should not be confused functionally with agents (though religious conceptual schemes sometimes include entries that conflate them ontologically; Boyer 2001). For example, a priest uses incense to sanctify a house or uses rocks of a particular shape to establish a temple site. While these instruments are not the agents, they often specify necessary conditions for the success of the agents' ritual actions. If so, it is only by virtue of their ritually mediated affinities with superhuman agency that they derive their efficacy. (Water that has not been consecrated is just plain old water.) The action representation system includes resources for representing the instruments agents employ (the water) as well as their qualities that the conceptual scheme defines as relevant (that it has undergone an earlier ritual sanctifying it). A complete representation of a ritual will, at least, include a representation of an agent with the requisite qualities acting upon a patient with the requisite qualities potentially using an instrument with the requisite qualities.

The most important of the requisite qualities of instruments are their own attachments to CI-agents through the performance of earlier rituals. Making sense of a religious ritual typically involves reference to a larger network of ritual actions. Performing earlier rituals enables the performance of the later ones. Because the priest has blessed the water in the font, participants can use it to bless themselves when they enter the vestibule of a church. These earlier rituals that fulfill necessary conditions for the performance of subsequent rituals are what we call "enabling rituals" (or, more generally, "enabling actions"). In everyday life, actions frequently presuppose the successful completion of previous actions, since those earlier actions fulfill necessary requirements for the performance of the action at hand. For example, operating a car presupposes that someone has put gas in the tank. If there is no direct reference to a CI-agent in a ritual's surface structure, then at least one of its elements must incorporate presumptions about its connections with one or more enabling rituals that eventually implicate a CI-agent. The classic rites of passage offer the best illustrations of these enabling relationships. Consider the sequence of initiation rites among the Zulu. In order for a Zulu male to be eligible for marriage, he has to go through a number of rites of passage, starting with the naming ritual and proceeding through the ear-piercing ritual, the puberty ritual, and the "grouping up ritual" (Lawson and McCauley 1990:113–121). No uninitiated person can initiate the newcomer. Ritual practitioners performing the initiation must have been initiated themselves. (Ritual practitioners are participants who hold some privileged religious status by virtue of which they are able to serve as the proximal agents in some rituals that other participants, who do not share their status, cannot.) Ultimately, the gods are responsible for the initiations through these ties to the ritual practitioner—that is, the immediate ritual agents who serve as the gods' intermediaries.

In the everyday world, the exploration of such presuppositions can go on indefinitely, either by tracing causal chains (the window broke, because the ladder fell and hit it, because the ground on which it rested was damp, and so on) or by concatenating reasons (John flipped the switch, since he wanted to see the room's contents, since he wanted to ascertain whether he could load them into the truck in the next ten minutes, since, if at all possible, he wanted to complete that job before the police arrived, since he wanted to avoid arrest). Religious rituals, while engaging the same representational resources, always presume an end point to such causal or rational explorations. With rituals, things come to an end. Causal chains terminate; reasons find an uncontroversial ground. In short, the buck stops with the gods. The introduction of actions involving CI-agents into the conception of an action introduces considerations that need neither further causal explanation nor further rational justification. Religious rituals can be accorded representational closure by terminating in the deeds of CI-agents. The actions of the gods ground religious rituals' normative force. Despite talk in the humanities and social sciences about civil religion, the religion of art, the rituals of football, or the theology of communism, such systems rarely engender such immediate authoritativeness. Our suggestion is that this is because they rarely involve such appeals to specific actions of CI-agents.

Finally, it is what the gods do that matters in religious ritual. Our theory of the cognitive representation of ritual provides descriptions for religious ritual actions, which are, in one respect, exhaustive. For participants, there is no more momentous cause to locate, no more crucial reason to propose. The actions of the gods guarantee the comprehensiveness of description, because their actions are causally, rationally, and motivationally sufficient for the ritual actions they inspire. The actions of the gods that serve these foundational roles are what our theory characterizes as *hypothetical* religious rituals. They are actions attributed to the gods to which humans appeal in the course of carrying out their own rituals. So, for example, the authority of popes might turn on Jesus's declaration that Saint Peter was the rock on which he would build his church. Participants appeal to such founding "hypothetical rituals" as actions enabling their own religious ritual practices.

Our ability to attribute the category of agency (and the inferences that accompany it) is the most significant piece of ordinary cognitive equipment deployed in the representation of religious rituals. The notion is fundamental in any theory of religious ritual, because it drives our most basic expectations about the form of any action. The identification of action turns critically on the identification of agents. The point is that we import all of our assumptions about agents and their actions when representing CI-agents and rituals. Participants' intuitive assumptions about the psychology of agents purchase them vast amounts of knowledge about CI-agents for free (Boyer 1996). So, for example, on the basis of knowing that some CI-agent desires X and believes that doing Y will enable her to obtain X, participants will know that it is likely that the CI-agent in question will do Y. Or knowing that the ancestors are easily offended if they are not offered the best available foods, and that they are likely to cause mischief in the community when they are offended, participants will recognize that they should ensure that the ancestors are well fed. Or, again, knowing that the gods have thought carefully about the laws they have instituted for human conduct, participants know that violations of those laws will likely provoke angry responses from the gods. The "specialness" of religious rituals, then, does not turn on anomalies in their basic action structures or with irregularities in the way that CI-agents exercise their agency. Qua agents, CI-agents are quite similar to human agents; that is why we can so readily draw inferences about their actions, their goals, their desires, and their other states of mind.

On a few fronts, though, CI-agents differ decisively from human agents, and it is those differences that make representations of religious rituals different from representations of ordinary actions. CI-agents possess various counterintuitive properties. As Boyer argues, those properties arise from violations of the default assumptions associated with basic ontological categories concerning the physical, biological, and psychological realms. So, for example, if something is an agent, then (normally) it is also a physical object and possesses all of the associated physical properties. CI-agents may differ from normal agents in that they *violate* the constraints this superordinate category, "physical object," imposes. Thus, they may pass through solid objects or be everywhere at once. CI-agents may violate constraints that other superordinate categories impose. CI-agents can be eternal, parentless, and capable of recovering from death, and they can know other agents' states of mind (Boyer 2001).

In our theory, then, very little distinguishes religious rituals from other sorts of actions. A religious system's conceptual scheme provides special entries for at least some of the slots in a description of a ritual's structure. For example, the specific acts carried out in religious rituals (such as sacrifices, blessings, consecrations, and so on) are often unique to religious conceptual schemes. Crucially, only with religious rituals do populations of participants carry out actions that routinely presume enabling actions by CI-agents with special counterintuitive properties; and what we might loosely call inquiry about the causal or rational foundations of religious rituals will always come to an end when they invoke the enabling actions of CI-agents.

It is the roles that CI-agents play in rituals' representations that are the critical variables that determine many of their important properties. Our theory identifies two principles for organizing this information about the impact of CI-agents' roles in religious ritual form. They jointly yield a typology of religious ritual forms that systematically organizes the rituals of *any* religious system and accounts for those properties.

The Principles of Superhuman Agency and Superhuman Immediacy categorize descriptions of rituals' structures that participants' action representation systems generate. At a first level of approximation, the Principle of Superhuman Agency (PSA) distinguishes between two kinds of ritual profiles: ones where CI-agents are ritually connected with the agent of a ritual and ones where they are connected with the ritual elements fulfilling one of the other two action roles. *Special agent rituals* are religious rituals in which the most direct link with the gods is through the current ritual's agent. Special agent rituals join the initial appearance of a CI-agent in the action representation with the entity fulfilling the role of the agent in the current ritual. These include such rituals as circumcisions, weddings, and funerals, as well as initiations, consecrations, and ordinations. In these rituals, the CI-agents are, so to speak, in on the action. The second kind of ritual profile concerns those rituals in which the most direct relationship with the gods is through either of the other two roles: through the patient or through the act itself (by way of an instrument). These will bind a CI-agent most directly with the items appearing in the second or third slots in the current ritual's structural description. *Special patient rituals* include sacrifices, rituals of penance, and the Eucharist. By contrast, rituals of divination and many blessings are examples of *special instrument rituals*.

The PSA concerns the character of CI-agents' involvement in a ritual. In assessing religious rituals' forms, the PSA focuses attention on the action role(s) of the current ritual that connects most directly with CI-agents' actions. Participants include at least one CI-agent somewhere in a ritual's full action representation—that is, a representation that includes not only the immediate ritual, but all of the enabling rituals on which it depends. The crucial question concerns where the entry for the CI-agent appears in a ritual's representation (figure 10.3). Whether a ritual is, on the one hand, a special agent ritual or, on the other, a special patient or special instrument ritual determines participants' judgments about numerous ritual properties. Determining which tie to CI-agents in the representation of a religious ritual constitutes the initial entry (the entry with the most "direct connection" to some element in the current ritual) is not too complicated. This is where the Principle of Superhuman Immediacy comes in.

The Principle of Superhuman Immediacy (PSI) states that the number of enabling rituals required to associate some element in the current ritual with an entry for a CI-agent determines that entry's proximity to the current ritual. Specifically, the initial appearance of a CI-agent in a ritual's full representation is the entry whose relationship to some element in the current ritual involves the fewest enabling rituals. For example, in a Christian baptism, at minimum the priest (the agent) and the water (the instrument) have ritually mediated attachments with God. The priest's affinity is more direct, however, since it is mediated by fewer enabling rituals. The water engages at least one additional level of ritual mediation in order to achieve its special status, which arises, after all,

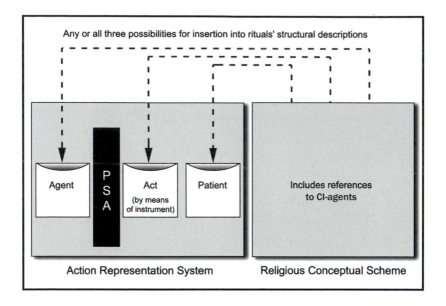

FIGURE 10.3. Principle of superhuman agency.

because it was a priest who consecrated it. So, according to the PSI, since the priest, who is the agent who performs the baptism, has a more direct ritual link with God than the water with which he carries out this ritual, baptism is a special agent ritual.

These two principles identify two aspects of religious ritual form. They concern (1) what role(s) in the current ritual enabling rituals are associated with and (2) how many enabling rituals are required to establish that association between an element in the current ritual and a CI-agent (which we shall refer to as a ritual's "depth"). The principal sources of complexity in rituals' full action representations concern the number and locations of embedded, enabling rituals. No formal considerations set any principled limits on the possible complexity of the full action representations of rituals that the action representation system can generate, though things like memory limitations probably set some practical limitations. The PSA addresses the action *role* (agent, act, or patient) with which enabling rituals establish the most direct connection with the actions of a CI-agent. By contrast, the PSI is concerned with the *number* of enabling actions necessary to establish such a bond. With the various concepts and principles presented above in hand, we can account for a variety of religious rituals' properties.

ACCOUNTING FOR VARIOUS PROPERTIES OF
RELIGIOUS RITUALS

Our comments in this section about our theory's possible ramifications for archaeology concerning the various ritual properties we address are occasional, brief, and speculative. This is the result of both limitations of space and of (our) imagination and competence.

A relationship between at least one element in the immediate ritual and the actions of CI-agents is critical to participants' assessments of both their rituals' well-formedness *and* their efficacy. Absent such presumptions, participants will not judge the ritual in question to be well formed and, consequently, they will judge it as ineffective. Unless eligible agents perform correct actions on eligible patients with the right tools, participants will not judge the ritual successful. Crucially, the eligibility of at least one of the ritual participants or the suitability of a ritual instrument will depend upon enabling actions that establish ties between them and the actions of a CI-agent. If an imposter performs weddings, the couples are not validly married in the eyes of the Church. If someone switches the specially selected bones a Zulu diviner uses, this will explain the diviner's failure to predict accurately.

Considerations of the well-formedness and effectiveness of religious rituals quickly demonstrate the importance of distinguishing between special agent rituals and special patient rituals. Well-formedness is only a necessary, but not a sufficient, condition for the effectiveness of a special patient ritual. Well-formed rituals, presumably, get the CI-agents' attention (Renfrew 1994b:51); however, although the well-formedness of ritual offerings to the ancestors is necessary for these gifts' acceptability, there is no guarantee that the ancestors will accept them (Whitehouse 1995). Similarly, even a casual survey reveals that the well-formedness of special agent rituals is considerably more constrained than special patient or special instrument rituals, since the former exhibit much less flexibility concerning ritual substitutions (see below).

The distinction between special agent rituals, on the one hand, and special patient and special instrument rituals, on the other, has important consequences. For example, individual participants need serve as the patients of special agent rituals only once, whereas participants can and typically do perform special instrument and special patient rituals repeatedly. Consider the difference between what are (typically)[8] once-in-a-lifetime initiations and the many sacrifices that ritual participants will perform as part of their religious obligations. In special agent rituals, CI-agents act, at least indirectly, through their ritually entitled middlemen. When the gods do things, they are done once and for all. By contrast, in special patient and special instrument rituals, the gods' closest associations are with the patients or the instruments of the ritual. Whatever ritually mediated connection the agent in such a ritual may enjoy with CI-agents is comparatively less intimate. Consequently, in these rituals the agents' actions carry no such finality. They are typically done again and again. Initiation into adulthood only happens once per participant, whereas participants will make offerings to the gods over and over and over.

Because the consequences of special patient and special instrument rituals are temporary only, it is unnecessary to have procedures (ritual or otherwise) for their reversal. Only the consequences of special agent rituals can be reversed. Defrocking priests, excommunicating communicants, expelling initiates, and dissolving marriages are all possible, but undoing Holy Communion or reversing a sacrifice is not. Only special agent rituals' consequences can be permanent, since in these it is CI-agents who have acted (usually through their intermediaries). These, then, are the only rituals whose consequences might ever need reversing.

It is not just the effects of special patient and special instrument rituals that are fleeting. That they are repeatable, and that often virtually every participant repeatedly performs them, signifies that nothing religiously indispensable turns on any one of their performances. Consequently, ritual substitutions often arise in these rites. Special patient and special instrument rituals are ones that human participants carry out with or on ritual elements that enjoy closer ritually established relationships with the gods than they. Nothing they do carries any lasting effects when their ritual attachments with CI-agents are less direct than are those of either the rituals' instruments or patients. In keeping with the importance the PSA accords the role of ritual agent, the special ritual connections of instruments or patients do not override the fact that it is the ritually less-well-connected participants who perform these rites (that is, who serve in the role of the ritual agent). These rituals' temporary effects (compared with the effects of special agent rituals) explain not only why these rituals are repeatable, but also why they often display greater latitude about their instruments, their patients, and even their procedures.

We suspect that this distinction would leave distinguishable traces in the archaeological record. Contemporary religious systems provide plenty of examples. A Muslim can use sand for a ritual washing in the desert, where water is a particularly scarce and valuable resource. Often, these rituals also permit substitutions for patients. Participants' consumption of

bread and wine for the body and blood of Christ is surely the most familiar illustration, but the ethnographic literature teems with examples.
Among the Nuer, it is particularly auspicious to sacrifice a bull, but since
bulls are valuable, a cucumber will do just fine most of the time (Evans-
Pritchard 1956; Firth 1963). These rituals may even display latitude about
the actual procedures involved. Humphrey and Laidlaw (1994) note, for
example, that the order of ritual actions in the Puja, its frequent performance notwithstanding, has manifested a good deal of variability over relatively short spans of time.

Research by Barrett and Lawson (2001) shows that subjects find
changes in agents more important to their judgments about ritual efficacy than changes in any other aspect of these rituals' structures. Special
instrument and patient rituals do not guarantee what we have called
"super-permanent" effects, that is, putative arrangements that exceed
even the spatial and temporal limits of participants' lifetimes (Lawson and
McCauley 1990:134, fn. 8). Those instruments and patients are not the
agents in these rituals. Whether participants use ritually consecrated
instruments or not, the primary consideration influencing subjects' judgments concerns the status of the current ritual's agent, even when that
agent's ties to CI-agents are comparatively less direct than those of the
other ritual elements.

Our theory suggests three closely related trends concerning ritual
substitutions. All are of a piece with the primacy that the detection of
agency enjoys in the representation of action. First, substitutions will typically apply to instruments and patients, as opposed to agents. After all,
some special patient rituals (e.g., the Eucharist) even substitute for CI-
agents—but only when they serve as the *patient* of the current ritual, not
as its agent. That substitutions turn on ritual roles as opposed to items'
inherent ontological statuses is a corollary of this first point. Second, substitutions will be less likely to arise for the agents in special agent rituals,
as opposed to special patient rituals. Finally, substitutions will more commonly concern the instruments and patients of special patient rituals, as
opposed to those of special agent rituals.[9] All three predictions readily
submit to both ethnographic and psychological tests. No doubt, archaeologists will be able to imagine consequences for a culture's material
record as well.

The PSI clarifies which among (potentially) multiple entries for CI-
agents within a ritual's full structural description is the initial one. The
different structural depths of these initial entries from one ritual to the
next will determine those rituals' comparative centrality to the overall

religious system. A ritual's centrality to a religious ritual system is inversely proportional to the depth of its initial entry for a CI-agent; hence, the least central rituals are the ones with the greatest depths. The greater a ritual's depth, the more distant are its connections with CI-agents, and, thus, the less central the ritual is to the religious system.

So, for example, a baptism a Catholic priest performs is valid because he has been ritually certified by the Church, which is attached ritually to the power and authority of Christ. (A variety of different scenarios has been and can be offered to justify that link.) Since the famous doctrine of transubstantiation establishes that the bread and wine are the very body and blood of Christ, Holy Communion, at least in orthodox Catholic views, is a ritual that requires no appeal to enabling actions in order to locate a CI-agent.[10] The CI-agent, Christ, is involved directly in the ritual at hand; consequently, a representation of a CI-agent arises in the very first level of this ritual's description. Hence, the Catholic Eucharist is one of the rituals that occur at the first level of structural depth in that religious system. By contrast, the baptism's representation has no CI-agent at its surface. (It is, after all, the priest who performs the baptism, not Christ himself.) Its description requires at least two embeddings of enabling actions (perhaps more, depending upon the preferred scenario) to establish the connection between the agent of that ritual (the priest) and a CI-agent. Consequently, it falls at no less than the third level of structural depth. It follows that the theory predicts that the Eucharist is a more central ritual to Catholicism than baptism is. (It also follows that Baptists' judgments should reverse these rituals' comparative centrality.)

This technical notion of the comparative centrality of religious rituals is valuable, because it both explains and predicts a variety of psychological, social, historical, and, we suspect, archaeological aspects of religious ritual systems. Claims about rituals' comparative centrality are readily testable. Multiple independent empirical measures correlate with a religious ritual's centrality.

The most straightforward cognitive gauge would simply be to elicit participants' judgments about such matters. This is not to say that participants have explicit knowledge about this abstract property of religious rituals or even about particular rituals' (absolute) depths. They do, however, possess a reservoir of pertinent tacit knowledge. Specifically, participants can offer a wide range of judgments about the comparative importance of various rituals. (So, for example, we predicted that the behavior of confirmed Catholics, by and large, will indicate that they regard the Eucharist as more central to their religious system than baptism.) That still might prove a fairly coarse measure, though, in light of a variety of extraneous variables that could influence participants' explicit judgments (such as performance frequency). Consequently, it would be especially valuable to design experiments that tap this intuitive knowledge by means of indirect behavioral measures while controlling for these potentially confounding factors.

Cognition is not the only source of evidence here, though. Aspects of ritual practice should also furnish evidence about rituals' centrality. For example, participants' knowledge about ritual prerequisites generally reflects genuine constraints on ritual practice. A Hindu cannot perform abbreviated Agnyadhana rituals in his home unless he has previously participated in an initial, full Agnyadhana. An Orthodox Jew's bar mitzvah really is a necessary condition for his becoming a rabbi. These points about ritual practice are so familiar that it is easy to lose sight of their theoretical significance. Because some of these rituals are prerequisites for others, they will ordinarily prove more central to these various religious systems. When apparent exceptions occur (e.g., the Catholic Eucharist), they should be explicable in terms of the theory's principles.

According to the insider-outsider criterion, religious rituals in our theory's technical sense are those religious activities that only participants in the system may participate in. Further restrictions on participation in or, perhaps, observation of religious rituals may also correlate with rituals' centrality. Hierarchies of participant eligibility turning on previous ritual accomplishments pervade religious ritual systems. Renfrew notes, for example, that "the concept of a communal ritual does not . . . imply that participation is open to the whole community. . . . The right of participation in specific rituals may be rigidly defined. Moreover, it is likely that some of the rituals carried out on behalf of the community will be conducted by one or more designated individuals" (Renfrew 1985:21). Participants' tolerance for variation in religious rituals is probably another measure. Presumably, that tolerance decreases with rituals' increasing centrality. History helps too. Ritual practice during periods of religious fragmentation may supply clues about rituals' various degrees of centrality. The perceived degree of upheaval within a religious system and the probability that diverging religious communities will refuse to identify with one another any longer will surely correlate better with the addition, alteration, or deletion of a comparatively central ritual than with one that is less central (Vial 2004).

Finally, we presume that supplementing the theory with a few plausible hypotheses, archaeology will often be able to provide evidence here. So, for example, when groups leave multiple, disparate ritual sites, it seems a reasonable hypothesis that more central rituals will more likely occur at major ritual sites, while less central rituals will more likely occur at less major ritual sites (Johnson 2004). The locations of ritual equipment and of discards at these special locations may exhibit patterns that will offer clues about such matters (Marcus and Flannery 1994:56). Presumably, the prominence of a ritual site will correlate with features such as size, proximity to population centers, comparative ornateness, and the like, though we defer to the archaeological professionals concerning which supplementary hypotheses to enlist.

We are not the first to have addressed these properties of religious rituals. We are, however, the first to offer a *single, unified theory that explains them all*. If our theory did nothing more than this, it should count as progress. However, the theory also explains additional properties of religious rituals that connect directly with the epidemiological considerations we raised early on. Recall that there we emphasized how in nonliterate cultures especially, the need to transmit rituals acts, in effect, as a mechanism of cultural selection, imposing constraints on ritual systems that will, among other things, assure particular rituals' memorability and participants' motivation to impart this religious system and its rituals to others (typically the next generation). In these settings, public representations of culture (including rituals) that do not satisfy these criteria will, quite likely, go extinct.

In the absence of literacy, the transmission of cultural representations is a tenuous process at best. Sperber argues that what we know about the variability and vicissitudes of human memory and communication counsel that the transformation of cultural representations in the course of transmission is the rule and that the faithful reproduction of mental representations occurs rarely, if at all. So, he concludes that it is primarily similarities in cultural representations persisting across generations that require explanation. He holds that "resemblance among cultural items is to be explained to some important extent by the fact that transformations tend to be biased in the direction of attractor positions in the space of possibilities" (Sperber 1996:108). The first step, then, is to locate those attractors.

The second step, as Sperber notes, is to explain them. "To say that there is an attractor is not to give a causal explanation; it is to put in a certain light what is to be explained: namely, a distribution of items and its evolution, and to suggest the kind of causal explanation to be sought: namely, the identification of genuine causal factors that bias micro-transformations" (Sperber 1996:112). The causal factors on which we focus are the cognitive dispositions of the human mind and the constraints that the process of transmission imposes. Because human minds have evolved in the directions that they have and because the necessary conditions for human life (such as food) are what they are, some sorts of mental and cultural representations recur again and again.

We have argued at length that the two most prominent considerations that enhance the probabilities that rituals will prove memorable are their performance frequencies and the levels of arousal (primarily emotional) that they elicit. (McCauley 1999b; McCauley and Lawson 2002). On the one hand, frequent performance does not produce outstanding memory for any particular instance, but it usually does ensure that we develop excellent procedural memory (at least) for the routine actions we are carrying out, whether they are religious rituals or not. On the other hand, occasions of high arousal can establish particularly vivid memories about specific events. Not all do, but those that we repeatedly rehearse in memory and recount to others and that concern events whose significance we continue to recognize over long periods of time often do. The classic illustration in the psychological literature is so-called flashbulb memories: memories for the circumstances under which people have learned about culturally significant events, such as the terrorist attacks on September 11, 2001 (Brown and Kulik 1977). Controlled experiments indicate that the vividness and confidence subjects associate with such memories do not guarantee their accuracy (Neisser and Harsch 1992). Just as in ritual, though, participating in, as opposed to observing, a momentous event seems to have a more substantial mnemonic impact. The experimental evidence reveals that precisely when flashbulb memories come from participation in such salient events, even when they are not particularly arousing at the time (for example, experiencing a major earthquake in a comparatively safe location), subjects' memories, by contrast, seem to be every bit as vivid and as accurate as they claim (Neisser et al. 1996).

We have argued that arousal in rituals may not be to consolidate memory so much as to signal that the ritual is significant, which, if corroborated by the artifacts in the vicinity (for example, images of the gods and of the gods' faces) and the participant's subsequent experience, does promote improved memory. The chief means for producing arousal in rituals is to stimulate participants' senses in order to excite their emotions; however, some religious systems also employ drugs, sexual arousal, and more (Marcus and Flannery 1994:59; Whitehouse 1995:110–114). We coined the term "sensory pageantry" to cover all of these ritual measures for arousing participants. It seems reasonable to expect that the means for producing such pageantry should leave detectable traces, if not patterns, in a culture's material record (Renfrew 1985).

If we construct a two-dimensional space of religious ritual possibilities with the two variables we have isolated, it is not difficult to locate two attractors (figure 10.4). To call these regions "attractors" means that the conditions they represent are conducive to the successful transmission of rituals, where "successful transmission" means at least that participants are satisfied with the continuity in the system over time.

These two attractors mirror the paradoxical associations that most people have about religious rituals. Reflection on ritual usually produces one or both of two reactions. The first is that rituals are boring, mindless activities that we do over and over again. The second is that rituals are rare, exciting occasions in which we are the center of attention and which mark some of the most significant moments in our lives. As the two attractors signify, both, in fact, are true. The numbers of the two attractors in figure 10.4 correspond to these two arrangements.

Looking to the same mnemonic considerations we stress, Harvey Whitehouse (1992, 1995, 2000) holds that performance frequency explains the different levels of sensory pageantry. This ritual frequency hypothesis proposes that the amount of sensory pageantry and, therefore, the amount of emotional arousal any religious ritual involves is inversely proportional to the frequency with which that ritual is performed (figure 10.5). We have argued[11] that, although the ritual frequency hypothesis

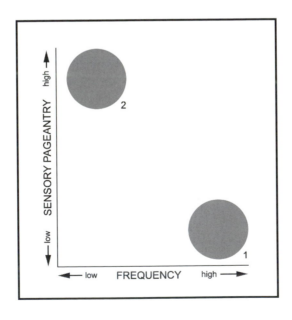

FIGURE 10.4. Two attractors.

makes sense of most rituals' positions in this space (which fall at one or the other attractor), it can neither make sense of the arrangements associated with the numerous rituals that do not fall near the line it defines (for example, the *Agnicayana*; McCauley 2001; Staal 1990), nor does it supply any account of rituals' performance frequencies.

By contrast, we have advanced the *ritual form hypothesis*, a corollary of the theory of religious ritual competence. In addition to providing a finer-grained analysis that enriches the space of ritual possibilities, the ritual form hypothesis also handles the ritual frequency hypothesis's first problem, makes significant headway with the second, and explains and predicts the evolution of ritual form in ritual innovation. The ritual form hypothesis states that for all religious systems, the *comparative* levels of sensory pageantry within *particular religious communities* will never be higher in special patient and special instrument rituals than it will be in special agent rituals. This hypothesis introduces an additional (discrete) variable—namely, ritual form—which aids in explaining the two attractors. This results in a three-dimensional space that offers a new perspective on both the positions of the attractors as well as the regions distant from the ritual frequency function (figure 10.6). As noted earlier, it also supplies some insight about what stands behind ritual frequencies, which the ritual frequency hypothesis leaves unaddressed. Specifically, because special

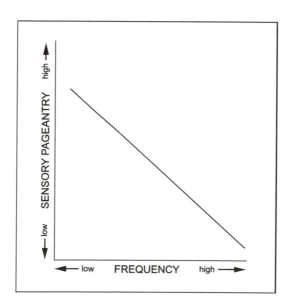

FIGURE 10.5. The ritual frequency hypothesis.

patient and special instrument rituals are repeatable (and most are frequently repeated), whereas special agent rituals are (typically) not (see
below), in highlighting ritual form the theory of religious ritual competence also isolates at least one of the variables that affects performance
frequencies.

The ritual frequency hypothesis has no means for explaining any
rituals that fall very far away from the line it defines[12] (figure 10.5). In
fact, it makes false predictions about most that do. Consider, for example, special patient and special instrument rituals with comparatively
low performance frequencies (figure 10.7). On the ritual frequency
hypothesis, their low performance frequencies would require that they
have *comparatively* high levels of sensory pageantry, but, in fact, they do
not (McCauley and Lawson 2002:146–155). Especially in the absence of
literacy, rituals that fall in this general area reliably require special cultural mechanisms for aiding their recall.

Or, by contrast, ponder special agent rituals with comparatively high
performance frequencies. *Prima facie*, this might seem conceptually inco-

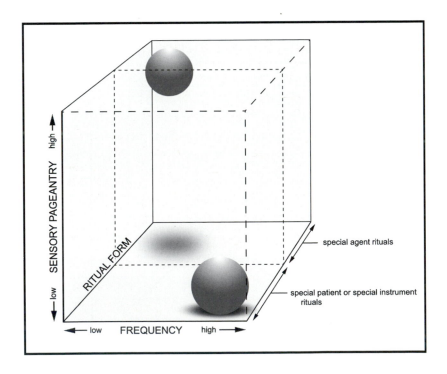

FIGURE 10.6. Ritual form as a discrete variable.

herent, since we have asserted that special agent rituals are not repeated, that participants are the patients of these various rituals only once (McCauley and Lawson 2002:155–178, 209). As the forms of these rituals suggest, they are not repeated typically, but religions have found a variety of strategies for circumventing this apparent conceptual barrier including

 a. limited repetition (of marriage) for some participants,

 b. juridical or ritual reversals of the effects of previously performed special agent rituals,

 c. substitutions for the patients of special agent rituals (see note 7 above), and

 d. determinations that earlier performances of special agent rituals failed.

Whitehouse's (1995) ethnography provides an excellent illustration of the last of these, about which the ritual form hypothesis makes correct

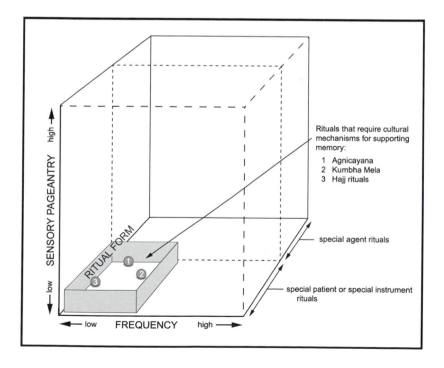

Figure 10.7. Special patient and special instrument rituals with low performance frequencies.

predictions but, ironically, the ritual frequency hypothesis does not (McCauley and Lawson 2002:166–178).

This point deserves emphasis, since at least one commentator fails both to attend to these possibilities and to appreciate their theoretical significance. Chris Knight (2003) is underwhelmed by our claims that special agent rituals (or more accurately, according to Knight, rites of passage) are (1) non-repeated rituals and (2) ones that have comparatively high levels of sensory pageantry. He asserts that these claims are "tautologies." Since such claims are certainly not tautologies (claims such as "a cat is a cat," which are true by virtue of their logical forms), nor are they even very good candidates for analytic truths[13] (claims that are true by virtue of the meanings of their terms, such as "a bachelor is an unmarried man"), presumably what Knight has in mind is that these are obvious truths (such as "dogs have four legs").

By now, though, the problem with *that* charge should be obvious. As we note above (and at length in our book), religions have found a variety of ways of eluding what Knight seems to think are conceptual necessities. Consequently, these claims, at least in their unqualified forms, are not only not obvious truths, they are not true at all (except when advanced as claims about the implications of ritual form, which is precisely how we advance them). We offered an extended discussion in our book of how the events described in Whitehouse's ethnography exemplify strategy (d) and of the peculiar earmarks of such cases,[14] but other examples abound. Many religions (such as Islam) permit multiple marriages (and weddings), illustrating strategy (a). Many also contain either ritual provisions or juridical provisions, or both, for reversing the effects of some special agent rituals, opening up the possibility of performing the special agent rituals again with the same ritual patients, illustrating strategy (b). We offered the consecration, desacralization, and reconsecration of St. Michael's in Cambridge, England, as one instance (McCauley and Lawson 2002:157). Consider, also, the nuptial histories of various Hollywood celebrities.

Knight's preference for the category "rites of passage" over our category "special agent rituals" is precisely to *miss* the theoretical point about the explanatory prominence of the critical cognitive variable our theory isolates—namely, *participants' representations of ritual form*. It is the properties these rites share with all other special agent rituals that matter for explaining and predicting the empirical patterns we have reviewed, since, among other things, those other special agent rituals exhibit the same patterns that the classic rites of passage do. Consider, for example, the evidence of comparatively high levels of sensory

pageantry that Joyce Marcus and Kent Flannery (1994:66) cite in association with non-repeated, "dedicatory offering" rituals marking the sanc-
tification of temples among the ancient Zapotec.

The classic rites of passage, assuredly, are prime examples of special
agent rituals, but they do not exhaust the category (McCauley and Lawson
2002:19). The force of what is, by now, a substantial array of empirical evidence—including experimental evidence—that we and others have mar-
shaled in support of our theory argues that it is by virtue of their status as
special agent rituals that the rites manifest these patterns. To allay any skep-
ticism as to whether these arguments, in fact, bear on the rites of passage,
we note that full members of the Church of the Latter Day Saints participate as the (substitute) patients in one rite of passage repeatedly, as they
undergo periodic, full immersion baptisms (as substitutes for departed
ancestors), illustrating strategy (c). Unwavering insistence on the preemi-
nence of classical categories (such as the rites of passage) and of classical
theorists and their theories (Marx, Durkheim, Turner, Rappaport, etc.)[15]
can blind researchers not only to the explanatory accomplishments of alternative approaches and theories, but even to *relevant facts* (McCauley and
Lawson 2002). Recognizing the relevance of facts and discovering new
facts regularly turn on exploring alternative approaches and testing new
theories. This is all difficult to see if in any particular field researchers are
so convinced by their favorite theories that they regard them as the embodiment of obvious conceptual truths (let alone tautologies).

We close with a few short comments about the ties between ritual
and motivation and some of their implications for religious ritual systems
overall. Under most conditions, the emotional arousal wrought by the
comparatively high levels of sensory pageantry in special agent rituals not
only serve to flag memorable events but to increase participants' motivation and commitment to transmit the religious system. Permitting
repeated participation (as the patient) in special agent rituals, therefore,
is—within limits—likely to result in highly motivated participants eager
to impart their religious representations. The dangers of habituation set
limits on effective "doses" of emotional arousal and effective frequencies.
Such opportunities for ritually induced arousal must occur infrequently
enough that participants will not need even greater levels of arousal the
next time in order to hold their interest. Violating those limits will result
in an escalation of frequency and sensory pageantry until the system
blows up (through what we have dubbed a "sensory overload ceiling")
either from the exhaustion of the resources necessary to produce these
sensory effects, from the exhaustion, disability, or death of the participants,

or from intervention from the outside (for example, civil authorities) (figure 10.8).

Oddly, figure 10.8 indicates that psychological challenges lurk in the locale of the first attractor too. Whitehouse (1995, 2000) argues that when all of a religious system's rituals are clustered at the first attractor, it reliably leads to instability owing to what he calls the "tedium effect." His ethnography recounts a splendid illustration. Performing rituals with little sensory pageantry day in and day out may facilitate participants' command of materials, but it also drains them of much motivation to continue in that mode.

Religions in literate cultures (or in cultures influenced by literate cultures) are usually more complicated.[16] Literacy brings advantages, such as the ability to write ritual manuals, instead of having to rely on participants' memories. It can also bring extra burdens, since "religions of the book" regularly include elaborate conceptual constructions, codified doctrines, theologies, and, probably, more rarified standards for what makes for faithful transmission of cultural representations (Rubin 1995). We have proposed that simultaneously assuring both participants' motivation and their facility with such conceptual materials requires that religious ritual systems include low-frequency, high-pageantry special agent rituals and high-frequency, low-pageantry special patient and special instrument rituals, respectively. All else being equal, such "balanced" religious ritual systems (which include rituals at both of the attractors in figure 10.6) will prove comparatively stable, since they have ritual means that address both of these requirements (McCauley and Lawson 2002:201–210). All of the so-called world religions exhibit such a pattern.

These consequences of our theory would seem to submit more readily to empirical assessment via archaeological evidence than many we have discussed. Three quick observations must suffice here. First, patterns among cultures' material remains concerning the artifacts and structured environments connected primarily with infrequently performed rituals accompanied by comparatively high levels of sensory pageantry should prove distinguishable from those connected primarily with frequently performed rituals accompanied by comparatively low levels of sensory pageantry. Because the ritual form hypothesis addresses the comparative levels of sensory pageantry associated with these rituals within particular religious communities, assessing relevant archaeological evidence will require ascertaining the local standards about what constitutes elevated levels of sensory pageantry, since these differ from one community to the next.

Second and more controversially, the material record should offer clues that the former are rituals of special agent form, whereas the latter

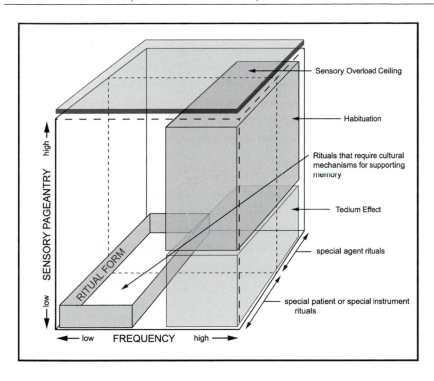

FIGURE 10.8. Psychologically problematic regions.

are rituals of special instrument and special patient forms. The differences would be between equipment useful for generating (comparatively) elevated levels of sensory pageantry (such as baptismal pools at the front of churches) and artifacts shaped and situated for regular and widespread use (such as votive candle holders in side chapels).

Finally, our speculations about the relative stability of such balanced systems imply that, all else being equal, such arrangements should contribute to the persistence of religious systems, compared, for example, with detectable variants and splinter groups that do not retain such patterns. This proposal would, among other things, encourage the calculation of correlations between two sorts of archaeological evidence—namely, between that bearing on the structures and settings of artifacts and that bearing on the persistence of particular religious systems. Across a sufficiently large stock of ritual sites, this proposal would predict (again, *ceteris paribus*) positive correlations between a religious system's longevity and evidence of it possessing a balanced ritual system in the sense discussed above. The ritual form hypothesis, in effect, suggests an avenue for discovering correlations between certain sorts of synchronic and diachronic patterns within particular bodies of archaeological evidence.

We fear, however, that this and other speculations above may reflect undue optimism about the number of available archaeological sites and about the availability, the condition, and the intelligibility of their materials. We have no doubts about the comparative range, severity, or immediacy of the difficulties associated with carrying out archaeological research.

GLOSSARY

action representation system: A fundamental, task-specific piece of cognitive equipment that all (normal) humans possess for representing the subset of events in their environments that qualify as actions. That capacity, in turn, relies on the ability to represent the subset of objects in their environments that qualify as agents (who can carry out those actions). The action representation system includes slots for at least three action roles: an agent, an act (with the option of including instruments that may be used in carrying out the action), and an [optional] patient of the action.

action role: One of three functions—agent, act, and (optionally) patient—required for representing any action's structure.

balanced religious ritual system: A religious ritual system that includes both special agent rituals, on the one hand, and special patient or special instrument rituals, on the other.

centrality (of a religious ritual): Inversely proportional to a religious ritual's depth in a religious ritual system, a religious ritual's centrality measures what rituals that ritual is capable of enabling. We have conjectured that centrality may also measure the degree of variation participants will permit in the performances of rituals, the probability of schisms (based upon the centrality of the rituals that are the points of controversy), and (all else being equal, such as where there are no ritual substitutions) participants' intuitions about the ritual's importance to the religious system.

depth (of a current religious ritual): The relative number of enabling rituals required to implicate a CI-agent with some action role (in the cognitive representation) of the current religious ritual. The more enabling rituals that are required, the greater the current religious ritual's depth.

effectiveness/efficacy (of a religious ritual): The ability of a (well-formed) religious ritual to accomplish its end (as characterized by the religious system's conceptual scheme).

counterintuitive agents (CI-agents): Agents putatively possessing counterintuitive properties.

counterintuitive properties: Properties that violate the constraints of, or are transferred across, domains within our basic ontological knowledge (that maturationally natural cognitive systems address). For example, a counterintuitive property attributed to a putative agent that *violates* our intuitive knowledge about the physical realm would be that agent's ability to walk on water. An example of a counterintuitive property of a putative agent that arises on the basis of a *transfer* of a psychological property to an entity (that is typically accorded physical and biological properties only) would be a snake that talks.

embedded ritual: An enabling ritual that is connected with an element fulfilling an action role in the current ritual and which appears below the surface in that current ritual's representation.

enabling ritual: A ritual that must be performed in advance of other rituals and whose successful accomplishment constitutes a necessary condition for the successful performance of the subsequent ritual(s). A current ritual's enabling rituals are embedded in its cognitive representation. So, for example, a priest's ordination is an enabling ritual in any of his subsequent performances of baptism.

hypothetical religious rituals: Enabling actions by putative CI-agents that may or may not have ever actually been performed but that are presumed in a religious system.

Principle of Superhuman Agency (PSA): Principle holding that the most direct connection of a CI-agent to an element fulfilling an action role in a cognitive representation of a religious ritual defines that ritual's form. (*See* Principle of Superhuman Immediacy, special agent ritual, special instrument ritual, and special patient ritual.)

Principle of Superhuman Immediacy (PSI): Principle concerning how many enabling rituals are required to establish a ritually mediated connection between a CI-agent (in an embedded enabling ritual) and an element fulfilling an action role in the current ritual. The PSI holds that the number of enabling rituals required to connect elements fulfilling action roles in the current ritual to an entry for a CI-agent determines the action role with the most direct connection to a CI-agent and, thereby, per the PSA, determines that ritual's form. (*See* Principle of Superhuman Agency.)

religious rituals (technical sense in the theory of religious ritual competence): The subset of repeated religious actions for which participants' cognitive representations include (1) CI-agents putatively figuring either directly or indirectly in an action role, and (2) the accomplishment of some explicitly describable (and inter-subjectively available) change in the religious world. So, for example, a baptism of a participant by a priest, who serves as the representative of God, by virtue of a series of earlier enabling religious rituals (in this technical sense), counts as the performance of a religious ritual. The baptism changes the participant's status in the religious world (in a way, for example, that pertains to what other religious rituals the participant is now eligible to participate in) that turns exclusively on the basis of the (inter-subjectively available) form of the religious ritual action in question and not, for example, on the priest's state of mind or intentions. Prayers, by contrast, fail to qualify as religious rituals in this technical sense, because they do not satisfy condition (2) above.

ritual form hypothesis: For all religious systems, the *comparative* levels of sensory pageantry within *particular religious communities* will never be higher in special patient and special instrument rituals than they will be in special agent rituals.

sensory overload ceiling: Limit on the levels of sensory pageantry associated with religious rituals, above which individual participants will either fall asleep, lapse into a coma, or die (depending upon the character of the sensory pageantry) or, with groups, the levels of sensory pageantry with which they exhaust the resources necessary for its subsequent production (see figure 10.8).

sensory pageantry: Material means for producing arousal (either emotional or cognitive) in ritual participants, usually by stimulating their senses (but also including the ingestion of psychoactive substances, sexual arousal, and the like).

special agent ritual: A form of religious ritual; those religious rituals in which the CI-agent who enjoys the most direct connection to the current ritual does so through the action role of the agent. Typically, a participant serves as the patient of such a ritual only once.

special instrument ritual: A form of religious ritual; those religious rituals in which the CI-agent who enjoys the most direct connection to the current ritual does so through the action role of the act. The same participants serving in the same action roles may, and typically do, participate in these rituals more than once.

special patient ritual: A form of religious ritual; those religious rituals in which the CI-agent who enjoys the most direct connection to the current ritual does so through the action role of the patient. The same participants serving in the same action roles may, and typically do, participate in these rituals more than once.

super-permanent effects (of a religious ritual): Putative effects of special agent religious rituals that exceed even the spatial and temporal limits of participants' lifetimes.

tedium effect: Psychological result of frequent repetition of special patient and special instrument rituals—only decreasing participants' interest in, engagement with, and motivation by the rituals in question and the religious system of which they are a part (compare Whitehouse 1995 and 2000).

well-formedness (of a religious ritual): The result of a religious ritual at some point (if not directly, then by enabling rituals at least) implicating a CI-agent with one of its action roles.

NOTES

1. Exceptions include some natural arrangements imbued with cultural valence. Some (such as Mt. Fuji) may undergo some minimal human manipulation. Others (such as the sun) do not (yet).

2. This is not to imply, however, that the relevant representations are either always or even usually consciously available to practitioners. For example, virtually no utterances involve a speaker's conscious awareness, in any sense, of the grammatical principles of the language in which the utterance has been formulated.

3. This point has genuine practical import. For example, moving the elderly from their homes, for which they have well-developed spatial memories not only for their layouts but particularly for the locations of the tools that we all require to get through a day, to assisted living facilities, for which they do not possess such memories, can result in the appearance or, worse, the misdiagnosis of dementia.

4. Undoubtedly, the development of language is our most fundamental accomplishment on this front; however, we will not discuss the role of spoken utterances in any systematic way, since they are not part of the persisting material culture that archaeologists can study (at least not until the development of audio recording in the last century).

5. Although much that he says could be construed as evidence for the claim, Barth does not consider the possibility that such (coded) symbolic relations simply do not exist (Sperber 1975).

6. The preservation of the metaphors and idioms by which Baktaman knowledge is communicated turns primarily on their employment in repeated communications (however vague) associated with the themes that underlie Baktaman ritual praxis. Still, neither Barth nor his informants (1987:26–27) hold that any cues or constraints, which the frequently confronted metaphors and idioms occasion, suffice to account for the similarities between two consecutive performances of initiations within any community. Barth and his informants agree that it is the attempts by the seniors responsible for staging these initiations to recall past performances that is the primary influence on the shape of the next one (Barth 1987:26).

7. Previously, we have referred to "culturally postulated superhuman agents" or CPS-agents. We abandon that usage, since cultures are not the sorts of things that postulate anything, so far as we can tell.

8. See the discussion of Knight (2003) below.

9. Note, though, that the latter do exist and sometimes make vital contributions to the persistence of religious systems (McCauley 2004).

10. Though it does require appeal to enabling actions in order to make sense of the substitution of the bread and wine for the body and blood of Christ. See the discussion of ritual substitution above.

11. See McCauley and Lawson 2002: Chapters 3–5. Whitehouse (2004) responds to some of these arguments. Space does not permit replies to those responses here; however, with respect to the points of contention about the cognitive grounds of religious ritual dynamics, as opposed to interpreting the various versions of Whitehouse's larger (interesting, but evolving) theory of religious modes, our

arguments for the superiority of the ritual form hypothesis stand unscathed. We should emphasize, however, that this is a family squabble among cognitivists. Regardless of which theory proves the more successful, the cognitive approach they share has yielded comparatively precise, testable theories that have generated illuminating programs of empirical research that bear on their assessment. Demonstrating *that* is what matters most in the long run.

12. In the three-dimensional space of possible ritual arrangements, the ritual frequency function defines a plane.

13. If Knight thinks that they are good candidates, then that is only further evidence for our argument three paragraphs below.

14. For example, unlike the repetition of special patient and special instrument rituals, repeated performances of special agent rituals with the same ritual patients as a result of the failure of an earlier performance will occasion a great deal of comment and explanation about both the need to perform the ritual again and why.

15. Our point here is not to slight the categories or the theories or the theorists. We note and address positions in Lawson and McCauley (1990) of five of six individuals Knight commends.

16. Whitehouse (2000) suggests that although religions with extensive doctrinal and ritual systems with low-pageantry, high-frequency rituals exist in what are basically nonliterate cultures (in Melanesia), the evidence he surveys suggests that they have only arisen in response to exposure to the literacy-based, doctrinal system of missionary Christianity. Karen Johnson (2004) argues that the archaeological evidence from prehistoric Iran, specifically at Choga Mish and Susa, suggests that religions exemplifying Whitehouse's doctrinal mode can arise completely independently of literacy.

REFERENCES CITED

Abbink, Jon
    1995   Ritual and environment: The *Mosit* ceremony of the Ethiopian
            Me'en people. *Journal of Religion in Africa* 25:163–190.
Baron-Cohen, Simon
    1995   *Mindblindness: An Essay on Autism and Theory of Mind*. MIT Press,
            Cambridge.
Barrett, Justin L., and E. Thomas Lawson,
    2001   Ritual intuitions: Cognitive contributions to judgements of ritual
            efficacy. *Journal of Cognition and Culture* 1:183–201.
Barth, Fredrik
    1975   *Ritual and Knowledge among the Baktaman of New Guinea*. Yale
            University Press, New Haven.
Barth, Fredrik
    1987   *Cosmologies in the Making: A Generative Approach to Cultural Variation
            in Inner New Guinea*. Cambridge University Press, Cambridge.
Bechtel, William
    1996   What should a connectionist philosophy of science look like? In
            The Churchlands and Their Critics, edited by Robert McCauley, pp.
            121–144. Blackwell Publishers, Oxford.

Boesch, Christophe, and Hedwige Boesch
    1993   Diversity of tool use and tool-making in wild chimpanzees. In *The Use of Tools by Human and Non-Human Primates*, edited by Arlette Berthelet and Jean Chavaillon, pp. 158–174. Clarendon Press, Oxford.
Boyer, Pascal
    1994a   *The Naturalness of Religious Ideas*. University of California Press, Berkeley.
    1994b   Cognitive constraints on cultural representations: Natural ontologies and religious ideas. In *Mapping the Mind: Domain-Specificity in Culture and Cognition*, edited by Lawrence A. Hirschfeld and Susan A. Gelman, pp. 391–411. Cambridge University Press, New York.
    1996   Cognitive limits to conceptual relativity: The limiting case of religious categories. In *Rethinking Linguistic Relativity*, edited by John Gumperz and Stephen Levinson, pp. 203–231. Cambridge University Press, Cambridge.
    1999   Cultural inheritance tracks and cognitive predispositions: The example of religious concepts. In *Mind, Evolution, and Cultural Transmission*, edited by Harvey Whitehouse, pp. 57–89. Cambridge University Press, Cambridge.
    2001   *Religion Explained*. Basic Books, New York.
Brown, Roger, and James Kulik
    1977   Flashbulb memories. *Cognition* 5:73–99.
Clark, Andy
    1997   *Being There: Putting Brain, Body, and World Together Again*. MIT Press, Cambridge.
Day, Matthew C.
    2004a   Religion, off-line cognition and the extended mind. *Journal of Cognition and Culture* 4:101–121.
    2004b   The ins and outs of religious cognition. *Method and Theory in the Study of Religion* 16 (3):241–255.
Donald, Merlin
    1991   *Origins of the Modern Mind: Three Stages in the Evolution of Culture and Cognition*. Harvard University Press, Cambridge.
Evans-Pritchard, Edward
    1956   *Nuer Religion*. Clarendon Press, Oxford.
Firth, Raymond
    1963   Offering and sacrifice: Problems of organization. *Journal of the Royal Anthropological Institute* 93:12–24.
Humphrey, Caroline, and James Laidlaw
    1994   *The Archetypal Actions of Ritual*. Oxford University Press, Oxford.
Hutchins, Edwin
    1994   *Cognition in the Wild*. MIT Press, Cambridge.
Johnson, Karen
    2004   Primary emergence of the doctrinal mode of religiosity in pre-

historic Southwestern Iran. In *Theorizing Religions Past: Archaeology, History, and Cognition*, edited by Harvey Whitehouse and Luther Martin, pp. 45–66. AltaMira, Walnut Creek, CA.

Knight, Chris
   2003   Trauma, tedium and tautology in the study of ritual. *Cambridge Archaeological Journal* 13:293–295.

Lawson, E. Thomas, and Robert N. McCauley
   1990   *Rethinking Religion: Connecting Cognition and Culture*. Cambridge University Press, Cambridge.

Leslie, Alan
   1995   A theory of agency. In *Causal Cognition: A Multidisciplinary Debate*, edited by Dan Sperber, David Premack, and Ann James Premack, pp. 121–147. Oxford University Press, New York.

Malley, Brian, and Justin Barrett
   2003   Can ritual form be predicted from religious belief? A test of the Lawson-McCauley hypotheses. *Journal of Ritual Studies* 17:1–14.

Marcus, Joyce, and Kent V. Flannery.
   1994   Ancient Zapotec ritual and religion: An application of the direct historical approach. In *The Ancient Mind: Elements of Cognitive Archaeology*, edited by Colin Renfrew and Ezra B. W. Zubrow, pp. 55–74. Cambridge University Press, Cambridge.

McCauley, Robert N.
   1999a   The cognitive foundations of religion and science. In *Religion im Wandel der Kosmologien*, edited by Dieter Zeller, pp. 55–67. P. Lang, Berlin.
   1999b   Bringing ritual to mind. In *Ecological Approaches to Cognition: Essays in Honor of Ulric Neisser*, edited by Eugene Winograd, Robyn Fivush, and William Hirst, pp. 285–312. Erlbaum, Hillsdale, NJ.
   2000a   The naturalness of religion and the unnaturalness of science. In *Explanation and Cognition*, edited by Frank Keil and Robert Wilson, pp. 61–85. MIT Press, Cambridge.
   2000b   Overcoming barriers to a cognitive psychology of religion. In *Method and Theory in the Study of Religion* 12:141–161.
   2001   Ritual, memory, and emotion: Comparing two cognitive hypotheses. In *Religion in Mind: Cognitive Perspectives on Religious Experience*, edited by Jensine Andresen, pp. 115–140. Cambridge University Press, Cambridge.
   2004   Four ways of achieving stability in religious ritual systems. Paper presented at the Midwest American Academy of Religion, DePaul University, Chicago, IL.

McCauley, Robert N., and E. Thomas Lawson
   2002   *Bringing Ritual to Mind: Psychological Foundations of Cultural Forms*. Cambridge University Press, Cambridge.

Michotte, Albert
    1963   *The Perception of Causality*. Metheun, Andover.
Mithen, Steven
    1996   *The Prehistory of the Mind*. Thames and Hudson, London.
    1997   Cognitive archaeology, evolutionary psychology and cultural trans-
            mission, with particular reference to religious ideas. In *Rediscovering
            Darwin: Evolutionary Theory and Archaeological Explanation*, edited
            by C. Michael Barton and Geoffrey A. Clark, pp. 67–74. American
            Anthropological Association, Arlington, VA.
Neisser, Ulric, and Nicole Harsch
    1992   Phantom flashbulbs: False recollections of hearing the news
            about *Challenger*. In *Affect and Accuracy in Recall*, edited by Eugene
            Winograd and Ulric Neisser, pp. 9–31. Cambridge University
            Press, New York.
Neisser, Ulric, Eugene Winograd, Erik Bergman, Charles Schreiber, Steve
            Palmer, and Mary Susan Weldon
    1996   Remembering the earthquake: Direct experience vs. hearing the
            news. *Memory* 4:337–357.
Penner, Hans
    1975   Creating a Brahman: A structural approach to the study of reli-
            gion. In *Methodological Issues In Religious Studies*, edited by Robert
            Baird, pp. 49–66. New Horizons Press, Chico.
Perner, Josef, Susan R.Leekam, and Heinz Wimmer
    1987   Three-year-olds' difficulty with false belief. *British Journal of
            Developmental Psychology* 5:125–137.
Renfrew, Colin
    1985   *The Archaeology of Cult: The Sanctuary at Phylakopi*. Supplementary
            Volume 18. The British School of Archaeology at Athens and
            Thames and Hudson, London.
    1994a   Towards a cognitive archaeology. In *The Ancient Mind: Elements of
            Cognitive Archaeology*, edited by Colin Renfrew and Ezra B. W.
            Zubrow, pp. 3–12. Cambridge University Press, Cambridge.
    1994b   The archaeology of religion. In *The Ancient Mind: Elements of
            Cognitive Archaeology*, edited by Colin Renfrew and Ezra B. W.
            Zubrow, pp. 47–54. Cambridge University Press, Cambridge.
    1998   Mind and matter: Cognitive archaeology and external symbolic
            storage. In *Cognition and Material Culture: The Archaeology of
            Symbolic Storage*, edited by Colin Renfrew and Chris Scarre, pp.
            1–6. McDonald Institute for Archaeological Research, Cambridge.
Renfrew, Colin, and Chris Scarre (editors)
    1998   *Cognition and Material Culture: The Archaeology of Symbolic Storage*.
            McDonald Institute for Archaeological Research, Cambridge.
Rochat, Philippe
    2001   *The Infant's World*. Harvard University Press, Cambridge.

Rubin, David
  1995   *Memory in Oral Tradition: The Cognitive Psychology of Epic, Ballads, and Counting-Out Rhymes.* Oxford University Press, New York.
Slone, Jason
  2004   *Theological Incorrectness: Why Religious People Believe What They Shouldn't.* Oxford University Press, New York.
Sperber, Dan
  1975   *Rethinking Symbolism.* Translated by Alice L. Morton. Cambridge University Press, Cambridge.
  1996   *Explaining Culture: A Naturalistic Approach.* Blackwell Publishers, Oxford.
Staal, Frits
  1990   *Rules without Meaning: Ritual, Mantras, and the Human Sciences.* Peter Lang, New York.
Tooby, John, and Leda Cosmides
  1992   The psychological foundations of culture. In *The Adapted Mind*, edited by Jerome Barkow, Leda Cosmides, and John Tooby, pp. 19–136. Oxford University Press, New York.
Vial, Theodore M.
  2004   *Liturgy Wars: Ritual Theory and Protestant Reform in Nineteenth-Century Zurich.* Routledge, London.
Wellman, Henry
  1990   *The Child's Theory of Mind.* MIT Press, Cambridge.
Whitehouse, Harvey
  1992   Memorable religions: Transmission, codification and change in divergent Melanesian contexts. *Man* (N.S.) 27:777–797.
  1995   *Inside the Cult: Religious Innovation and Transmission in Papua New Guinea.* Clarendon Press, Oxford.
  2000   *Arguments and Icons: The Cognitive, Social, and Historical Implications of Divergent Modes of Religiosity.* Oxford University Press, Oxford.
  2004   *Modes of Religiosity: A Cognitive Theory of Religious Transmission.* AltaMira, Walnut Creek, CA.
Whitehouse, Harvey, and Luther Martin (editors)
  2004   *Theorizing Religions Past: Archaeology, History, and Cognition.* AltaMira, Walnut Creek, CA.
Wimmer, Heinz, and Joseph Perner
  1983   Beliefs about Beliefs: Representations and constraining function of wrong beliefs in young children's understanding of deception. *Cognition* 13:103–128.

11.

SACRIFICE AND RITUALIZATION

Caroline Humphrey and James Laidlaw

The ethnographic case of a rite of animal sacrifice (taxilag) *in a Buddhist monastery temple in Inner Mongolia, together with other associated rites from the same region, is used to test a theory of ritualization put forward by the authors in previous publications, where the ethnographic case was the quite different and contrasting Jain* puja, *from Western India. This prompts some clarifications to the analytical category of sacrifice, and a clear distinction between it and ritualization. The ritualization of the ceremony in which a sacrifice is performed need not imply or require ritualization of the sacrifice itself.*

In the summers of 1998 to 2002 we[1] were investigating sacred landscapes in Inner Mongolia. The southern side of the Mona Uula mountain range, running parallel to the *Huang-He* (Yellow) River, is an area believed by Mongols to be densely permeated with spirit powers. These, called "masters" (*ejid*), inhere in rivers, spring, crags, animal trails, waterfalls, caves, tops of mountains, and especially in green and bushy trees. There are also various artifacts in this landscape, such as *stupas*, victory flag-staffs, and round stone cairns called *oboo*, where the same or similar "masters" dwell or can be called into presence. It was impressed on us that the most obvious thing the local people do with regard to these sites and objects is to offer them, or the spirits in them, "sacrifices." More exactly, they hold events called *taxilag* (from the verb *taxi-*, to propitiate), which we identified with the anthropological idea of sacrifice. Most of these occasions involve the killing of a domesticated animal, the offering of certain of its organs to the spirit power, and the subsequent consumption of the edible parts of the dead beast. Clearly ritual and clearly sacrifice, one might think. But as we observed the haphazard, *ad hoc* character of these taxilag, which nevertheless include certain extremely formalized sections, and when we considered the range of activities that can be called a taxilag—an event that sometimes deliberately omits the killing of an animal—we began to query both of the key terms. What was "ritualized" about these events? And what was "sacrificial"? The more we thought about these questions, the more "sacrifice" and ritual" seemed to drift apart. In this paper, we explain how the Mongolian example has persuaded us that these categories should be understood as different and separate.

The argument is an extension of ideas put forward in our book, *The Archetypal Actions of Ritual* (Humphrey and Laidlaw 1994; Laidlaw and Humphrey 2006), which developed the theory that "ritual" is a quality that action can come to have, rather than being, as many other theorists had assumed, a definable category of distinctive kinds of events. Noting both that an extraordinarily wide range of actions, events, and processes can be ritualized and also that "rituals" are always ritual-somethings (that is, they always consist of actions that can be performed in unritualized ways), we suggested that the key questions a theoretical treatment of ritual needs to answer are: What happens when you perform an act *as* a ritual? What is it about ritual acts that makes them ritual? (Humphrey and Laidlaw 1994:72). Our answer to these questions elaborates upon a central claim that ritualization involves the modification—an attenuation but not elimination—of the normal intentionality of human action. Ritual is action in which intentionality is in a certain way displaced so that, as we summarize the matter, participants both are and are not the authors of their ritual actions. This accounts, we argue, for many of the often-noted features of rituals: the distinctive ways in which they are rule governed; the fact that component actions have a certain object-like quality, can be repeated, have their order changed and reversed, be lengthened and shortened; and thus, the fact that to those who perform them they can seem not to be merely the outcome of what they themselves do but instead to be preexisting or archetypal entities which they somehow aim at replicating, or achieving, or entering into. There are reasons, deriving from the fact that these "archetypal actions" can have highly complex meanings attributed to them but also can be performed in abstracted or dissociated states of mind, why religion uses ritual very widely and pervasively. These same reasons also explain why religions are often ambivalent about ritual or downright hostile to it. But it is an important corollary of our argument that understanding what is distinctive about ritual is separate from understanding the nature of the acts or processes that are ritualized. This is as true of religious acts, such as sacrifice, as it is of political or social actions. Entirely non-religious actions, such as taking up citizenship of a new country, can be highly ritualized (or not), just as religious actions may be ritualized (or not) (Humphrey and Laidlaw 1994:65–67).

Our book expounded its theory through a single ethnographic case, that of the Jain *puja* (a sequence of rites of worship and offering) in

Western India. This had its advantages in terms of the coherence of the materials and the detail we were able to draw on to explain issues concerning rules, mistakes, purposes, and meanings. But the disadvantage was that it was difficult to convey or substantiate the generality of our claims about ritualization as a modification of the intentionality of human action. It was possible for readers to see the Jain puja as a special case, that of a liturgy-based, particularly "doctrinal" ritual (Whitehouse 1995, 2004; Whitehouse and Laidlaw 2004). So what better place to explore the generalizability of our ideas than in the wildly different society of rural Inner Mongolia? The taxilag, with its cheerful tramping up craggy mountains, matter-of-fact killing of livestock, fascination with blood and guts, lighthearted improvisation, and its feasting with plentiful downing of strong alcoholic spirits, seemed a world away from the precise, serious, and, one might say, almost prim activities of the Jain puja. Would our ideas about ritual apply in the Mongol case too?

A further advantage of the comparison is that it enables us to demonstrate the range and plurality of "sacrifice," since both the Jain puja and the Mongol taxilag can be understood as varieties of this idea. This article does not aim, however, to provide a theory of sacrifice, if any such single theory were even possible. Several powerful arguments have, in very different ways, seen "sacrifice" as the kernel of religion (Girard 1977; Burkert 1983, 1987; Valeri 1985, 1994; Bloch 1986, 1992). These propositions have their own value, but our concern here is that they are weakened by conflation of the actions of the sacrifice-religion complex they are really trying to explain on the one hand and the phenomenon of ritual on the other. Bloch, of course, has made substantial contributions to the anthropological understanding of ritual (see, for example, Bloch 2004), but these are quite separate from his theory of sacrifice and "rebounding violence." Theorists of sacrifice, because they confuse sacrifice with ritual in general, often mistakenly assume that if their theories are successful, they have explained the latter too. It sometimes even appears as if sacrifice is not just the core of religion but of ritual as well (Girard 1977:300). By disentangling these two anthropological categories, we hope to be able to show that our account of ritualization does apply to contexts very different from the Jains, and also to clarify some issues in the relation between sacrifice and religion.

ETHNOGRAPHIC AND HISTORICAL CONTEXT

The ethnographic context for the present study was the Buddhist Monastery of Mergen Süm and its surrounding villages and settlements in southwestern Inner Mongolia. Before the revolutions and wars of the twentieth century, this was a large and wealthy monastic community, with seven reincarnated lamas, an elaborate hierarchy of several hundred other monks, extensive landholdings, and a fine walled complex of temples and residential buildings. The community was destroyed and disbanded, and the buildings badly damaged, in mid-century, but following the end of the Cultural Revolution, one surviving reincarnated lama, the Chorji Lama, who lives permanently in the nearby city of Bautou, has now reasserted his claims, and a small monastic community has been reestablished.

In this region sacrifice is prominent, perhaps even central to religious life. Of course, it is well known that "spirit cults" coexist with Buddhism in many Asian societies (Tambiah 1970; Spiro 1971) and that in some regions of what is called "ethnographic Tibet," Buddhist communities still offer blood sacrifices to local deities, despite the centuries-long disapproval by lamas (Mumford 1989). Nevertheless, it was arresting to us to find blood sacrifice taking place inside a famous *Gelugpa* establishment—the Gelugpa being the reformed and most strict of the monastic traditions in North Asia. Here, the crucial organs of the carcass are laid out in the inner sanctum of a temple, right beside the Buddhist altar (see figure 11.1). Furthermore, the taxilag ceremony (or at least that part of it taking place inside the temple) is carried out by the lamas with cheerful goodwill and without a hint of condemnation. In other words, this is what seems an ideological impossibility: a Buddhist sacrifice.

Yet it is not the ideological contradiction of animal sacrifice with a religion of compassion for all living things that interests us here; and nor is this apparent ethical paradox the reason for our argument that sacrifice and ritualization should be understood as separate processes. We would make the same argument even in cases where prevalent religious values and the practice of sacrifice are in perfect harmony. And, in fact, an argument to this effect could be made for the people of Mergen district. Although disagreements about the advisability of blood sacrifice are not altogether absent, as we discuss further toward the end of this paper, we found that there is a generally accepted, long-lived, and stable tradition of "Buddhicized sacrifice" in this area. It is necessary first to give a brief account of this phenomenon historically, before proceeding to our own argument.

The Mergen Monastery is the home of the line of reincarnations of the Mergen Gegen, of whom the third, Lubsandambijalsan, was particularly innovative in the early eighteenth century in composing texts to celebrate local deities and "spirit masters" of the land. Crucially, this creative outpour-

FIGURE 11.1. Goat sacrifice laid out in front of the battle standard,
Mergen Monastery, 1998.

ing was included within the Buddhist cycle of rituals conducted by the
lamas. A poet who rejected the Tibetan-language liturgy, which was—and
still is—predominant over the whole of Inner Asia, the Third Mergen
Gegen deepened and extended an earlier tradition in this monastery of
using the Mongolian language for liturgy. His lyrical prayers included
paeans of praise and propitiatory addresses to the local mountains, rivers,
crags, and so on, mentioned earlier, as well as to a number of fierce protector deities of the Buddhist pantheon. Not only do the lamas use these same
texts today, but also several of the eulogies have been adopted as folk songs

by local people, which they sing at weddings and other festivals. The possibility of confluence between the Buddhist deity-image and the physical landscape around the monastery is seen in the fact that Lubsandambijalsan is said to have acquired a personal deity, *Öxin Tengger*, when he experienced a transformative vision of her as "being" on the slope of a nearby hill. He constructed a stupa (*suburgan*) to her honor on this hill. Öxin Tengger is the Mongolian name of the Buddhist goddess known in Tibetan as *Baldan Lhamo*. The hill is also called Öxin Tengger. Though the stupa was destroyed in the Cultural Revolution, a kind of benign power is attributed to the hill itself, in the context of a landscape strategically dotted with sacred objects constructed to suppress evil spirits. In short, the Mergen Gegen validated the worship, in a "common cycle," of deities and landscape objects that are usually, in other Buddhist regions, seen as separate and different.

Now the Gegen's prayers acknowledge the *dokshit* ("fierce") character of many of the deities involved. For example, one text advised for use at the sacred cairn (*oboo*) includes the words:

> Collect and absorb
> The whole great power of Buddha and Bodhisattva,
> And become the emperor of fury,
> Bluish colored, fiercely angered...
> Showing your eye teeth,
> Flashing your tongue,
> Staring with your three eyes. . . .

Although the Gegen had criticized blood sacrifices at the oboo as "dirty" and "sinful" and advised making taxilag offerings without them, evidently local people in the eighteenth century had thought that only blood sacrifice could appease such local land gods. The same is still true today, with the difference that now even the Mergen lamas agree. Thus, the taxilag rite should be carried out in a "red" (blood) or a "white" (milk and grain products) variant, according to whether the deity addressed is considered to be dokshit or not. The essential point is that a variegated repertoire of ritual actions extends right across the spectrum, from blood sacrifice offered to the "fierce" warrior-like master spirit of the nearby mountain peak of Shar Oroi to offerings for the great "fierce" and "peaceful" (*nomxon*) Buddhist deities such as Tara. The term *taxilag* is used for all of these rites, and the same idea lies behind the variety of offerings. The deity should be propitiated (*taxi-*) by whatever means it will appreciate.

Looking at the number and regularity of rites, it is fair to say that most of the time the idea of ferocious gods who protect one from harm is at least as compelling to the people in this region as the wisdom and compassion associated with the peaceful ones. Furthermore, the Buddhist "fierce" deities coexist with, and sometimes seem to elide into, images of ancestral warriors and the spirits of battle standards (as well as the spirits of the land). It is because one such battle standard (tug)[2] is kept in the Janghan Temple[3] at the Mergen Monastery, its spirit requiring blood propitiation, that we discovered the seeming anomaly of the goat carcass beside the altar.

The ethnographic materials used for this article include our own detailed participant observation of the taxilags for Shar Oroi Peak (1998) and the battle standard (2000 and 2002), as well as of a non-sacrificial ritual held annually at the Mergen Monastery, the Mani ceremony of 2000. Besides these, we have had access to videotapes and descriptions of a variety of "red" and "white" taxilags to a sacred tree, a spring, and a cairn (oboo), and another example of the Shar Oroi mountain ritual, all from 1999.[4]

INTRODUCING THE ARGUMENT

With this ethnographic introduction, it is now possible for us to outline our argument in brief. The taxilag for the battle standard is perhaps the most elaborate "ritual" we observed, but we argue in the following section that the ritualization seen here is not, for the most part, ritualization of the sacrifice. The sacrifice itself remains comparatively unritualized, and the crucial killing of the animal, on the occasion we observed it, was entirely practical (that is, it did not even incorporate those ritual elements the Mongols told us "should" take place on such occasions). Instead, as we suggest in the subsequent section, the complex and elaborate ritualization of the tug (battle standard) ceremony derives from its incorporation in the cycle of Buddhicized worship. That is, it derives from the assimilation of the spirit of the battle standard to the pantheon of fierce (dokshit) deities and hence of the tug rites into the "Buddhist" repertoire of the lamas. In other words, the offering to the tug includes a whole range of rites also used in many other standard Buddhist ceremonies. This point is demonstrated by a comparison of the tug rites with the non-sacrificial Mani ceremony. Although the latter is explained locally by entirely different purposes from those attributed to the tug sacrifice—one version is the attaining of spiritual completeness—an identical array of ritualized actions are employed in it (along with some others that are different). In both the tug and the Mani ceremonies, we see the characteristic features of ritualization:

the preset "nonintentional" character of ritual acts, the presence of stipu-
lating constitutive rules, the dividing up of action into discrete acts that
may be moved or displaced, and the attribution of different meanings to
the same ritualized act (Humphrey and Laidlaw 1994; Laidlaw and
Humphrey 2006). Thus, in both the tug and the Mani, we found the repetition of the same discrete, highly ritualized actions, such as manipula-
tions of an arrow, mirror, grains, and sacred water, and rites of "penitence"
(*namanchilag*) and receiving empowered, blessed objects (*adis*). These
"movable" ritual acts (meaning those that can be injected into many different ceremonies) are interspersed with others that are particular to a
given rite and with some actions that are not ritualized at all. And in all
the rites we observed, it is the movable acts that predominate, taking up
the great majority of time. Yet, for many of these movable ritual acts, it is
difficult even for the Mongol participants to conceptualize their relevance
to any of the events at issue: in the cases of the tug sacrifice and the Mani,
respectively, the worship of a fierce deity and the attainment of spiritual
completeness. In fact, ritualization here goes further than in the Jain case,
to the point of virtually obliterating any coherent conception of the overall structure of the event. As a result, the rationale for including, or not
including, any given ritual act in the sequence becomes weak. Uncertainty
among the lamas, even on the days of the rite, about what would be in it
and therefore how long it would last, is an indication of the highly ritualized, formulaic character of these "archetypal actions" in their repertoire.

   These ideas may be discussed in relation to theories of sacrifice.
Bloch's (1992) account of "rebounding violence," for instance, is one of
the most persuasive recent anthropological works on the nature of sacrifice. However, it applies much more clearly to less ritualized than to
more ritualized instances. This is true whether it is the sacrificial killing
itself, or, as in the Mongol battle-standard case, the encompassing event
(the offering as a whole) that is ritualized. Thus, to some extent, ritualization is a process that works against the symbolic/ideological dynamic
that authors such as Bloch and Valeri identify in sacrifice. The more ritualized a series of actions, the more they need to be decoded by the
anthropologist in order to show that such a theory applies, because the
rite as performed decreasingly resembles the underlying event or process
that has been ritualized—the sacrifice. The meaning and coherence of
the underlying event is obscured, dissipated, and dispersed by ritualization. Therefore, we conclude, the more a sacrifice is ritualized, the less
clearly it is sacrificial in a religious sense.[5]

URAD MONGOL SACRIFICE

The claim that the key event of sacrifice, the killing of the living being, can be relatively little ritualized may seem surprising, because we tend to assume that people generally ritualize what is important to them. In this section, we show first that sacrifice as such is highly important to the Mongols of the Mergen area, and secondly, that it does not constitute the most highly ritualized part of the taxilag (even though the latter can be described as a whole as a "ritual sacrifice"). For descriptive purposes, we define "sacrifice" here as comprised of three related sequences:[6] the killing of a live being, the offering of its life (or some concept such as its "life energy") to a spirit or deity, and the subsequent acquiring of benefit or fortune of some kind through the consumption of parts of the offering (Bloch 1992).[7]

One could argue that sacrifice is central to the identity of the people of Mergen considered historically. These are Urad Mongols, a group claiming descent from Chingghis Khan's brother Habt Hasar, who were sent from their homeland in the far north near the Russian border by the Manchu Qing Dynasty in the seventeenth century to conquer and guard their present lands. Until the early twentieth century, the Urad Mongols comprised three Banners[8] in the Qing imperial structure, and most of their territories are still known as "Banners" (*Hoshuu*) today.[9] When one considers that these are incomers, for whom "conquering" and "guarding" territory was central to their *raison d'être* in the area, it makes a certain sense that the lay Mongols have chosen "fierce" gods as their primary objects of worship and that they devote so much energy to the propitiation of the spirits of the land. The profound meaning of sacrifice for the success of their endeavor—that is, the reproduction of the good fortune (*xishig*) of a victorious people in a land beset by spirit and human enemies—is indicated by certain Mongols' claim that the original sacrifices were of human beings. They speak of human sacrifice with horrified fascination and say it was productive of a terrible power.

We were told that the very first sacrifices for the battle standard, the spirit of the Huang-Ho River, and the Banner *oboo* (the stone cairn where regular gatherings of the Urad groups were held) consisted of the killing of human enemies. Such sacrifices are said to have been necessary to provide spiritual strength in times of extreme danger. The 1940s, with fighting between Communists, Republicans, and so-called warlords, were another such time. We met an elderly man who said his uncle had been deputed to find a human victim for the Banner oboo sacrifice but had been unable to do so, and therefore the Banner had to resort to the usual substitution, an ox, which was the custom in more peaceable times. According to accounts of the human sacrifice, the victim should be male, an enemy,[10] and ideally covered with unusually copious body hair (the word for animal fur was used for this). This victim was made drunk, then tightly and completely bound from the feet upward, forcing the blood into the head. He was dispatched by the Banner leader who would spear the skull, producing a spectacular spurt of blood. This blood, spattered on the standard or the cairn, was said to give invincible power to the ancestral and other spirits who would assure the victorious existence of the Urad Mongols. These events were described to us with some embarrassment, since everyone has been educated to think of them as the height of "superstition." Some people claimed they were "just stories." Yet few people locally doubt that human sacrifice has indeed taken place on rare occasions. They say that their present sacrifices of livestock to the standard and the oboo are direct continuations of the same rite. The substitution of animal for human victims happens because in more peaceful times less extreme sacrifices are necessary.

Two things seem to us to follow from this account: first, that killing and the offering of blood are central to the Mongols' concept of sacrifice; and second, that sacrifice as an event is integral to their beliefs about the successful reproduction of their existence in times of danger. It is impossible to speculate with any degree of reliability about the degree to which the human sacrifices in the past were ritualized. But in the present rites—which, let us remember, people say are a direct continuation of these human sacrifices—the actual killing is hardly ritualized at all. In effect, the event of "sacrifice" is hidden amid a thicket of other ritualized acts.

THE SACRIFICE TO THE BATTLE STANDARD

The central example for this paper is the taxilag for the tug (battle standard), which is kept in the most sacred inner sanctum of the Janghan Temple. This tug is said to have belonged to a seventeenth-century ancestor called Jargal Baatar, and it is preserved along with his armor and clothing. The ceremony lasts for most of a day and consists of four ritual sections, called *chig* by the lamas. Each chig is separated by a break in the ritual, when the lamas leave the temple and retire to their quarters to rest. As described to us the day before the taxilag, each chig is supposed to comprise a number of specific named rites. Yet evidently, as will be detailed below, some of these rites can be left out, while others may be repeated, thus lengthening or shortening the section and the ritual as a whole. These decisions are taken as the day proceeds and, as far as we could gather, according to the mood of the directing lama.[11]

We were told that a yellowish sheep would be the best offering to the tug, and that the killing of the animal was due to take place during the first chig. What actually happened was that the man deputed to obtain a yellowish sheep could not find one and bought a white goat. The goat was unceremoniously dispatched, in a residential compound in the monastery, during the gap between the first and second chigs, by a layman. Meanwhile, the first chig proceeded as a series of rites initiated by the blowing of a conch shell and clashing of cymbals outside the doors of the Janghan Temple. The lamas and the entire congregation then proceeded into the temple for the taxilag rites. Although the four chigs can be lengthened or shortened at will, it seems that the actual sacrifice, the killing of the animal, is not one of these rites. Both by virtue of its timing (between chigs) and its spatial location (outside the temple, though inside the monastery), the physical killing is in a sense excluded from the taxilag. The sacrificial meat is included only as one element in a list of various offerings made later in the rite to the deity of the standard, all the rest of which are what we have called "movable" elements found also in other Buddhist rituals.

The tug taxilag in the temple started with the *megzem* (a prayer to Padmasambhava), the *itgel* (vow of belief), and the *chain taxil* (offering of tea to the lamas). The head lama then enumerated the offerings in ritual units called *ja*, a foreign term used by lamas for "share." The offerings on this occasion were listed as "a sheep one unit" (despite the fact that everyone knew a goat was in the offing), "salt three units," "tea two units," "milk six units," and other items such as money and buns. The use of special, non-everyday terms for these items, the counting in the unfamiliar units of ja, and the evident divorce between the list and the actual offerings it ostensibly described, indicate that the act of listing was itself ritualized. This listing of items was immediately followed by the *daatgal*, a short standard text by which people hand over their lives (or some activity of central importance to them) to the total protection of a god. The daatgal was repeated many times. The lamas then swung into a series of chants, each for a named dokshit deity, which they read from the Mergen Gegen's Mongolian texts. These greatly exceeded the earlier rites in length and fervor. With musical encouragements, the low roar of long trumpets, the thud of the large drum, clashing cymbals, ringing of bells, and rattling of hand-drums, each dokshit deity was described and invoked at length. One deity in this series was the well-known fierce protector god *Yamandaga*.[12] Another was *Gagch Baatar*

(Lone Warrior Hero), also a deity well known in the Buddhist pantheon. After about an hour of these invocations, the music rose to a loud crescendo and then chanting ceased. At this point, as we were later told, the gods descended (*burxan buudaj baina*). After a final, more subdued prayer to the calm (*nomxon*) deity, White Tara, the first chig ended.

In the interval following the first chig, as we sat around having tea in the compound of the Chorji Lama, some distance from the temple, the goat was brought in and dispatched beside us. A specialist butcher (a layman) was employed, and he killed the animal by slitting its chest, reaching in his arm, feeling for the aorta, and tearing it apart. He made no protective, purificatory or other ritual preparations; nor were there any preparatory rites of purification of the goat, such as we were later told "should" take place for sacrifices. In fact, the goat sacrifice was done in exactly the same way that Mongols normally kill animals (for regular food). They always try to employ a specialist slaughterer, and they always use the tearing of the aorta method. Now this method may look ritualized to one unfamiliar with Mongolia, simply because it seems a strange way of killing an animal. In fact, though, it has a practical purpose, which is the conservation of the blood within the carcass for later use as food. The "management of blood" appears to have been a key concern in the human sacrifice too, even though the method of dispatch in the latter case seems far more bizarre. This became apparent to us when we heard the details of a threat of "human sacrifice" from a distant region in northern Mongolia (Morten Pedersen, personal communication). During the 1930s, a Communist activist had strayed into this remote area of fierce resistance. He was captured and threatened with death. The locals described how they would kill him: by binding him tightly from the feet upward to his lower chest, and then from the top of his head downward to his upper chest. The blood would be concentrated in the area of his heart. When his chest was slit, his heart would spring out from between his ribs with a jet of blood. This horrifying act was to be dedicated to the battle standard of the rebels. We see that what is aimed at here is a practical and shocking effect, even a symbolic effect, and that this can be achieved in different ways. What is important here are the act itself and the intention behind it, not the performance of a standardized convention, as is characteristic of ritualization.

In the tug sacrifice, if the actual killing of the goat is more or less unritualized, the offering of its parts to the deity is distinctly more so. Parts and named actions are specified in advance and are the same as those used in other blood sacrifices, such as those to the mountain deity.

It is specified that "red" offerings must include the *jülde*, the *chus*, and the *chüs*. The jülde is said to consist of "the five organs" *(taban tsol)*, those parts held to sustain life (the heart, lungs, liver, kidneys, and head), to which, for some reason no one could explain, the right foreleg and the four right top ribs should be added. The ankles and hooves with the entire skin must be included in the offering as a sign that the whole animal is being offered. The chus (blood) is represented by a small jar of raw blood, and the chüs (bile) is likewise placed uncooked in a jar for offering. The main lama gave laconic instructions to the butcher on how to excise these parts correctly. When laid out in the temple, the jülde is wrapped in the goatskin, the hairy side inward, with the head facing toward the battle standard. Slits are made in the skin so that the eyes can "see" the tug. The goat's eyes are therefore kept open, as is its mouth, the latter being a sign that the goat can vomit out its "five organs" to the god. Immediately after the killing, this entire offering is brought into the temple and laid out before the battle standard, just to the right of the Buddhist altar, together with butter lamps.

We wondered throughout this ritual exactly to whom or to what the sacrifice was being given. People had spoken to us of the battle standard itself (tug), which is a pole some 7 feet in height topped with a metal trident. Just below the trident is a metal circle, from which dangles long, tangled, black hair (said to be human hair). They also said the addressee of the sacrifice might be the spirit *(sülde)* of the tug, or a Buddhist deity, *Gungga*, locally called *Tavan Khan*, said by some to be the "master" of the tug.[13] The lama who carried in and laid out the jülde made three soundless prostrations to the Buddhist altar, which bears representations of many deities, among them Tavan Khan. After numerous fruitless inquiries, we were forced to admit that the designee of the sacrifice was unclear.[14] Certainly Tavan Khan never rose to particular prominence in the liturgy as the tug taxilag rites continued.

The second chig now began with a rite that had no apparent relevance to the sacrifice at all. This was the "confession to the four fierce gods" *(dörbön dokshit-yn namanchilag)*.[15] The namanchilag are long texts, chanted according to the words and melodies of the Mergen Gegen, which describe and call upon each god to forgive known and unknown sins. We noted that the lamas were chanting for their own sins to be forgiven, whereas it was the laity who had made the goat offering, which seemed to be entirely ignored during this section. Lay worshipers continued to arrive, stood around briefly in silence, and perhaps offered some money to a lama or placed it on an altar, before being seated behind the chanting lamas. Some, but not all, stayed through the remainder of the ceremony. After around an hour of the confession chants, the lamas moved to a rite called *xariguulag*, whereby a deity is implored to "fight back" and vanquish devils. A xariguulag was chanted for each of the well-known "fierce" Buddhist gods. The second chig concluded with the throwing out of *balings* (cone and phallic-shaped dough models, said to be offerings). We were told that many godlings and spirits gather when a taxilag is held. The balings are thrown out at several points during the ritual. They are scattered in all "15 directions," as well as onto the roof of the temple, to appease hovering spirits, with the idea: "Be happy and keep away, leave us to perform this ritual in peace." Other people, however, interpreted the balings as "weapons" thrown like spears to attack evil spirits.

We hope that enough has been said, without an exhaustive description of the entire taxilag, to indicate the relatively peripheral role in it of two of the three key elements of sacrifice—namely, the killing of a live being and the offering of its parts to the deity. The third core element of the sacrifice, consumption of parts of the offering by the congregation, occurs, however, in parts that are rather highly ritualized. This can be seen from the fact that the essential operation—ingestion of the offering returned back from the deity and transformed as blessing or fortune (Bloch 1992)—is divided by the Mongols into several different rites and actions. However, the result of this ritualization is that these various actions are so separate from the acts of killing and offering, and from one another, that the logic of "the sacrifice" is obscured.

The main act of consumption, the feast *(xool)*, is hardly ritualized at all. The ritual appropriate to this occasion is the same as that obtaining at feasts in general. We ate the cooked meat of the goat at a cheerful and entirely secular feast out of doors in the Chorji Lama's compound during the interval between the second and third chig, a meal to which all and sundry were invited.

Similarly unritualized is the "consumption" of the jülde, the symbolic parts of the animal laid before the deity. We were told that the jülde should be taken away by the *gonir* lama[16] and, in private after the ritual, eaten in its entirety, including the eyes, the idea being that nothing offered to the god should be thrown away.[17] But this provision—that it should all be eaten—is the only prescription he appears to be under.[18]

Another, highly ritualized act of consumption does take place, however, in the main body of the temple during the third chig. This happens in the context of the ritual act of "beckoning of fortune" (*dalalga*). While the Chorji Lama waves an "arrow of heaven" and holds a bowl of grains,[19] the lay patron or offerer of the sacrifice holds up a platter with the dalalga foods and, with a circular gesture, calls in the blessing (*xeshig*) of the god(s). The contents of the platter go to this patron and should be taken home for consumption within the immediate family and on no account given to outsiders. Now "logically" the platter should contain parts of the goat offering which should, therefore, be kept back from the collective feast. Lamas said that the cooked right foreleg should be part of the dalalga meat—and at a taxilag we attended for the deity of the Shar Oroi mountain peak, this indeed was the case. At the tug ritual in 2000, however, the dalalga platter contained bread, dates, cheese, and dried cream, and thus bore no evident relation to the goat sacrifice. The "movable" character of the dalalga rite in general is indicated by the fact that it can take place on its own, as well as in conjunction with many other ceremonial sequences aside from the taxilag: for example, at funerals, at the giving away of a bride, or at the calling-in of migratory birds in the spring (Chabros 1992).

So far we have shown that the "consumption" phase of sacrifice is divided into three (or two if we exclude the jülde, as Valeri would argue). The communal meal, so central to many theories of sacrifice—from Robertson Smith to Detienne and Vernant (1989) and Valeri (1994)—is separated from the consuming of the parts actually offered to the god and, more singularly, from the rite of ingestion of good fortune by the offering participants. The taxilag contains a further type of consumption. This is *adis*, the ceremonial handing out of fortune-conveying foods to the congregation by the lamas. One explanation of adis is that it is the blessed leftovers of the deity. The nearest equivalent to this we know from other cultures is the *prasad* or *prabhavana* distributed in Indian temples. Like the dalalga, the giving out of adis is a "movable" ritual act that occurs in many diverse situations. The adis at the goat sacrifice was distributed twice, first to lamas alone during the third chig, and afterward to the laity outside the temple. It consisted of biscuits and a brownish, sweet tea-like liquid, poured by a lama from a brass pot onto a peacock feather. The liquid was then dripped onto the palms of the lamas or lay participants, who then licked it up.

To convey to our readers how these various rites of consumption were distributed among other, unrelated rites at the tug taxilag, let us simply list the sequence of rites in the third chig, many of which, the reader will notice, have also occurred during the first two chigs: (1) smoke offering (*ünesen sang*); (2) chant for ghosts (*totxor*); (3) offering of balings; (4) a chant called *sülde* (spirit or soul-inspiration); (5) libation of alcohol (*altan taxil*); (6) prayer to Mon Khan, the deity of the Shar Oroi Mountain; (7) the "beckoning" of dalalga; (8) repetition of smoke offering; (9) washing the face of god (*nuur ugaalah*); (10) chant for raising the spirit (*sülde devdeh*); (11) giving of adis; (12) repetition of "washing the face";[20] (13) prayer to Yamandaga; (14) chant to the White Tara goddess; (15) adis biscuits given out to all lamas, but not to lay people; and finally, (16), a rite called *gurim* or "the triple repulse" (*gurvan xariuulag*), which was tacked on at the request of one of the laity to get rid of a personal misfortune. This was rapidly chanted from memory—the lamas were already folding up the trumpets and wrapping up their texts.

This having been done, the lamas silently told their prayer beads and put their hands together. They clapped three times, and with this the tax-ilag ended. It turned out to our surprise that the fourth chig had effective-ly been compressed into the third. We were told later about how one rite, the "wind horse" (*xii mori*), which should have been part of the fourth sequence, had been amalgamated with the sülde chant in the middle of the third chig. The reason for the shortening of the whole ritual may have been simply that the lamas were tired after many hours of chanting.

To summarize, let us briefly assess this description of the taxilag to the battle standard in respect, first, of the structure of sacrifice and, second, in relation to our theory of ritualization.

It was stated earlier that sacrifice consists of at least three elements: the killing of a consecrated live being, the offering of its life energy to the deity, and the ingestion by the congregation of the transformed substance of the offering as a blessing. In the case at hand, the acquisition and dis-patch of the victim was, in effect, not ritualized and was carried out out-side the ritual space of the taxilag. The symbolic offering of the life force of the animal (jülde), on the other hand, was brought centrally into the rit-ual space. But the spiritual designate of the sacrifice was never clear, and hence it was not evident which of the ritual chants was the one whereby the jülde was offered up. As for the third element, certain rites of incorpo-ration of fortune by the participants were included in the taxilag. But this function of blessing-giving consumption was dispersed into four separate elements (the communal feast, the "beckoning fortune" rite, the giving of adis, and the eating of the jülde), two of which took place outside the rit-ual space and time of the taxilag (the feast and the eating of the jülde).

Meanwhile, the elements of sacrifice that were incorporated in the taxilag ceremony as a whole were mixed up with numerous other rites that greatly exceeded them in number, complexity, auditory and visual salience, and length of time involved. This was particularly obvious in the final sequence, as the acquisition of spiritual fortune or blessing was—

according to our informants—gained as much through the "wind horse" and "raising the spirit" ritual chants as from the more clearly sacrificial elements (the feast, the dalalga, and the consumption of adis). In such ways, the line of "logic" of the sacrifice was dispersed and obscured.

CONCLUSION

Our theory of ritual mentioned earlier applies without difficulty to the case of Mongolian sacrifice. We see in this case the crucial role of ritual space, for example, where the terrain is divided into the highly sacred temple sanctum, the less sacred space inside the temple, and the relatively non-sacred area of the Chorji's compound. The siting of actions in one or another of these spaces is significant. That the killing of the animal, for example, took place in the least sacred area is certainly not an accident and surely is related to the Buddhist disapproval of killing (however subdued such disapproval is in this monastery). Our idea that highly ritualized acts are "nonintentional" in the sense of being stipulated in advance, necessary for the achievement of the ritual, and open to a variety of meanings and purposes, was also confirmed by the tug ceremony. This ritual sequence of sacrifice contained rites that are commonly performed as parts of quite other ceremonies, and there is no clear reason for their incorporation here other than the idea that, by established tradition, they have to be done.

As for sacrifice, while the tripartite structure of actions mentioned above is manifested in the battle-standard ceremony, these actions are only patchily ritualized. The relation between such blood sacrifices and "religion" can certainly be questioned in the Mongol case, given their similarity to the dispatch of victims in actual fields of battle, on the one hand, and their uneasy juxtaposition with Buddhism, on the other. Considering Mack's claim (1987:8) that ritual is by definition a reenactment of a "prior event," it might be possible to argue that sacrifice in the Mongolian case should not be considered ritual in this sense. The human sacrifices were not thought by participants to be reenactments but contingent actions undertaken to deal with particular, dire circumstances. Possibly, for the Mongols, sacrifice in general always has something of this character, even when it is conducted regularly. Even if we concede that such blood sacrifices are in some sense religious, it would be quite another matter to "identify" them with ritual. We have argued that ritualization is a separate process, one that is injected into sacrificial action at certain points and not others. The interesting question then becomes, why are certain acts so much more ritualized than others?

GLOSSARY

adis: Empowering blessing, usually bestowed by a lama, and objects so empowered.

baling: Small cone- and phallus-shaped dough shapes, often red in color, offered in temple rituals.

chig: Section of a lengthy ritual.

dalalga: Plate of meat, blessed during a sacrificial ritual, through which blessing is conveyed to the patron and his or her family.

dokshit: "Fierce" deities, requiring blood offerings. Contrast *nomxon*.

ejid: Literally "masters." Spirits residing in rivers, animal trails, mountaintops, and other features of the landscape.

jülde: Parts of the corpse of a sacrificed animal, laid out as an offering, and consisting of the five life-sustaining organs (heart, lungs, liver, kidneys, and head), wrapped in the animal's skin.

Mani: Annual Buddhist ceremonial rite, during which small edible pellets, later taken away and consumed by worshipers, are endowed with spiritual power (*adis*) by means of recitation of sacred texts by lamas.

namanchilag: Rite of propitiation and penitence, characteristically to appease fierce (*dokshit*) deities.

nomxon: "Peaceful" deities, requiring vegetarian offerings. Contrast *dokshit*.

oboo: Semi-spherical monument, usually of undressed stones, wherein reside *ejid* (spirits).

puja: Rite of worship, often before a temple image, in Hinduism and Jainism.

taxilag: Sacrifice; sacrificial ritual.

tug: Battle standard.

NOTES

1. The team included, at various times, Caroline Humphrey, James Laidlaw, Balzhan Zhimbiev, Christopher Evans, and A. Hürelbaatar from Cambridge, and Nasanbayar, Gai Zhe-yi, and Mönhbuyan from Huhhot, Inner Mongolia.
2. The battle standard (*tug*) is different from the victory flag-mast (*darchug*), a post with colored cloth streamers. The latter are erected in the landscape to suppress evil forces. Most of them were destroyed in the Cultural Revolution, but one or two have started to appear again, for example opposite the main door of the (sadly now late) Lama Lubsansengge's house in a village not far from Mergen. The tug, by contrast, celebrates human victories over human enemies. The most noted examples in Inner Mongolia are kept at the Chinggis Khan mausoleum in the Ordos.
3. The Janghan Temple is the smaller of the two currently working temples at the Mergen Monastery. The other temple notably contains a huge statue of the Maitreya Buddha and is not used for sacrifices. The allocation of one separate

temple for sacrifices, often called the Deity Temple, is common in Mongolian and Buryat Buddhist monasteries.

4. The 1999 field observations were made by our colleague Hürelbaatar, who also accompanied us to Mergen in 1998, 2000, and 2002.

5. This argument may be compared with Girard's theory (1977) that violence is the manifestation of the sacred in a dual mode: (a) the terror of uncontrolled killing, and (b) the control of violence effected by rituals of sacrifice. Ritual—that is, "control"—is thus necessary to transform killing into sacrifice. Thus far, we would agree with Girard, insofar as this argument preserves a distinction between the action (killing) and ritualization. What is more problematical is his assumption that sacrifice is central to ritual in general (1977:300).

6. Valeri (1994) offers a slightly different list of four components. However his first—induction or preparation of the victim—is, as we shall see below, absent in this case. His others are taking of the life, renunciation (which may include giving to a deity) of part of the victim, and consumption of (the rest of) it. These correspond to Bloch's three elements.

7. Clearly, many different actions have been counted as "sacrifice" in European historical contexts, and they are so varied that it is difficult to specify a root meaning of the term. This can be seen if one considers the divergent meanings attributed to the Christian Eucharist when it is defined as a (symbolic) sacrifice. It should be noted that neither "sacrifice" nor "ritual" is a concept with an exact Mongolian equivalent. We use Bloch's definition here for heuristic purposes.

8. A Banner was an administrative division responsible for providing troops and other dues to the state.

9. The Mergen Monastery was formerly in the Urad West Banner. In a recent administrative reorganization designed to extend the territories subject to cities in Inner Mongolia, the Mergen lands were incorporated in the urban district of Baotou city.

10. Normally, we were told, this victim was a Chinese. It was said by Mongols that an elderly man would volunteer to be a sacrificial victim, since this was an honorable way to die and would assure the good fortune of descendants.

11. Although the reincarnated Chorji Lama was the highest-ranking lama present, and therefore presided in a formal sense, the practical direction of the ceremony was in the hands of another, very senior, knowledgeable and liturgically experienced, but not reincarnated, lama.

12. In Tibetan Buddhism, Yamandaga is generally held to be of higher status than the other dokshit deities. A *yamad* (= Skt. *ishta*) is a chosen or personal deity. See Samuel 1993:166.

13. *Tavan Khan* (Five Kings) consists of five fierce (dokshit) gods, said to belong to the "red root" of Tantric Buddhism (Sodubilig 1996:208). The group of deities Tavan Khan belongs to is considered to be lower than the Four Dokshit. The significant fact about Tavan Khan is that this deity is both a Buddhist god and a spirit-master of the land (Naranbatu, personal communication). Thus, some oboos in the Mergen area are said to have Tavan Khan as their spirit.

14. This is true also in many other traditions. See Heesterman 1993:13 on ancient India; Yerkes 1953:74–79 on ancient Greece; and Valeri 1985:61; 1994:107, for general discussion.

15. The number four here appears to be liturgically specified, but arbitrary in relation to the number of dokshit recognized by the Mergen lamas and worshiped during the taxilag.

16. The office of *gonir lama* in a Mongolian Buddhist monastery has attached to it the duties of a temple custodian, including, especially, looking after offerings.

17. Only the bones of the sacrifice are not eaten. They are not thrown away but should be carefully burned.

18. At first sight, this stipulation might appear to contradict Valeri's (1994:107–108) insistence on distinguishing the part of the victim that is "renounced" from that which is "consumed," but the gonir lama, in this role, is not a patron or normal participant in the rite, and the rule that he should consume the food, and do so out of sight, appears to be basically a method of "secure disposal" of the offering which, now belonging to the gods, should be neither consumed "normally" as food nor left to decompose. The same concern, interestingly, is found among the Jains. Offerings made in a temple may never be taken away or consumed by observant Jains, but are eaten by paid Hindu temple servants (*pujaris*). It does, therefore, make sense, in Valeri's terms, that this part of the animal and the remainder that is eaten collectively in the feast are kept separate and "consumed" differently.

19. The dalalga arrow is not a practical artifact but a symbolic object with five notches and five colored streamers, known widely in Buddhist rituals from Tibet to Manchuria. In Tibet, the arrow and the vessel of grain represent the male and female elements, respectively (Nebesky-Woykowitz 1975:365).

20. The "washing the face" rite was done continuously during the last phase of the third chig in the inner hall of the temple, while the other chants were being carried out in the outer hall. "Washing the face" was said by one informant to be a rite of respectful farewell to the deities, with the idea, "We have called you to our temple. You have come through the dusty world. Now we cleanse you before sending you back."

REFERENCES CITED

Bloch, Maurice
   1986   *From Blessing to Violence: History and Ideology in the Circumcision Ritual of the Merina of Madagascar*. Cambridge University Press, Cambridge and New York.
   1992   *Prey into Hunter: The Politics of Religious Experience*. Cambridge University Press, Cambridge
   2004   Ritual and deference. In *Ritual and Memory: Toward a Comparative Anthropology of Religion*, edited by Harvey Whitehouse and James Laidlaw, pp. 65–78. AltaMira, Walnut Creek, CA.

Burkert, Walter
   1983   *Homo Necans: The Anthropology of Ancient Greek Sacrificial Ritual and Myth*. University of California Press, Berkeley.
   1987   The problem of ritual killing. In *Violent Origins: Ritual Killing and Cultural Formation*, edited by Robert Hamerton-Kelly, pp. 149–176. Stanford University Press, Stanford.

Chabros, Krystyna
   1992   *Beckoning Fortune: A Study of the Mongolian Dalalga Ritual*. Otto Harrassowitz, Wiesbaden.

Détienne, Marcel, and Jean-Pierre Vernant
1989   *The Cuisine of Sacrifice among the Greeks*. University of Chicago Press, Chicago.

Girard, Réné
1977   *Violence and the Sacred*. Translated by Patrick Gregory. Johns Hopkins University Press, Baltimore.

Heesterman, Jan C.
1993   *The Broken World of Sacrifice: An Essay in Ancient Indian Ritual*. Chicago University Press, Chicago.

Humphrey, Caroline, and James Laidlaw
1994   *The Archetypal Actions of Ritual: A Theory of Ritual Illustrated by the Jain Rite of Worship*. Clarendon Press, Oxford.

Laidlaw, James, and Caroline Humphrey
2006   Action. In *Theorising Rituals: Issues, Topics, Approaches, Concepts*, edited by Jens Kreinath et al., pp. 265–283. Brill, Leiden.

Mack, Burton
1987   Introduction: Religion and ritual. In *Violent Origins: Ritual Killing and Cultural Formation*, edited by Robert Hamerton-Kelly, pp. 1–72. Stanford University Press, Stanford.

Mumford, Stan Royal
1989   *Himalayan Dialogue: Tibetan Lamas and Gurung Shamans in Nepal*. University of Wisconsin Press, Madison.

Nebesky-Wojkowitz, Rene de
1975   *Oracles and Demons of Tibet: The Cult and Iconography of the Tibetan Protective Deities*. AkademischeDruck-u. Verlagsenstalt, Graz.

Samuel, Geoffrey
1993   *Civilized Shamans: Buddhism in Tibetan Societies*. Smithsonian Institution, Washington, DC.

Sodubilig
1996   *Shashin-nu toli*. Huhhot: Inner Mongolian Educational Press.

Spiro, Melford
1971   *Buddhism and Society: A Great Tradition and Its Burmese Vicissitudes*. Allen and Unwin, London.

Tambiah, Stanley J.
1970   *Buddhism and Spirit Cults in North-East Thailand*. Cambridge University Press, Cambridge.

Valeri, Valerio
1985   *Kingship and Sacrifice: Ritual and Sacrifice in Ancient Hawaii*. University of Chicago Press, Chicago.

1994   Wild victims: Hunting as sacrifice and sacrifice as hunting in Huaulu. *History of Religions* 34:101–131.

Yerkes, Royden Keith
1953   *Sacrifice in Greek and Roman Religions and in Early Judaism*. A. & C. Black, London.

Whitehouse, Harvey
    1995   *Inside the Cult: Religious Innovation and Transmission in Papua New Guinea*. Clarendon Press, Oxford.
    2004   *Modes of Religiosity: A Cognitive Theory of Religious Transmission*. AltaMira, Walnut Creek, CA.
Whitehouse, Harvey, and James Laidlaw (editors)
    2004   *Ritual and Memory: Toward a Comparative Anthropology of Religion*. AltaMira, Walnut Creek, CA.

12.

RESPONSE:
DEFINING THE NEED FOR A DEFINITION

Catherine Bell

This piece responds to the ideas and themes expressed so well in the Cotsen Advanced Seminar conference papers and conversation. It explores the benefits and liabilities for archaeology of more culturally detailed arguments about the nature of ritual, while underscoring the basic theory of a practice approach to ritual.

One of the first realizations the Cotsen Advanced Seminar brought home to me is ritual theory's relative ignorance of archaeology in the formulation of its reigning theories. Moreover, our weak attention to what archaeology has had to say about ancient ritual is matched by a concomitant misunderstanding of archaeology's needs with regard to a theory of ritual. The few major studies of Neolithic ritual that have addressed the topic of ritual in terms broad enough to engage multiple fields have been extremely speculative, with imposed agendas marked by the paucity of empirical data; so cultural theorists may have been rather quick in their assessments. Recently, of course, a fresh wave of interest, stirred by scholars of cognitive theory (the most common term used), has depicted the function of prehistoric ritual using evolutionary assumptions. Most of these accounts eschew questions of meaning in favor of a focus on the adaptive qualities of ritual as a form of communication. And, to the extent that these studies speculate about the beginnings of ritual in the earliest human communities (or simply those communities that only archaeology can find), they must work without a net, so to speak; only the credibility of their arguments can assure further interest in their line of reasoning. In a recent overview of what is happening in the study of ritual today, I have tried to assess many of these cognitive approaches; and I found that, for all their emphasis on adaptive functions, they have been content, like some colleagues in Classics or even in the nineteenth-century study of religion, to remain almost entirely speculative, with no serious engagement of archaeological works (Bell 2005). So I have learned a great deal at this conference about the many other ways in which archaeologists are thinking about ritual and the concrete problems they face.

Despite this convergence of interests, I am not sure that I can contribute significantly to archaeology's particular problems and dilemmas. In fact, it occurred to me to wonder why archaeologists are so eager to complicate the fairly straightforward definition of ritual, used for over a hundred years and expressed in a very adequate version by Professor Colin Renfrew—namely, rituals are those activities that address the gods or other supernatural forces. Has archaeology today achieved so much consensus on methods and interpretive strategies that it is seeking insecurity elsewhere? Or having trained something like two generations of archaeologists to be widely read in cultural theory, is it ready to push the envelope into this no-win area of study? In any case, here is a self-consciously scientific enterprise where its own good logic gets it involved in cultural questions.

To an historian of religions, archaeology must work with so little clear data that the simplest of definitions might seem the most useful. My field can get lost in the overabundance of detail. It wanders from analysis of the rites of American UFO cults to analysis of the installation rite of the last emperor of China, Pu Yi, in 1908—a complicated affair involving the exigencies of crowning a child, court strategies, national politics, the demands of Manchu tradition, and more than a thousand years of Chinese textual resources. And if one were to wander out onto the streets of Beijing at that time, there would be a variety of activities going on that had ritual-like features, such as divination consultations, lighting incense and tossing moon blocks in small temple settings, or transactions to secure priestly talismans to protect a newborn son from the possibilities of soul-stealing. In some of these situations, the participants would argue that their activities were not rituals at all—but custom. In fact, just such arguments are common, even among scholars, as in a disagreement between two scholars of Japanese religion concerning the practice of leaving small wooden plaques at the local temple inscribed with requests to the gods (Reader 1991). Of course, an abundance of religious activity can be no clearer than scarcity when trying to define ritual. So, in most cases, the old familiar definition will be espoused by historians or sociologists. Would analyses of excavated ruins, or elaborate coronations, be any easier or clearer by questioning the definition of ritual?

Much depends on the problem identified as fundamental, analysis of which is inevitably constrained by very practical issues. Some questions need very little in the way of theorizing ritual; others would depend on it completely. My work on ritual was originally written very much in the mode of a "thought experiment," to use a phrase suggested recently by

Mary Beard. It was particularly integral to that experiment that I avoid a definition of ritual. To some reviewers, this has been such an incorrigible and incomprehensible stumbling block that I often need to underscore how deliberate it was. Refusing to define ritual is not just a failure of nerve or a lack of academic integrity. As I have written elsewhere, my method does not "offer a definitive interpretation of a set of ritual actions" because it is more concerned to demonstrate the multiple ways in which activities integral to a performance can be intended and experienced. "This approach can, therefore, actually undermine reliance on concepts like ritual, especially the notion of ritual as a universal phenomenon with a persistent, coherent structure that makes it tend to work roughly the same way everywhere" (Bell 1998:218). I will circle back to this issue as I go on to discuss some other terms that we have used.

SYSTEMS

The seminar papers and our conversations about them frequently referred to belief systems and ritual systems. Yet I have to ask myself, what systems? Few beliefs held by any group of people actually form a system, with the exception, perhaps of Thomistic theology and some tomes of political ideology. Much more frequently, there is some attempt at coherence, and even when quite questionable, coherence is extolled. But rarely are beliefs sufficiently consistent with one another to make a system credible, although people often need to believe they are. Beliefs are, for the most part, built up with historical layers and cultural borrowings, both the expedient and the highly inconvenient, which are socially and culturally generative. They are not internalized as a whole on the basis of reasoned discourse and clear instruction. The same is true with ritual systems. Rites are totally redesigned every once in awhile, as they were by the "reforming" clerics of the sixteenth-century Council of Trent; but such systems exist largely on paper even when they are thoroughly promulgated. We understand that we do not really mean "system"; the term actually intends something quite partial for any number of realistic reasons. Yet even when used heuristically, it will mislead us. Qualifications are apt to disappear even within one's own monologue as one presses for a convincing conclusion.

Under the most controlled conditions, we would find variations in the correct, even published, rules for how to do rituals, as in Pope Gregory VII's eleventh-century promulgation of the Roman Rite or Stalin's twentieth-century effort at people's rituals. Both situations attempted to put together dissimilar parts, expecting perfect compliance. Various parts of a system people might know well from some degree of

regular, shared performance; unfamiliar parts can evoke the alien styles
of other regions or even the sheer awkwardness of recent invention. We
know there are always variations, both intended and unintended; there
are misinterpretations and misunderstandings; and there are various
forms of resistance to anything meant to be sweeping, regularized, and
mandated. This is not to say that beliefs and rites are always unsystemat-
ic. I just want to argue that "system" is a word that can appear useful, but
it is apt to send us off with a misleading set of connections. For example,
do we interpret artifacts by linking them to those beliefs that show the
greatest coherence? In this way, Marija Gimbutas's female figures
appeared to attest to a coherent pre-Indo-European understanding of
fertility that was interpreted to build a more coherent and compelling
system with each new find—no matter how diverse the settings, styles,
time periods, or lack of supporting evidence from outside the data system (Gimbutas 1989).

MEMORY

Some papers and discussions have raised the very interesting issue of
memory, a topic that many fields have begun to take more seriously, or
self-consciously, since Connerton's (1989) provocative *How Societies
Remember*, among others. Humphrey and Laidlaw (1994) in *The Archetypal
Actions of Ritual* and McCauley and Lawson (2002) in *Ritual on the Mind*
also look to memory as a critical aspect of the social life of ritual practices.
I have not thought of memory in these terms. I suppose I have seen it as
a matter of the schemes and strategies that people absorb, both consciously and unconsciously, as from the architecture about them, for example.
They do not recognize fully how the architecture was created or modified
according to shared schemes that are socially and culturally effective,
schemes that can be learned simply from using the space as it is designed.
This was particularly apparent in our discussions of the "plaza." We may
not know exactly what was done in some ancient Mesoamerican plazas,
but the types of activities they would afford give us a very different set of
social possibilities than those generated by a city laid out with a strict grid
formation and a central Great Bath, as in the city of Mohenjodaro. The
plaza differs so dramatically from the linked caves, small and isolated on
mountaintops, that one begins to look for other instances in which
schemes of similar contrasts are used. Or a central plaza may suggest a
public replication of some domestic form (as may the caves, of course).
The sense of centrality may be one of human commonality, as in one peo-

ple politically defined, or an organized marketplace for exchanges among peoples who do not trade in a linked line of villages. In such a case, a plaza could actually harbor a pecking order, with each village having its place, while the whole existed by the grace of the urban authorities sponsoring the plaza. So the ritualized interactions with the gods that are evoked at the type of center generated by a plaza may display a logic of communality or hierarchy, or a mixed message of both. With these different scenarios for how bodies might move in and out and around a plaza, there is the internalization of specific social values (nothing more than Bourdieu's idea of "how things are done") that quietly argue for their synchrony with the nature of power in the cosmos.

If people are absorbing schemes through the way their architecture makes them socialize, then the schemes they internalize and express in their more ritualized practices help us understand not only memory, but also belief. It would be a rather limited project to uncover the ritual schemes of the plaza unless one can continue to track how these schemes are used outside or beyond the rite, the ritual space, and the ritualized occasions. How do the internalized schemes of a center for gathering, vs. the division of households and perhaps the influence of class distinctions, create a flexible working reality with usefulness in other situations, like setting prices on one's goods or organizing gender relations in the extended family? How do they enable one to interpret situations and better respond to them? If these schemes are at all important, then the individuals internalizing them, undoubtedly quite idiosyncratically, would have to have some sort of advantage in dealing with all the other social demands facing them. A ritual-induced scheme does not always have to work well outside the rite, but if it hardly *ever* works well somewhere, I cannot imagine it will not be dropped as irrelevant, old-fashioned, and meaningless. I am not forgetting that such ritual-induced schemes and strategies can be said to *shape* the very social situations in which they are found to be so useful. I would encourage the view that the expression or externalization of the embodied strategies, so intensified in ritualized situations, provides people with a creative repertoire of ways of construing and acting outside the rite. Therefore, I do not think it makes any sense to say a rite molds people. Rather, the repertoire of resources that ritualized agents come to possess may be mechanical for some and imaginative for others, but unlikely to be exactly the same for any two individuals by virtue of individualized ways of projecting, embodying, and experiencing the efficacy of aspects of these schemes.

CROSS-CULTURAL DIMENSIONS

We have also spoken about the usefulness of more cross-cultural evidence to help explain a ritual or the ways in which an activity might have been ritualized. One of my teachers was Mircea Eliade, perhaps the most famous "cross-culturalist" since Sir James Frazer, with all the strengths and weaknesses implied by such a title. I tend to regard cross-cultural studies as indispensable background knowledge. Likewise, someone could use my list of "six common ways to ritualize" to tick off the characteristics found at, say, a formal "high" dinner at a Cambridge college, and it would not be a useless exercise (Bell 1997:138–163). But both the cross-cultural and the structurally focused analysis should look beyond the ritualized practice in question to examine it in regard to something else—other cultural events or other logically possible ways of acting. I would emphasize the primary importance of maintaining, as much as possible, the location of the practice within a larger semiological field that is created by that practice in that particular cultural community. A break-of-day offering on stones atop a hill? Knowledge of such things in other cultures will help identify possibly relevant dimensions to this one practice. And from ritualization lists like the one I published, you might find it significant that the routinization involved in this offering does not seem to entail any particular formalization. Yet perhaps the most important dimension is the offering's place in a field of ways of acting in that community: other offering practices, other hilltop activities, other daybreak or dusk activities, as well as evidence of the history of such related practices. The restoration of the daybreak hilltop rite to as large an immediate cultural and historical context as can be handled might seem something to be taken for granted by the modern archaeologist. Yet there can be too much attention given to the more mechanical and time-consuming aspects of cross-cultural parallels or listed ritual features, both of which detract from how the practice is operating in its own context. We must remember that there is no basic (*Ur*) or key example of a practice that can explain supposed parallels or derivations. In cultural *bricolage* there is no best or first example. I have argued, for better or worse, that all practice is a constant "riff" on aspects of its context. Ritualization is a play on the cultural situation; what generalities or tendencies we can locate exist because of the commonalities in either the human condition or the viewer's perspective. So we should use them sparingly.

I think the most challenging tangle of issues was raised by the phrase, uttered in passing, "But we will never know what it meant to them anyhow." That sentiment implies, of course, that there is a certain type of meaning that we cannot really expect to go after because it would be so hard to find or even know if we had found it. But I also think in its banality the phrase suggests that the real meaning of the ritual is what the ancient participants thought of it, rather than all the other ways the ritual might be analyzed. Of course, we could immediately appreciate what a small victory this view could be said to represent. At times, it has been assumed with great authority that the practitioners do not know much at all about what they are doing—it is the professional who can explain it. But there are other optical complications to this correction of one form of shortsightedness. The sentiment that we will never know what some practices really meant to the practitioners was evoked more to defend the need for archaeology to set up its own category and definition of ritual. The importance of being able to talk to one another clearly was another justification for this top-down approach to definition.

For archaeologists working at ancient sites where there is so little to help illuminate the function of the place and the lives of the people who used it, it is often probably quite accurate to conclude that we will never know what a place and its activities meant to the generations who lived there. But we do not want to be saying "so we are not going to look there; we are not going to ask those questions." We have to say "that's one of the areas where it is really hard." Because if we were to conclude that we are not going to look there, then we would likely fall back on our own imposed assumptions and categories, with all the justification of an unexamined retreat from some impossible morass. This is a dubious method for working at the ability to talk to one another clearly. Several speakers argued that we need to define ritual so we can better talk to one another, *as if our problems interpreting a ritual site lay in communicating with one another.* A clear definition, they suggest, will establish clarity in the discipline and in all the thousands of conversations of which it is composed. This position reminds me of a colleague of mine who did much to establish the study of ritual in the 1970s and ever since then has argued that we will get nowhere without a clearer definition of ritual. In 2000, he was still ruing a lack progress in ritual studies which he linked to a failure in this critical area (Grimes 2000:259–270).

Well, we are never going to agree on a definition of ritual. We do not want to, nor will doing so solve the problems we face. Requests for such definitions will continue to sound sensible, but they will be ignored—they always are. No field ever moves forward because a good number of people agree on the definition of some central concept that then allows them to get down to work. Those who are interested and invested in ritual, from any perspective or discipline, will continue to evoke different aspects of the phenomenon. We will disagree quite fundamentally; we will talk past one another quite blithely; we will think we are in agreement and go off in quite different directions. It is very frustrating for those who think definitional order is a necessary first step. Thinking and talking and writing about ritual and ritualization, all of which define a field of inquiry, will proceed in a very untidy and disorganized manner. There are endless examples among comparable terms, such as myth, religion, culture, and nature. Someone will propose a definition, someone else will disparage it; both sides will make some good points; but there will be no consensus at the end of the day. Elsewhere, in regard to the idea of religious "performance," I have written, "Critical terms are not critical because they contain answers but because they point to the crucial questions at the heart of how scholars are currently experiencing their traditions of inquiry and the data they seek to encounter." Currently "we are entering an era in which what we want to learn cannot be learned if our terminology overdetermines the theater of engagement" (Bell 1998:220–221).

I am arguing that a clear, generally accepted definition is useful only in those projects that are focusing on something else. In an examination of domestic space, we might agree that "society" means such-and-such, but we would hesitate to agree to any a priori meaning of "the family," even though it would seem to make the project easier.

WHOSE PROJECT?

The issue of a clear definition of ritual as an initial or central project raises a more difficult question. In talking together about ritual and ritualization, are we looking for heuristic terms for the field to use, which is a necessary enterprise for communication and understanding, or do we want terms that will help us uncover what our ancient peoples might have thought about the sort of things we think they were doing in a ritual-like way?

In one example mentioned, an excavation revealed a room with a high bench that may have held some figurines; the bench does not look like it was used for normal household activities, assuming those were food preparation, storage, sleeping, and the like. What terms and what conceptual associations do we have to help us flush out the possible uses and implications of this bench? I have previously proposed the term "ritualization" for just this purpose—not because it better captures a Cycladic sense of what the activities at the bench were or what they meant to the locals, but because it is better at keeping those questions in front of us. A priori definitions of ritual can impose too many assumptions. The language of ritualization tries to minimize these assumptions. If the Cycladians were doing something other than what we would consider straightforward food storage or some comparable domestic routine, then they were making distinctions among their ways of acting. Ritualization keeps our terminological focus on their distinction-making, a key to their understanding and creation of a world. I would like to keep our current disciplinary terms very loose in order to apply them to many forms of performance—until we are able to understand their terms and distinctions. With such a loose language, the discipline would have areas of agreement and disagreement, and even sub-conversations content to remain independent of the larger chaos. If some consensus does emerge, it signals either the demise of interest in ritual per se, or a weariness that will yield to a new crop of challenges before too long.

Is the loose heuristic language of ritualization able to rise to the challenge thrown out to us at the beginning of this seminar by Professor Renfrew? He asked, how would one defend the claim that a particular structure is a temple? A definition of ritual is needed, he argued, to demonstrate a temple. That is a very "real-world" challenge. The language of ritualization is useful in describing a space that is a building but not domestic space, perhaps by being too small or too large, among other features. Ritualization makes us focus on what is different and similar within the semiology of architecture that this one site exhibits. If this society made no distinctions at all between addressing their gods for fertility and filleting fish for a meal, then it might be hard to argue for temples or religion as distinguished cultural entities in that society. There are societies that work very hard to rid themselves of any significant distinction between the sacred and the profane, by either sacralizing everything or profaning it. In Hasidic communities, men will tie their shoes in the morning in a particular order with specific prayers. There are Zen meditations for emptying one's bowels, a functional reminder that no realm is outside the practice of Zen. Initial distinctions between technical activities and ritual activities can give us very clear descriptions of a temple but in many cases would lead us astray in trying to understand the cultural distinctions with which a society was constantly engaged.

The Zen and Hasidic examples are uncommon ones for the so-called modern world, where secularity tends to reign. We do not know about the ancient world. Cross-cultural knowledge would make us look at a possible temple site in terms of its location and altars for gods and offerings. Any anthropologist who has noticed the symbolic organization of domestic space understands how it expresses cosmological and sociological values in ways that make the inhabitants embody them and then re-express them. What is different about a temple or ritualization? Less in my theory than in many others: what is different is just what the social actors would invoke to distinguish their domestic spaces from other ones—closed or open—where mundane interactions with gods or other powers are possible. Like Professor Renfrew, we would all look for evidence of supernatural forces to identify a temple, but if there is any evidence to be had, it should speak to us about how the sacred is distinguished, or not; it should not simply be important because it conforms to broader understandings of what is likely.

I do not think all ritualization is religious, although I am never quite sure what that word means. But I think people do ritual instead of other things, and they often do it when they think to invoke or identify other sources of power as accessible to them. Even if an event is ritualized very marginally, such as the example of the installation of a Cambridge don, the ritualization will be sufficient in form or symbolism to invoke the authority of medieval clerical power and prestige; but both its form and symbolism will not be so developed or consistent with church rites as to imply any real conviction that church authority is at stake in the current situation. The separation of the secular and the religious will be observed with its own set of ritualized distinctions. Yet the installation's slight echoing of the extra authority of the religious sphere is necessary for constructing the actual authority and prestige meant to be accorded the position. We could not give it any real rank if we sent an email thanking the lucky person for taking on the job. The echoing of either religious or military orders is a particularly common way of imparting the authority of those institutions to other social positions that have no particular claim to being religious or military. Ritualizing helps us analyze a possible temple site as well as the places that may have played on the symbolism of the temple to create other forms of temple-like authority.

POWER

There were a few references to political power and political control in the seminar. I reminded myself that power is also not a system, nor does it trickle, or crash, down from one direction; rather, it works to lock people into intricate tangles. I have been reexamining some of my earlier work in light of the pronouncement that we have entered a post-postmodern and certainly a post-Foucaultian world (Bell 1992:199–223). How does a post-Foucaultian context enable a more delicate or calibrated argument about the operations of power in society? I have maintained that ritual is the thing to do when one is negotiating for authority, and when the power that one needs to tap must have an extra-communal source. Yet everyone has to be empowered in some way or to some extent by such an appeal in order to bring power into the community from outside it. You do ritual when you are not exercising other forms of authority, control, or coercion. People gather for what seems to be a rather top-down power play in the enthronement ceremony of a king or queen, as opposed to some grass-roots endorsement. Citizens bow their heads because they are forbidden to watch the emperor's carriage go by. In these situations, the ritualization of activities assures the citizens that in some culturally convoluted way, each of them participates a bit in the schemes that identify and channel the power entering their community. The empowerment that comes with these forms of ritualization may be fairly marginal, even quite illusionary to our eyes; but to be effective, and hence a real social option, everyone has to emerge from the rites with a sense of having participated in something that leaves them feeling a bit empowered too, able to deploy schemes of authority, even if they do not believe in or profit by everything said and done. It's a bit like a conference, actually.

Of course, as one person mentioned, the community may not understand what is happening. Certainly Caroline Humphrey's paper reminds us that the agent of ritual action is only minimally the agent of what is happening; the agent did not write the script—he or she is just following it, and usually with no particular intentions about it. I do not contest much in that analysis; I have identified some of the same points in my own explanation of misrecognition. Yet I would emphasize how the agent is still the author of these actions, at least as much as we are the authors of anything we do; it is a continuum of authorship, perhaps, but I would want to recognize the creativity and complexity of the actor as actor, even when acting in the role of a so-called follower. This difference in our theories points to a conundrum. I tend to answer such conundrums by assuming the actors and agents are more like me than they are different. Of course, we have been taught the importance of recognizing the totality of cultural and historical difference, but when in doubt I assume similarity. So the way we participate in a conference, for example, can probably be a rough guide to how ancient people participated in long-winded ritualizations for the fertility of the harvest. I learned much from Victor Turner's wonderfully thick descriptions of the interaction of personalities and the power grabs, all played out in a multi-village circumcision of a group of young Ndembu boys (Turner 1967:151–279). In other words, the differences between us and them cannot make us assume we are acting very differently. What we do culturally can be the best guide to what people at any other time or place have done—*as long as we are conscious that we are acting as culturally as they, and as prone to the same human baggage of biases and rationalities.* Indeed, that was the argument of my first book: that we cannot analyze ritual fully if we do not simultaneously analyze theory-making and understand its similarities to—and differences from—ritual, or ritual-making, as a cultural practice. I have enjoyed thinking about ritual primarily because of the foil it provides theory. And I enjoyed thinking about ritual theory in this context of archeological evidence and interpretation because of the foil it provides the theoretical practices of my own field, where the focus on "religion" identifies so little as hard evidence—like an unearthed pot or a central plaza—that we generate interpretations of interpretations, like applying "liminality" to random examples of so-called missionizing activity. I would love to stub my toe against something a bit more earthy.

REFERENCES CITED

Bell, Catherine
   1992   *Ritual Theory, Ritual Practice.* Oxford University Press, Oxford.
   1997   *Ritual: Perspectives and Dimensions.* Oxford University Press, Oxford.
   1998   Performance. In *Critical Terms for Religious Studies*, edited by Mark C. Taylor. Chicago University Press, Chicago.
   2005   Ritual (Further Perspectives). In *Encyclopedia of Religions*, revised edition, Vol. 11, edited by Lindsay Jones, pp. 7848–7856. Macmillan, New York.
Connerton, Paul
   1989   *How Societies Remember.* Cambridge University Press, Cambridge.
Gimbutas, Marija
   1989   *The Language of the Goddess.* Harper, San Francisco.
Grimes, Ronald L.
   2000   Ritual. In *Guide to the Study of Religion*, edited by William Braun and Russell T. McCutcheon. Cassell, London.
Humphrey, Caroline, and James Laidlaw
   1994   *The Archetypal Actions of Ritual: A Theory of Ritual Illustrated by the Jain Rite of Worship.* Clarendon Press, Oxford.
McCauley, Robert N., and E. Thomas Lawson
   2002   *Bringing Ritual to Mind: Psychological Foundations of Cultural Forms.* Cambridge University Press, Cambridge.
Reader, Ian
   1991   What constitutes religious activity? *Japanese Journal of Religious Studies* 18 (4):373–376.
Turner, Victor
   1967   *The Forest of Symbols: Aspects of Ndembu Ritual.* Cornell University Press, Ithaca.

13.

ARCHAEOLOGIES OF RITUAL

Evangelos Kyriakidis

Of all the overarching, overlapping, and sometimes overworked themes of this book, there are three that I would like the reader to keep in mind. First are issues of definition and the relationship between ritual and religion. Second is the discipline of archaeology itself, the material it deals with, and the ways it is influenced by that material as a discipline, with certain given abilities, limitations, and interests. And, last come the various perspectives of study, some new and others old, that could be seen as fruitful avenues for future research, different archaeologies of ritual. In this final chapter, I will discuss mainly the first and the third themes, though still referring to the second (for which see also chapter 2).

A DEFINITION OF RITUAL AND ITS IMPLICATIONS

The thorny issue of the definition of ritual is arguably the most important, as it affects the research interests of most, if not all those engaged in this field; it is also the most difficult in that it may be seen to depend on a certain consensus. A consensus regarding the definition may prove impossible to achieve; but I for one do not believe that a definition need be universally accepted to be useful. Indeed, few of the views on ritual find all scholars in agreement. The background of each scholar varies, much like the backgrounds of the subjects of the study of ritual. Consequently, the perceptions of what ritual is vary both among scholars and performers.

The lack of a definition of ritual is responsible for a great deal of the problems any discussion of the topic faces. Discussants often find that they are talking about partly, or even entirely, different things. What are the non-specialists expected to do in this turmoil of ideas and conflicting views? Are they to use the term at all, and if so, with what meaning? If they are to be understood by others, it is important that scholars include a definition of their use of the term. Bell, offering an alternative view (here chapter 12), eschews the need for a definition, believing such an effort to be a waste of valuable time that could be used to discuss what ritual does and how it can be used.

In my view, abolishing definitions and avoiding the issue of what is meant by ritual is counterproductive. It means that we encourage vagueness and that we do not facilitate critical arguments. To study the effects of ritual without a definition is tantamount to the common philosophical crime of having an epistemology that is not derived from the ontology. As Davidson put it, "disputes over values . . . can be genuine only when there are shared criteria in the light of which there is an answer to the question who is right" (2004:50). Definitions do vary and people always disagree, but this is by no means discouraging. Using definitions should not be a tedious obsession, but an integral part of any argument. A short explicit or implicit definition before the main argument will always clarify where people stand and how they use the term. Without that, only nebulous observations and arguments can be made discouraging scholars from using ritual in their work. To make ritual useful, to study it, learn from it, and to convey this learning, one needs to have a clear idea of what it is.

So what is ritual? Having argued for the usefulness of a definition in the study of ritual, it would be hypocritical to stop short of proposing one. Before I do, however, it would be helpful to examine the relationship between ritual and religion.

In this volume, McCauley and Lawson (chapter 10) and Bell (chapter 12) are inclined to see ritual as an exclusively religious activity, whereas Kyriakidis (chapter 2), Marcus (chapter 4), Humphrey and Laidlaw (here chapter 11), and Renfrew (chapter 6) have a different view. Although the two groups are by no means entirely in opposition, the former takes for granted the relevance to the supernatural, while the other argues that rituals can be as much non-religious as religious. As we shall later see, many of the things said exclusively referring to religious rituals would be equally applicable to secular rituals.

Some of those who claim that ritual is always religious go as far as to say that an activity that is similar to ritual but is not religious is "ceremony." To me these two terms are largely tautologous. Indeed, of their Latin equivalents *ritus* and *caerimonia*, it is the latter that is consistently religious, whereas *ritus* can also mean habit, tradition, or custom. Today, however, the words "rite," "ritual," and "ceremony" have so much semantic overlap that they can be treated as largely synonymous. I would agree to one term being used to mean religious ritual and the other secular ritual, as long as it is understood that we are talking about comparable things.

One common reaction to the claim that rituals can be non-religious is that in these instances they are ex-religious. That is, it is conceded in such cases that rituals can be non-religious, but if so, then they must have once been religious and are fossils of the past. Therefore, in order to distinguish a ritual from a non-ritual, according to this view, one would need to have the special knowledge that the ritual in question is, or at least was, a religious activity.

My position is that as long as you cannot distinguish between two identical things, they are the same. So, how would a student distinguish among a ritual that she knows is religious, another that she knows was religious, and a third that an omniscient being (and by that I mean the fictitious being often conjured in philosophy for the sake of argument) would know was religious but the student does not? Privileged knowledge cannot really be a criterion for the definition of ritual, not if it is to be a meaningful analytical category. I claim that all three cases would and should be identified as rituals, together with many other activities that can be called ritual but neither were nor shall be religious. The identification should not be made through privileged knowledge or intuition, but through the successful application of criteria.

So what type of activity is ritual? Many believe that any activity can become a ritual. I would go further and argue that the term "ritualization," which is often used by the likes of Bell (here chapter 12) and Bourdieu in different ways, is just a particular way in which any activity may become institutionalized, crystallized, or established.[1] But this by no means implies that an activity's crystallization (institutionalization or establishment) terminates with its becoming a ritual. The establishment of ritual itself can, indeed, be assessed and is a fruitful way to see and understand ritual (Kyriakidis 2005:68–76). In fact, the distinction between performance- and liturgy-centered rituals, as drawn by Hastorf (here chapter 5), touches on these different degrees of ritual establishment, "performance-centered" being less established and "liturgy-centered" being more so. Another way that some activities can become established is when they become prescribed by technology; in this way, technology may become a meaningful comparison to ritual (Nikolaidou, here chapter 9).

If a ritual does not emerge through the slow, progressive, and incremental crystallization of a non-ritual action, but through a deliberate invention, it is still promoted as set (crystallized). This is also the case with the extreme example of my invention of a "ritual of manhood" which consists of just shaving once and declaring, "Now I am a man." This is a ritual that is not expected to be repeated (as I have done it only once in this way and it is unlikely to be ever repeated). It is still a set activity, in the sense that by declaring this to be the ritual of manhood, I also mean that this is my (as of now) set way of becoming a man. Although often elusive, it is this set aspect of ritual that is most visible to archaeology (Kyriakidis 2005:33, 75–76).

If we consider ritual as set or crystallized action, then ritual becomes an important link between things and people, as Hastorf comments (chapter 5). If action has an effect on items, set action has even more so. This is particularly interesting for archaeology, which primarily works with material culture and makes inferences as to human actions.

Moreover, if ritual is the crystallization of any activity in a particular way, then this particular way may be the one that would distinguish ritual from non-ritual. It is here that I would like to turn to a recent contribution to the understanding of ritual by Humphrey and Laidlaw (in press; this volume, chapter 11). They argue that ritualization of action involves in each case "a specific modification in the intentionality of human action." They elaborate, saying that "[r]itual is action in which intentionality is in a certain way displaced so that, as we summarise the matter, human agents both are and are not the authors of their ritual actions" (Humphrey and Laidlaw 1994:70–71). This particular displacement of intentionality takes place in the following way. The understanding of the intention-in-action is normally based on the beholder's skill to interpret the wide array of possible actions in any configuration and context. In ritual, however, the identification of the intentions of the performer, as Humphrey and Laidlaw stress, is not an interpretation of the performer's feelings, thoughts, and attitudes, but a reference to the public and culture-specific knowledge about such actions, through prior stipulation. This prior stipulation, however, is not the only ingredient for the identification of ritual.

I would tend to modify Humphrey and Laidlaw's theory in order to tackle many of the problems of the term "ritual." Two of these problems are (1) the aforementioned dispute regarding the association of ritual with religion, and (2) the differing definitions of an activity by various groups of people; that is, there may be some activities that outsiders may be inclined to call rituals, but that their performers do not consider as such. Indeed, there is a relatively frequent divide between etics and emics (Lett 1990) in the characterization of an activity as "ritual." One further problem of the term is that the various definitions given have a predominantly Western perspective, failing to account for the possibility that there might be activities that we ourselves do that we never consider rituals but that others might consider as such.

It seems that part of the problem of the term "ritual" is that it is largely an etic category. It characterizes activities that are related to certain groups of people (if we are to avoid the also nebulous terms "culture" and "culture-specific") and are set, much like customs. Yet, unlike some customs, they are not considered as normal, rational, contiguous, causal, or logical by those etic observers. Ritual has also become an emic category, but this is more of an acknowledgment that this customary activity may not appear "rational" or "normal" to the etic beholder.

It is at this point that the modified intentionality would find its best fit for this theory. Emic observers, given their familiarity with certain actions in certain contexts, readily identify the intentions-in-action. They may give different descriptions of that action with varying amounts of knowledge assumed. For example, in the Jain dip-Puja ritual as described by the well-informed etics Humphrey and Laidlaw (2006), "a Jain woman in a temple, performing puja, stands before an idol, takes a small oil lamp in her right hand, lifts it up and holds it towards the statue." Those with access to the relevant knowledge could alternatively describe this activity as "lamp-worship," drawing reference to prior knowledge. A similar situation however, could be encountered in an office at an aircraft factory, in which a designer is drawing a tube. Those with the relevant knowledge of the situation could describe this activity as the designer helping to build a more effective piloting system, a result with no contiguity or causal link for the non-initiate etic, much like the identification of "lamp worship" in the first example. What I am arguing here is that these activities would not be readily recognizable by non-initiates through reference to the universals of human experience, and therefore need some reference to specific, insider's prior knowledge. Jain light worship is as clearly understandable as aeroplane piloting systems are to many others, and the understanding of the intention-in-action in both cases refers to specific shared prior knowledge or conceptual framework. This does not mean to imply that improving the aeroplane piloting system is not a ritual, while Jain light-worship is. On the contrary, both can be *seen* as rituals or as non-rituals by different people with access to different kinds of knowledge.

The last comment needs a little elaboration. It is easy to understand how designing a tube may be seen by non-initiate outsiders or complete strangers as a ritual, especially if it is mistaken for a customary activity; after all, the category "ritual" does not only belong to us or to those who partake in Western culture. But how is it possible to claim that some insiders may not take Jain light-worship to be a ritual? In fact, many may believe that there is no difference between light-worship and any other activity— that light-worship is not special, but merely a part of the fabric of everyday life. Indeed, it is conceivable that many of those attending rain-making rituals do not consider them special—or, at any rate, different from everyday activities. So if the insiders are not aware of alternative pathways of action, they may consider that the intention-in-action in what we call "rituals" is entirely normal, rational, causal, or contiguous, and that what we recognize as a ritual, to their eyes, is not.

In a definition where ritual is defined as an etic category, an emic group is always implied. Rituals are clearly associated with specific groups of people, and quite often, as we will discuss later on, they are characteristic of these groups. The term "culture-specific" would also be useful, if the word "culture" were not so vague.

Therefore, to attempt the entire definition, *ritual is an etic category that refers to set activities with a special (not-normal) intention-in-action, and which are specific to a group of people.*

This definition also clarifies the frequent association of religion with ritual. It is common in the Western world to take religious practice as special, not normal, even in some cases irrational. Moreover, religious practice, like religion, is always associated with a specific group of people. Following this definition, therefore, set religious practice can always be seen as ritual. Since not all but a great deal of religious practice is set, then religious practice is often seen as synonymous with ritual. But neither is all religious practice ritual—for example, the Crusades were a religious practice yet not a ritual—nor is all ritual practice religious—for example, civil wedding ceremonies are ritual but not religious.

It would be fair to say, therefore, that this definition, even though it may not satisfy everybody, addresses many of the difficulties and problems of the topic.

We now turn to that last part of the definition—namely, that rituals are specific to a group of people—and discuss further some of its repercussions for the term. In other words, we shall study the relationship between ritual and society. There is a two-way relationship between groups of people and rituals; groups of people create, continue to perform, or alter certain rituals, yet the identity of these groups is often defined by their ritual participation. Moreover, the same groups may perform different rituals that are thus linked and can be usefully grouped together for analytical purposes.

RITUAL AND SOCIETY

It is common in the social sciences to treat the terms "society" and "social group" in the same way. In this sense, each person is linked to others in many different ways and is thus a member of many different societies. This will depend on his or her place of origin, interests, ambitions, and, most importantly for our discussion, experiences. Indeed, it is often the case that there are social groups within social groups—for instance, the inhabitants of Elounda in Crete are also a subgroup of the inhabitants of Crete and of Greece. It is also common for membership to different groups to overlap. Those Christians who see themselves as belonging to the Church of Crete, those speaking or understanding the Cretan dialect, and those who live in Crete today are, with some exceptions, largely the same people.

The shared experience of participating in rituals forms a link between people, and thus ritual participation defines the membership to certain social groups (see also Renfrew, chapter 6). For example, the participants in a specific wedding ceremony are all linked and thus become members of a group through their shared experience of this ritual.[2]

It is often the case that the members of a social group defined on the basis of participation in a certain ritual will also be members of other social groups that are based on different rituals. Say, for instance, that the people who go to Sunday Church of England services are largely the same as those who attend Church of England christenings. These social groups also can be seen under an umbrella grouping of the Church of England that includes all those who attend, or pretend to attend, its Christian rituals.

Rituals that have roughly the same audiences are also often linked in other ways. They tend to share a number of elements (such as chants, paraphernalia, and location) due to a centripetal power of assimilation (see Kyriakidis, here chapter 2). They are also frequently dependent on one another, some being the condition for the participation in others (for example, baptism is a condition to participation in the ritual of appointing a priest) (McCauley and Lawson, here chapter 10). Rituals that are closely linked in these ways can be usefully classed together as a "ritual system," thus aiding the study of social groups and their ideologies.[3]

Indeed, it is often the case that the beliefs accompanying rituals within a system are the same or complementary and can themselves be grouped together into belief systems. These belief systems, or the repeated performance of one of the rituals in the corresponding ritual system, are forces that can strengthen the membership to an umbrella society. For example, the rituals of baptism, funeral, Sunday mass, wedding, and so on encourage and renew the membership to the churchgoers' society. It is notable that these umbrella societies, of which the members have multiple, parallel links to one another through the ritual system, are particularly strong and become even stronger if they also have a shared belief system, such as a religion, in common.

As mentioned above people are frequently members of several social groups and there is often a large overlap between them. The membership of a ritual-system umbrella group, for example, will often overlap with that of groups whose members are linked through their specific preferences (the types of products they buy, the type of food they prefer), political or ideological beliefs, identities (national or other), and ambitions. The reason for such an overlap can be coincidence (such as a historical coincidence), though it can also be a manifold expression of membership and a distinction between members and non-members in specific societies (Bourdieu 1996). It is obvious that the larger and stronger the membership of these groups, the greater their importance, political or otherwise.

The societies that are defined by multiple links among their members use their constituent links to demonstrate membership. For example, societies that are defined on the basis of both ritual and ethnic links may use their rituals as a manifestation of their ethnic identity.

While rituals can define social groups and thus unite their members, they also draw boundaries. Boundaries unite and divide at the same time and are often contested, doubted, fenced, protected, and/or embellished. They have been much discussed in archaeology through various perspectives (e.g., Hodder 1987). Although different types of boundaries and diffusion patterns overlap, they rarely correspond. Ritual borders, however, are defined in at least two ways: the boundaries of the ritual system as a whole, and the boundaries of each specific ritual site in the case of a great number of homologous ritual sites or ritual institutions that divide the landscape (for instance, parishes). Memory is particularly significant in such a division of landscape, not only in the sense of a device for the recognition of boundaries by individuals, but also because social memory and lore keep old ritual sites and old boundaries alive. Ritual boundaries are often fuzzy, unclear, non-continuous, or patchy.

The ability of ritual to both unite and divide renders it particularly relevant to studies of nationalism, colonialism, and political manipulation. But we shall return to these themes below.

TRACING RITUAL

Having extensively discussed the elements of the definition of ritual, it is time to briefly consider its repercussions to the ways archaeology can trace a ritual. Since the archaeologist is commonly the etic, he or she would have to discover a "special," set activity that is associated with a group of people. The group of people will not be of much use for archaeology, since most patterned activity that archaeology normally uncovers is anyway associated with a group of people. "Special" means not normal; it is thus the task for archaeology to trace what is normal and then compare it to what is not. Alternatively, it is up to archaeologists to decide that a certain activity is, for them, unreasonable or non-contiguous, as long as they make clear that they are studying things from their own perspective. Finally, and most importantly, rituals are a set category. I have extensively discussed elsewhere the aspects of ritual that are related to their property of being "set" or established. In fact, Bell has observed that rituals tend to be repeated, invariant, rule-governed, formal activities with an air of tradition, among other things. All these aspects are related to this crystallized, or set, property of ritual. If we can trace these things in archaeology and we can distinguish these crystallized or set activities from normal activities, then we are looking at a ritual (Bell 1997:138–169; Kyriakidis 2005:28–40).

A reconstruction of practice through the material record is difficult for archaeology. A reconstruction of special practices such as rituals is also difficult, though because these practices are set, it may occasionally be somewhat easier (Kyriakidis, here chapter 2). Archaeologists use various techniques of "cheating" for prehistoric archaeology, where no written records are available.

The main conjecture archaeologists use in order to "cheat" is continuity. It is often assumed that a recorded practice reflects the ways in which this practice was performed and the attitudes toward it through both time and space. Certainly, both are fallacious arguments if taken to extremes. That is, the views or practices of a certain individual may generally reflect attitudes and ways of the society in which he or she belonged, but this can only be in a general and abstract way. Likewise, the greater the time distance between two compared practices, the less likely that their elements will be the same or will have the same connotations. Though there is no doubt that continuity can, and indeed does, exist, it has to be proven in every case and cannot be considered a given for any society.

Continuity claims commonly come through the use of history, ethnohistory, and the drawing of parallels between periods with significant time gaps. The use of ethnohistory, be it in archaeology of the New or Old World (for examples from India, see Chakrabarti 2001:35), has the additional complication that it is written by outsiders to the given society, adding an extra layer of ignorance and bias to our own. Thus, ethnohistory

is certainly useful as an extra piece of evidence (see Hastorf for a praise of
moderate ethnohistory, in chapter 5, and a note of caution from Marcus,
chapter 4, and Fogelin, chapter 3) and as an alert for the different possibilities, but it can by no means be uncritically used as the starting and finish-
ing point in any research.

In fact, the search for the origins of ritual practices, a common goal
of many using ethnohistory in an uncritical way, is futile, as the "origin of
practice" is a contradiction in terms and is unenlightening since it does
not offer any further information either about that practice or the society in which it was produced. It can also be dangerous, as it can lead to sectarian (Fogelin, here chapter 3) or nationalist claims. Indeed, on some
occasions it may be inspired from such nationalistic tendencies.
Nationalism is one of these potential greater themes in the study of ritual in archaeology; to which we shall turn below.

Having offered one definition for ritual, and having briefly discussed
some of the repercussions of this definition, it is now time to discuss and
comment on other themes raised that pertain to the archaeology of ritual or rather the different archaeologies of ritual. These themes are conflicting and contrasting: physical and cognitive dimensions, political
manipulation and political separation, nationalism and globalization. It is
my intention here to highlight the value of these themes, in anticipation
of future studies that will give them the appropriate treatment.

PERSPECTIVES ON RITUAL AND ARCHAEOLOGY

Physical and Cognitive Dimensions

Archaeology is largely the study of material remains and of material culture in general and does not have any direct access to beliefs. An archaeology of religion, if one takes religion to be a system of beliefs, cannot
therefore have as much scope as an archaeology of ritual, which is more
accessible to us, if one takes ritual to be a practice or action (see also
Renfrew, here chapter 6). This is because practice has a direct effect on
materials, whereas belief has an effect on materials only through practice.
In other words, for the study of practice we need to make fewer deduc-
tions than for the study of belief.

Having said that, beliefs are always a constituent part of understanding the people of the past and a key aspect of enriching our views on
ancient societies. Rituals are almost always accompanied by attitudes
toward them, as well as by beliefs about the rituals themselves and about
other things in relation to these rituals including, in some instances,

religious beliefs. An attempt to access the accompanying beliefs, and more generally the cognitive dimension of rituals, is an integral part of ritual research.

One way in which the rapport between the physical and the cognitive in ritual is revealed is in the relation of ritual with landscape. Meaning is created through the interaction of multiple sign-systems with the beholder (Goodwin 1997:129). Landscape is thus perceived in a way that an additional sign-system completely alters the meaning of the landscape. Rituals are such sign systems. Indeed, rituals—especially communal ones—create cultural space, a *topos*, much like monuments. They may not affect the landscape physically, but they certainly affect it cognitively. Rituals, literally, take place; they are performed in a specific location and are inscribed in the memories of the participants. Those rituals that are repeated, renew this cognitive space in memory. This cognitive change of the landscape has a multitude of effects: sentimental, perceptual, associational, territorial, historical, and so on. Moreover, the changes in the landscape resulting from the performance of rituals—be they the erection of features or monuments, deforestation, the discarding of items used in ritual, or the tending to the land and nature (regular cleaning, conservation, etc.)—have a visual effect on the landscape. Such visual changes act as markers and memorials, enforce collective memory, and can aggressively appropriate the landscape.

Thus, a landscape as presented by Fogelin (here chapter 3) that is filled with clusters of Buddhist cairns will ascribe new information, religious, ethnic or other, to the notional "biography" of the cultural and cognitive landscape. It will also constitute the coordinates of meaning through the concentration of those clusters and their relation to other ritually significant monuments such as monasteries and stupas, or to resources, settlements, and geographical features (peaks, ravines, water sources, and the like).

Ritual defines cognitive space in the large scale as described above, but it also defines space in the small scale (for example, within a building). If ritual is a practice that is often constituted of a repeated series of actions, then each of these actions often takes place in a specific micro-scale location (such as the pulpit of a church or a sacrificial table). Ritual gives meaning to, or rather enriches the meaning of, the various features in the location where it takes place. In Christian churches, there are adyta or sacrosanct areas, chapels, special areas for prayer, specific places where participants kneel, particular places where they receive Communion, locations for the choir or the cantors, and locations for specific artifacts.

The invention and production of artifacts in turn involves a complex cognitive process that can betray the mental background of its makers, while their presence facilitates the memorization and evocation of thoughts or actions. "Since we discover almost none of our tools in nature fully formed, it seems fairly clear that activities inside human heads bear the principal responsibility for getting this synergistic relationship between our mental states and aspects of the external environment rolling" (Boesch and Boesch 1993; McCauley and Lawson, here chapter 10; Mithen 1996). Thus, the techniques employed, the particular style, the choice of colors, metals, and shape of a ritual incense burner may reflect not only the mental and physical abilities of the maker, but also his or her attitudes toward that item, toward previously made items of the same type and the ritual in which it partakes.

The temporal properties constitute another cognitive dimension of ritual (Renfrew, here chapter 6). Rituals have a rhythm that manifests itself not only in the frequency of the ritual's performance, but also in the tempo of the internal sequence of acts within each ritual. As time is a meaningful parameter of events (Bourdieu 1977:15), the frequency of repetition is particularly important, both for the ascription of meaning to the performance and for its mnemonic effects, as McCauley and Lawson support (here chapter 10). On the other hand, the internal tempo may evoke certain moods and affect the experience of the performance. The temporal aspect of rituals can be elusive materially and thus archaeologically; a frequent repetition can be traced, but the intervals between the repetitions cannot be always determined with accuracy.

Further cognitive aspects of ritual that may occasionally be traceable in archaeology are offered in this volume by McCauley and Lawson (here chapter 10), following up on their book on ritual (2002). Many of their ideas are relevant to religious rituals only, but some can be adapted for understanding secular ones as well. For example, their *Principle of Superhuman Agency* assesses the ties that various rituals have with the superhuman, a significant cognitive dimension of all religious rituals (here chapter 10). With this principle they distinguish three types of rituals: special agent rituals, in which the most direct link with the superhuman is through the current ritual's agent (such as a priest); special patient rituals; and special instrument rituals, whereby the most direct relationship with the superhuman is, respectively, through the patient or the act itself (often by way of an instrument) (McCauley and Lawson, here chapter 10). These three categories could indeed be partly adjusted also for non-religious rituals. An inauguration ceremony—for instance, in which a mayor cuts a ribbon to formally open a building—could be described as a special agent ritual.

Various papers in this volume have offered rich food for thought on the cognitive aspects of rituals. The constant challenge for the archaeologist is to seek a balance between using the material constructively in order to pursue greater understanding, and ensuring that claims and reconstructions are sufficiently supported by the evidence.

POLITICS AND POLITICAL MANIPULATION

It is common for those studying ritual, including archaeologists, to consider ritual a political tool that reaffirms "institutional facts" in a given society (Marcus and Flannery 2004; Renfrew, here chapter 6; Searle 1995), and an influencing mechanism that creates identities and influences beliefs (Hastorf, here chapter 6; Kyriakidis 2005:68–76). There is no general consensus, however, on whether the social structures and beliefs influence the rituals or vice versa. The truth, as usual, is probably to be found somewhere in the middle. Ritual influences the beliefs of its participants, and precisely for this reason it is also a prime target for political manipulation. Rituals with a wide participation base influence a large number of people and have a significant political consequence. Societies whose membership is defined by these communal rituals are ideal targets for lobbying and manipulation. In this context, it is interesting to see as an example the process by which the local interlinked Odissi and Oriya ritual dances seem to have increasingly become a prime target and thus an agent of the Hinduization that is "sweeping through contemporary" India, subsuming or marginalizing local identities (Lopez y Royo, here chapter 8). A broader view of ritual is possible, however, whereby it is not necessarily a deliberate target but rather a receptacle of a myriad of influences. In this sense, Odissi ritual dances have come to merely reflect these dominating Hinduization practices, whether willfully targeted or indirectly influenced. Irrespective of how that influence came about, a major political change may influence ritual practice, and likewise, change in an important ritual may influence the political structures. It is fair to say, therefore, that ritual change often reflects social and political change (Kyriakidis 2002:11–48; 2005:60–76; Marcus and Flannery 2004; Renfrew, chapter 6).

One major social change that some rituals can bring about is establishing and creating acceptance for ritual institutions. These institutions tend to also perform non-ritual activities. Monasteries are an example of this, wherein the majority of the space is used for non-ritual purposes.

With their production and consumption of wealth, personnel, and territory, ritual institutions are interesting subjects for the study of ritual, which are often accessible to archaeology (Kyriakidis 2005:99–101, 111). Their mobilization of a workforce, and its use for increasing an institution's wealth or for conducting ritual ceremonies, also renders them significant players in the ideological or political landscape of an area and occasionally also in the financial and military realms. At this point, rituals not only reflect or serve a sociopolitical order or change, but they also constitute it.

As we mentioned earlier, rituals not only define social groups and thus unite their members, but also divide groups, by drawing boundaries. The use of ritual to separate groups along ethnic lines is a feature particularly common in colonization, where the colonized seek to assert their independent identity from the colonizers in all sorts of ways. Sometimes this can be evident in the archaeological record. For instance, evidence suggests that at the time of the second Greek colonization of the Mediterranean, the indigenous Sicilian population apparently continued to perform non-Greek rituals as a statement of nonconformity with the colonizers (Morris 1999; Papadopoulos and Lyons 2002; Smith 2003).

One way that ritual can maintain old identities and create new ones is through its ability to inscribe mnemonic landscapes and to create cultural environments through its performance, much like other types of crystallized and memorable activity (McCauley and Lawson, here chapter 10). The mountain peak that has been used for ritual will always be a special peak for the performers, as long as they recall that performance (Kyriakidis 2005:113–119).

Being prime targets for political manipulation as well as excellent political tools for influencing and forging identities, rituals can offer insights for the study of social and political dynamics as seen through the material record. Due to this special link with identity, nationalism can also be closely associated with ritual and its study, a theme to which we now turn.

NATIONALISM AND GLOBALIZATION

If globalization is a relatively new term, the dialectic between the forces of the local and those of the international is very old, and the study of ritual in archaeology is touched by its repercussions in several ways.

Because rituals are so often closely connected with identities, many studies have had a vested interest in demonstrating that the rituals currently associated with a specific area can be traced back to the distant past. Although it is not inappropriate to argue in favor of continuity of practice through a rigorous contextual study of several comparable practices separated by only a small time-gap, it is common for such studies to claim continuity for rituals separated in time by hundreds of years. In these cases, continuity is both taken for granted and sought for—the perfect recipe for a circular argument. Moreover, and much along the lines of what was mentioned earlier, continuity of ritual practice can be exploited for its political value, "proving," for instance, the existence of a specific group in a particular place in the remote past. By contrast, few studies explore the changes of ritual in the changing contexts, the ways in which practice and belief have been transformed through history, the multiple influences from neighboring or similar practices, and the ways in which new elements are then emulated. Nationalism, if not parochialism, has therefore instigated much research on ritual that is, unfortunately, largely research with blinkers.

If the forces of the local frequently influence the study of ritual, they also directly affect ritual practice. Above we have already touched on how ritual can be a target and a tool for political manipulation, and on how rituals can preserve or reinforce distinct identities. As local rituals can be a tool of resistance and rebellion against colonizers, they can also be manipulated to the ends of creating a distinct national identity. A large number of rituals are created, adapted, or adopted in order to create a sense of belonging among participants that is distinct from that of neighboring areas (see Lopez y Royo here chapter 8).

Currents of globalization have also had a significant effect on ritual research in that they have given to many a superficial understanding of and familiarity with other groups across different parts of the world, and have aroused a superficial interest in peculiar customs, rituals, and religions. In this sense, the study of ritual shares common ground with several different agendas that can be linked to globalization, the emergence of "ethnic" culture, global tourism, post-colonialism, and Americanization: namely, the exoticization and commodification of local culture. These have had a profound effect on folk music, for instance, which is often termed "ethnic" and is sold in "World Music" series or promoted in festivals like WOMAD (World of Music, Arts & Dance). The commodification of music has a series of consequences that are relevant to the study of ritual. The lyrics and the contexts are largely ignored, while the aesthetic element of the music is separated from meanings and associations. Moreover, certain pieces become international hits, and their performance becomes widespread. Regardless of their local authenticity, some performers thus become celebrated world figures, overshadowing the local celebrities and the criteria for their promotion.

The same forces have a similar and sometimes even more profound effect on rituals. Some rituals are particularly successful at arousing the senses. As McCauley and Lawson argue, the arousal of the senses attracts the attention of the performers (here chapter 10), and this, consequently, leads them to better memorize these rituals. But it also attracts the attention of tourists, tour operators, anthropologists, filmmakers, and others who, enchanted, become followers of these rites, record them, idealize them, and lend to them the "eye of the world." This, of course, has multiple effects on the rituals of any society. It means that rites that please the senses have a greater likelihood of surviving in the modern world than others. In a quickly globalizing society where a lot of the old traditions are rapidly being forgotten, rituals do not stand much chance of survival if they are not commodified. Those elements in them that arouse the senses will thus tend to be artificially increased as if in order to attract outside attention. Moreover, all rites will go through a process of so-called purification toward what is considered original, old fashioned, "local," and "non-Western" (see Schiller 2001:72), with "no outside influences," as well as a beautification so that they become more attractive. In other words, in today's globalized society, rituals have a tendency to become shows.

But that is not all. The ruthlessness of the globalized environment is such that old rituals, even those that have been commodified, purified, and beautified, will still be considered no more than well-packaged commodities with a nice story on the label. They will still be on the same footing as any other invented performance, with a fabricated ritual "history." In fact, it may be that such fabricated performances will outperform the old and "refurbished" rituals.

The claim of a long-standing tradition can only be substantiated with the study of the past. It is here that history and archaeology start playing an increasingly important role. Due to their apparent objectivity, archaeology and, in some cases, history are seen as successful intermediaries between different cultures. They are, therefore, often expected to play a role in claims for long-standing traditions and can also be manipulated to these ends.

It is often the case that claims of tradition are voiced with professional efficiency, sometimes using the techniques of archaeology and of the subdiscipline of museum studies. In the words of Lopez y Royo, the aforementioned Odissi dance "has been thus reconstructed, re-created, restored [cf. archaeology]—a metaphorical ancient temple rearranged and re-erected on new grounds [cf. museum studies] . . ." (brackets mine). In other words, academic archaeology and its methods have influenced the ways in which ritual traditions are fabricated and, in their turn, have been manipulated by those who purposefully aim to create ritual traditions.

Another way in which academic archaeology and globalization have an effect on rituals is through the choice of "worthwhile" sites. The choice of UNESCO world heritage sites, a subjective procedure conducted by academics or academically informed individuals, gives ritual and other sites a global value, which decontextualizes their meaning and importance. Awarding such sites international acclaim, much like the creation of the aforementioned world music "ethnic" celebrities, is a superficial process that takes place beyond the system that created them (cf. post-modernism; Jameson 1991:1–54). Such a procedure, like the one described by Terence Ranger (here chapter 7) for the candidateship of Zimbabwe's Matopos Hills, is useful for the advertisement of the country internationally, and for the creation of conservation projects and income through tourism, but it does not guarantee and may in fact jeopardize the preservation of the prior human and ritual environment (see chapter 7).

Elements of globalization are inherent in all scholarship that strives to obtain an objective, critical distance from its observed subject and attempts to place it in a global comparative framework. Ritual scholarship is no exception. But ritual itself is, if one accepts our definition of ritual as an etic category, most closely associated with and affected by the global. We can all share the feeling of having observed many of these special activities that have a superficial similarity to others across the world. This gives us the confidence to talk about rituals to one another as if we were impartial. Categories of ritual are often named—for example, "passage rituals" or "calendrical rituals"—which gives the false impression that superficially comparable rituals, irrespective of context, are similar in essence.

Although it is important to draw similarities and to seek to study the effects of ritual practice and the ways it is influenced in general terms, the study of ritual in archaeology will not be able to draw meaningful comparisons without regard to local context. As researchers we must also be aware of our own subjectivity and of how our work is inevitably shaped by innumerable forces, local and global. The challenge for archaeologists is how to present past rituals, whether in scholarship, museums, or archaeological sites, in a way that is accessible to a global audience, while being based upon and promoting an understanding of the local context, past and present. Archaeologists, and indeed all those who present rituals to a global audience, also need to be aware of the impact that this attention may come to have on the local context in the future.

This volume has been host to a number of conflicting yet inspiring views on ritual and archaeology. The differing opinions, themes, and agendas developed should not be discouraging to the reader, as they do reflect the multivocal discourse on the subject. Indeed, it seems quite clear that one of the largest contributions of such an effort is not to solve the problems with which the study of ritual in archaeology is riddled, but to enrich the discourse with new ways to approach an old theme. In this chapter, several of these many approaches were explicitly commented on, while others were only mentioned in passing. In the future, these diverging research themes for archaeologies of ritual should and shall be explored in greater detail.

NOTES

1. Indeed Bourdieu (1977:163) uses the terms "institutionalization" and "ritualization" in his text to mean something like crystallization of practice. The view proposed here, however, is that ritualization is a particular way for the institutionalization or crystallization of practice; so any ritualized activity is crystallized, yet not every crystallized activity is necessarily ritualized.
2. Societies based on ritual may reflect two types of links: those of common beliefs (which accompany the rituals) and those of common experience (that of ritual participation and/or preparation). Like any other social group, some ritual societies may renew their affiliation with their members, while others die away with time. As some rituals are never repeated, the experience-based affiliation of their participants with one another may wither in time and be forgotten. Conversely, the oft-repeated rituals renew the experience-based affiliation of their participants frequently and thus remain strong. The belief-based affiliation of members in a society may be renewed through other means and is not based solely on ritual repetition.
3. The term "system" has been challenged by Bell (here chapter 12), who finds the word "systematic" (etymologically derived from the word "system") as not descriptive of these rituals that are grouped together. Indeed, rituals can by no means be described as systematic. But if the discussion is predicated on etymology, then the term "system," coming from Greek σύστημα—verb συνίσταμαι, to be comprised of συν (like co-) ίσταμαι (exist), or "coexist"—means no more than a totality, a group. So, without intending to mean "systematic," "system" can be used to describe, as above, a group of rituals.

REFERENCES CITED

Bell, Catherine
1997   *Ritual: Perspectives and Dimensions*, Oxford University Press, Oxford
Boesch, Christophe, and Hedwige Boesch
1993   Diversity of tool use and tool-making in wild chimpanzees. In *The Use of Tools by Human and Non-Human Primates*, edited by Arlette Berthelet and Jean Chavaillon, pp. 158–174. Clarendon Press, Oxford.
Bourdieu, Pierre
1977   *Outline of a Theory of Practice*. Translated by Richard Nice. Cambridge University Press, Cambridge.
1996   Distinction. Routledge, London.
Chakrabarti, Dilip K.
2001   The archaeology of Hinduism. In *Archaeology and World Religion*, edited by Timothy Insoll, pp. 33–60. Routledge, New York.
Davidson, Donald
2004   The objectivity of values. In *Donald Davidson: Problems of Rationality*, edited by Donald Davidson, pp. 39–52. Oxford University Press, Oxford.
Goodwin, Charles
1997   The Blackness of Black: Color Categories as Situated Practice. In *Discourse, Tools and Reasoning: Essays on Situated Cognition*, edited by Lauren Resnick, Roger Säljö, Clotilde Pontecorvo, and Barbara Burge, pp. 111–140. Springer-Verlag, New York.
Hodder, Ian
1987   The contextual analysis of symbolic meanings. In *The Archaeology of Contextual Meanings*, edited by Ian Hodder, pp. 1–10. Cambridge University Press, Cambridge.
Humphrey, Caroline, and James Laidlaw
1994   *The Archetypal Actions of Ritual*. Oxford University Press, Oxford
2006   Ritual action. In *Theorizing Rituals: Classical Topics, Theoretical Approaches, Analytical Concepts*, edited by Jens Kreinath, J. A. M. Snoek, and Michael Strausberg. Brill, Leiden.
Jameson, Fredric
1991   *Postmodernism or, The Cultural Logic of Late Capitalism*. Duke University Press, Durham.
Kyriakidis, Evangelos
2002   The ritual and its establishment: The case of some open air Minoan rituals. Ph.D. dissertation, University of Cambridge.
2005   *Ritual in the Aegean: The Minoan Peak Sanctuaries*. Duckworth, London

Lett, James
  1990   Emics and etics: Notes on the epistemology of anthropology. *Emics and Etics. The Insider / Outsider Debate*, edited by Thomas N. Headland, Kennelth L. Pike, and Marvin Harris, pp. 127–142. Frontiers of Anthropology, Vol. 7. Sage Publications, Newbury Park, CA.
Lyons, Claire, and John Papadopoulos
  2002   *The Archaeology of Colonialism*. Getty Research Institute, Los Angeles.
Marcus, Joyce, and Kent V. Flannery
  2004   The coevolution of ritual and society: New ^{14}C dates from ancient Mexico. In *Proceedings of the National Academy of Sciences of the USA* 101 (52):18257–18261.
McCauley, Robert, and Thomas Lawson
  2002   *Bringing Ritual to Mind: Psychological Foundations of Cultural Forms*. Cambridge University Press, Cambridge.
Mithen, Steven
  1996   *The Prehistory of the Mind*. Thames and Hudson, London.
Morris, Ian
  1999   Negotiated peripherality in Iron Age Greece: Accepting and resisting the east. In *World-Systems Theory in Practice*, edited by Nick Kardulias, pp. 63–84. Rowman and Littlefield, Lanham.
Papadopoulos, John, and Claire Lyons
  2002   *The Archaeology of Colonialism*. Getty Research Institute, Los Angeles.
Schiller, Ann
  2001   Mortuary monuments and social change among the Ngaju. In *Social Memory, Identity and Death: Anthropological Perspectives on Mortuary Rituals*, edited by Meredith Chesson, pp. 70–79. Archaeological Papers of the American Anthropological Association 10.
Searle, John
  1995   *The Construction of Social Reality*. Allen Lane, Harmondsworth.
Smith, David G.
  2003   How the West was one: The formation of Greek cultural identity in Italy and Sicily. Ph.D. dissertation, Stanford University.

INDEX

NOTE: Bold page numbers indicate where terms are defined or receive significant treatment. Italic page numbers indicate where terms are illustrated.